FOR HICCUPS!
WHOK
WHAT WAS *THAT* FOR?!
SORRY. BUT ARE YOUR HICCUPS GONE?
THE ONE WITH HICCUPS IS *UZUME*!
HIC

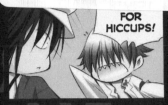

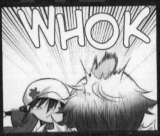

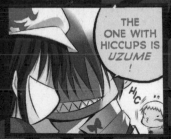

ITSUWARIBITO

Volume 22
Shonen Sunday Edition

Story and Art by
YUUKI IINUMA

ITSUWARIBITO ◆ UTSUHO ◆ Vol. 22
by Yuuki IINUMA
© 2009 Yuuki IINUMA
All rights reserved.
Original Japanese edition published by SHOGAKUKAN.
English translation rights in the United States of America and Canada
arranged with SHOGAKUKAN.

Translation/John Werry
Touch-up Art & Lettering/Susan Daigle-Leach
Design/Matt Hinrichs
Editor/Gary Leach

The stories, characters and incidents mentioned
in this publication are entirely fictional.

Printed in the U.S.A.

Published by VIZ Media, LLC
P.O. Box 77010
San Francisco, CA 94107

10 9 8 7 6 5 4 3 2 1
First printing, December 2017

www.viz.com
WWW.SHONENSUNDAY.COM

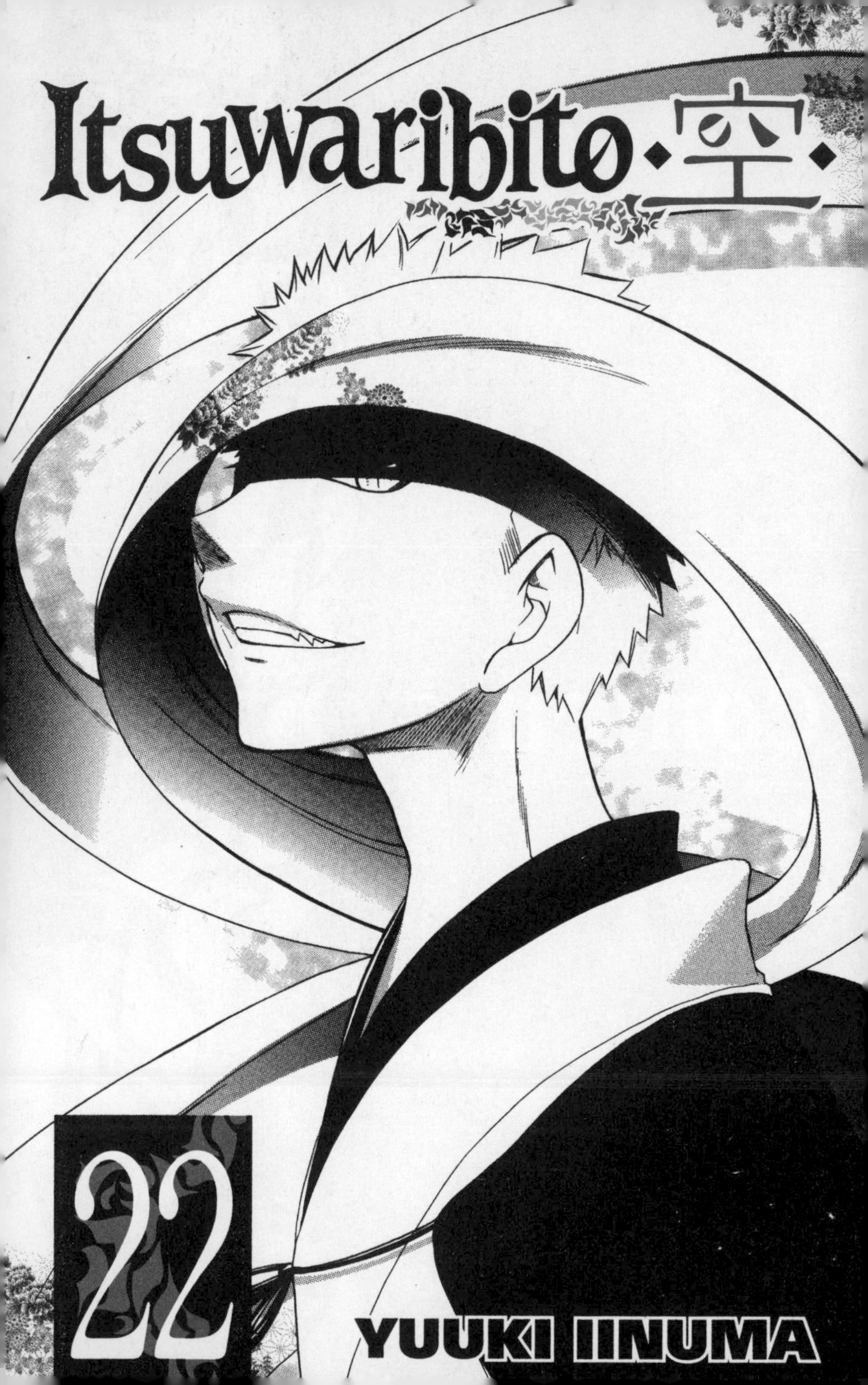
Itsuwaribito·空·
22
YUUKI IINUMA

Contents

Chapter 206 God's Isolation

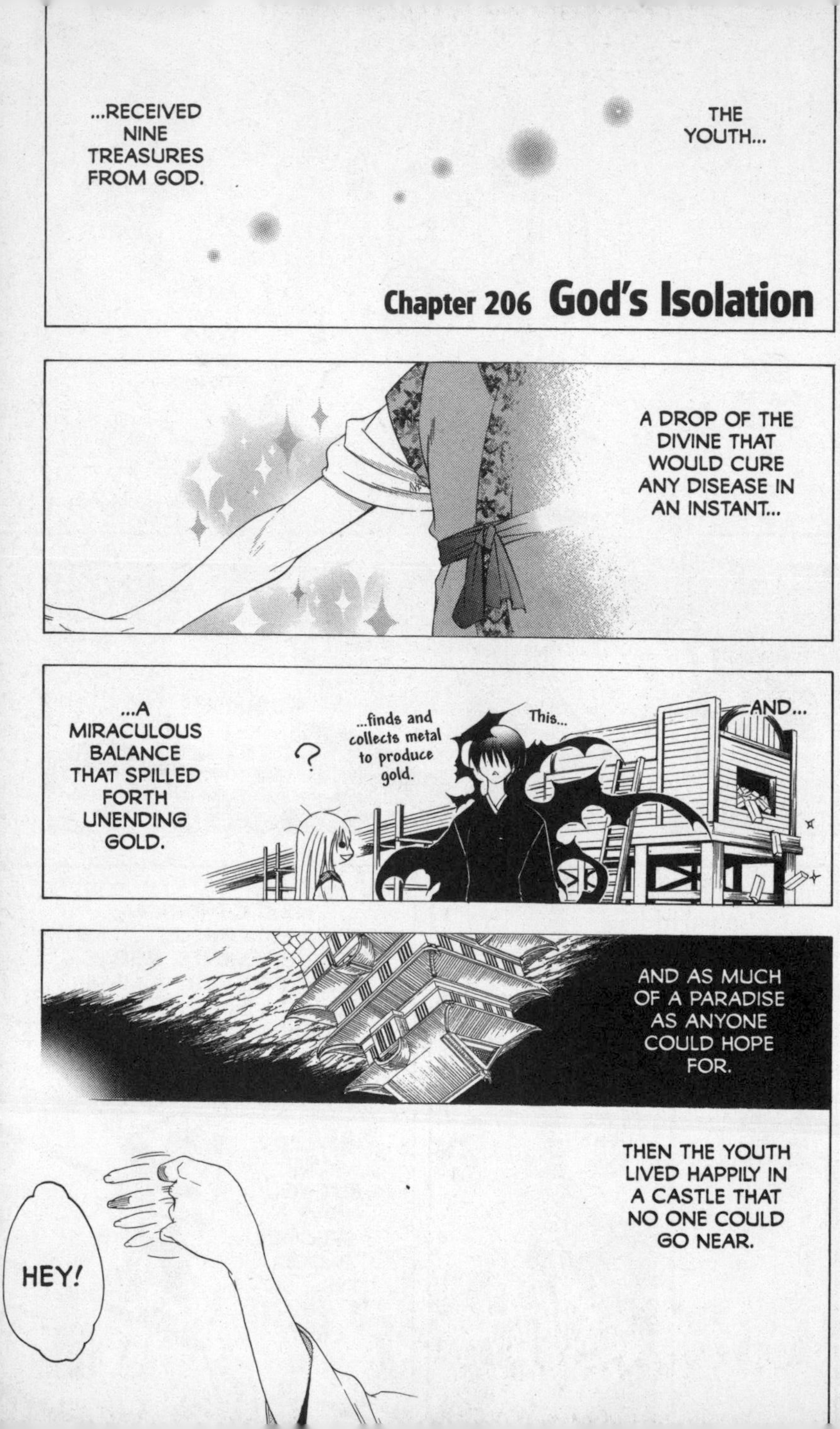
THE YOUTH...
...RECEIVED NINE TREASURES FROM GOD.
A DROP OF THE DIVINE THAT WOULD CURE ANY DISEASE IN AN INSTANT...
AND...
This...
...finds and collects metal to produce gold.
?
...A MIRACULOUS BALANCE THAT SPILLED FORTH UNENDING GOLD.
AND AS MUCH OF A PARADISE AS ANYONE COULD HOPE FOR.
THEN THE YOUTH LIVED HAPPILY IN A CASTLE THAT NO ONE COULD GO NEAR.
HEY!

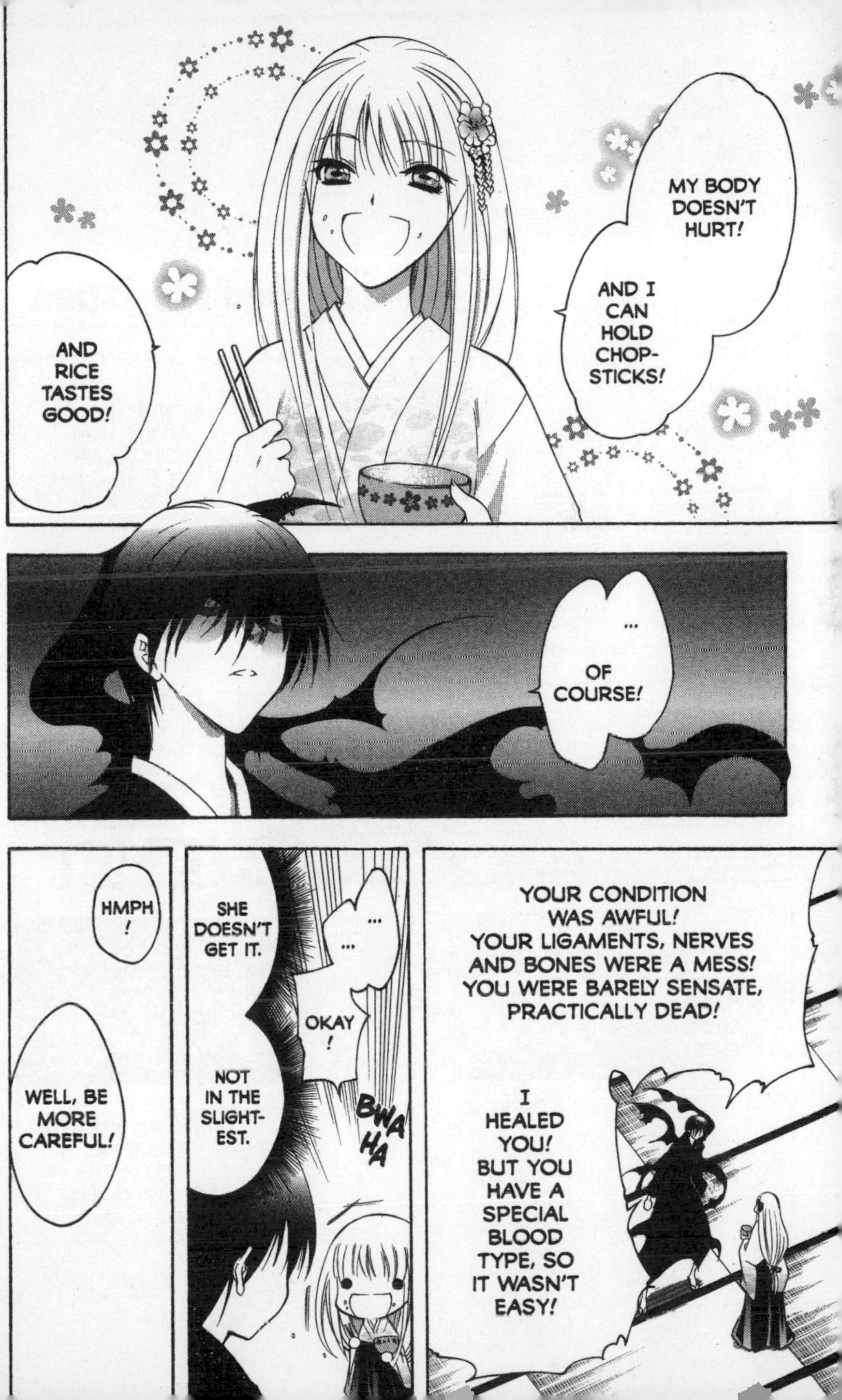
MY BODY DOESN'T HURT!
AND I CAN HOLD CHOP-STICKS!
AND RICE TASTES GOOD!
... OF COURSE!
YOUR CONDITION WAS AWFUL! YOUR LIGAMENTS, NERVES AND BONES WERE A MESS! YOU WERE BARELY SENSATE, PRACTICALLY DEAD!
I HEALED YOU! BUT YOU HAVE A SPECIAL BLOOD TYPE, SO IT WASN'T EASY!
... ...
SHE DOESN'T GET IT.
OKAY!
BWA HA
NOT IN THE SLIGHT-EST.
HMPH!
WELL, BE MORE CAREFUL!

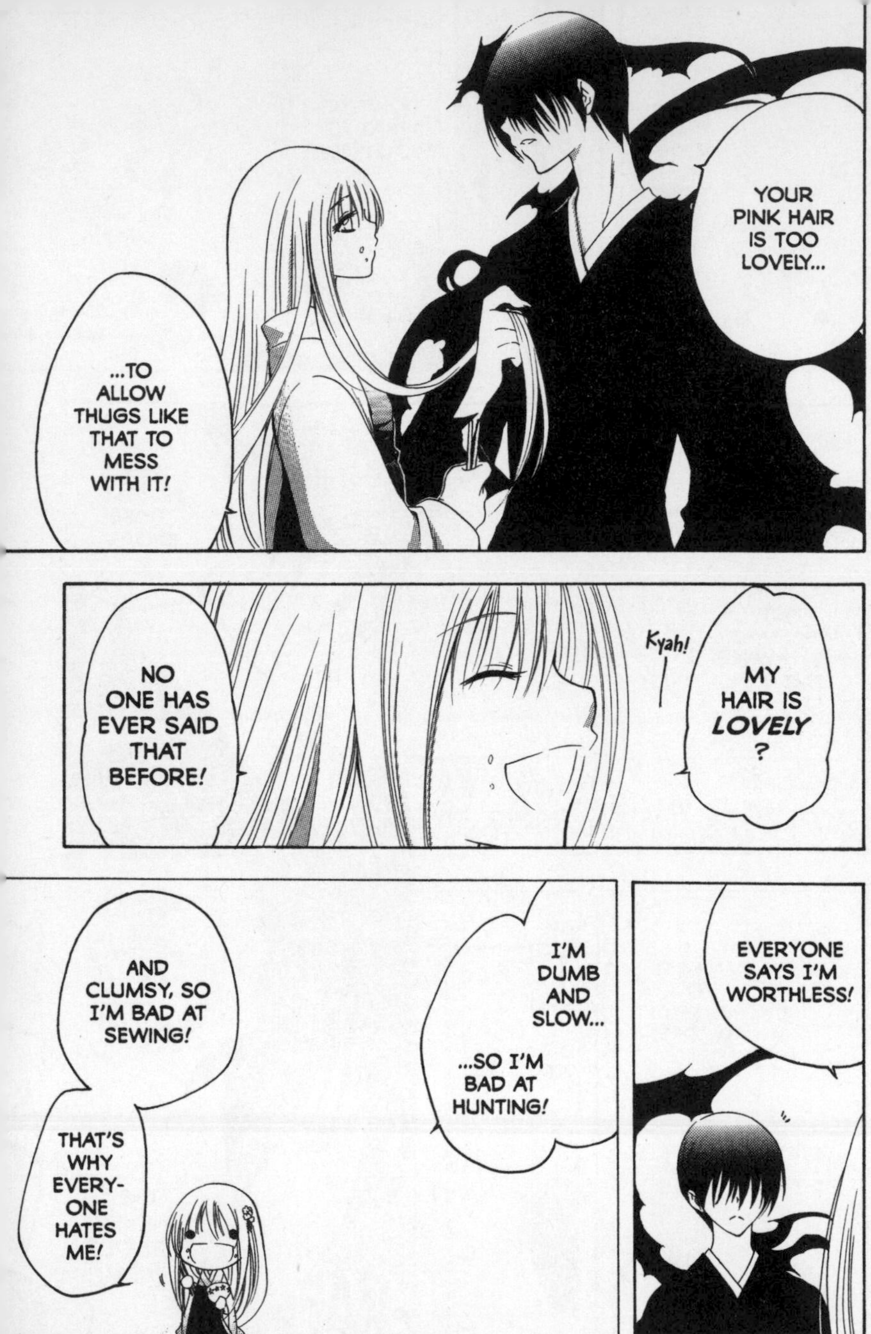
YOUR PINK HAIR IS TOO LOVELY...
...TO ALLOW THUGS LIKE THAT TO MESS WITH IT!
Kyah!
MY HAIR IS *LOVELY*?
NO ONE HAS EVER SAID THAT BEFORE!
EVERYONE SAYS I'M WORTHLESS!
I'M DUMB AND SLOW...
...SO I'M BAD AT HUNTING!
AND CLUMSY, SO I'M BAD AT SEWING!
THAT'S WHY EVERY-ONE HATES ME!

PAT

BUT THOSE THINGS BOTHER YOU, DON'T THEY.

DON'T DO THAT TO YOURSELF!

GROAN MOAN MOAN

WELL, FORGET THOSE IDIOTS.

THEY WOULDN'T KNOW WHAT WAS WORTHWHILE IF IT BIT THEM.

ANYWAY, YOU MUSTN'T WORRY.

I...

...AM HERE TO HELP YOU.

OOPS. SORRY.

PEOPLE LOVE TO PRATTLE ABOUT LOFTY IDEALS...

...BUT THEY NEVER EXEMPLIFY THEM!

GRAH

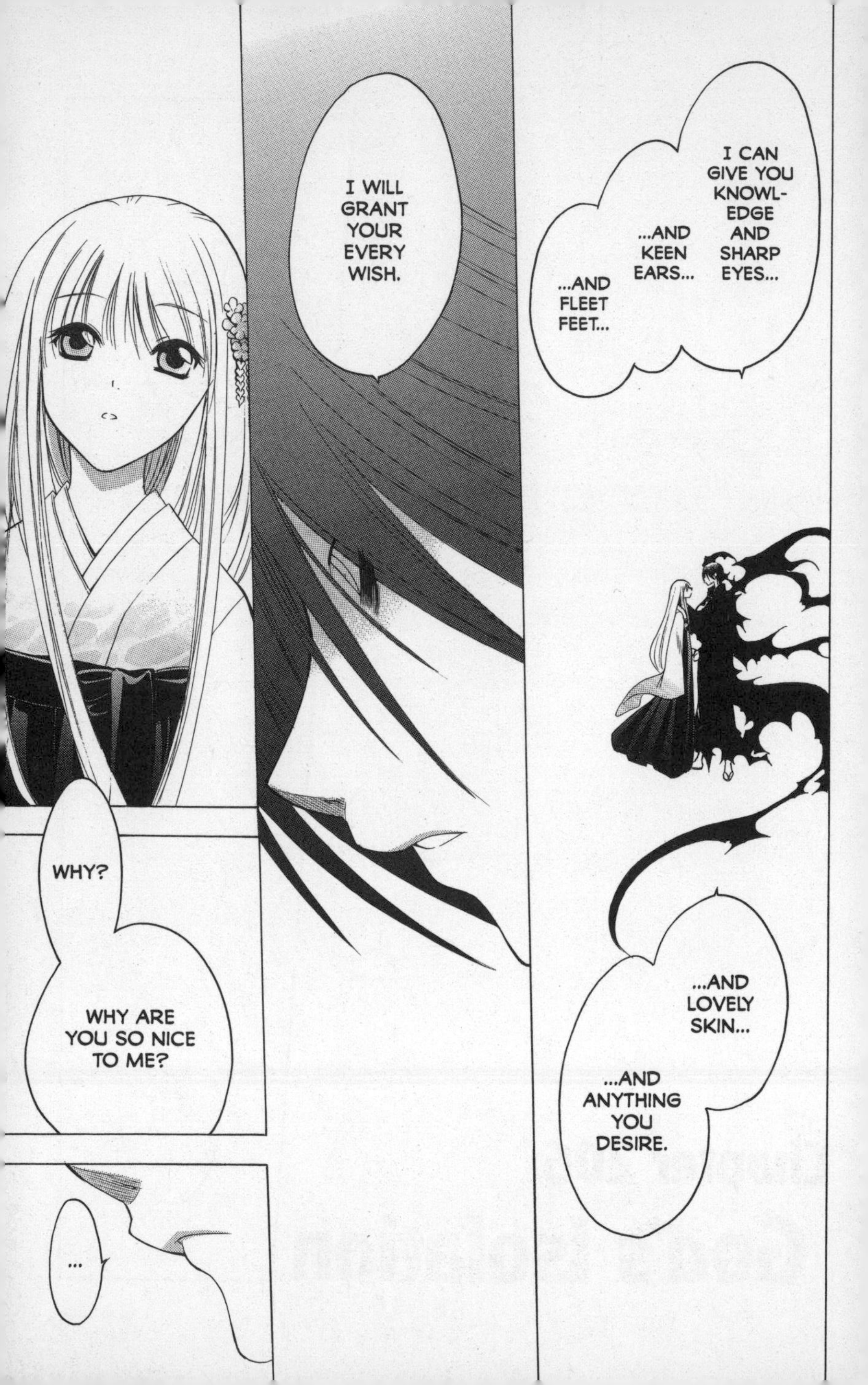
I CAN GIVE YOU KNOWL-EDGE AND SHARP EYES...
...AND KEEN EARS...
...AND FLEET FEET...
...AND LOVELY SKIN...
...AND ANYTHING YOU DESIRE.
I WILL GRANT YOUR EVERY WISH.
WHY?
WHY ARE YOU SO NICE TO ME?
...

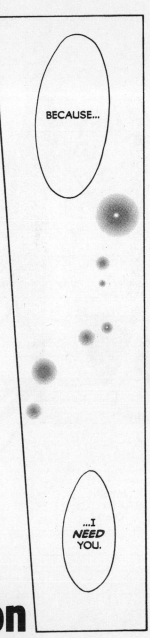

Chapter 206
God's Isolation

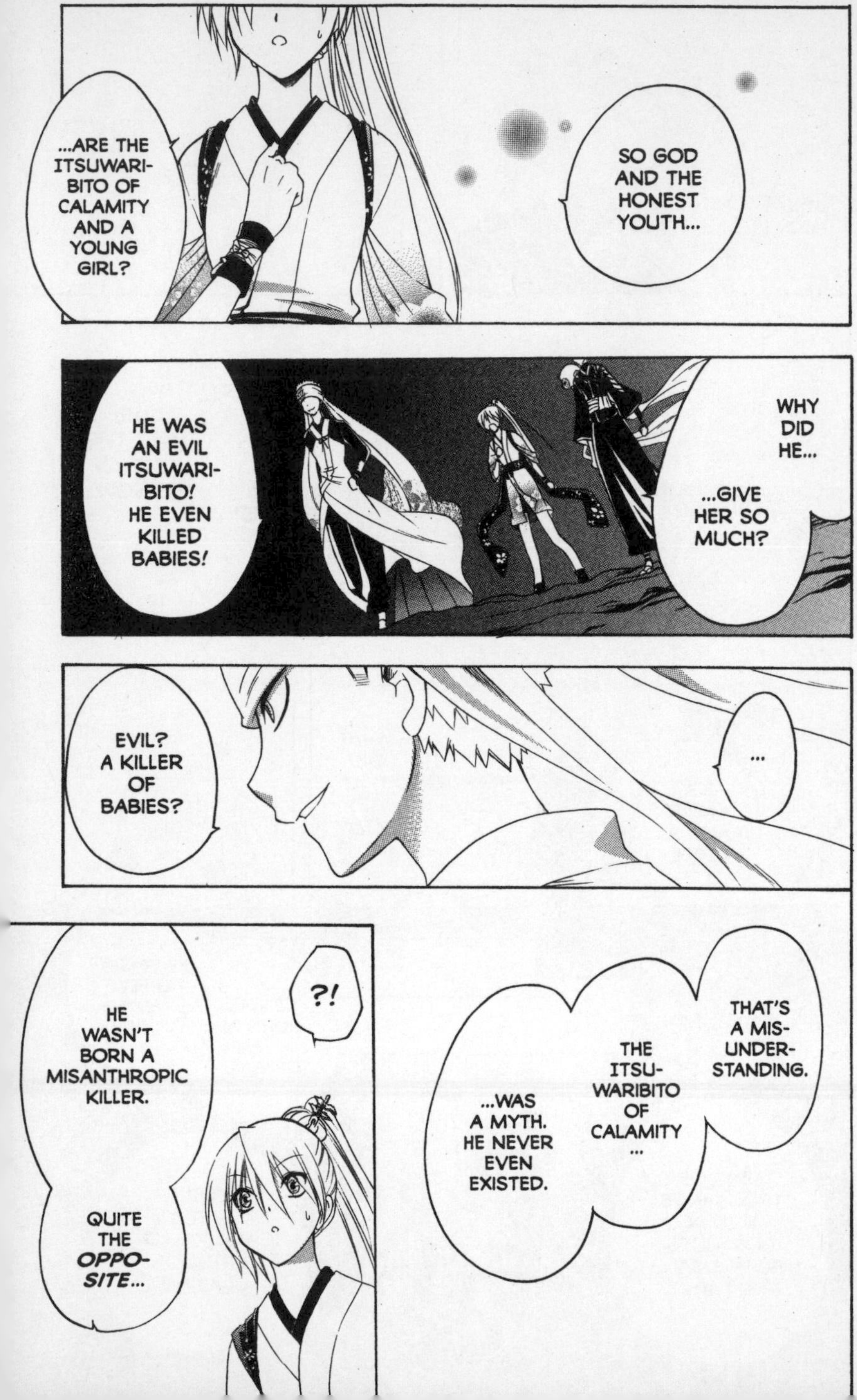
SO GOD AND THE HONEST YOUTH...
...ARE THE ITSUWARIBITO OF CALAMITY AND A YOUNG GIRL?
WHY DID HE...
...GIVE HER SO MUCH?
HE WAS AN EVIL ITSUWARIBITO! HE EVEN KILLED BABIES!
...
EVIL? A KILLER OF BABIES?
THAT'S A MISUNDERSTANDING.
THE ITSUWARIBITO OF CALAMITY...
...WAS A MYTH. HE NEVER EVEN EXISTED.
?!
HE WASN'T BORN A MISANTHROPIC KILLER.
QUITE THE *OPPOSITE*...

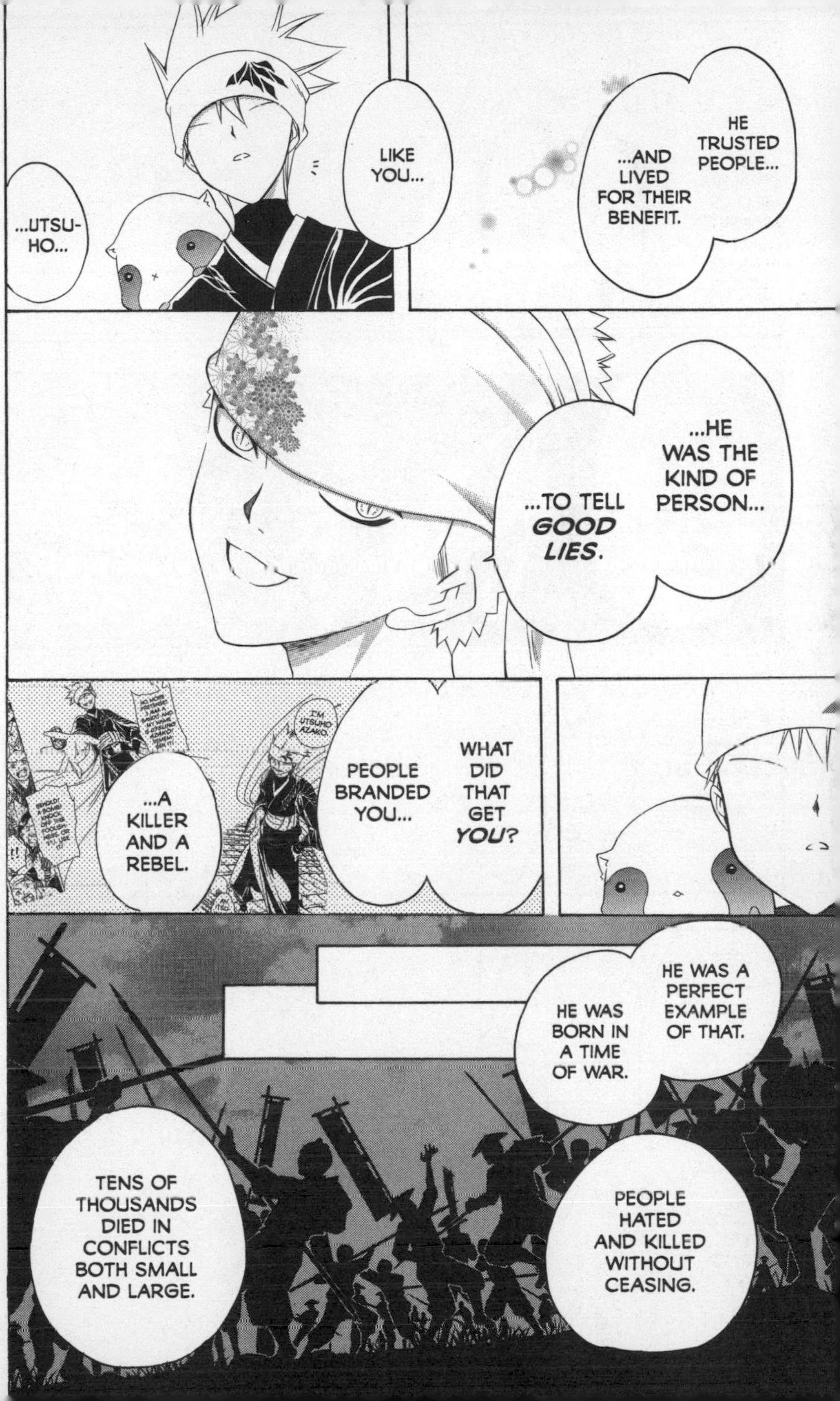
HE TRUSTED PEOPLE...
...AND LIVED FOR THEIR BENEFIT.
LIKE YOU...
...UTSU-HO...
...HE WAS THE KIND OF PERSON...
...TO TELL *GOOD LIES*.
WHAT DID THAT GET *YOU*?
PEOPLE BRANDED YOU...
I'M UTSUHO AZAKO.
...A KILLER AND A REBEL.
HE WAS A PERFECT EXAMPLE OF THAT.
HE WAS BORN IN A TIME OF WAR.
PEOPLE HATED AND KILLED WITHOUT CEASING.
TENS OF THOUSANDS DIED IN CONFLICTS BOTH SMALL AND LARGE.

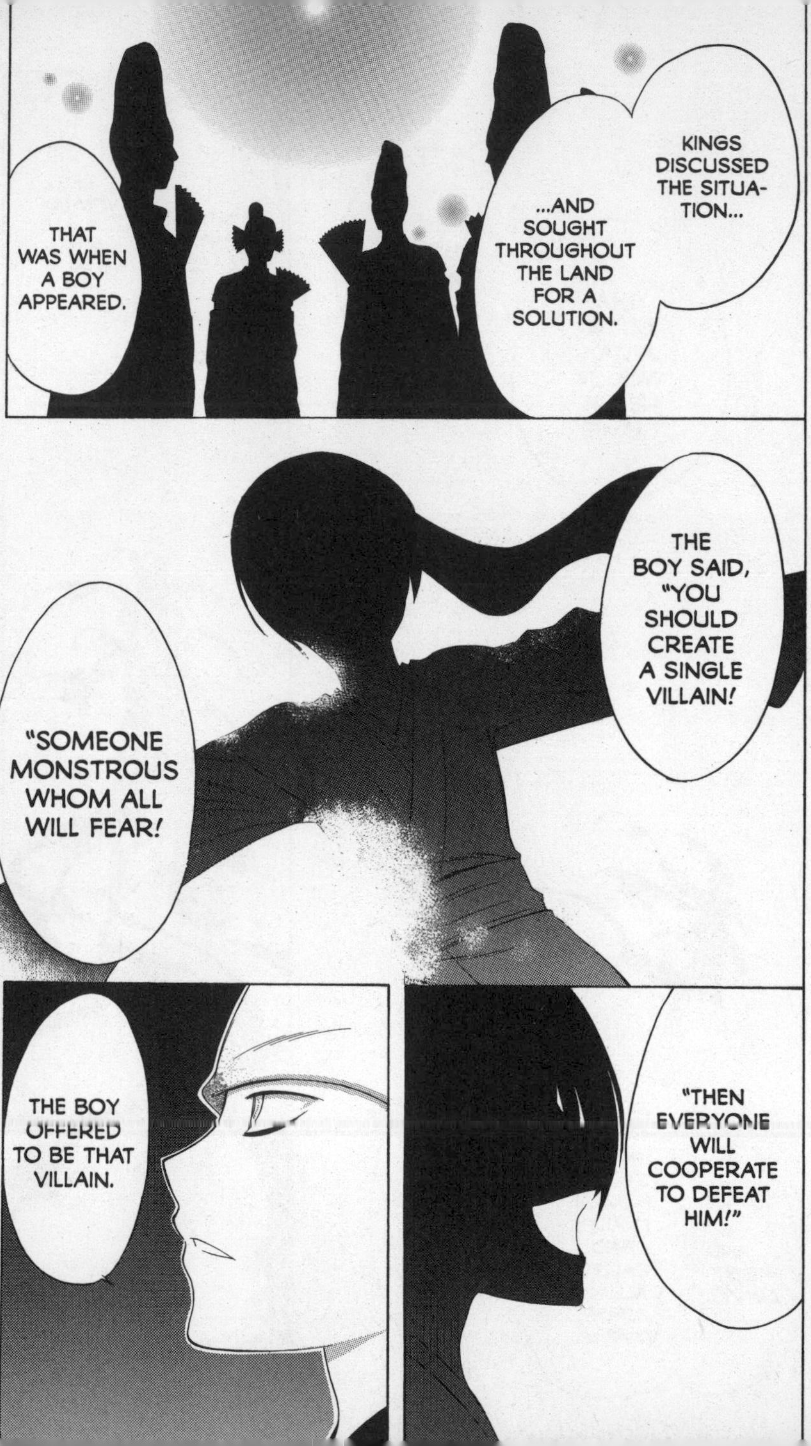
KINGS DISCUSSED THE SITUATION...
...AND SOUGHT THROUGHOUT THE LAND FOR A SOLUTION.
THAT WAS WHEN A BOY APPEARED.
THE BOY SAID, "YOU SHOULD CREATE A SINGLE VILLAIN!
"SOMEONE MONSTROUS WHOM ALL WILL FEAR!
"THEN EVERYONE WILL COOPERATE TO DEFEAT HIM!"
THE BOY OFFERED TO BE THAT VILLAIN.

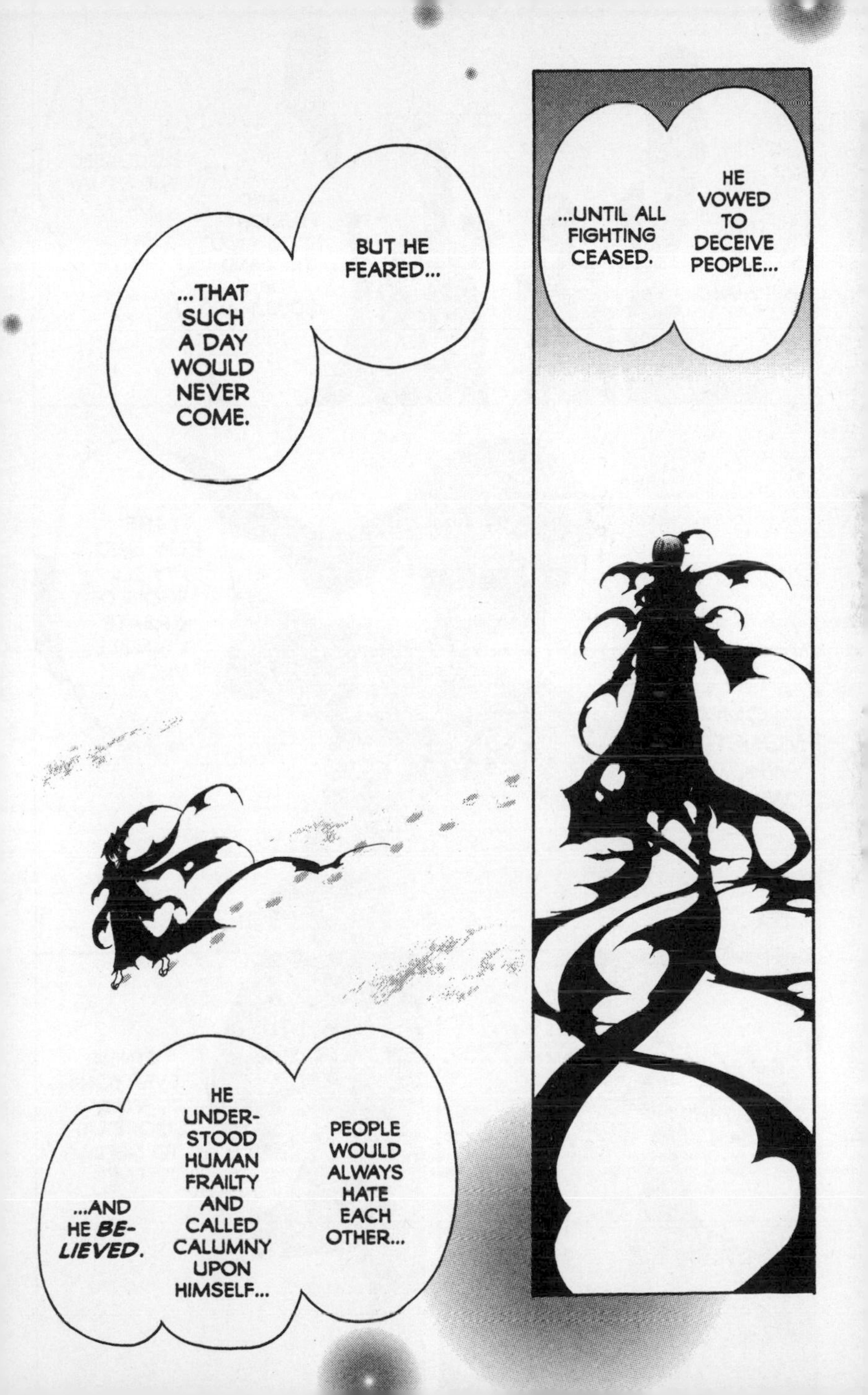
HE VOWED TO DECEIVE PEOPLE...
...UNTIL ALL FIGHTING CEASED.
BUT HE FEARED...
...THAT SUCH A DAY WOULD NEVER COME.
PEOPLE WOULD ALWAYS HATE EACH OTHER...
HE UNDER-STOOD HUMAN FRAILTY AND CALLED CALUMNY UPON HIMSELF...
...AND HE *BE-LIEVED*.

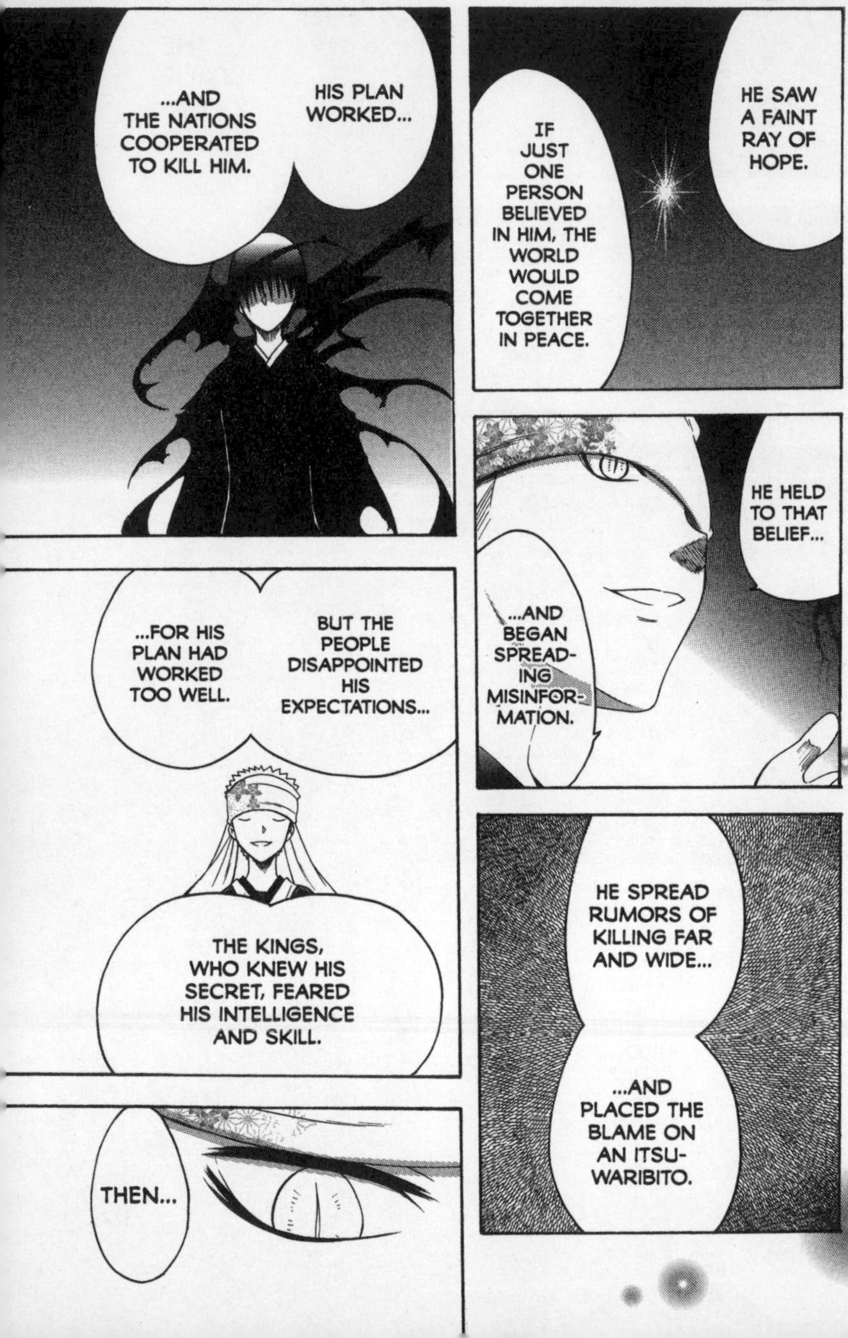
HE SAW A FAINT RAY OF HOPE.
IF JUST ONE PERSON BELIEVED IN HIM, THE WORLD WOULD COME TOGETHER IN PEACE.
HE HELD TO THAT BELIEF...
...AND BEGAN SPREAD-ING MISINFOR-MATION.
HE SPREAD RUMORS OF KILLING FAR AND WIDE...
...AND PLACED THE BLAME ON AN ITSU-WARIBITO.
HIS PLAN WORKED...
...AND THE NATIONS COOPERATED TO KILL HIM.
BUT THE PEOPLE DISAPPOINTED HIS EXPECTATIONS...
...FOR HIS PLAN HAD WORKED TOO WELL.
THE KINGS, WHO KNEW HIS SECRET, FEARED HIS INTELLIGENCE AND SKILL.
THEN...

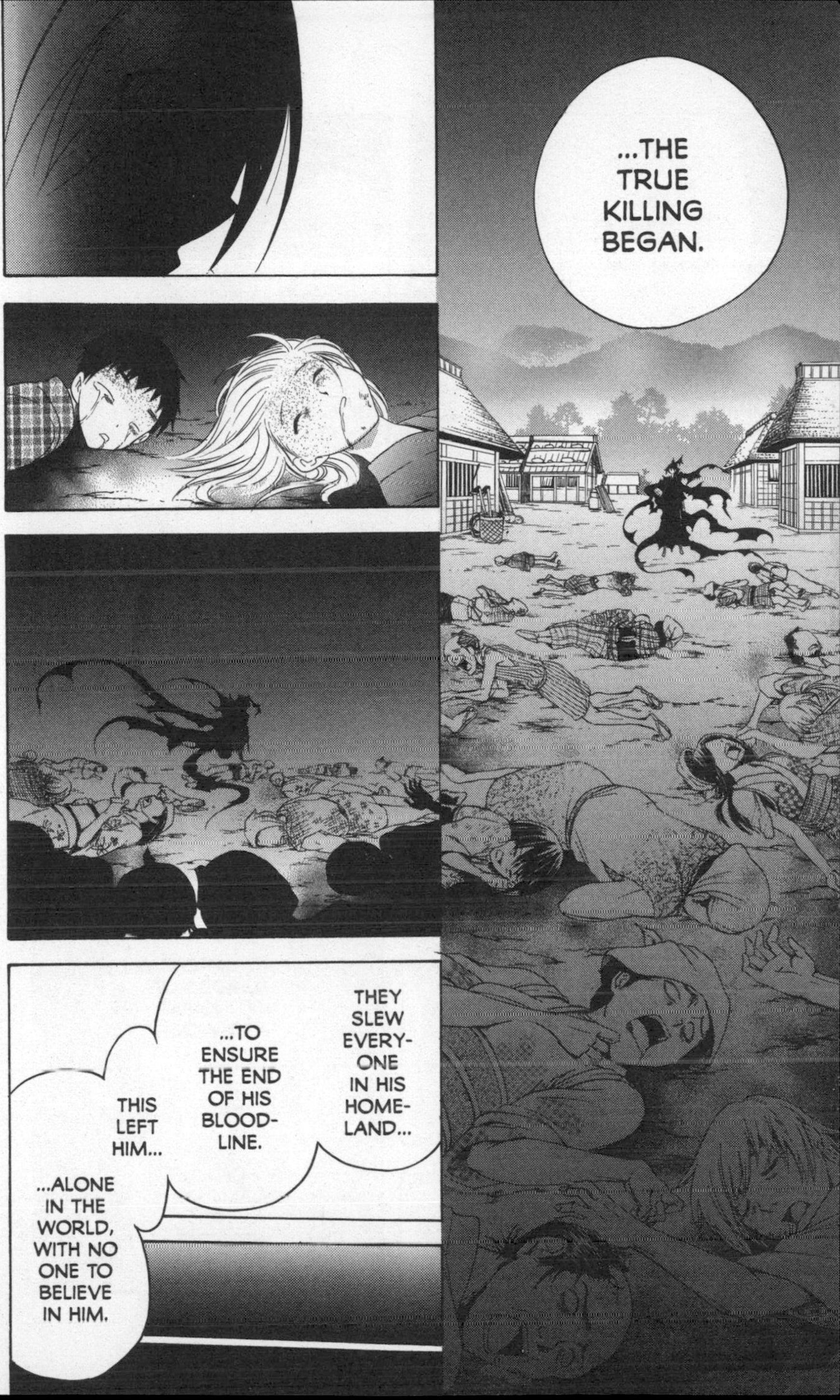
...THE TRUE KILLING BEGAN.
THEY SLEW EVERYONE IN HIS HOMELAND...
...TO ENSURE THE END OF HIS BLOODLINE.
THIS LEFT HIM...
...ALONE IN THE WORLD, WITH NO ONE TO BELIEVE IN HIM.

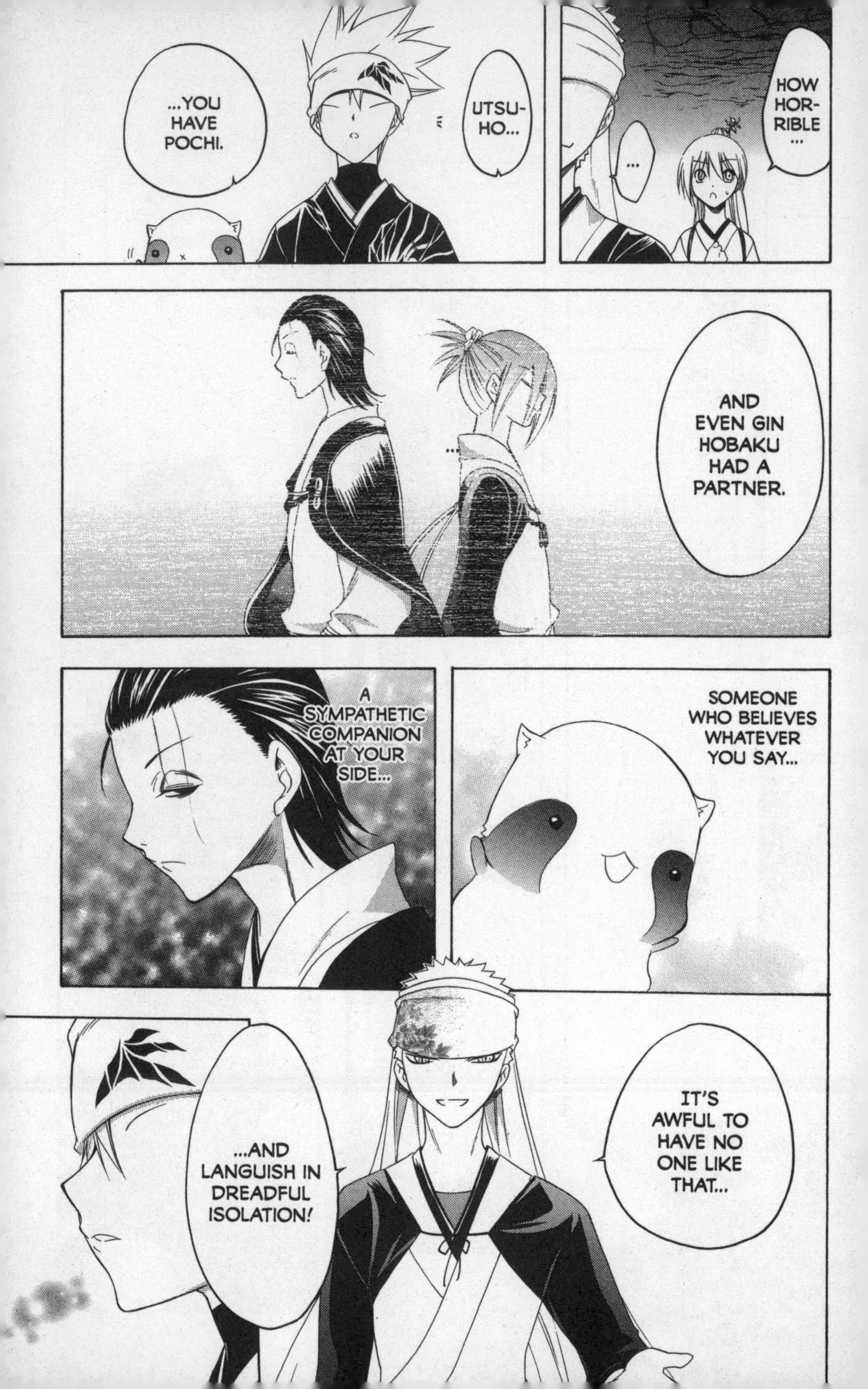
HOW HOR-RIBLE...
...
UTSU-HO...
...YOU HAVE POCHI.
AND EVEN GIN HOBAKU HAD A PARTNER.
...
SOMEONE WHO BELIEVES WHATEVER YOU SAY...
A SYMPATHETIC COMPANION AT YOUR SIDE...
IT'S AWFUL TO HAVE NO ONE LIKE THAT...
...AND LANGUISH IN DREADFUL ISOLATION!

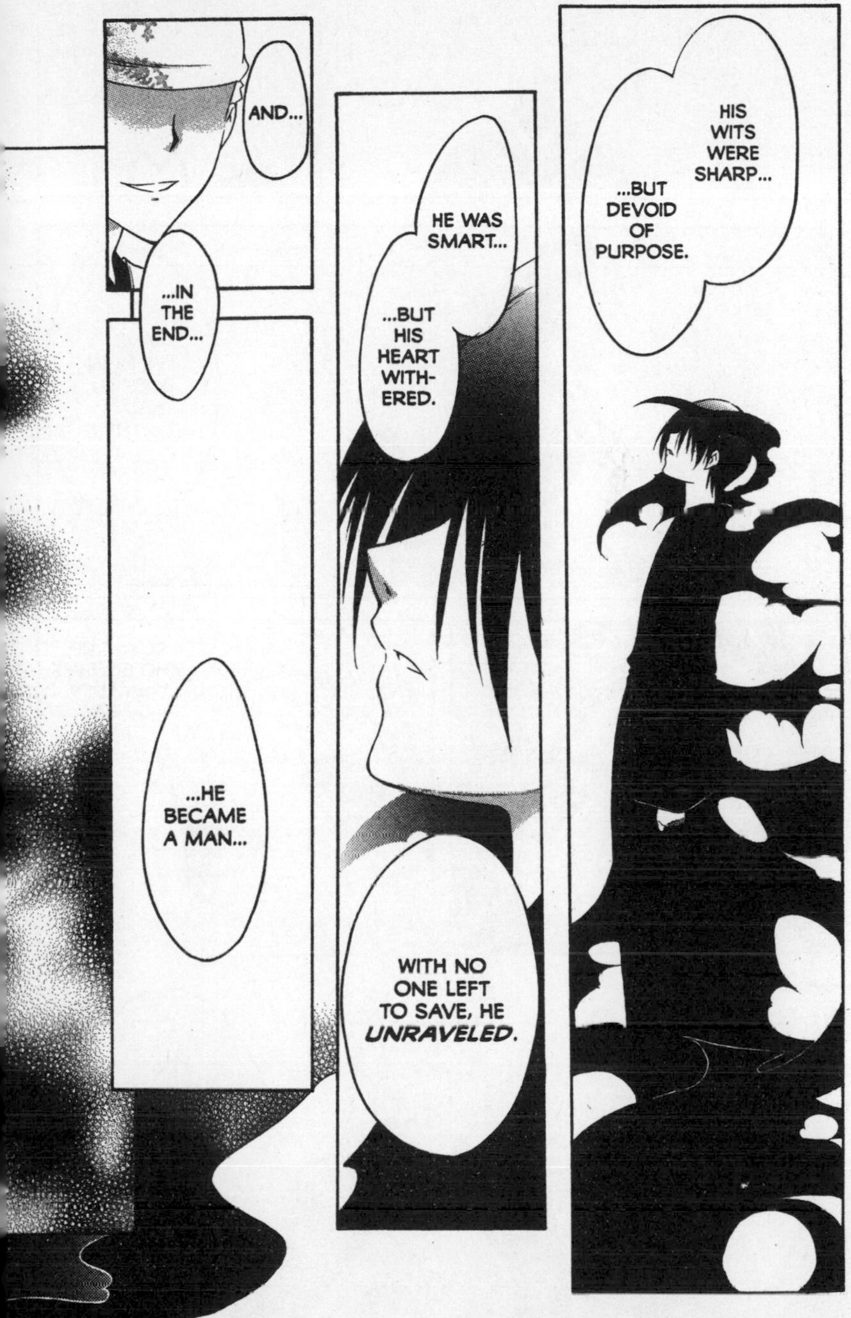
HIS WITS WERE SHARP...
...BUT DEVOID OF PURPOSE.
HE WAS SMART...
...BUT HIS HEART WITH-ERED.
WITH NO ONE LEFT TO SAVE, HE *UNRAVELED*.
AND...
...IN THE END...
...HE BECAME A MAN...

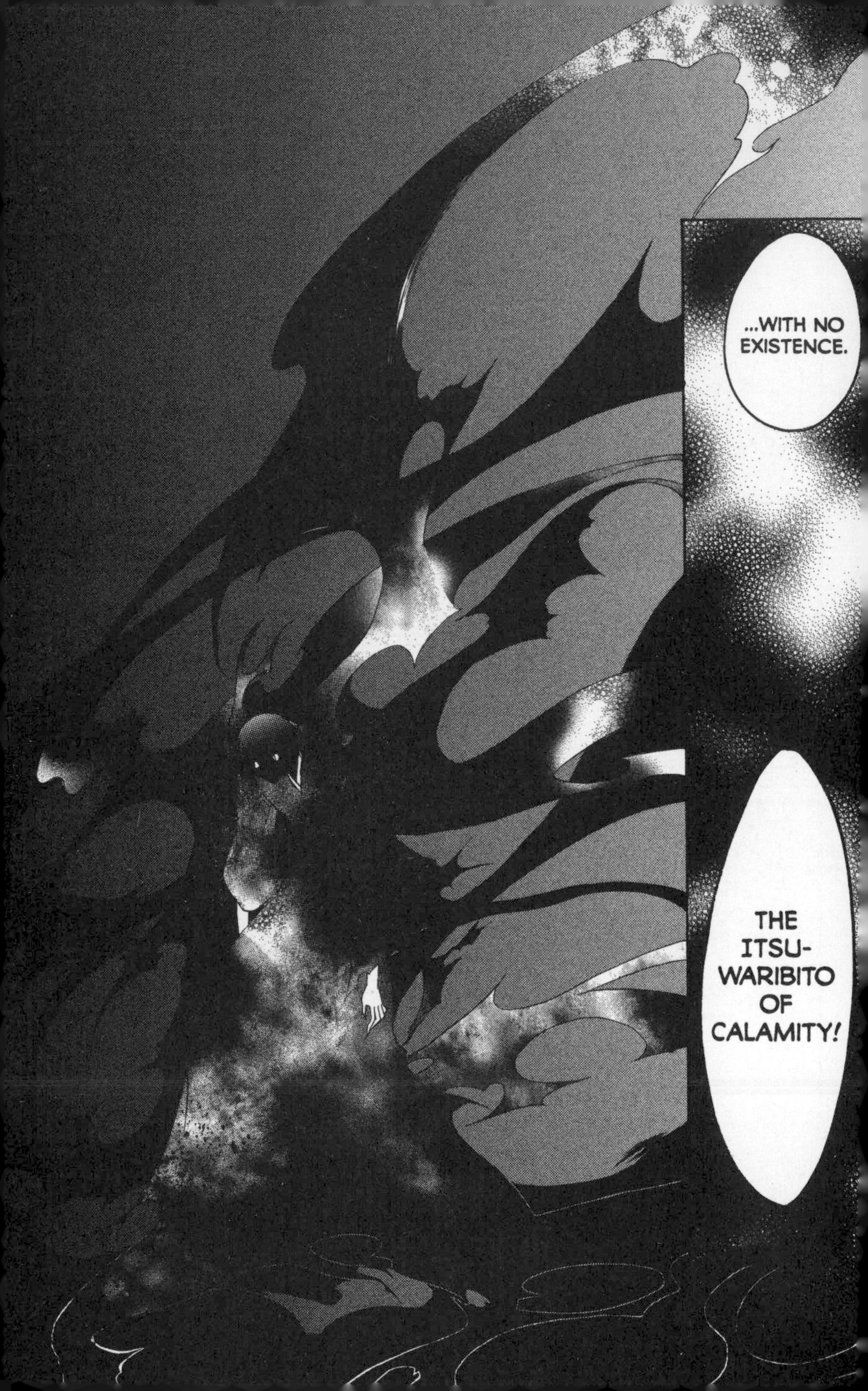
...WITH NO EXISTENCE.
THE ITSU-WARIBITO OF CALAMITY!

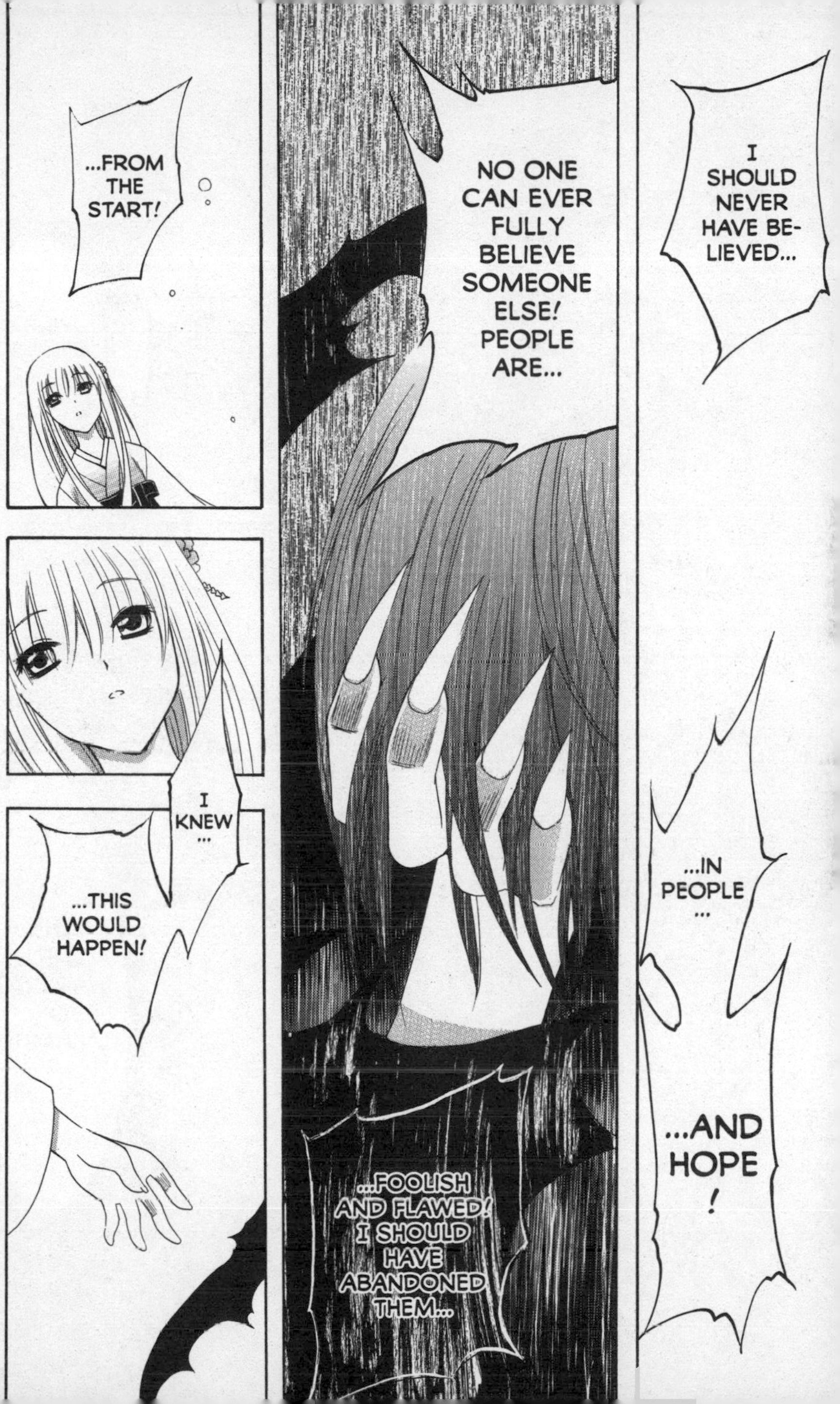
I SHOULD NEVER HAVE BELIEVED...
...IN PEOPLE...
...AND HOPE!
NO ONE CAN EVER FULLY BELIEVE SOMEONE ELSE! PEOPLE ARE...
...FOOLISH AND FLAWED! I SHOULD HAVE ABANDONED THEM...
...FROM THE START!
I KNEW...
...THIS WOULD HAPPEN!

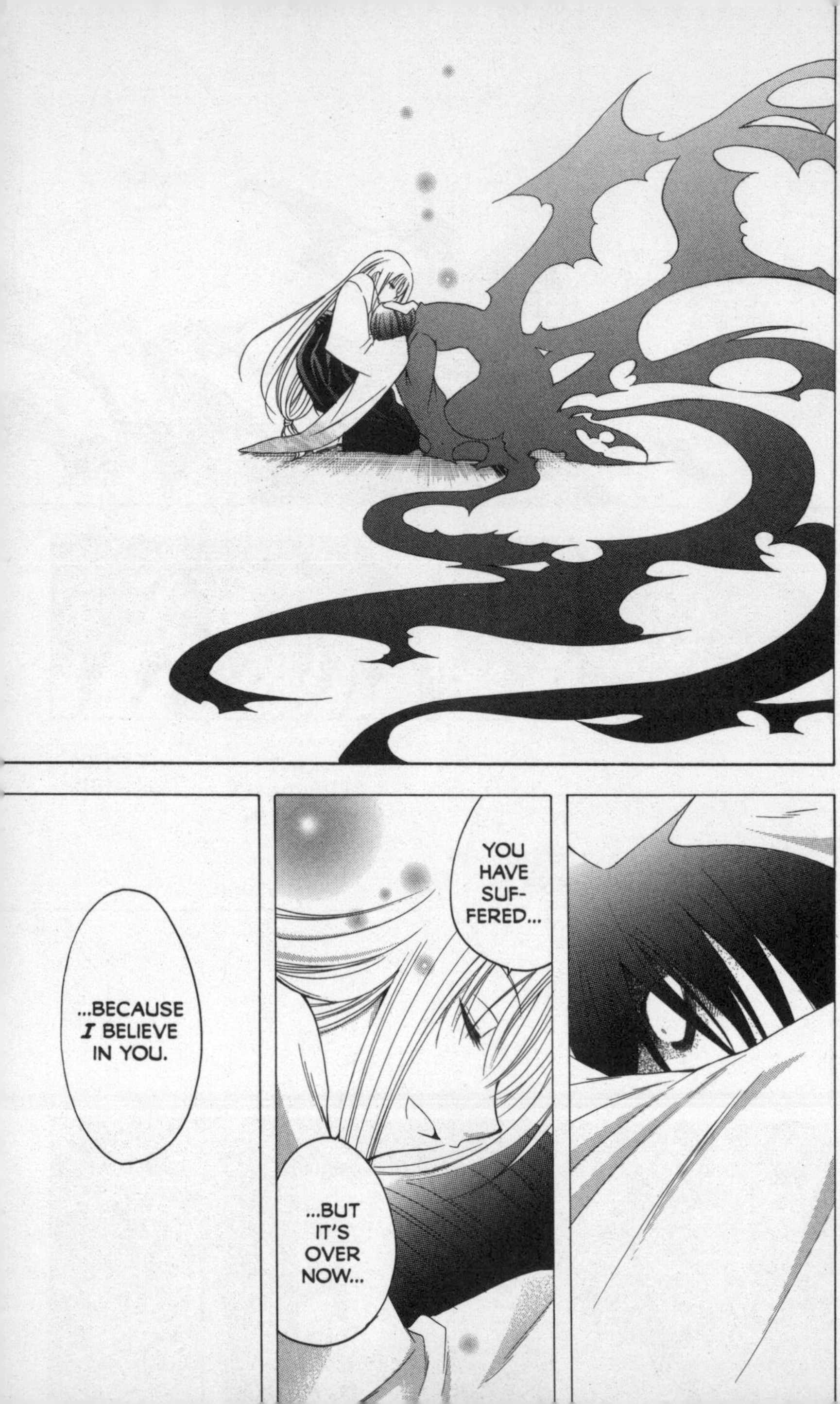
YOU HAVE SUF-FERED...
...BUT IT'S OVER NOW...
...BECAUSE *I* BELIEVE IN YOU.

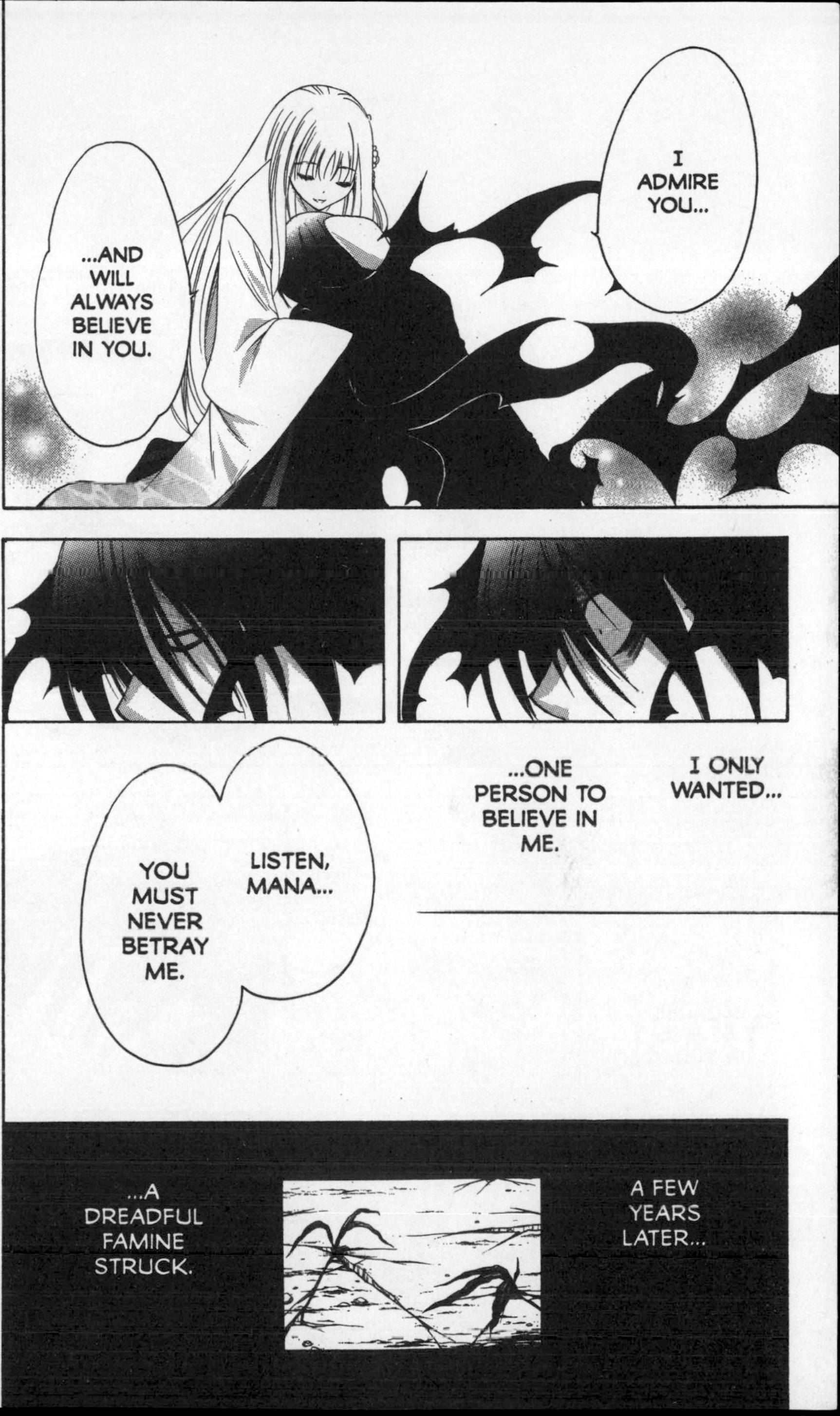
I ADMIRE YOU...
...AND WILL ALWAYS BELIEVE IN YOU.
I ONLY WANTED...
...ONE PERSON TO BELIEVE IN ME.
LISTEN, MANA... YOU MUST NEVER BETRAY ME.
A FEW YEARS LATER...
...A DREADFUL FAMINE STRUCK.

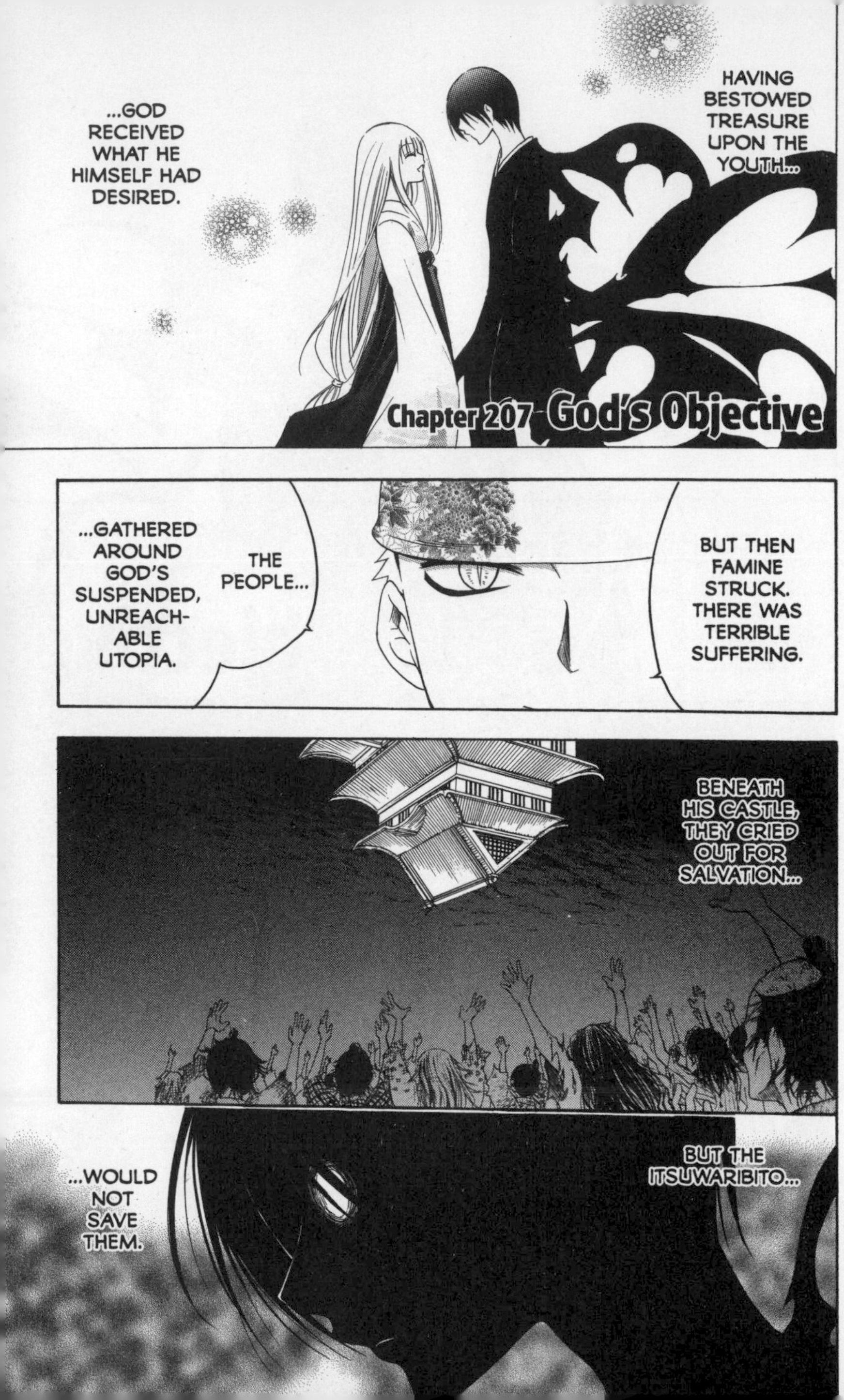
HAVING BESTOWED TREASURE UPON THE YOUTH...
...GOD RECEIVED WHAT HE HIMSELF HAD DESIRED.
Chapter 207 God's Objective
BUT THEN FAMINE STRUCK. THERE WAS TERRIBLE SUFFERING.
THE PEOPLE...
...GATHERED AROUND GOD'S SUSPENDED, UNREACHABLE UTOPIA.
BENEATH HIS CASTLE, THEY CRIED OUT FOR SALVATION...
BUT THE ITSUWARIBITO...
...WOULD NOT SAVE THEM.

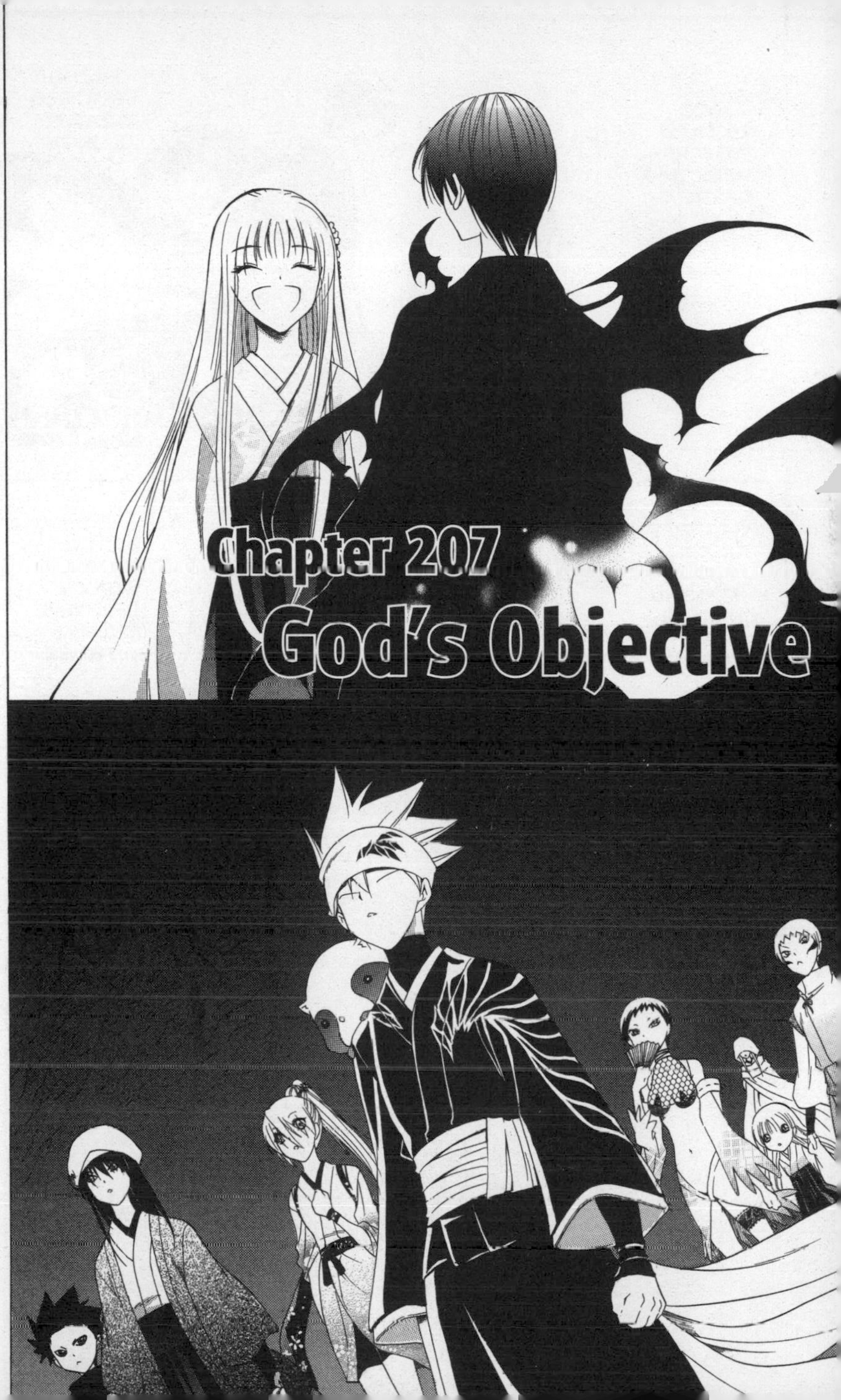
Chapter 207
God's Objective

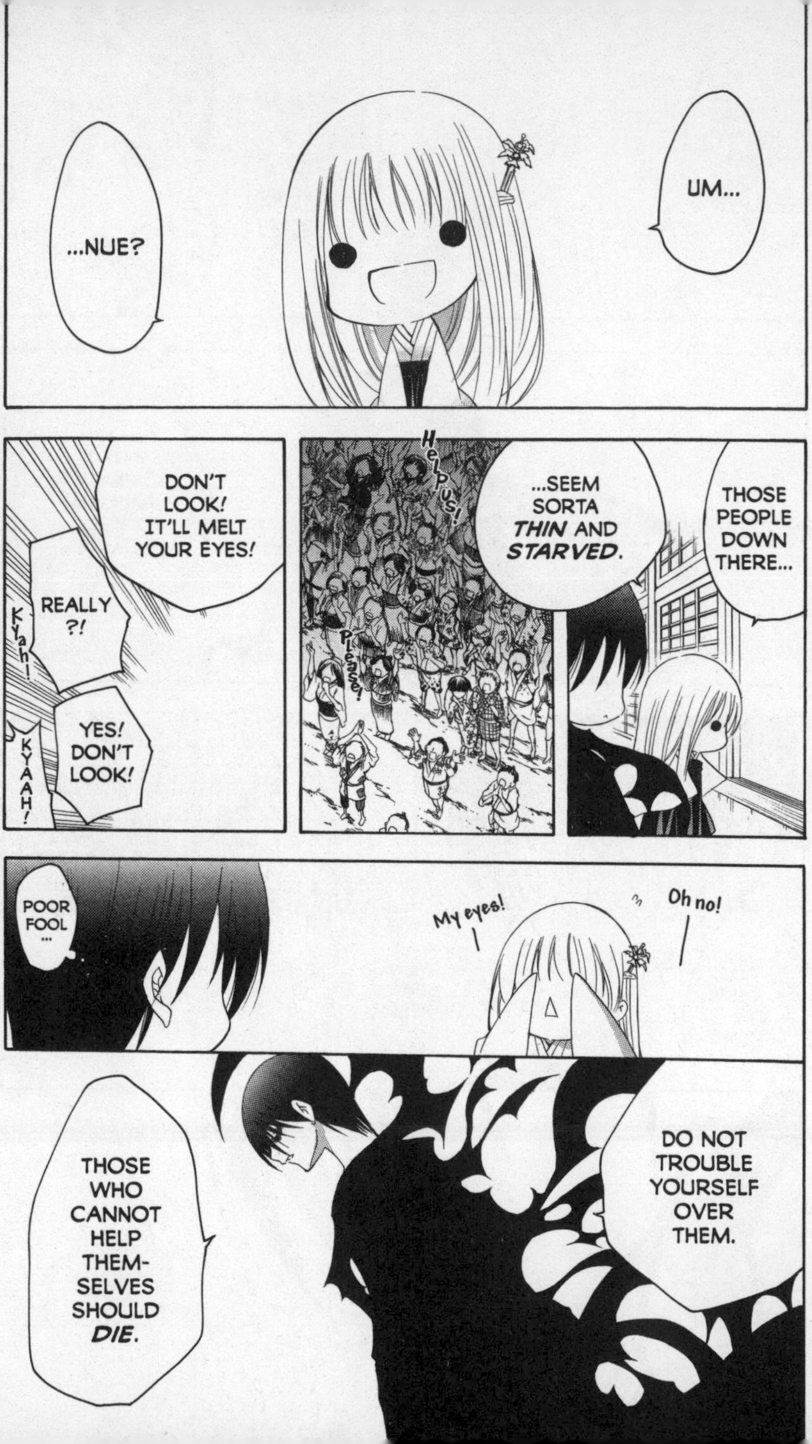
UM...
...NUE?
THOSE PEOPLE DOWN THERE...
...SEEM SORTA *THIN* AND *STARVED*.
Help us!
Please!
DON'T LOOK! IT'LL MELT YOUR EYES!
REALLY?!
Kyah!
YES! DON'T LOOK!
KYAAH!
Oh no!
My eyes!
POOR FOOL...
DO NOT TROUBLE YOURSELF OVER THEM.
THOSE WHO CANNOT HELP THEM-SELVES SHOULD *DIE*.

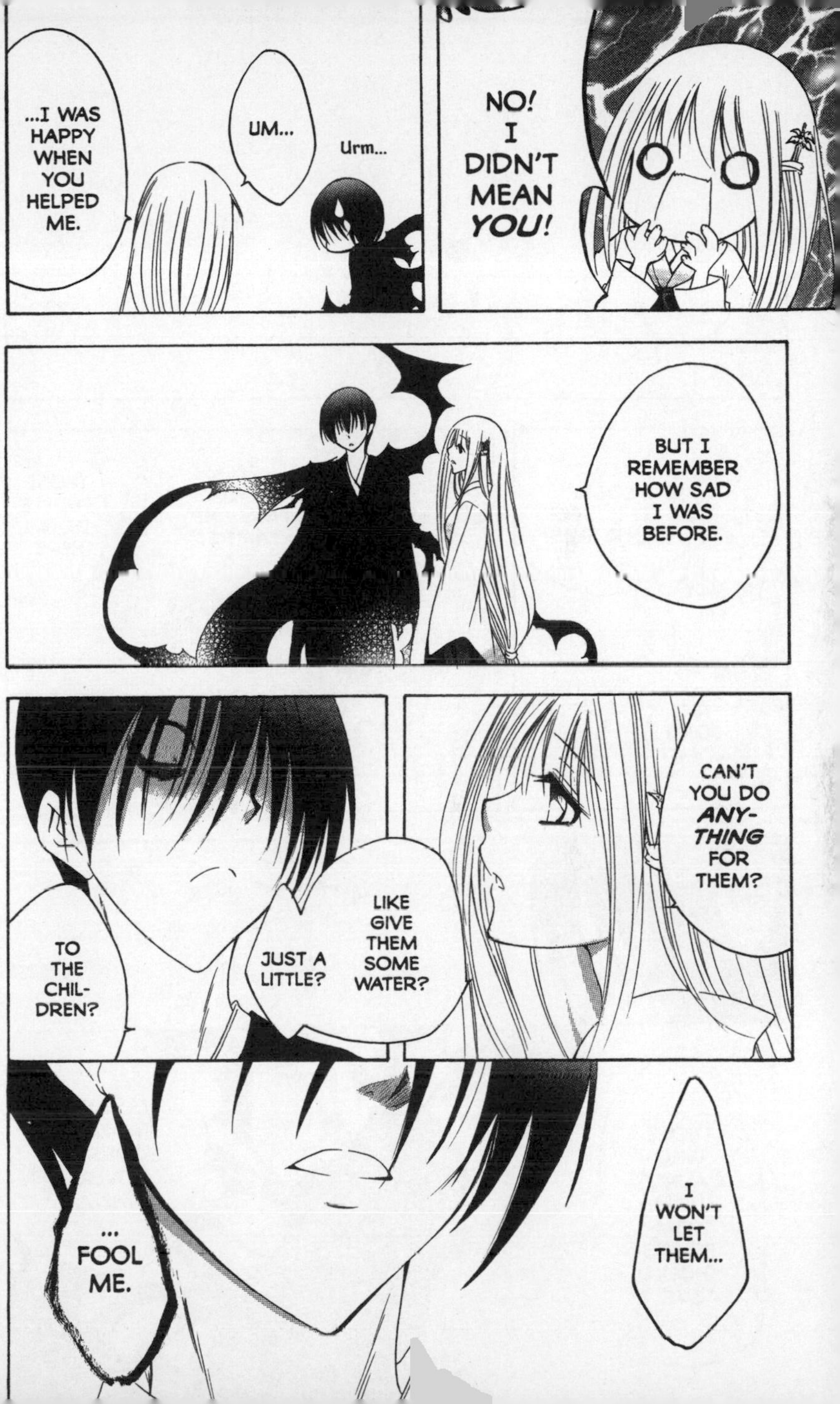
NO! I DIDN'T MEAN YOU!
UM...
Urm...
...I WAS HAPPY WHEN YOU HELPED ME.
BUT I REMEMBER HOW SAD I WAS BEFORE.
CAN'T YOU DO ANYTHING FOR THEM?
LIKE GIVE THEM SOME WATER?
JUST A LITTLE?
TO THE CHILDREN?
I WON'T LET THEM...
...FOOL ME.

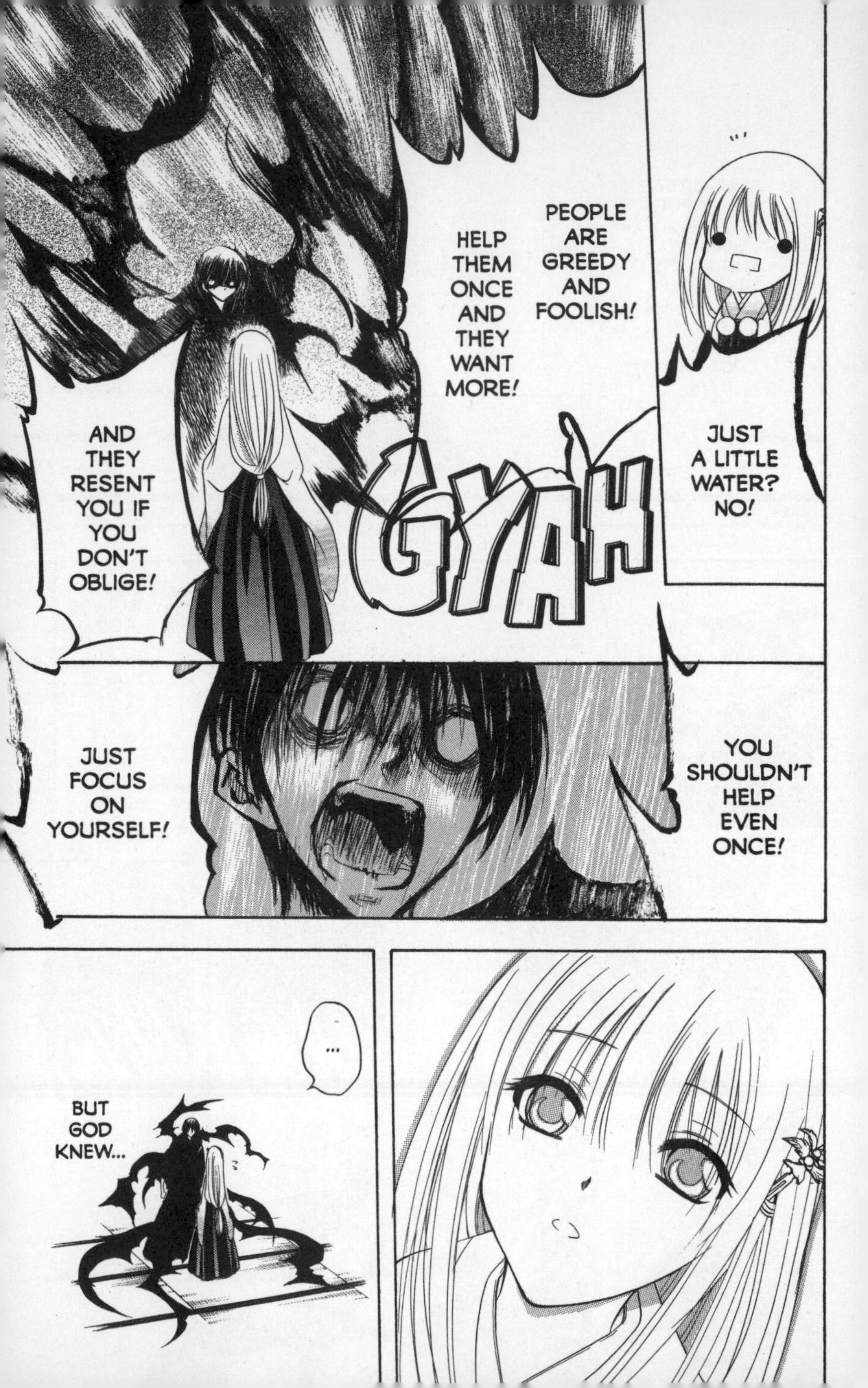
JUST A LITTLE WATER? NO!
PEOPLE ARE GREEDY AND FOOLISH!
HELP THEM ONCE AND THEY WANT MORE!
GYAH
AND THEY RESENT YOU IF YOU DON'T OBLIGE!
YOU SHOULDN'T HELP EVEN ONCE!
JUST FOCUS ON YOURSELF!
...
BUT GOD KNEW...

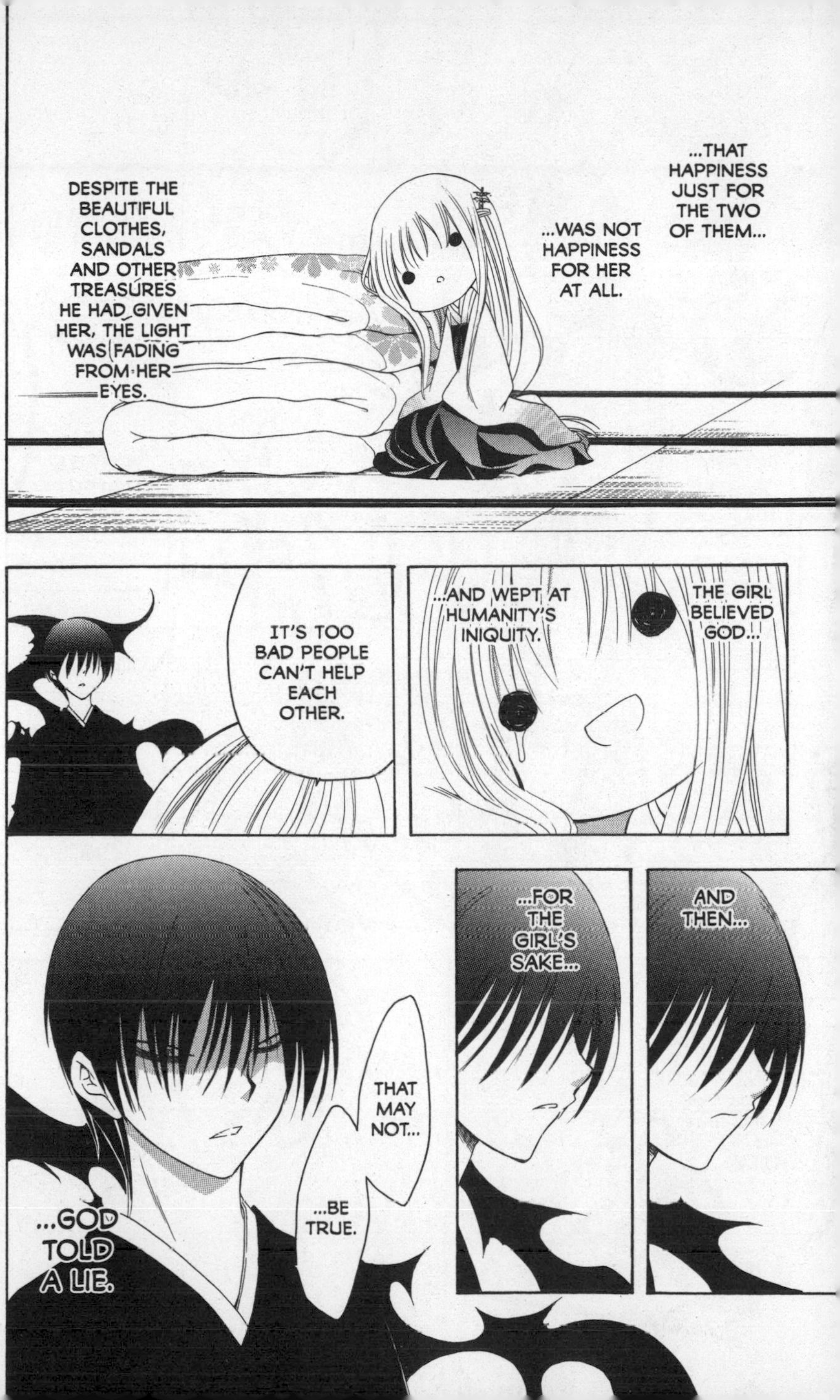
...THAT HAPPINESS JUST FOR THE TWO OF THEM...
...WAS NOT HAPPINESS FOR HER AT ALL.
DESPITE THE BEAUTIFUL CLOTHES, SANDALS AND OTHER TREASURES HE HAD GIVEN HER, THE LIGHT WAS FADING FROM HER EYES.
THE GIRL BELIEVED GOD...
...AND WEPT AT HUMANITY'S INIQUITY.
IT'S TOO BAD PEOPLE CAN'T HELP EACH OTHER.
AND THEN...
...FOR THE GIRL'S SAKE...
THAT MAY NOT...
...BE TRUE.
...GOD TOLD A LIE.

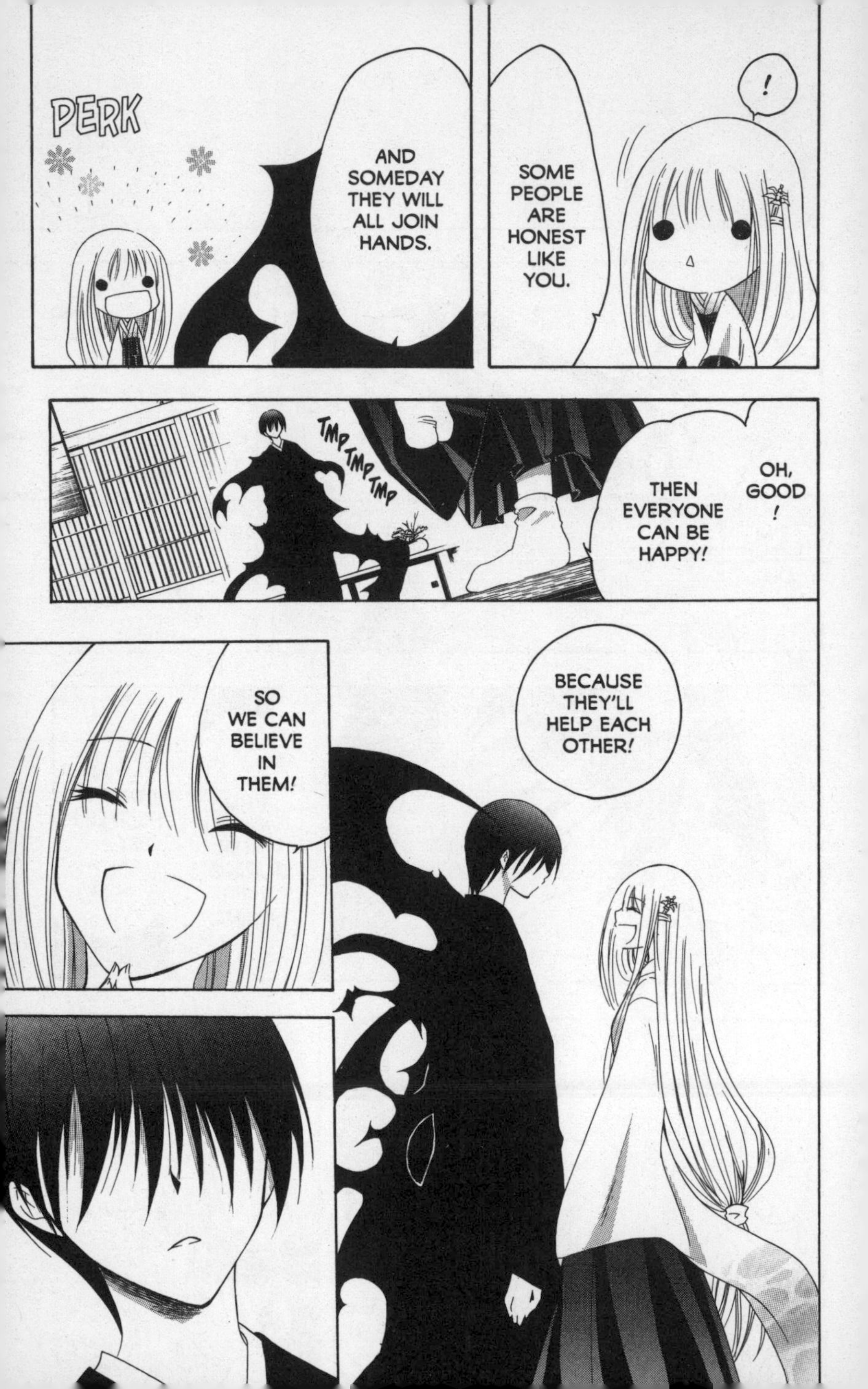
!
SOME PEOPLE ARE HONEST LIKE YOU.
AND SOMEDAY THEY WILL ALL JOIN HANDS.
PERK
OH, GOOD!
THEN EVERYONE CAN BE HAPPY!
TMP TMP TMP TMP
BECAUSE THEY'LL HELP EACH OTHER!
SO WE CAN BELIEVE IN THEM!

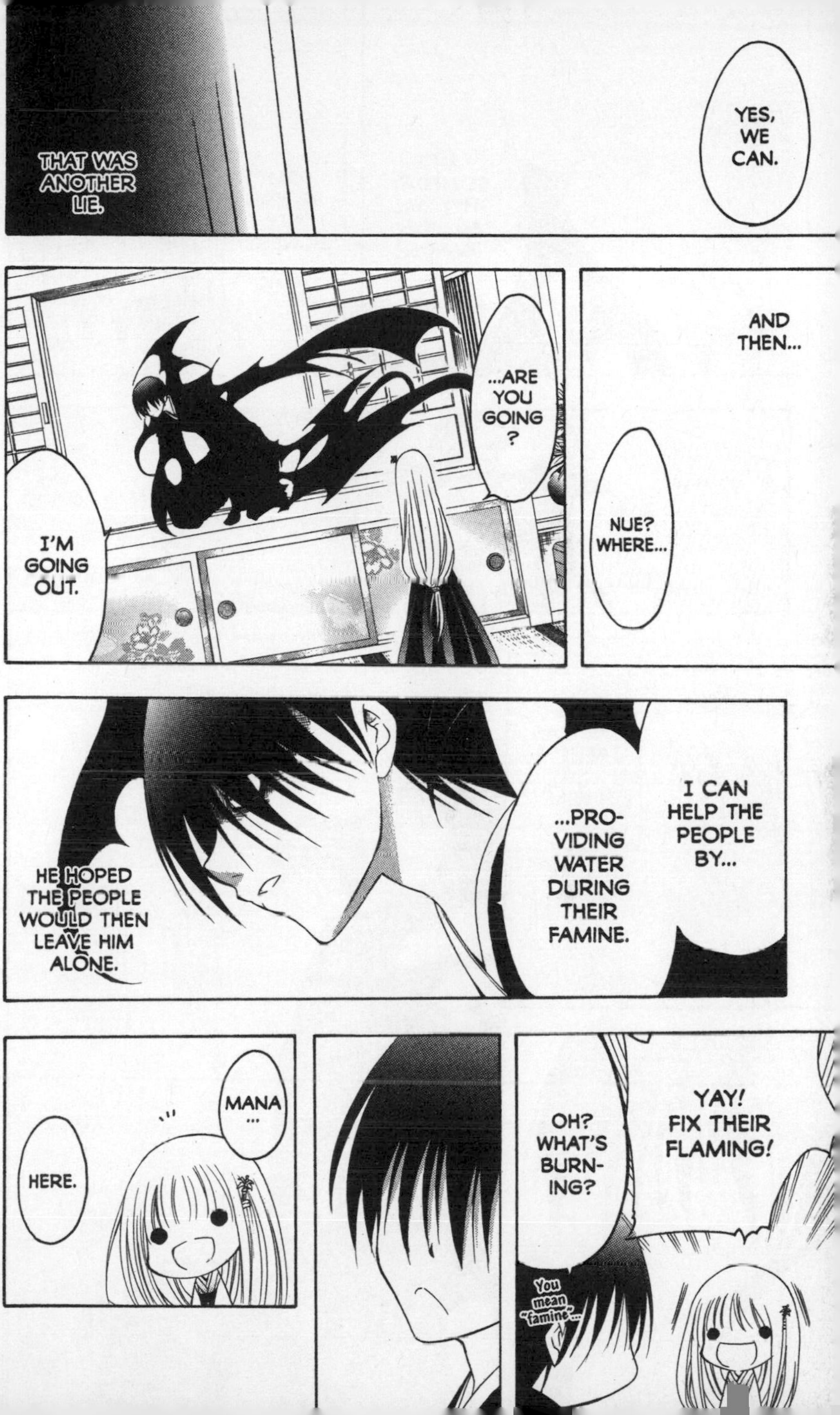
YES, WE CAN.
THAT WAS ANOTHER LIE.
AND THEN...
NUE? WHERE...
...ARE YOU GOING?
I'M GOING OUT.
I CAN HELP THE PEOPLE BY...
...PRO-VIDING WATER DURING THEIR FAMINE.
HE HOPED THE PEOPLE WOULD THEN LEAVE HIM ALONE.
YAY! FIX THEIR FLAMING!
OH? WHAT'S BURN-ING?
You mean "famine"...
MANA...
HERE.

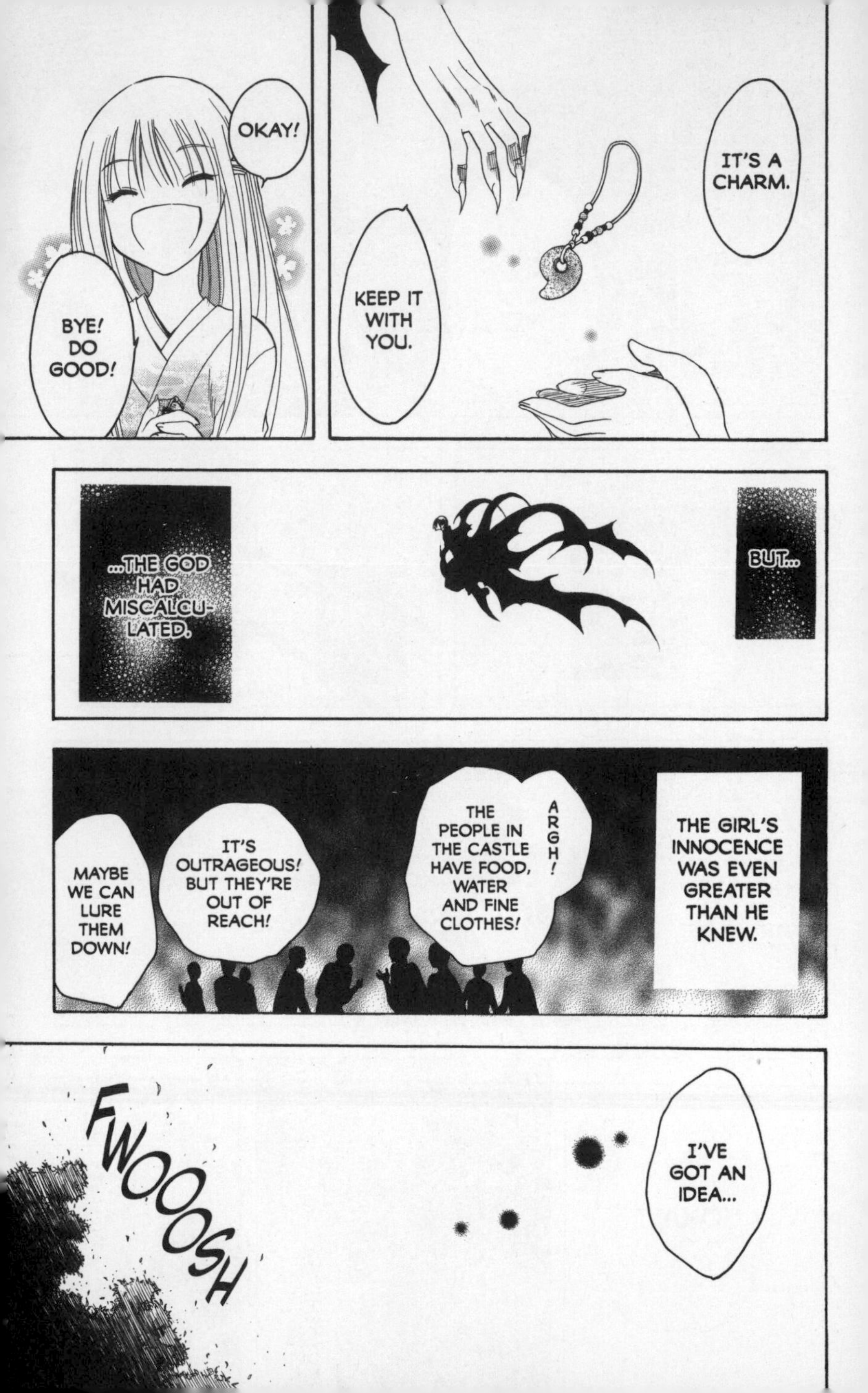
IT'S A CHARM.
KEEP IT WITH YOU.
OKAY!
BYE! DO GOOD!
BUT...
...THE GOD HAD MISCALCULATED.
THE GIRL'S INNOCENCE WAS EVEN GREATER THAN HE KNEW.
ARGH!
THE PEOPLE IN THE CASTLE HAVE FOOD, WATER AND FINE CLOTHES!
IT'S OUTRAGEOUS! BUT THEY'RE OUT OF REACH!
MAYBE WE CAN LURE THEM DOWN!
I'VE GOT AN IDEA...
FWOOOSH

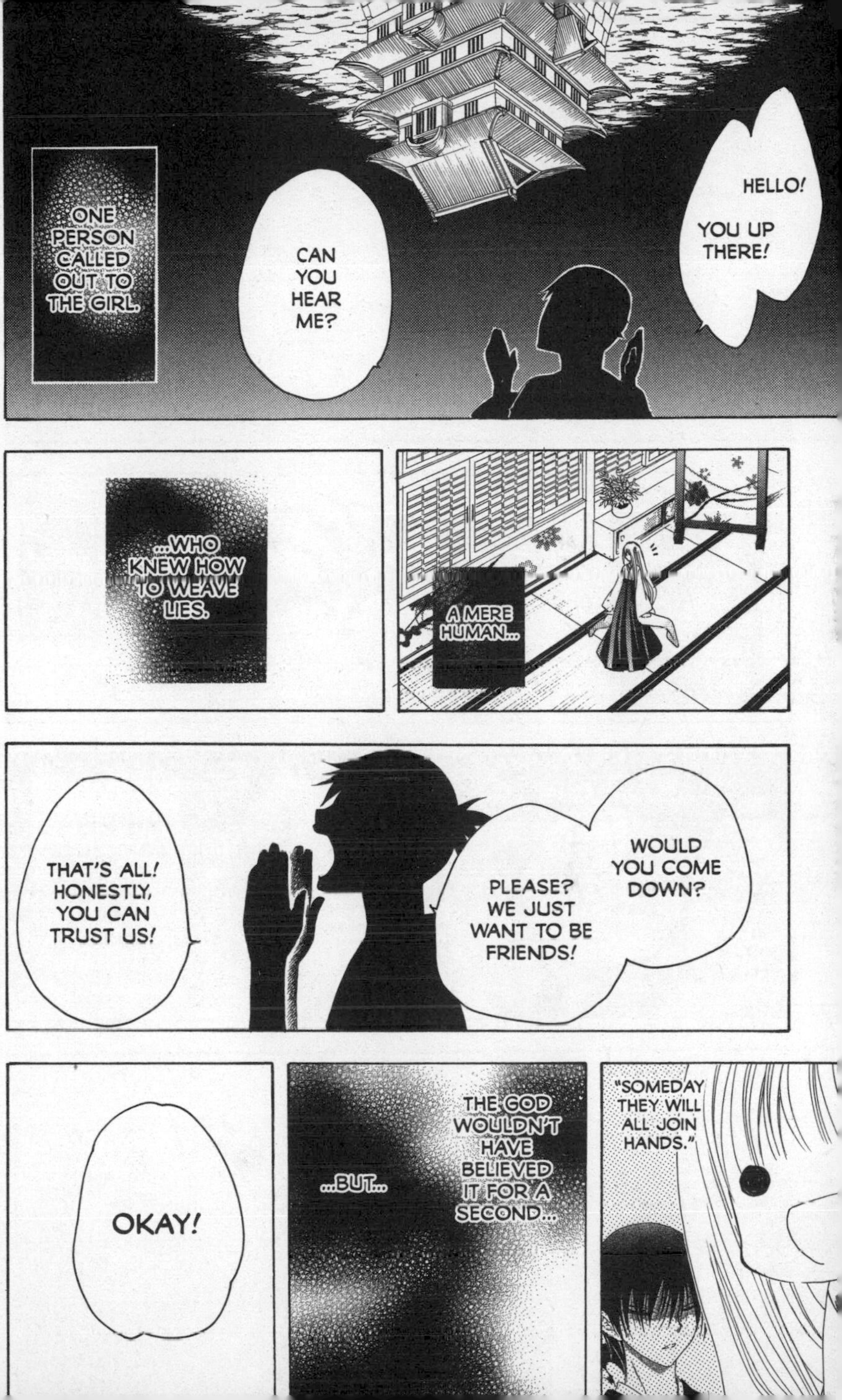
HELLO! YOU UP THERE!
CAN YOU HEAR ME?
ONE PERSON CALLED OUT TO THE GIRL.
A MERE HUMAN...
...WHO KNEW HOW TO WEAVE LIES.
WOULD YOU COME DOWN?
PLEASE? WE JUST WANT TO BE FRIENDS!
THAT'S ALL! HONESTLY, YOU CAN TRUST US!
"SOMEDAY THEY WILL ALL JOIN HANDS."
THE GOD WOULDN'T HAVE BELIEVED IT FOR A SECOND...
...BUT...
OKAY!

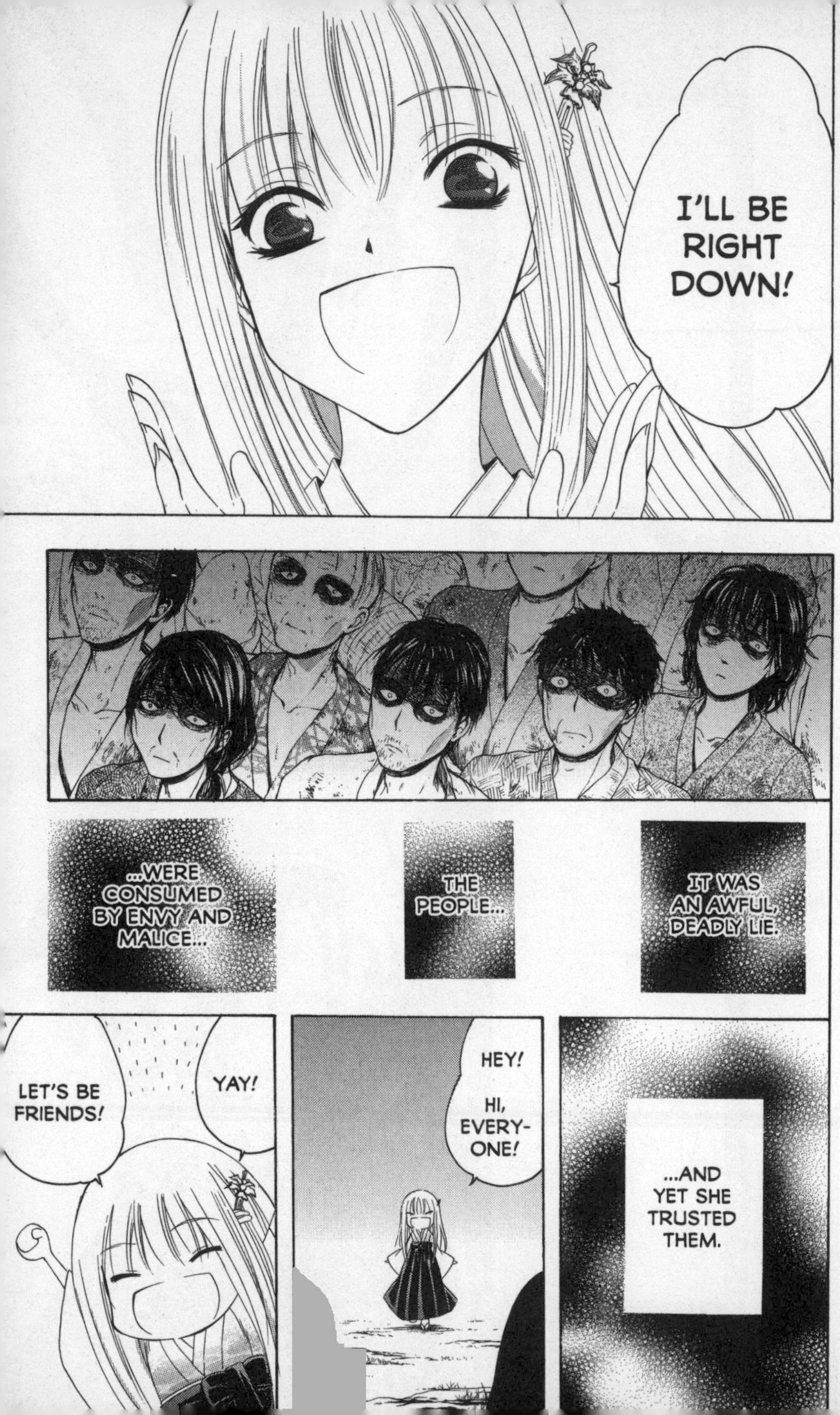
I'LL BE RIGHT DOWN!
IT WAS AN AWFUL, DEADLY LIE.
THE PEOPLE...
...WERE CONSUMED BY ENVY AND MALICE...
...AND YET SHE TRUSTED THEM.
HEY!
HI, EVERYONE!
YAY!
LET'S BE FRIENDS!

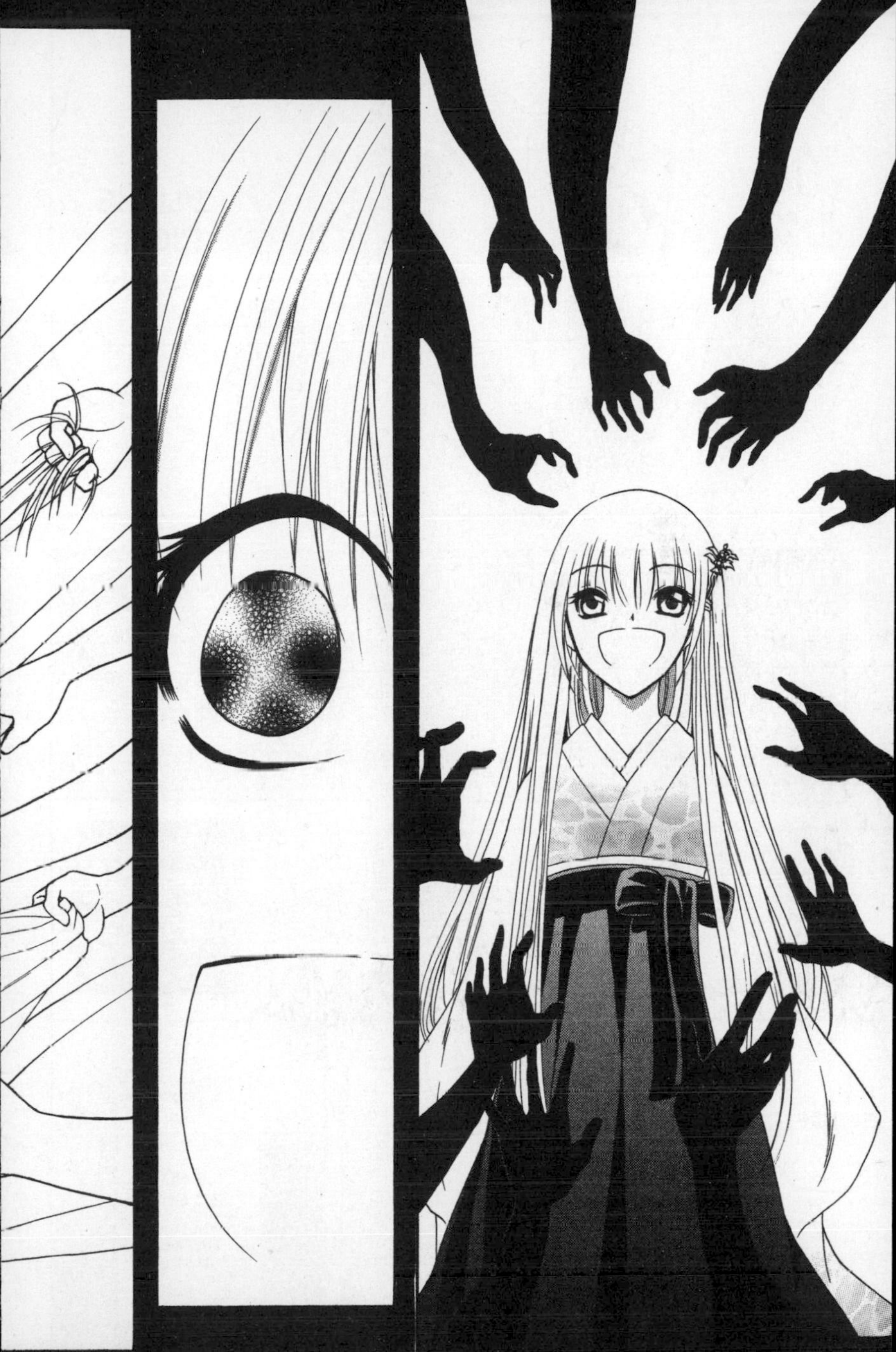

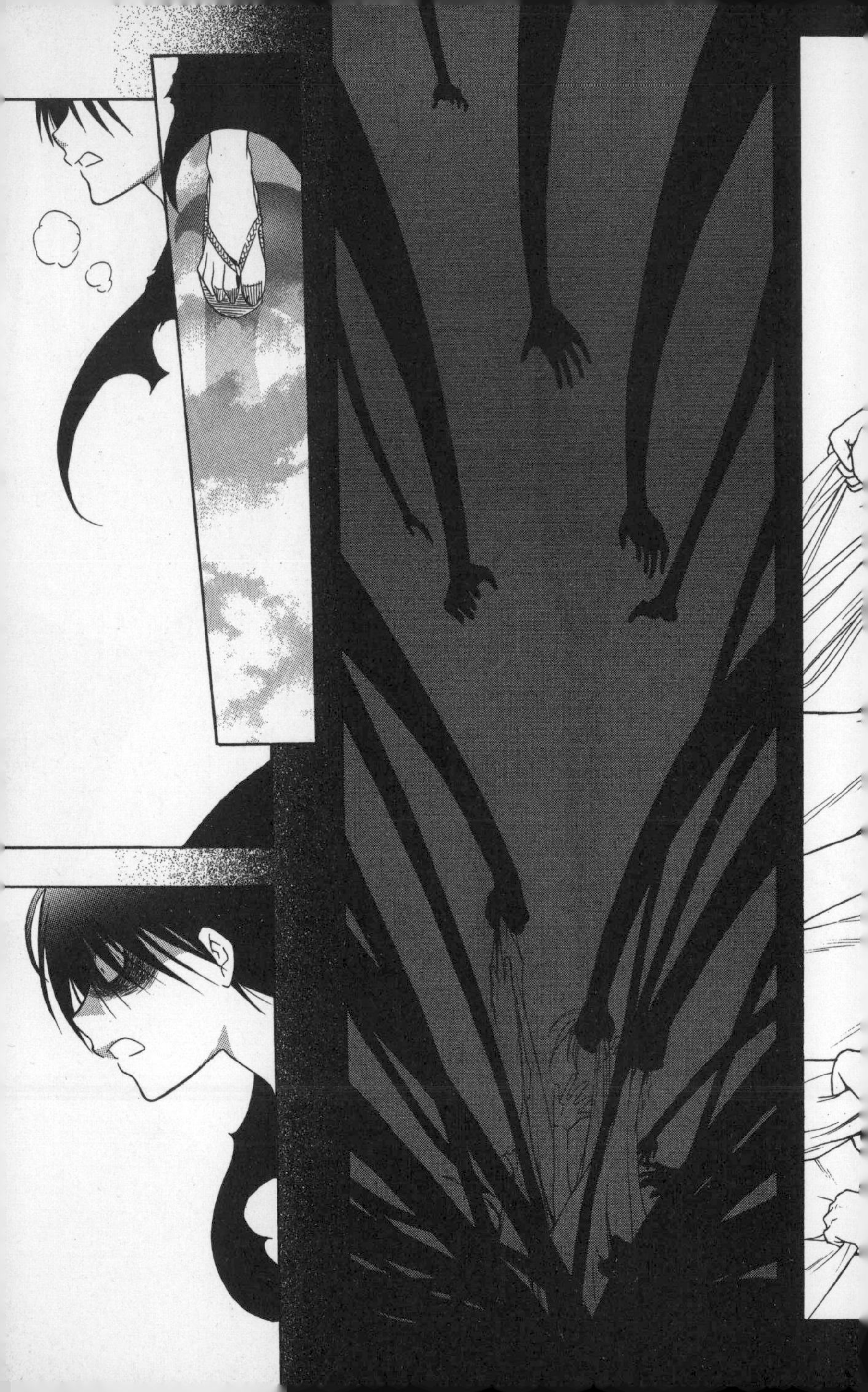

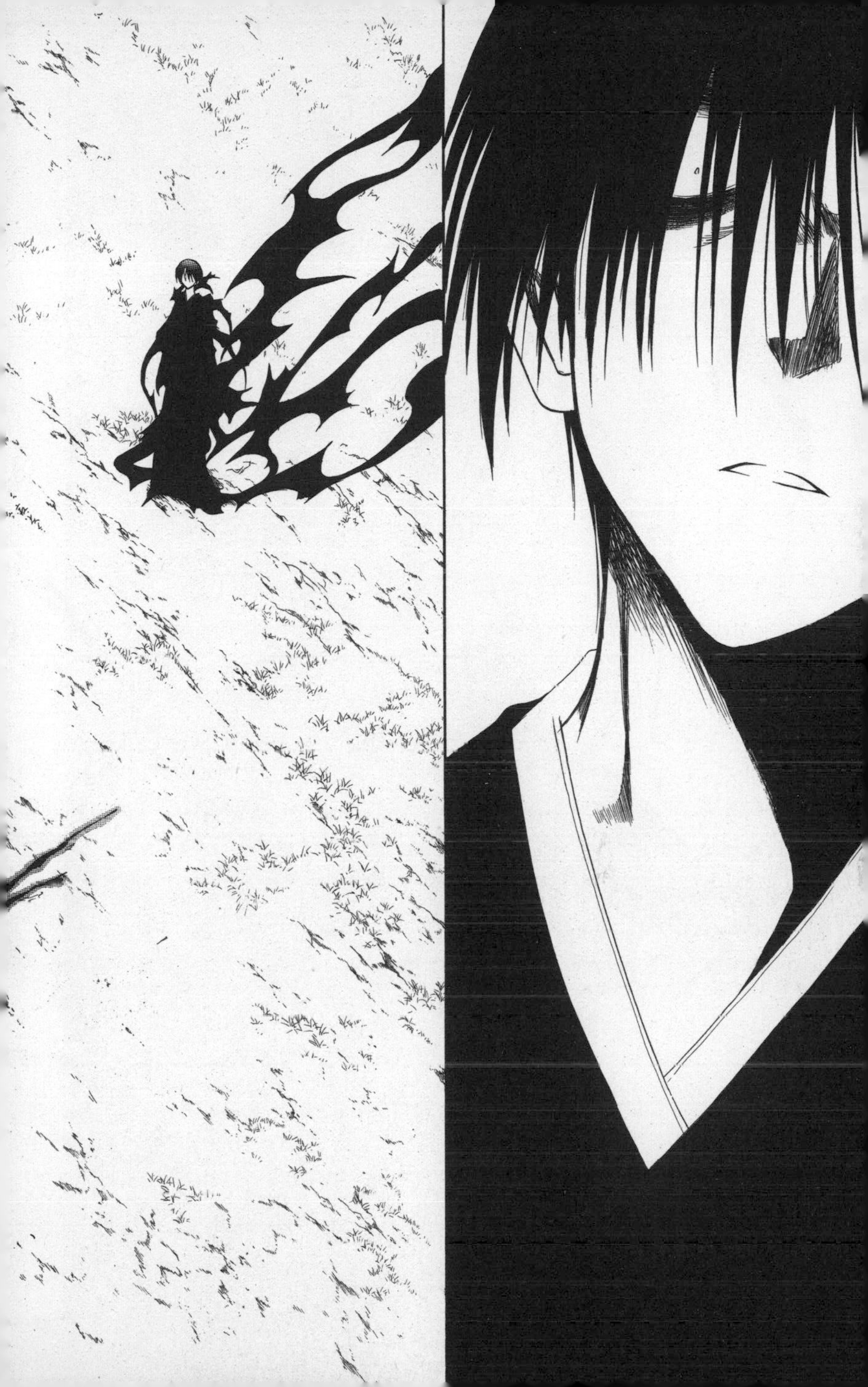

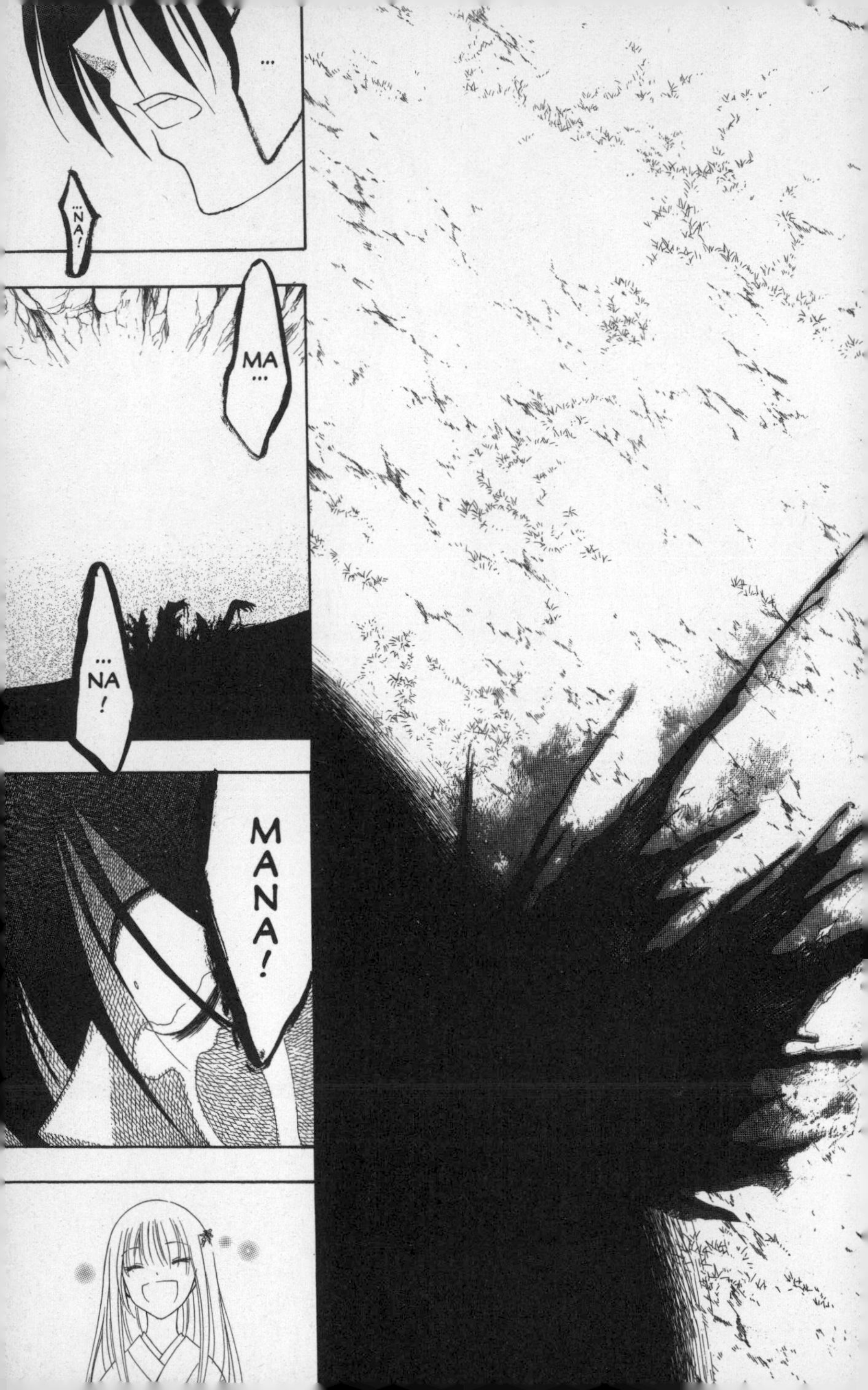
...
...NA!
MA...
...NA!
MANA!

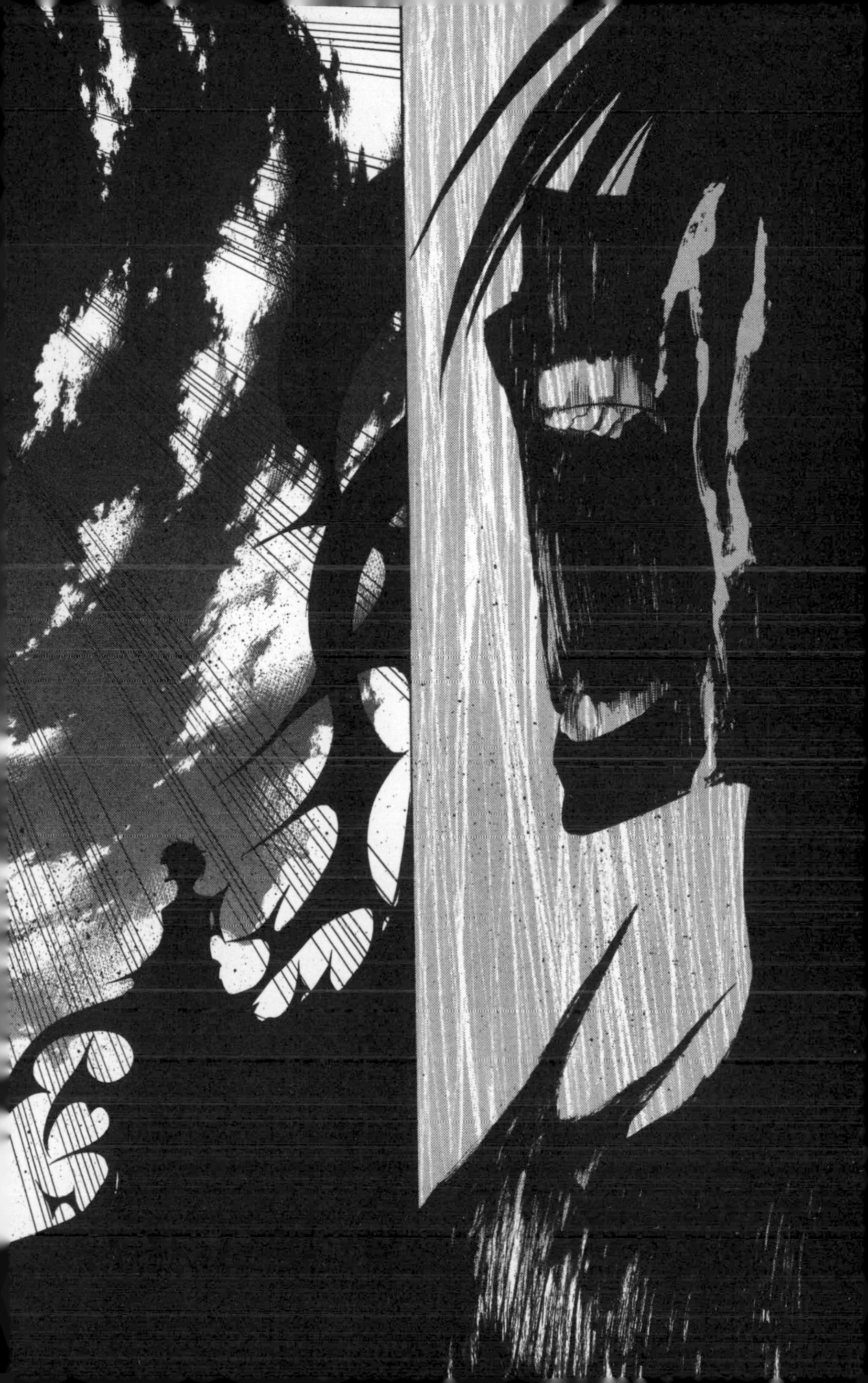

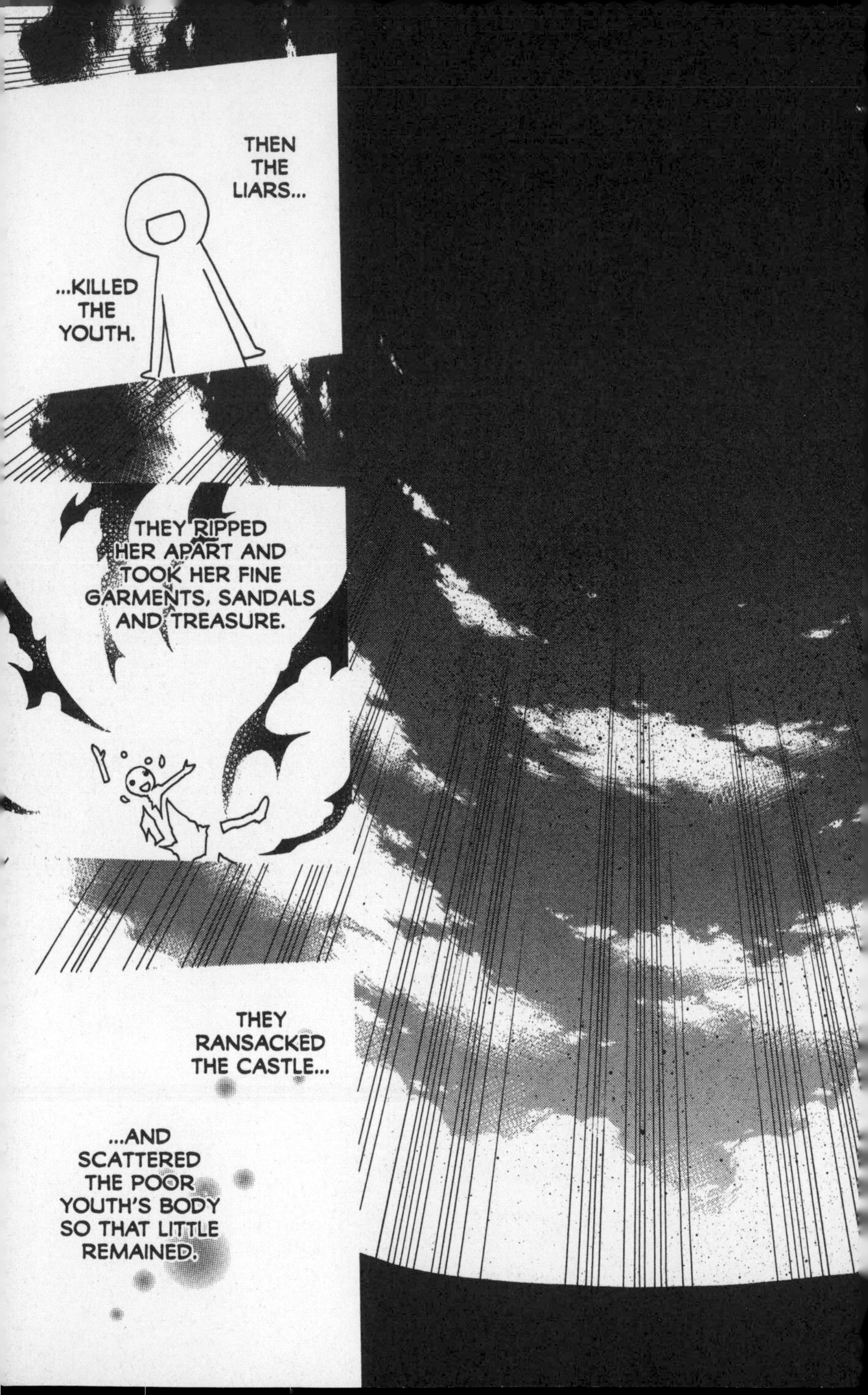
THEN THE LIARS...
...KILLED THE YOUTH.
THEY RIPPED HER APART AND TOOK HER FINE GARMENTS, SANDALS AND TREASURE.
THEY RANSACKED THE CASTLE...
...AND SCATTERED THE POOR YOUTH'S BODY SO THAT LITTLE REMAINED.

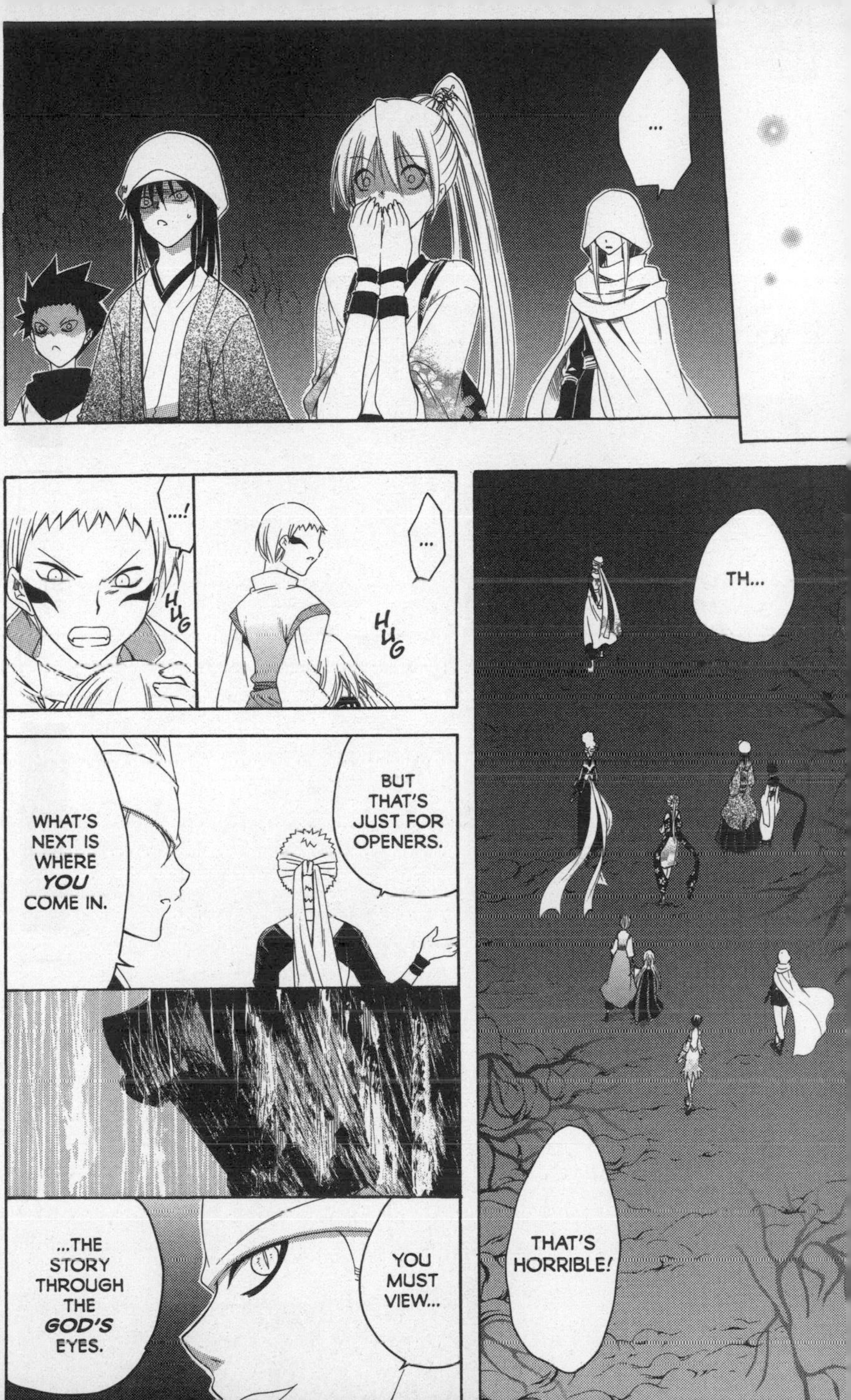
...
TH...
THAT'S HORRIBLE!
...
HUG
...!
HUG
BUT THAT'S JUST FOR OPENERS.
WHAT'S NEXT IS WHERE *YOU* COME IN.
YOU MUST VIEW...
...THE STORY THROUGH THE *GOD'S* EYES.

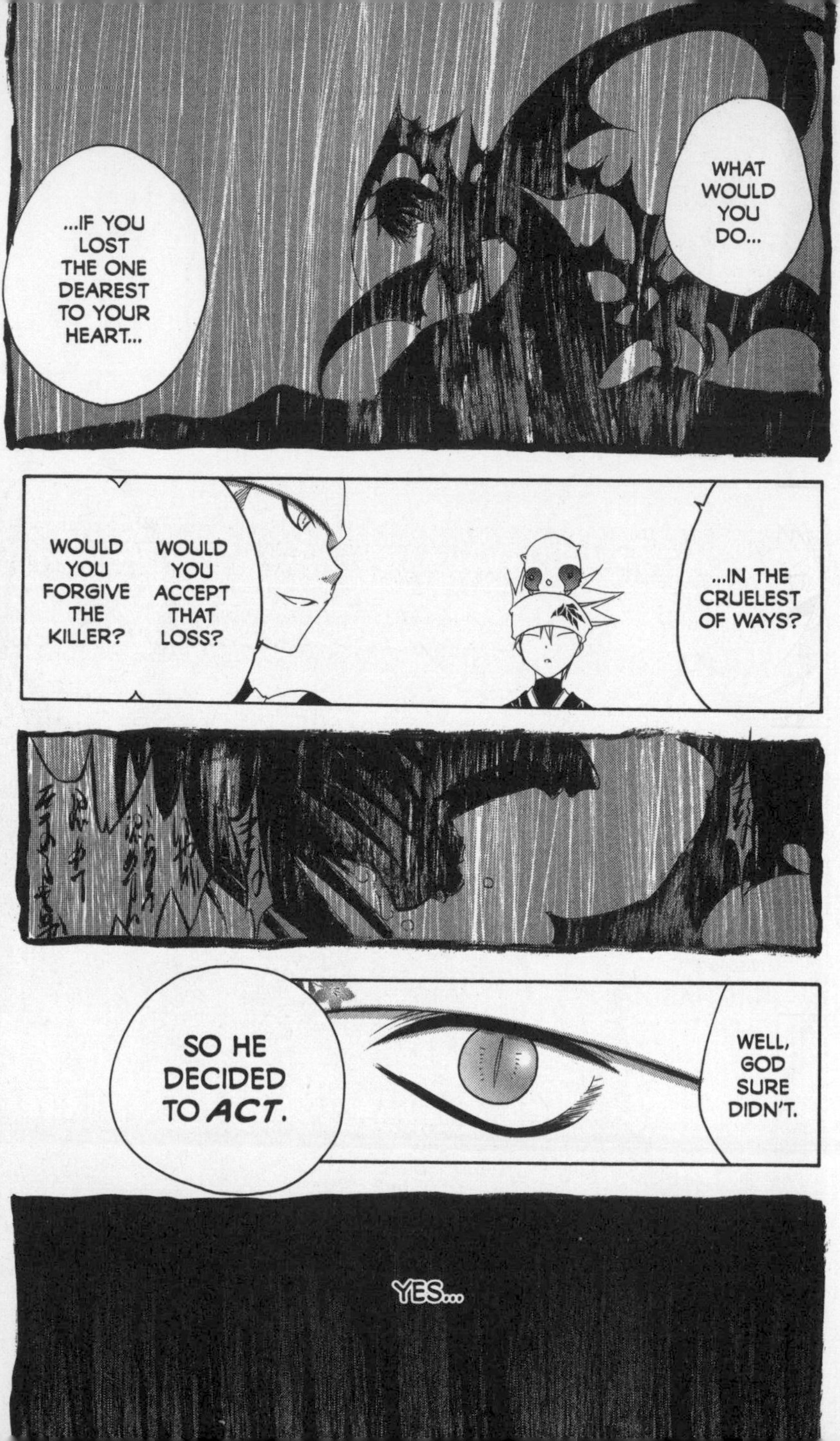
WHAT WOULD YOU DO...
...IF YOU LOST THE ONE DEAREST TO YOUR HEART...
...IN THE CRUELEST OF WAYS?
WOULD YOU ACCEPT THAT LOSS?
WOULD YOU FORGIVE THE KILLER?
WELL, GOD SURE DIDN'T.
SO HE DECIDED TO ACT.
YES...

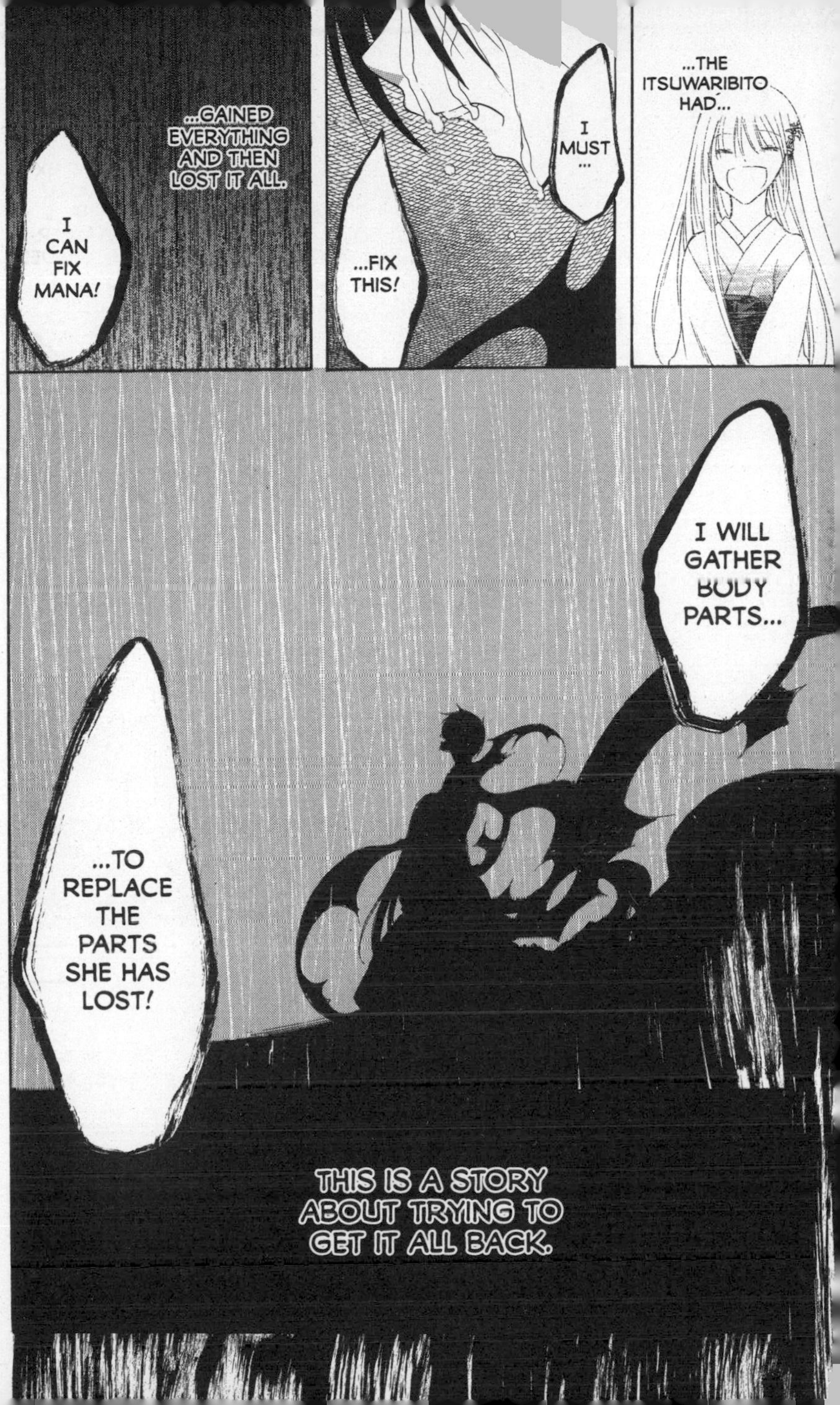
...THE ITSUWARIBITO HAD...
I MUST...
...FIX THIS!
...GAINED EVERYTHING AND THEN LOST IT ALL.
I CAN FIX MANA!
I WILL GATHER BODY PARTS...
...TO REPLACE THE PARTS SHE HAS LOST!
THIS IS A STORY ABOUT TRYING TO GET IT ALL BACK.

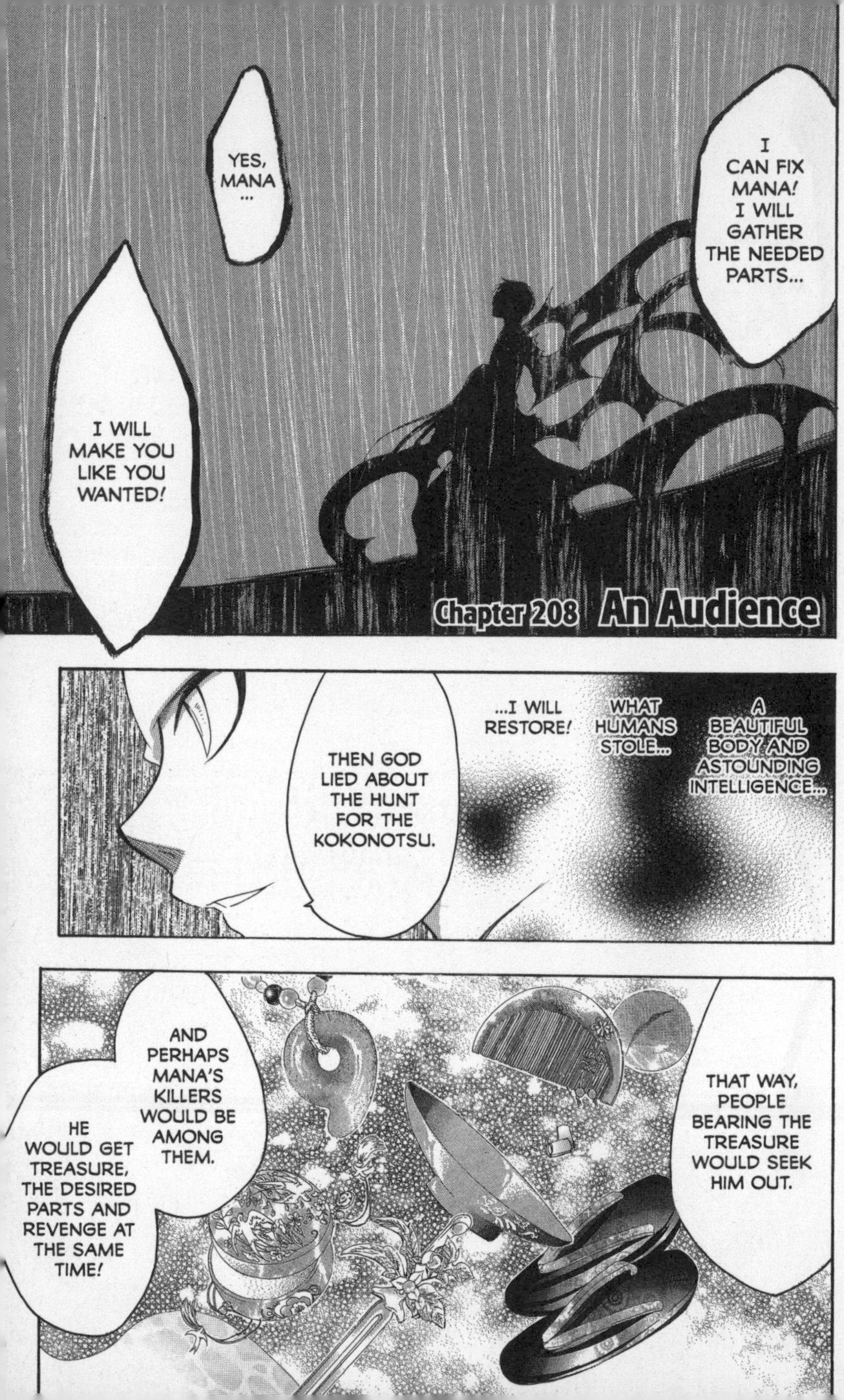
I CAN FIX MANA! I WILL GATHER THE NEEDED PARTS...
YES, MANA ...
I WILL MAKE YOU LIKE YOU WANTED!
Chapter 208 An Audience
A BEAUTIFUL BODY AND ASTOUNDING INTELLIGENCE...
WHAT HUMANS STOLE...
...I WILL RESTORE!
THEN GOD LIED ABOUT THE HUNT FOR THE KOKONOTSU.
THAT WAY, PEOPLE BEARING THE TREASURE WOULD SEEK HIM OUT.
AND PERHAPS MANA'S KILLERS WOULD BE AMONG THEM.
HE WOULD GET TREASURE, THE DESIRED PARTS AND REVENGE AT THE SAME TIME!

Chapter 208
An Audience

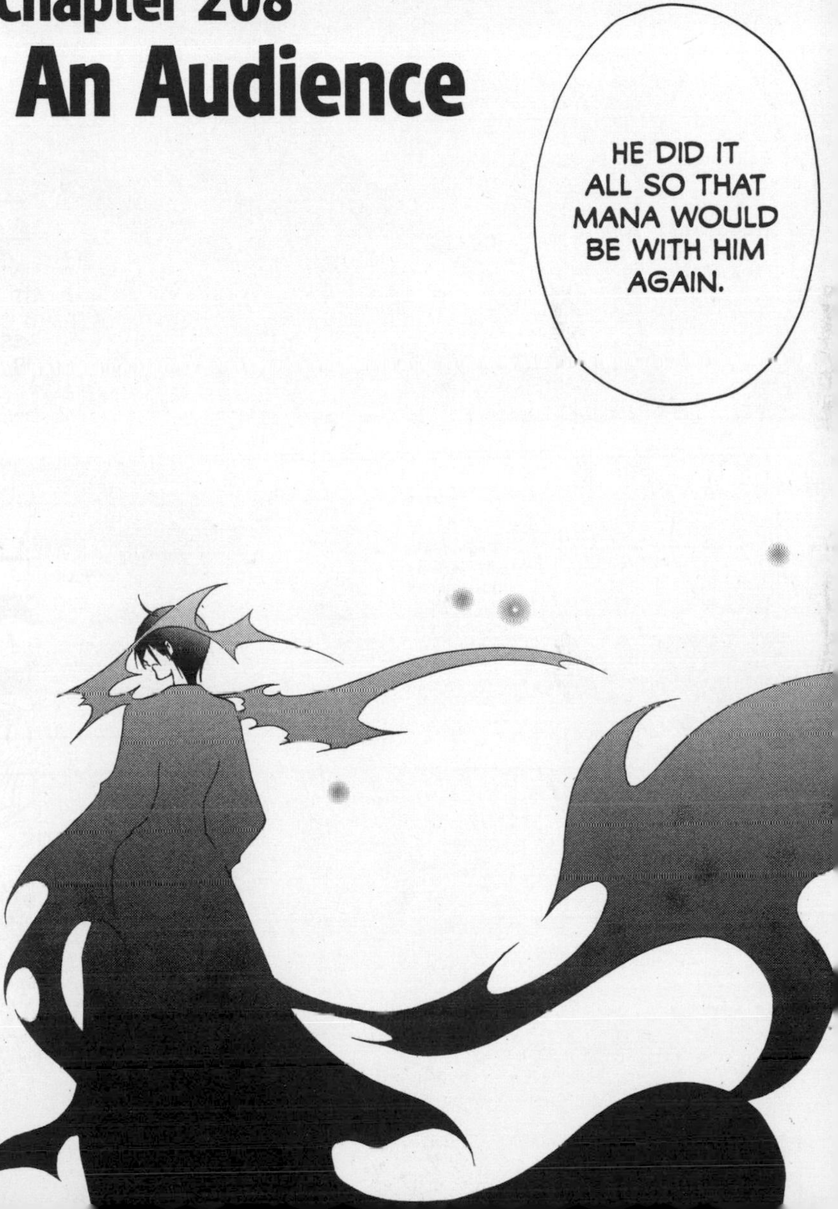
HE DID IT ALL SO THAT MANA WOULD BE WITH HIM AGAIN.

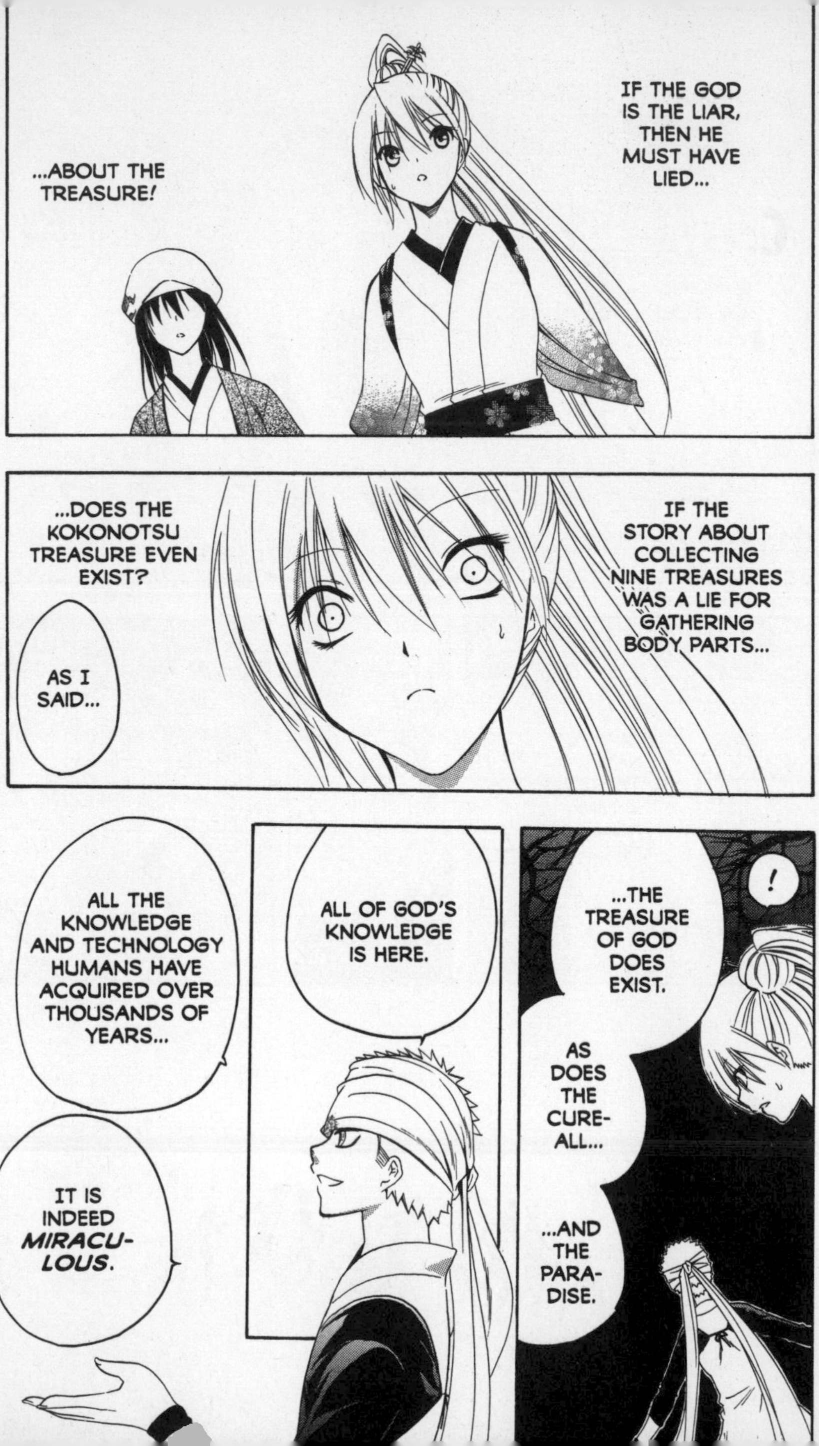
IF THE GOD IS THE LIAR, THEN HE MUST HAVE LIED...
...ABOUT THE TREASURE!
IF THE STORY ABOUT COLLECTING NINE TREASURES WAS A LIE FOR GATHERING BODY PARTS...
...DOES THE KOKONOTSU TREASURE EVEN EXIST?
AS I SAID...
!
...THE TREASURE OF GOD DOES EXIST.
AS DOES THE CURE-ALL...
...AND THE PARA-DISE.
ALL OF GOD'S KNOWLEDGE IS HERE.
ALL THE KNOWLEDGE AND TECHNOLOGY HUMANS HAVE ACQUIRED OVER THOUSANDS OF YEARS...
IT IS INDEED *MIRACULOUS*.

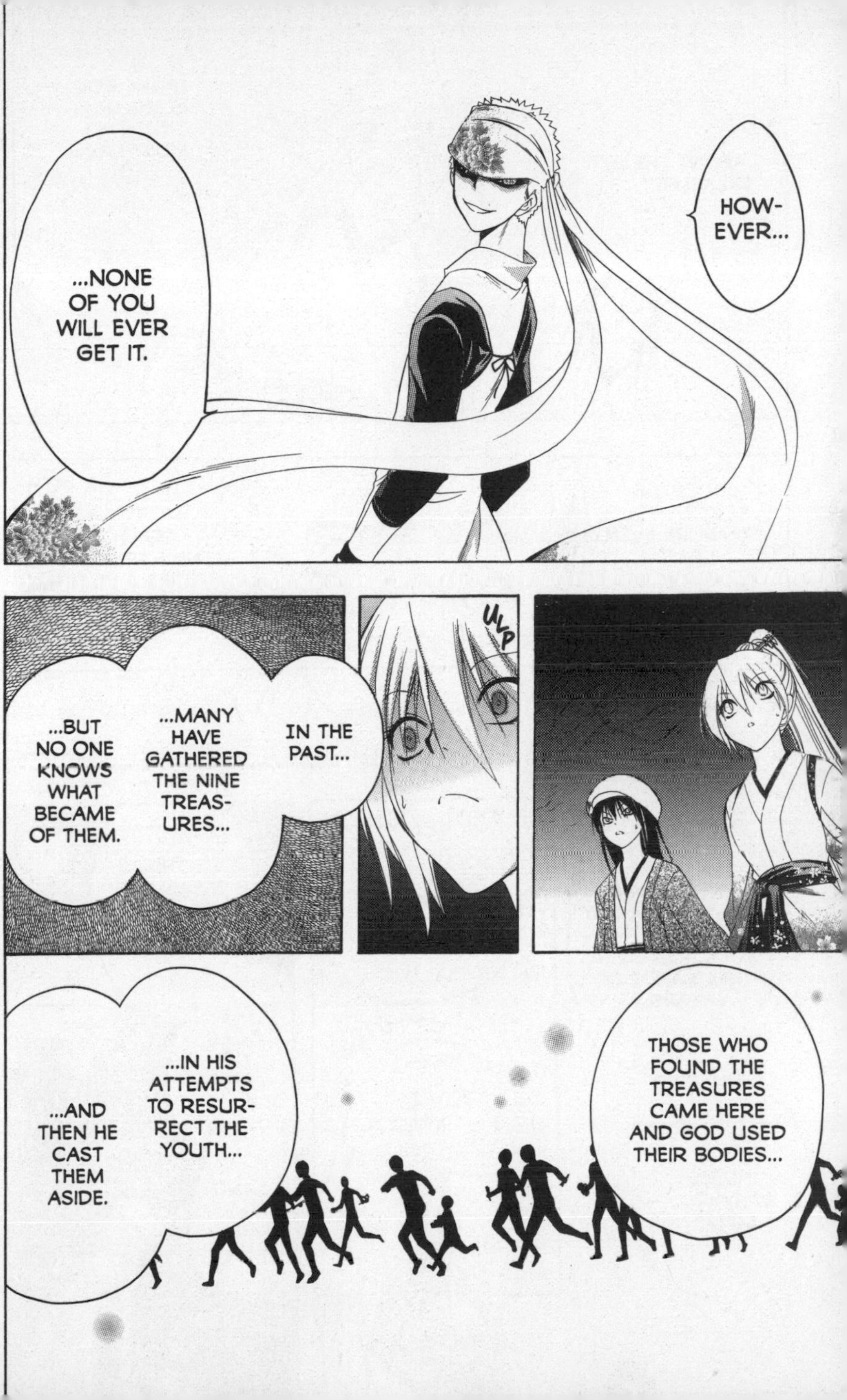
HOW-EVER...
...NONE OF YOU WILL EVER GET IT.
UVP
IN THE PAST...
...MANY HAVE GATHERED THE NINE TREAS-URES...
...BUT NO ONE KNOWS WHAT BECAME OF THEM.
THOSE WHO FOUND THE TREASURES CAME HERE AND GOD USED THEIR BODIES...
...IN HIS ATTEMPTS TO RESUR-RECT THE YOUTH...
...AND THEN HE CAST THEM ASIDE.

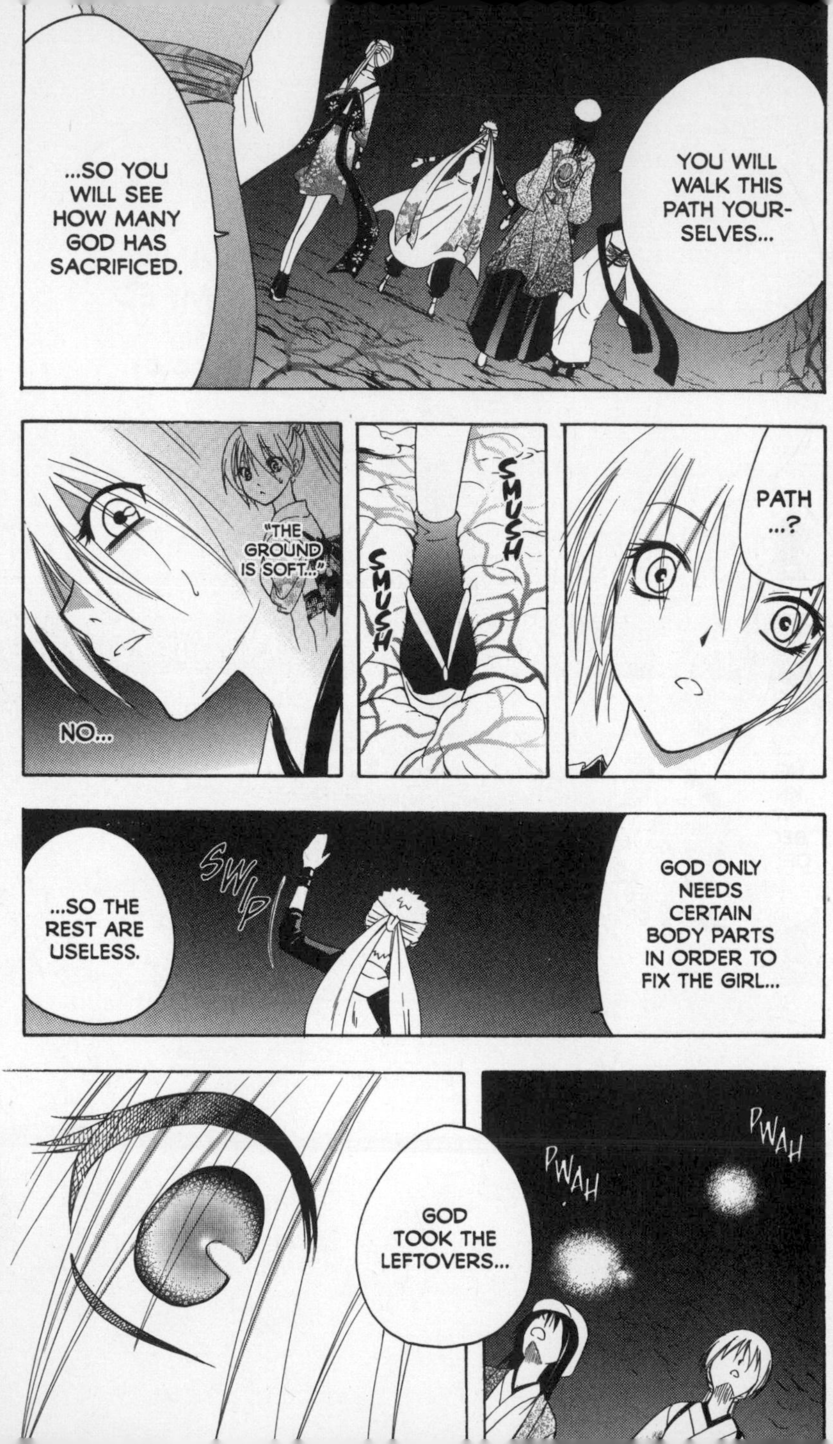
YOU WILL WALK THIS PATH YOUR-SELVES...
...SO YOU WILL SEE HOW MANY GOD HAS SACRIFICED.
PATH ...?
SMUSH
SMUSH
"THE GROUND IS SOFT..."
NO...
GOD ONLY NEEDS CERTAIN BODY PARTS IN ORDER TO FIX THE GIRL...
SWIP
...SO THE REST ARE USELESS.
PWAH
PWAH
GOD TOOK THE LEFTOVERS...

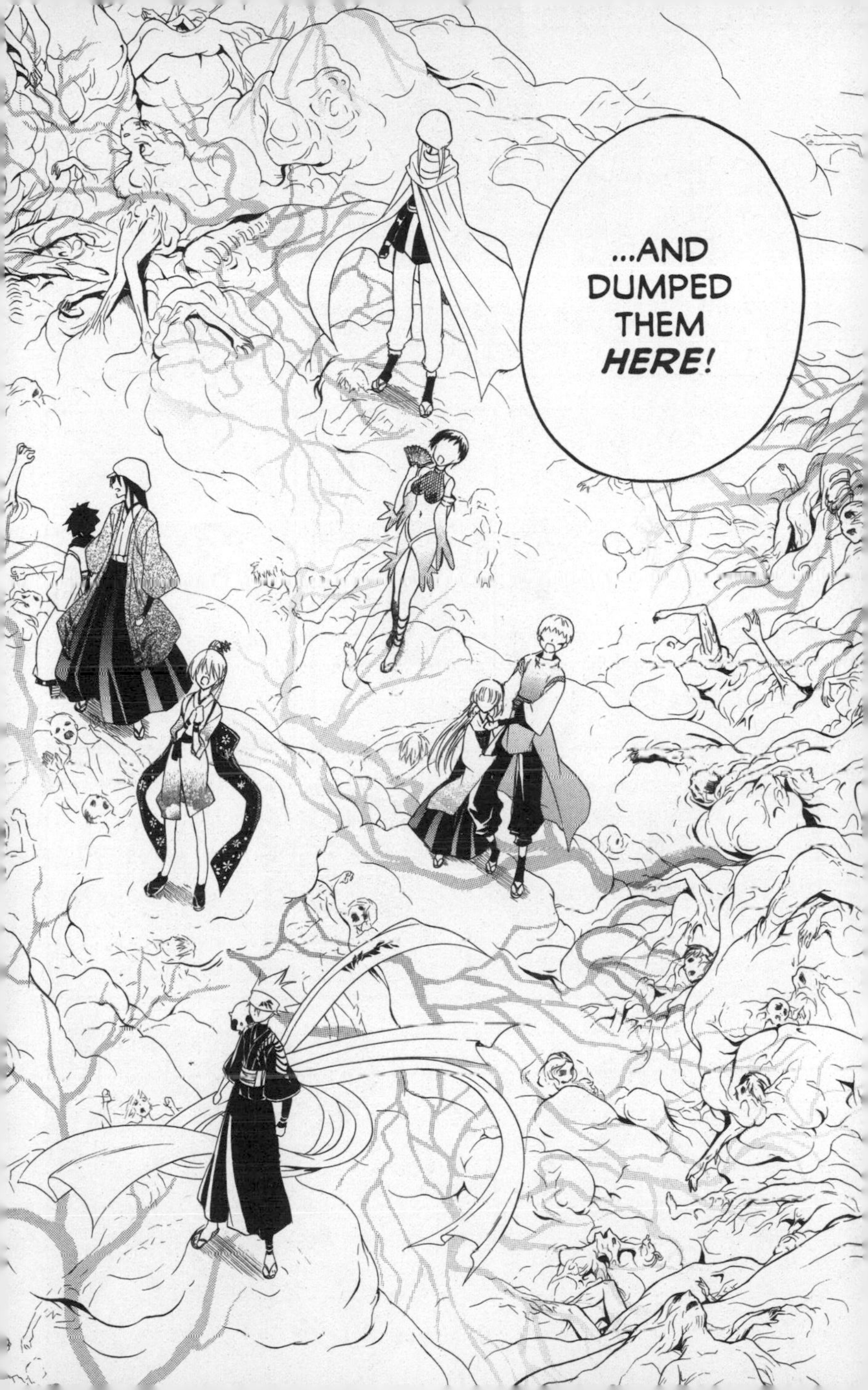
...AND DUMPED THEM *HERE!*

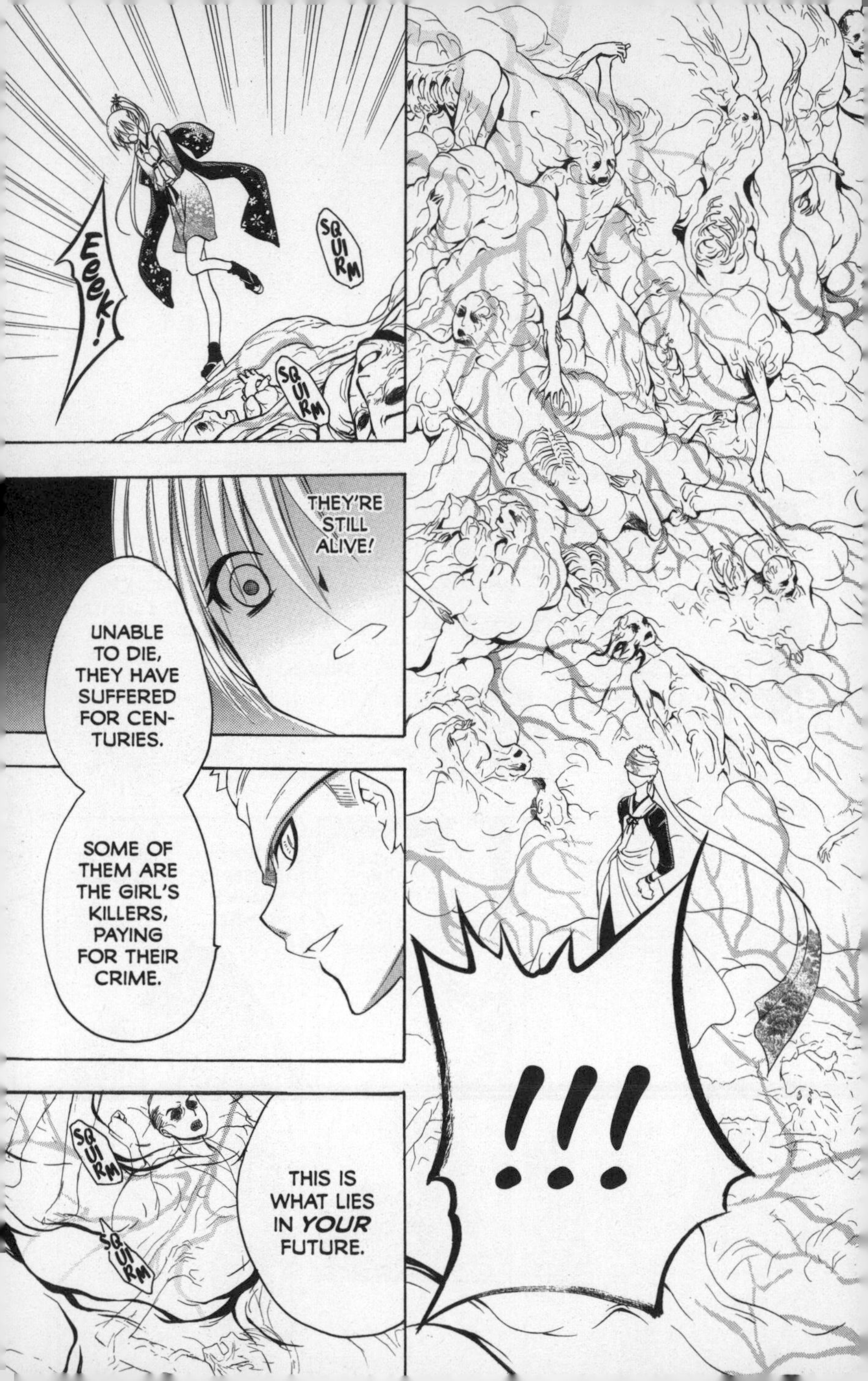
!!!
SQUIRM
Eeek!
SQUIRM
THEY'RE STILL ALIVE!
UNABLE TO DIE, THEY HAVE SUFFERED FOR CENTURIES.
SOME OF THEM ARE THE GIRL'S KILLERS, PAYING FOR THEIR CRIME.
THIS IS WHAT LIES IN *YOUR* FUTURE.
SQUIRM
SQUIRM

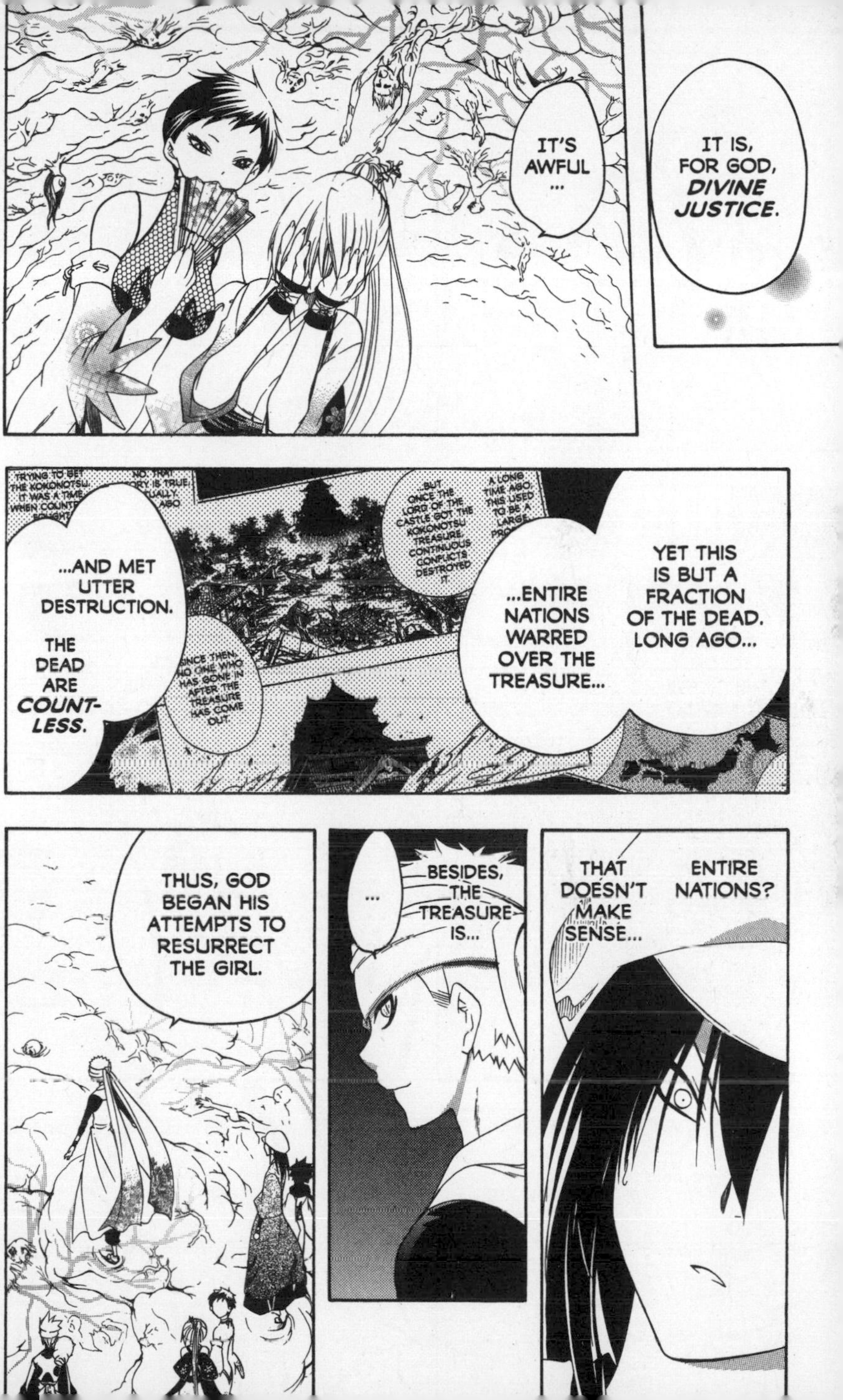
IT IS, FOR GOD, DIVINE JUSTICE.
IT'S AWFUL ...
YET THIS IS BUT A FRACTION OF THE DEAD. LONG AGO...
...ENTIRE NATIONS WARRED OVER THE TREASURE...
BUT ONCE THE LORD OF THE CASTLE GOT THE KOKONOTSU TREASURE, CONTINUOUS CONFLICTS DESTROYED IT.
SINCE THEN, NO ONE WHO HAS GONE IN AFTER THE TREASURE HAS COME OUT.
...AND MET UTTER DESTRUCTION.
THE DEAD ARE COUNTLESS.
ENTIRE NATIONS?
THAT DOESN'T MAKE SENSE...
BESIDES, THE TREASURE IS...
...
THUS, GOD BEGAN HIS ATTEMPTS TO RESURRECT THE GIRL.

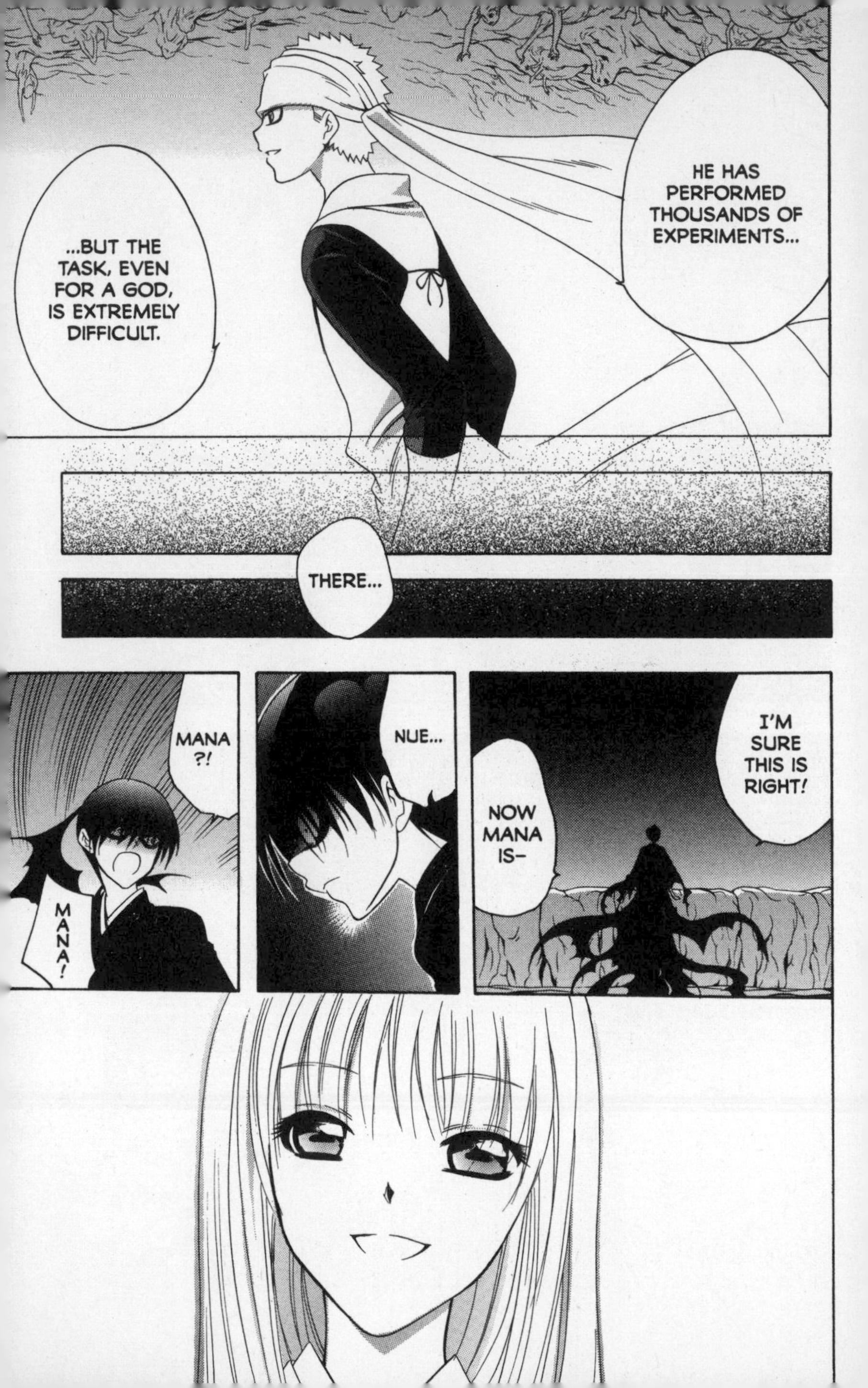
HE HAS PERFORMED THOUSANDS OF EXPERIMENTS...
...BUT THE TASK, EVEN FOR A GOD, IS EXTREMELY DIFFICULT.
THERE...
I'M SURE THIS IS RIGHT!
NOW MANA IS–
NUE...
MANA?!
MANA!

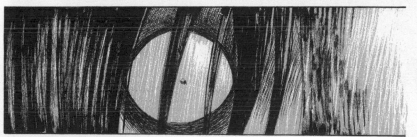

SHE WAS SIMPLY...

...TOO DAMAGED.

MA...

...NA...

NUP...

KOFF *X*!

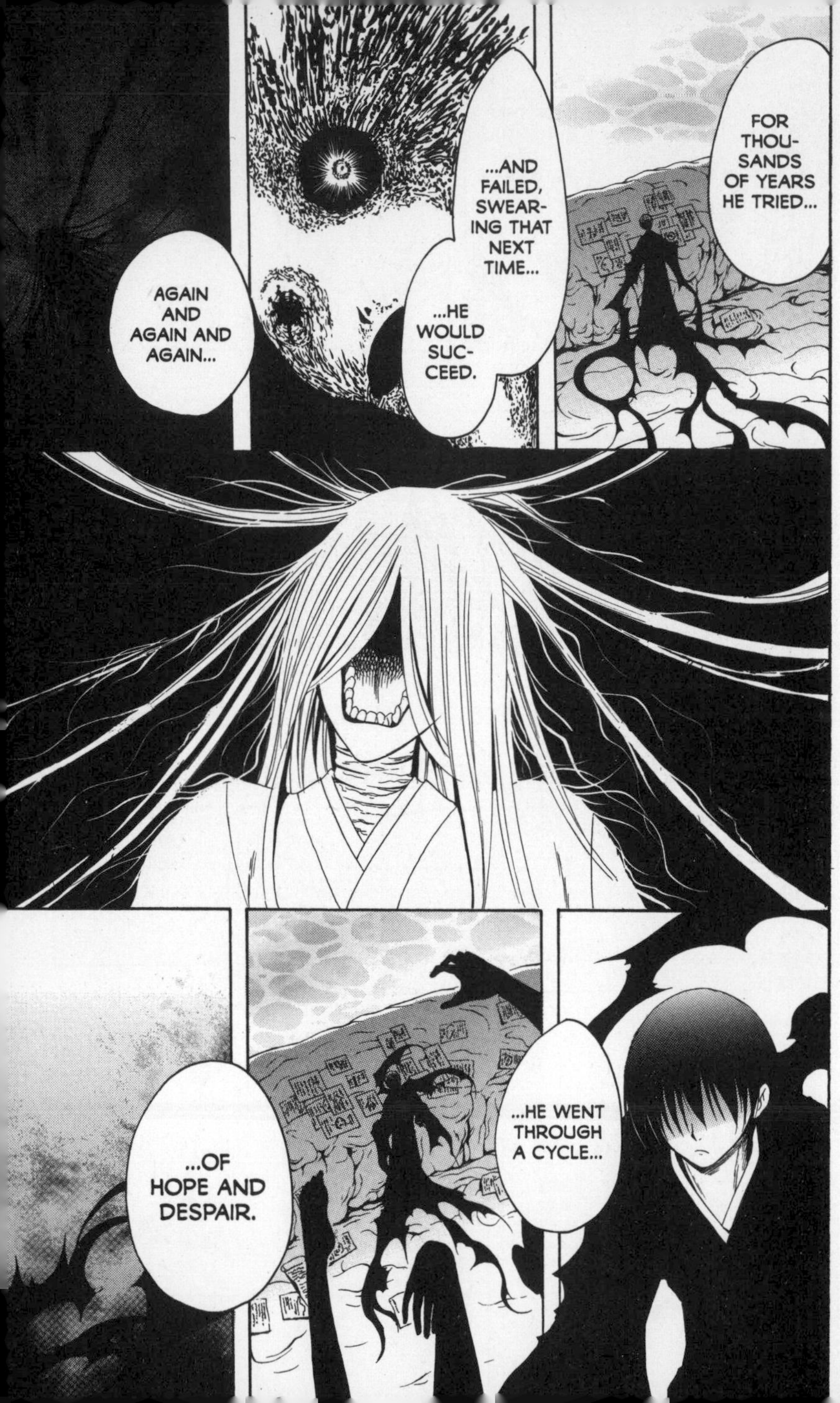
FOR THOUSANDS OF YEARS HE TRIED...
...AND FAILED, SWEARING THAT NEXT TIME...
...HE WOULD SUCCEED.
AGAIN AND AGAIN AND AGAIN...
...HE WENT THROUGH A CYCLE...
...OF HOPE AND DESPAIR.

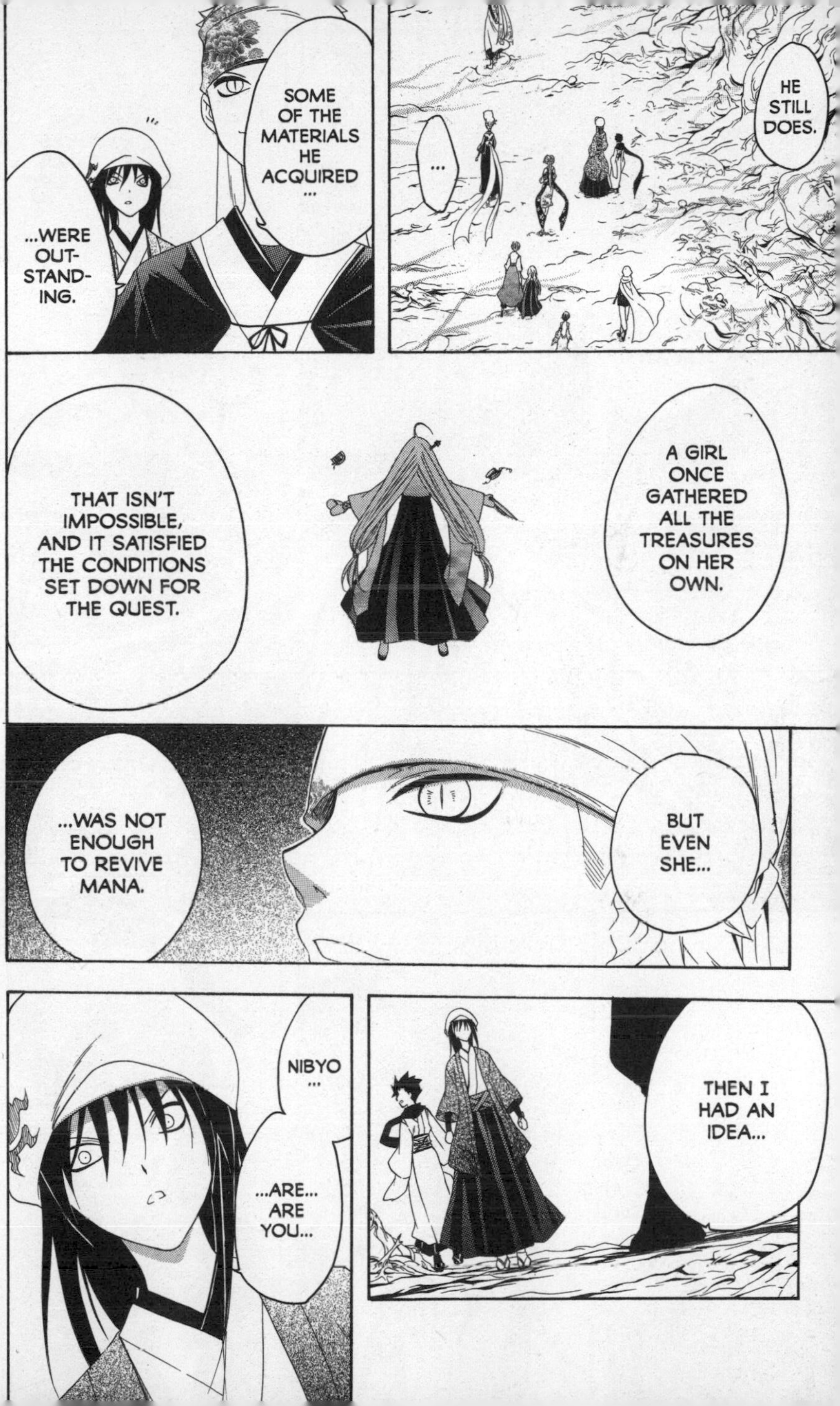
HE STILL DOES.
...
SOME OF THE MATERIALS HE ACQUIRED ...
...WERE OUT-STAND-ING.
A GIRL ONCE GATHERED ALL THE TREASURES ON HER OWN.
THAT ISN'T IMPOSSIBLE, AND IT SATISFIED THE CONDITIONS SET DOWN FOR THE QUEST.
BUT EVEN SHE...
...WAS NOT ENOUGH TO REVIVE MANA.
THEN I HAD AN IDEA...
NIBYO ...
...ARE... ARE YOU...

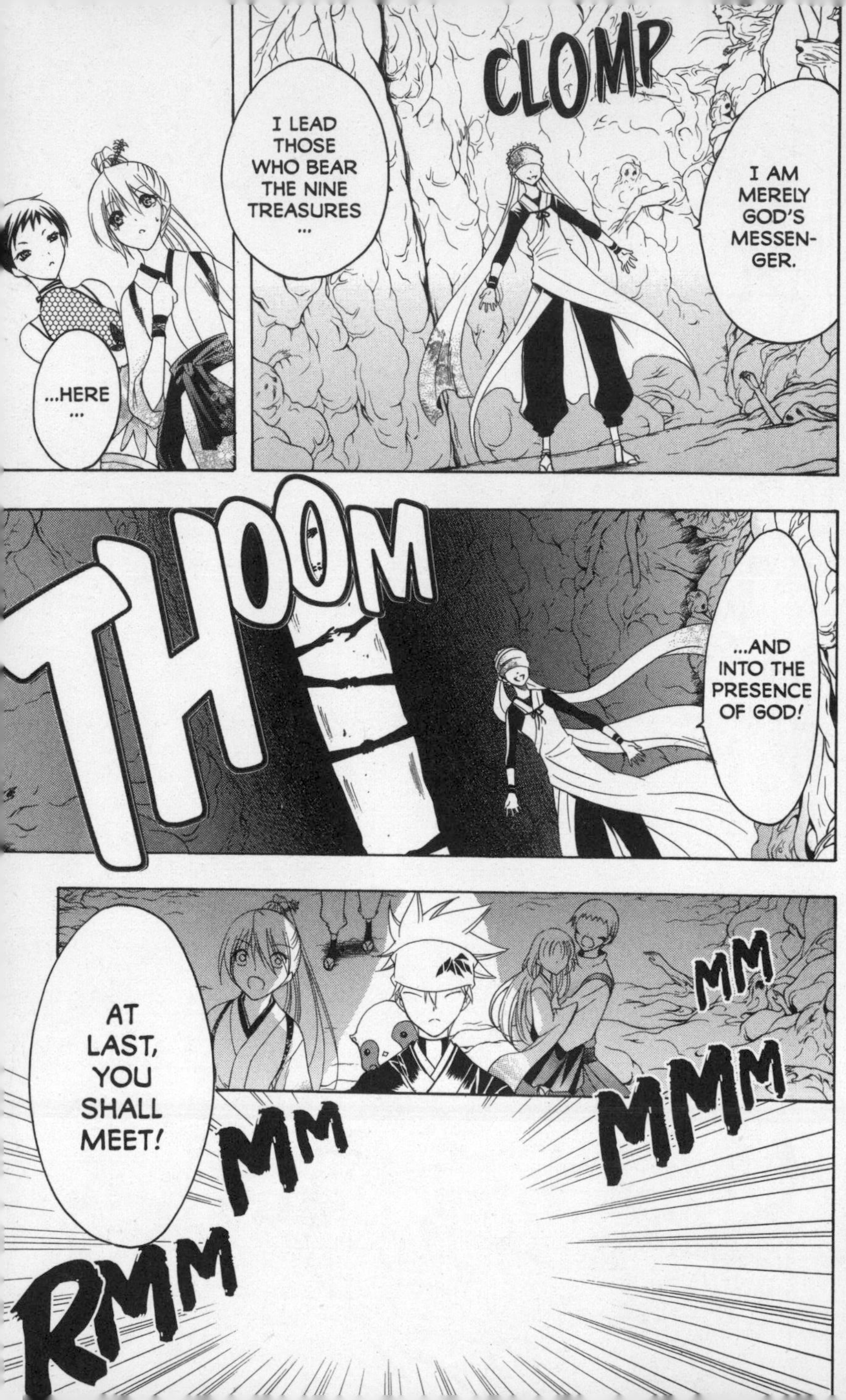
I AM MERELY GOD'S MESSEN-GER.
CLOMP
I LEAD THOSE WHO BEAR THE NINE TREASURES ...
...HERE ...
...AND INTO THE PRESENCE OF GOD!
THOOM
AT LAST, YOU SHALL MEET!
MM MMM
RMM MM

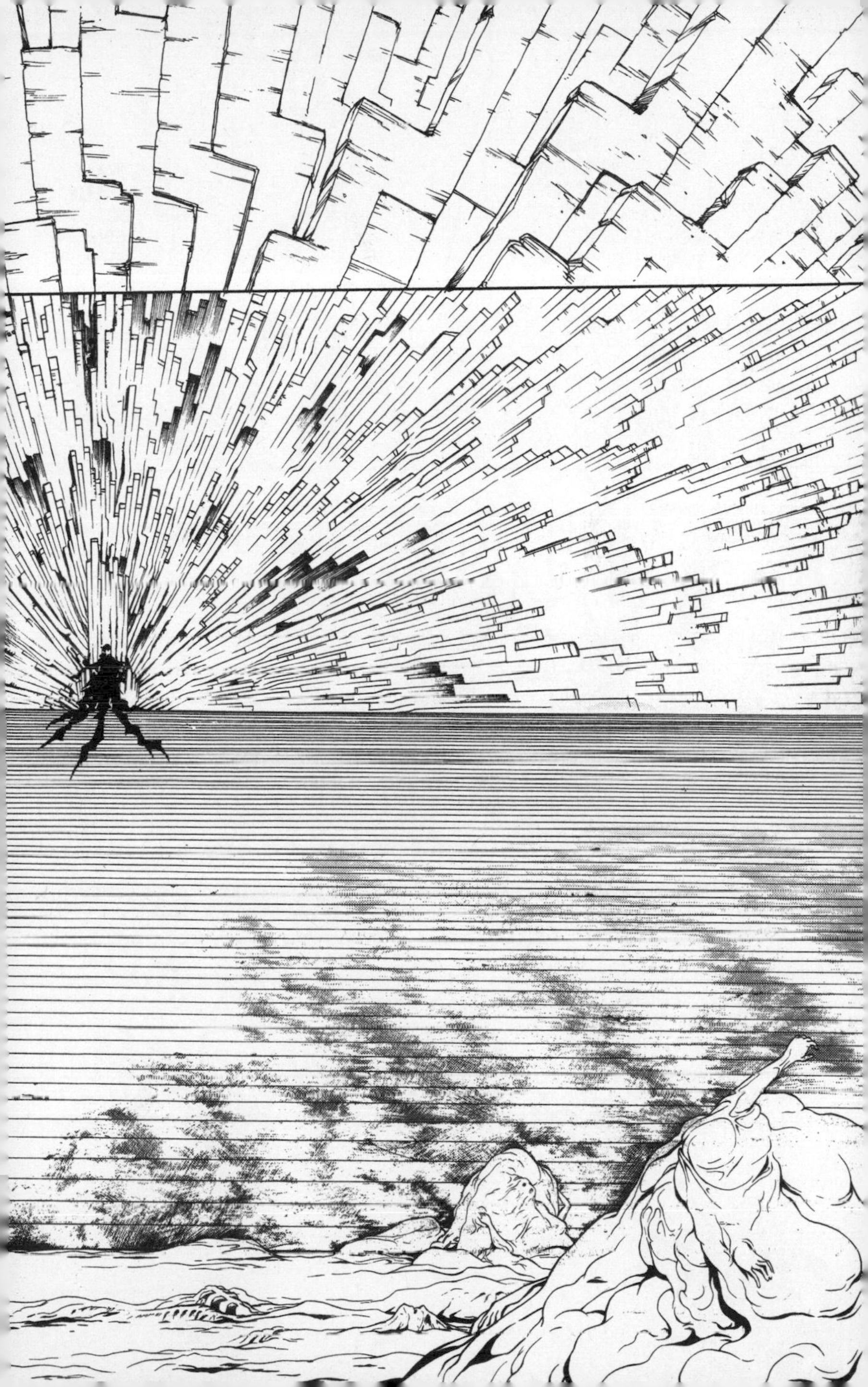

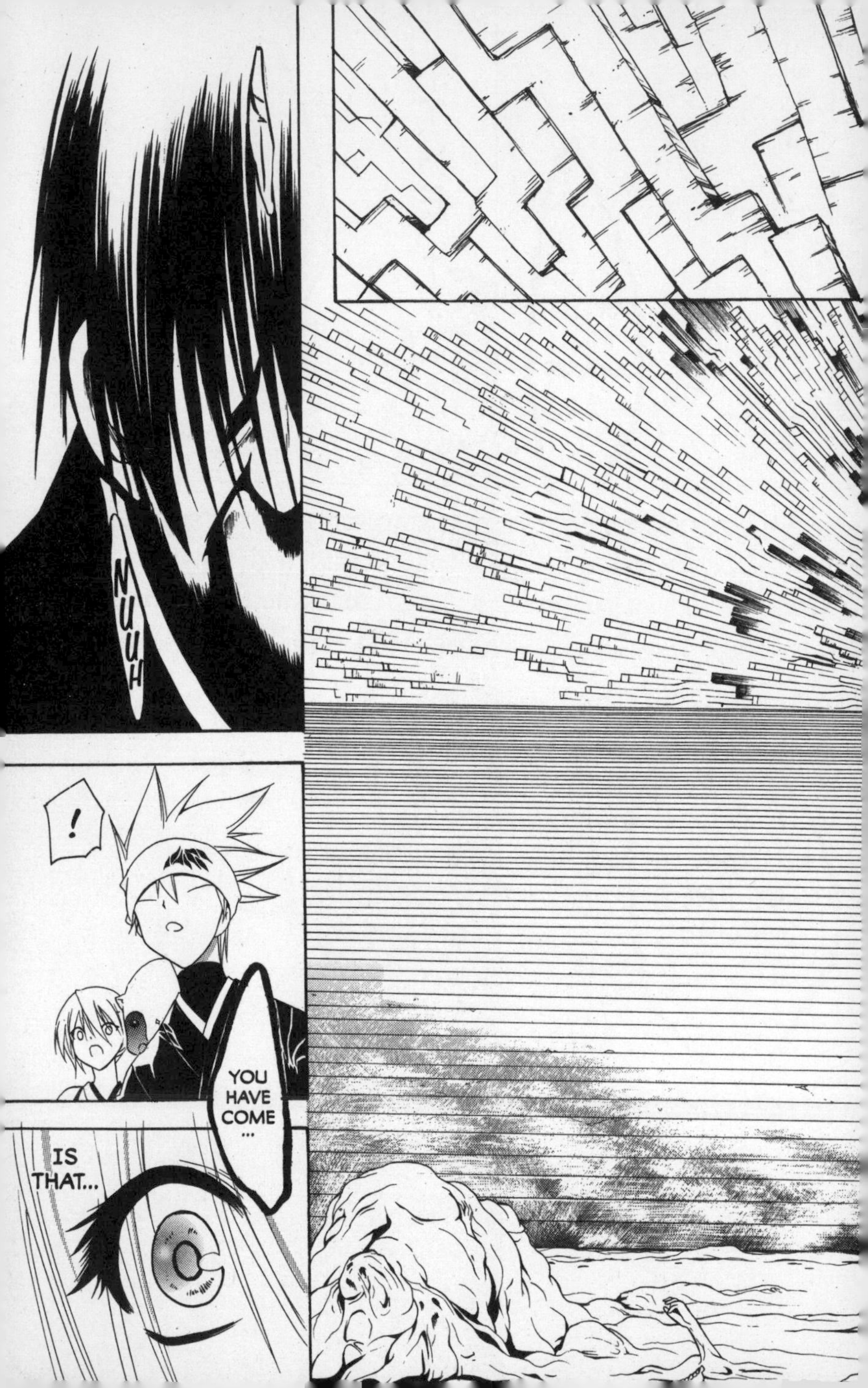
NUUH
!
YOU HAVE COME ...
IS THAT...

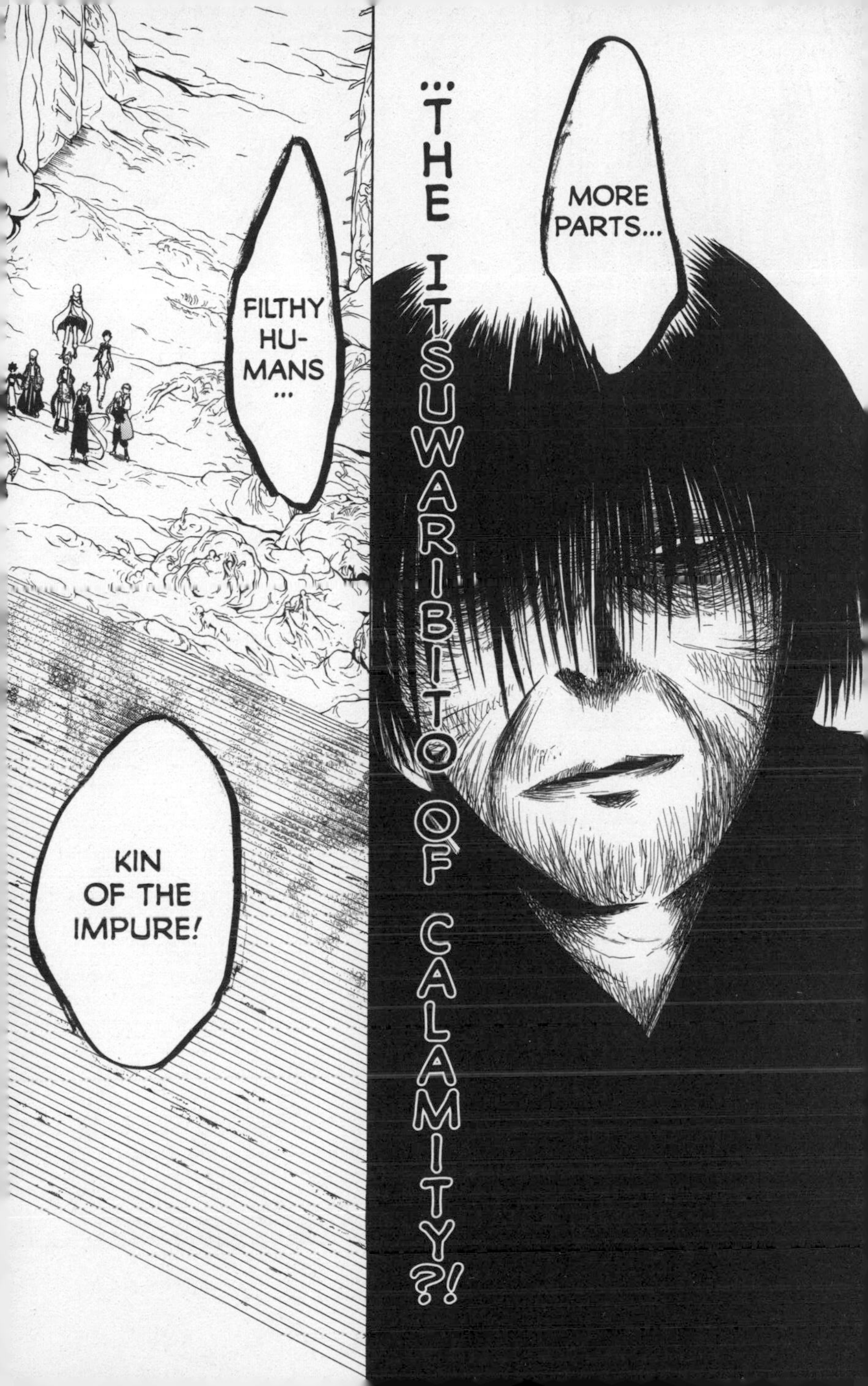
MORE PARTS...
...THE ITSUWARIBITO OF CALAMITY?!
FILTHY HU-MANS...
KIN OF THE IMPURE!

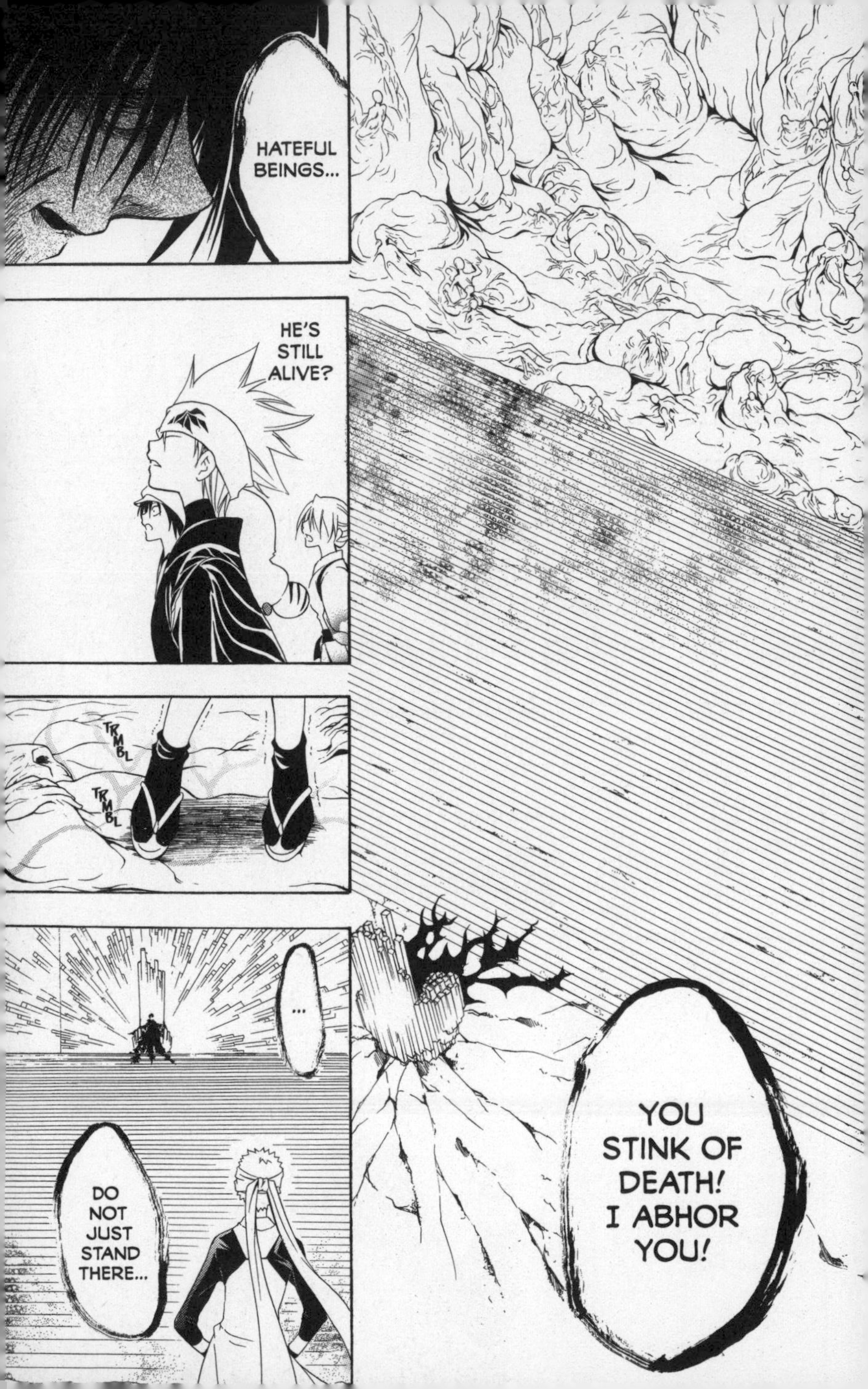
YOU STINK OF DEATH! I ABHOR YOU!
HATEFUL BEINGS...
HE'S STILL ALIVE?
TRMBL
TRMBL
...
DO NOT JUST STAND THERE...

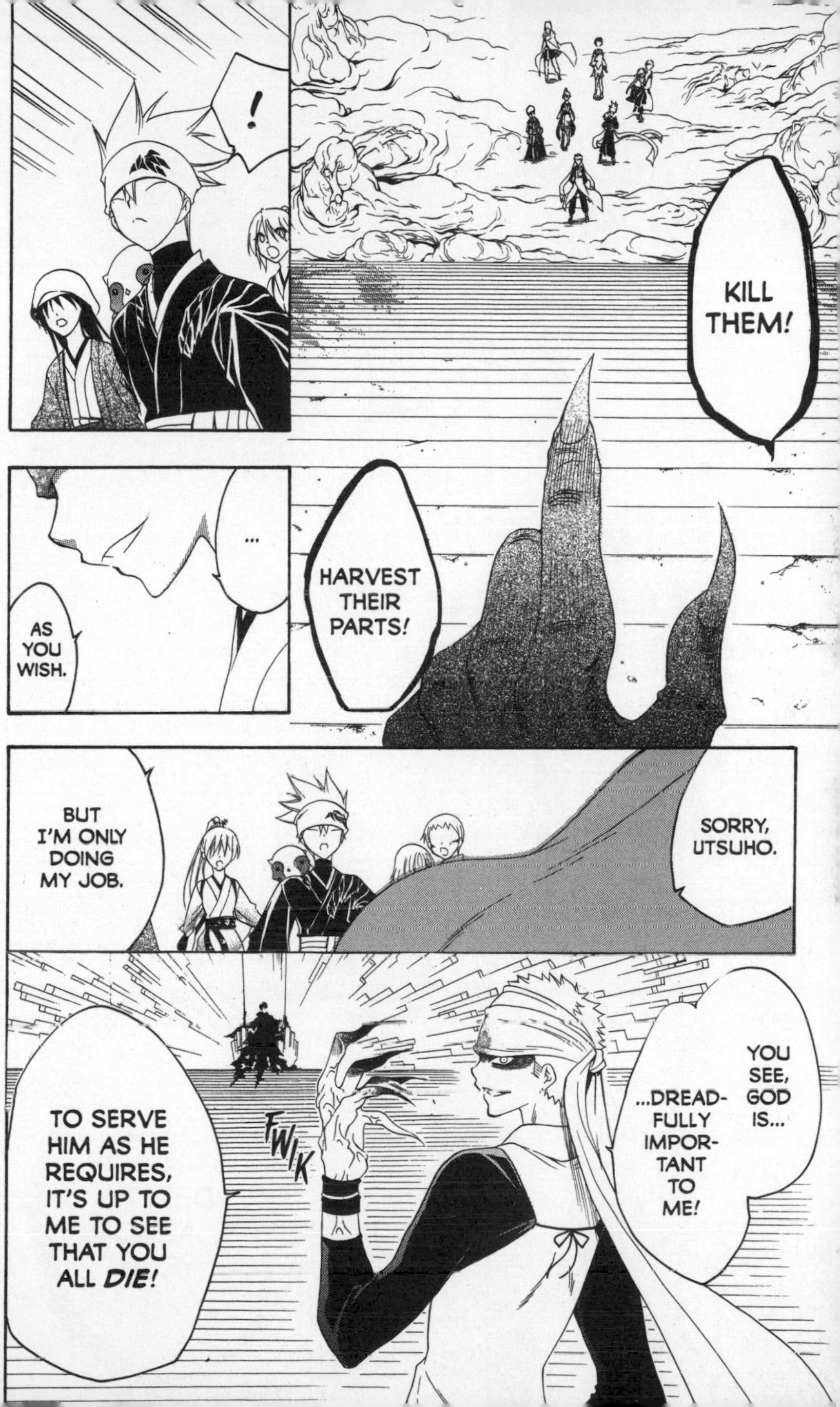
KILL THEM!
!
HARVEST THEIR PARTS!
...
AS YOU WISH.
SORRY, UTSUHO.
BUT I'M ONLY DOING MY JOB.
YOU SEE, GOD IS...
...DREAD-FULLY IMPOR-TANT TO ME!
FWIK
TO SERVE HIM AS HE REQUIRES, IT'S UP TO ME TO SEE THAT YOU ALL *DIE*!

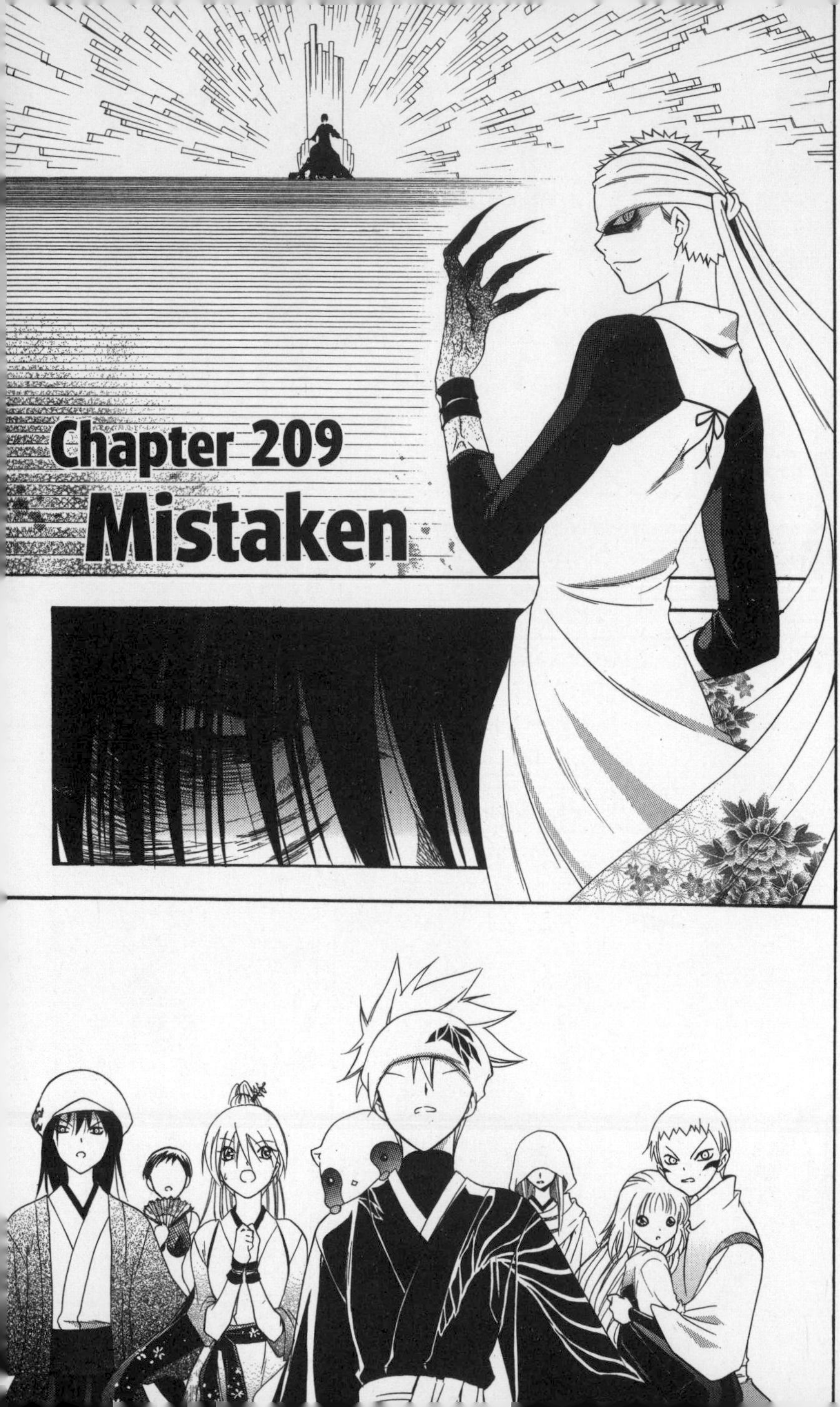
Chapter 209
Mistaken

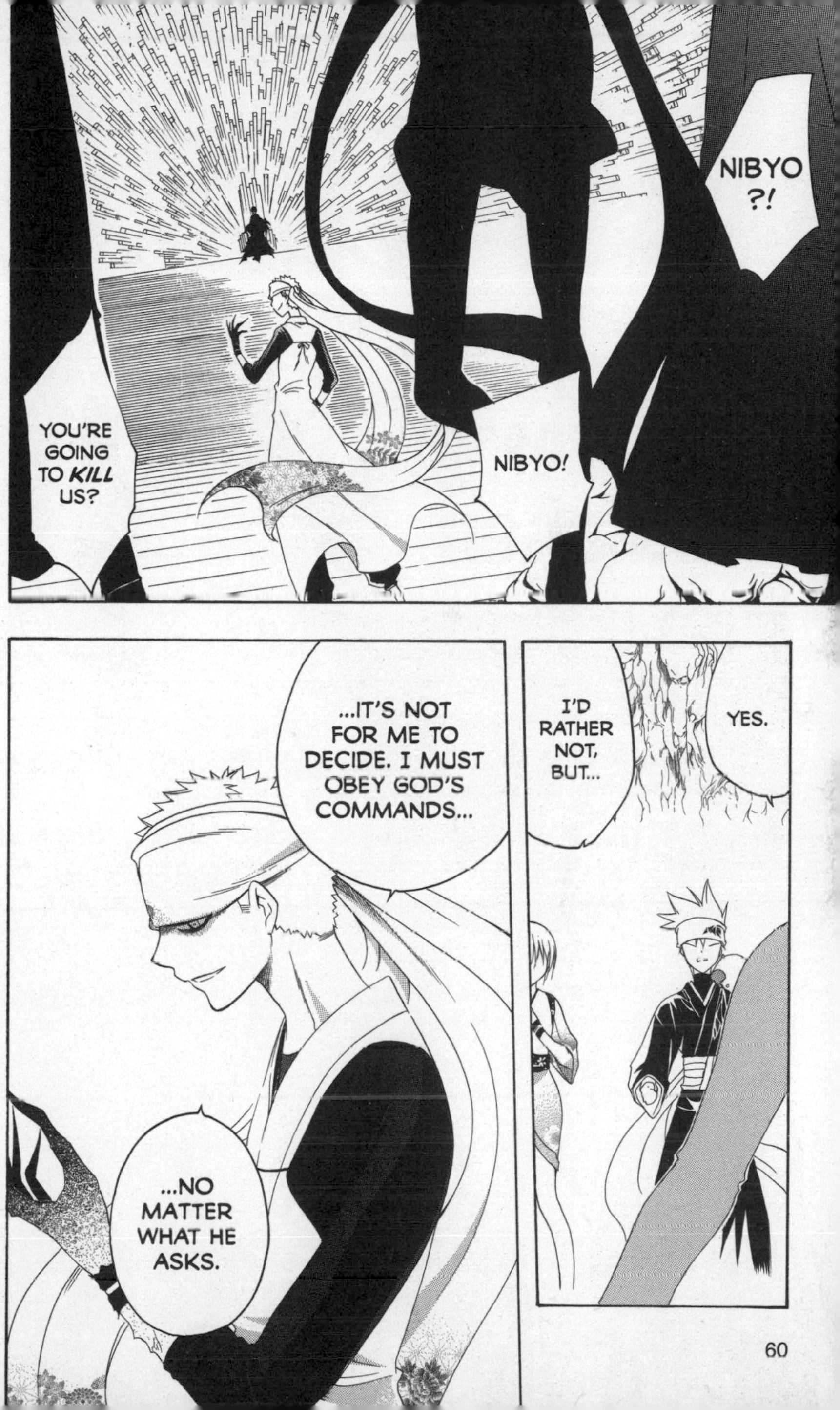
NIBYO ?!
NIBYO!
YOU'RE GOING TO *KILL* US?
YES.
I'D RATHER NOT, BUT...
...IT'S NOT FOR ME TO DECIDE. I MUST OBEY GOD'S COMMANDS...
...NO MATTER WHAT HE ASKS.

I'VE HEARD YOUR STORY, BUT–

...

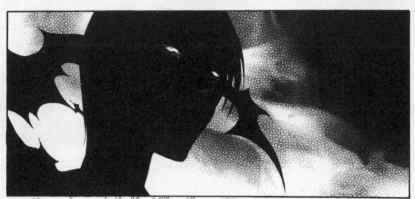

OH NO...

I CAN'T TALK...

I CAN'T EVEN MOVE!

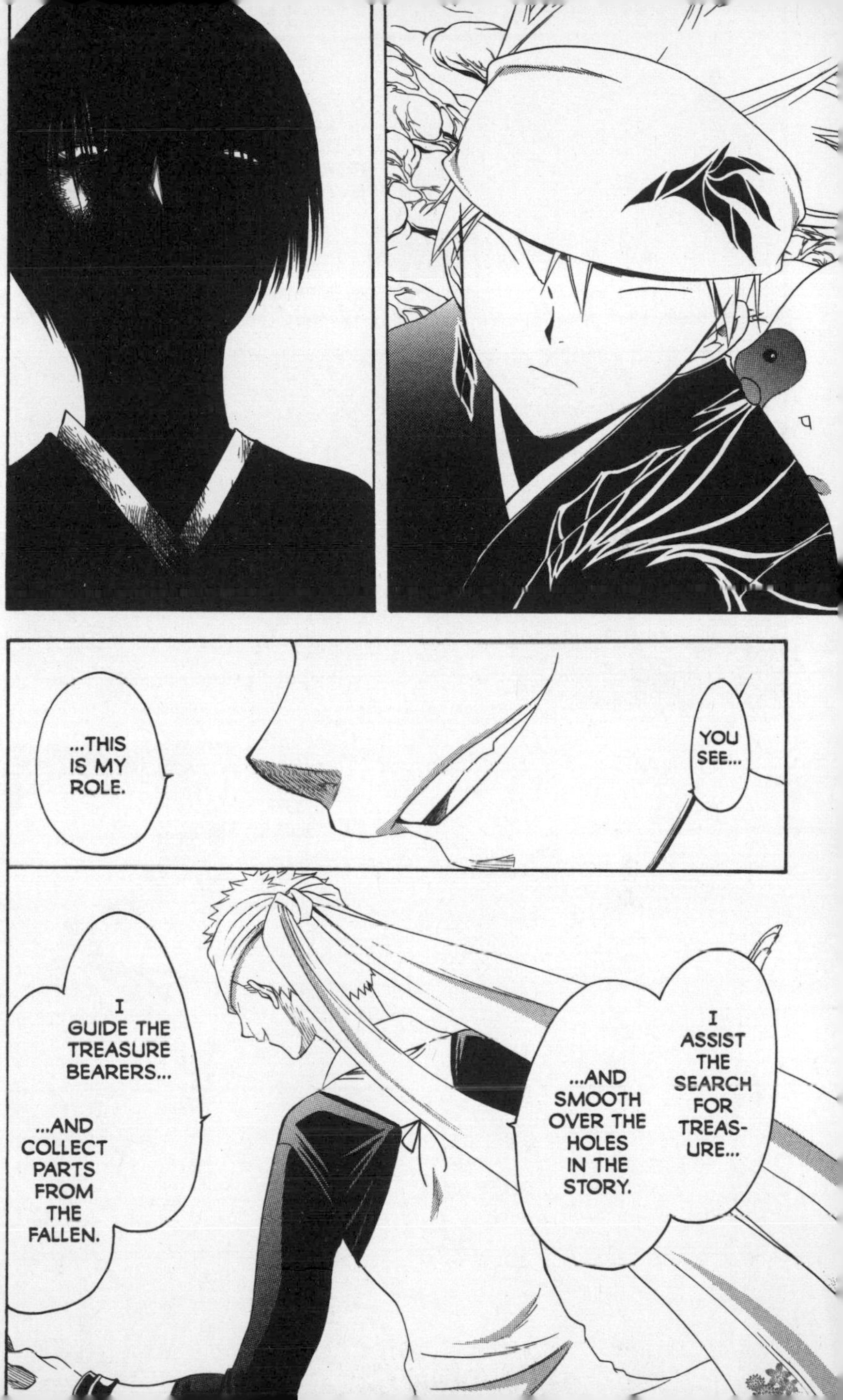
YOU SEE...
...THIS IS MY ROLE.
I ASSIST THE SEARCH FOR TREAS-URE...
...AND SMOOTH OVER THE HOLES IN THE STORY.
I GUIDE THE TREASURE BEARERS...
...AND COLLECT PARTS FROM THE FALLEN.

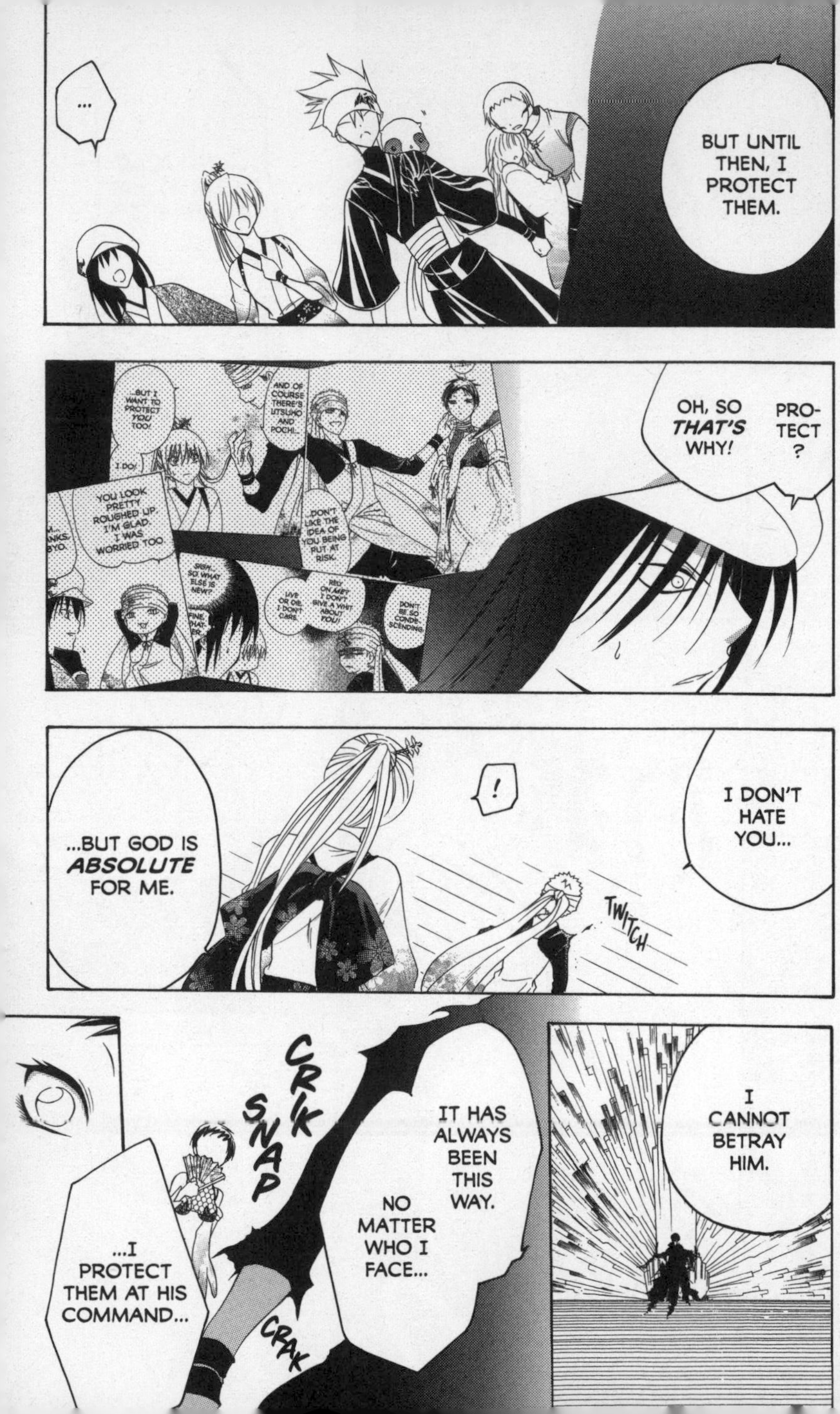
BUT UNTIL THEN, I PROTECT THEM.
...
PROTECT?
OH, SO *THAT'S* WHY!
AND OF COURSE THERE'S UTSUHO AND POCHI...
...BUT I WANT TO PROTECT *YOU* TOO!
I DO!
...DON'T LIKE THE IDEA OF YOU BEING PUT AT RISK.
YOU LOOK PRETTY ROUGHED UP. I'M GLAD. I WAS WORRIED TOO.
DON'T BE SO CONDESCENDING.
RELY ON *ME*? I DON'T GIVE A WHIT ABOUT *YOU*!
LIVE OR DIE, I DON'T CARE.
SIGH... SO WHAT ELSE IS NEW?
I DON'T HATE YOU...
!
TWITCH
...BUT GOD IS ***ABSOLUTE*** FOR ME.
I CANNOT BETRAY HIM.
IT HAS ALWAYS BEEN THIS WAY.
NO MATTER WHO I FACE...
CRIK
SNAP
...I PROTECT THEM AT HIS COMMAND...
CRAK

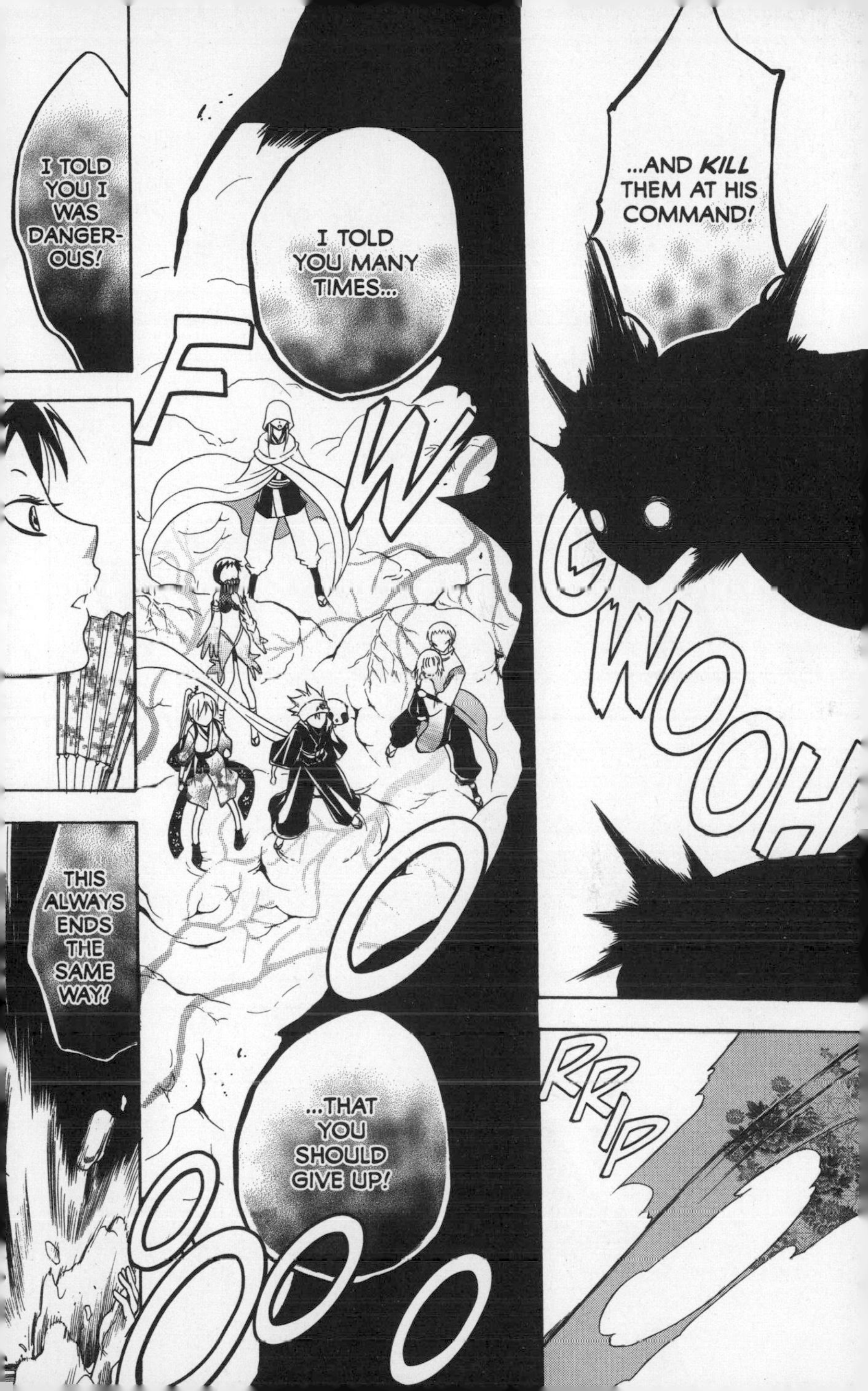
...AND KILL THEM AT HIS COMMAND!
GWOOOH
RRIP
I TOLD YOU MANY TIMES...
FWOOOOOOO
...THAT YOU SHOULD GIVE UP!
I TOLD YOU I WAS DANGER-OUS!
THIS ALWAYS ENDS THE SAME WAY!

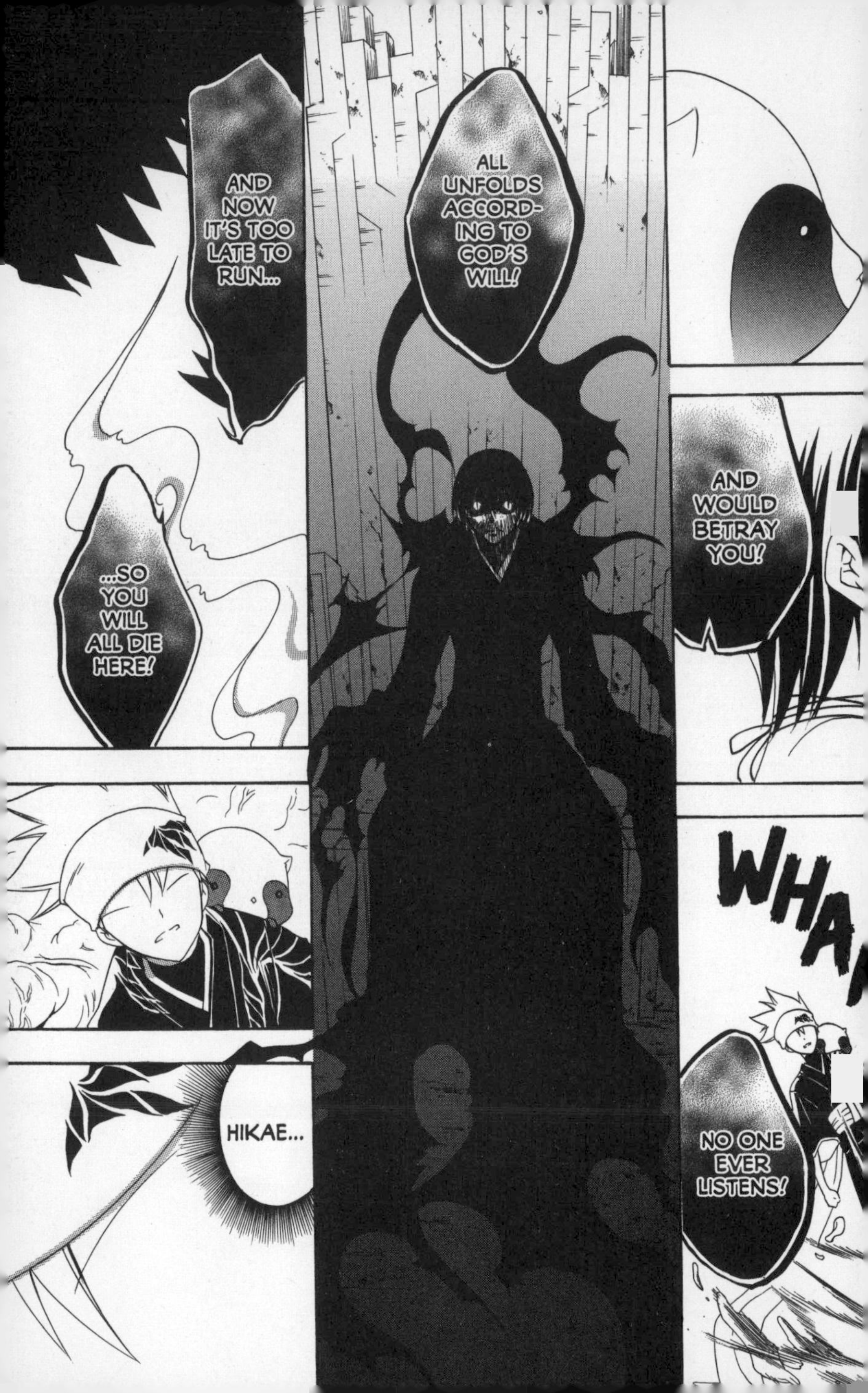
AND WOULD BETRAY YOU!
WHA
NO ONE EVER LISTENS!
ALL UNFOLDS ACCORD-ING TO GOD'S WILL!
AND NOW IT'S TOO LATE TO RUN...
...SO YOU WILL ALL DIE HERE!
HIKAE...

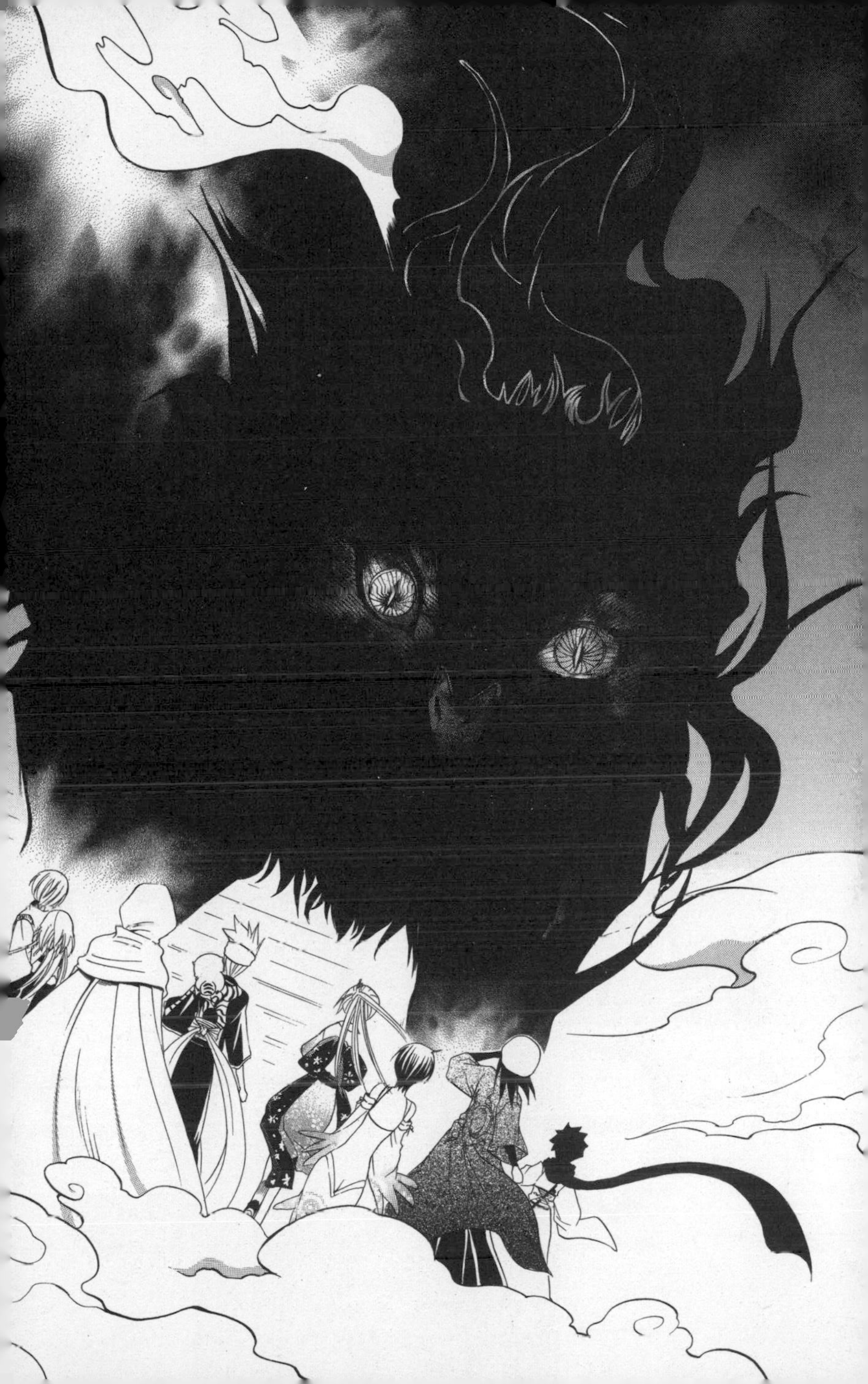

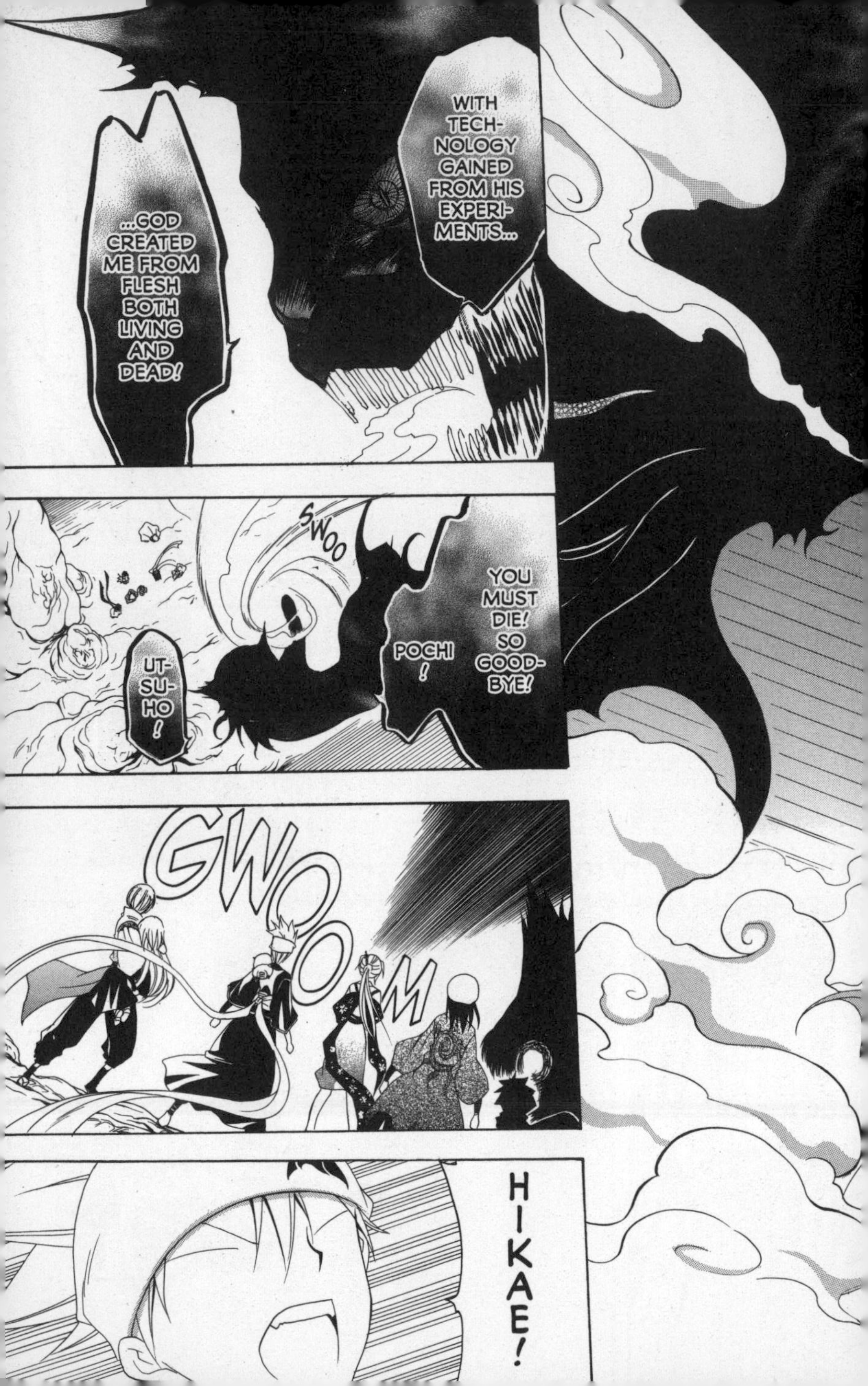
WITH TECH-NOLOGY GAINED FROM HIS EXPERI-MENTS...
...GOD CREATED ME FROM FLESH BOTH LIVING AND DEAD!
SWOO
YOU MUST DIE! SO GOOD-BYE!
POCHI!
UT-SU-HO!
GWOOOM
HIKAE!

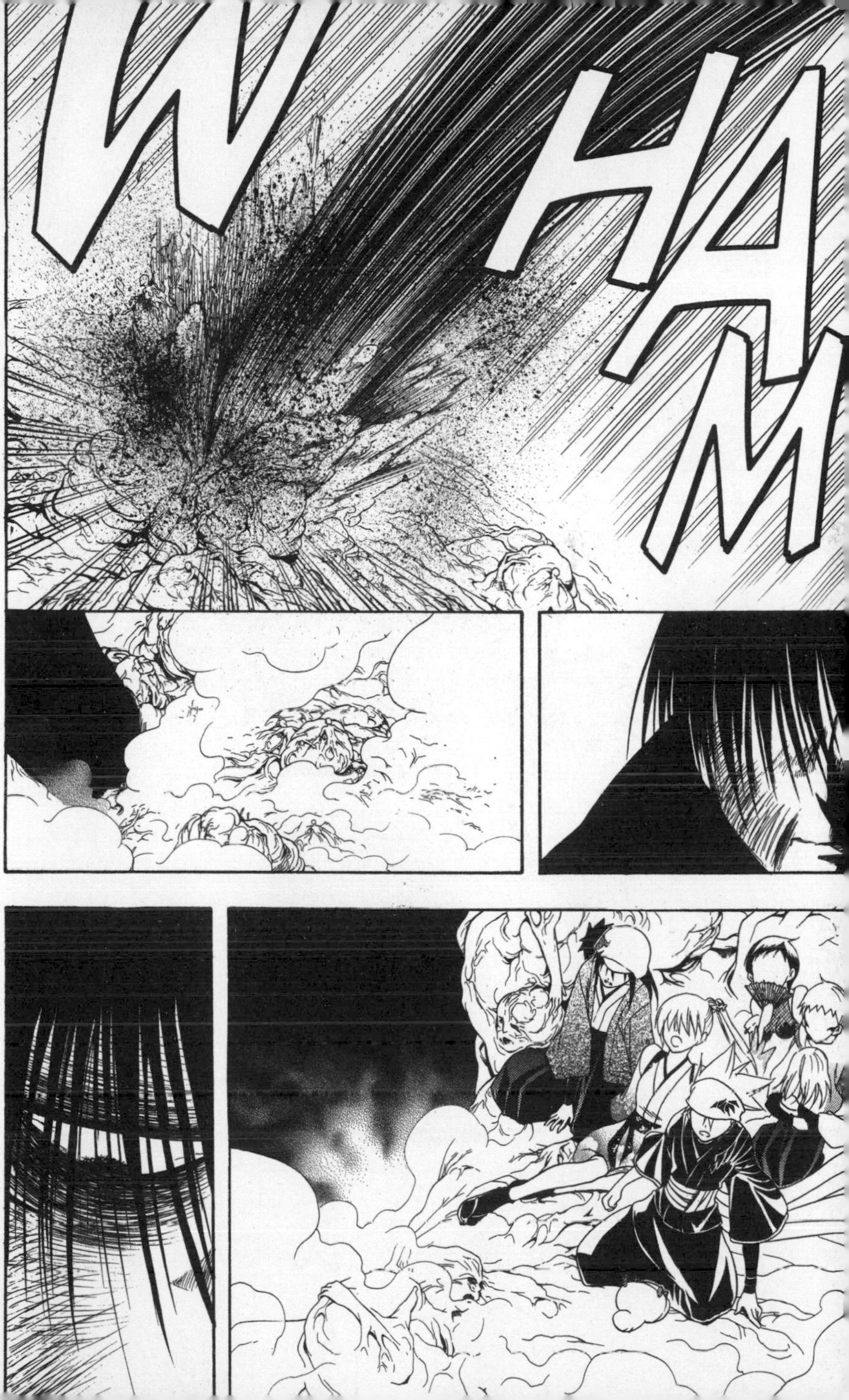
WHAM

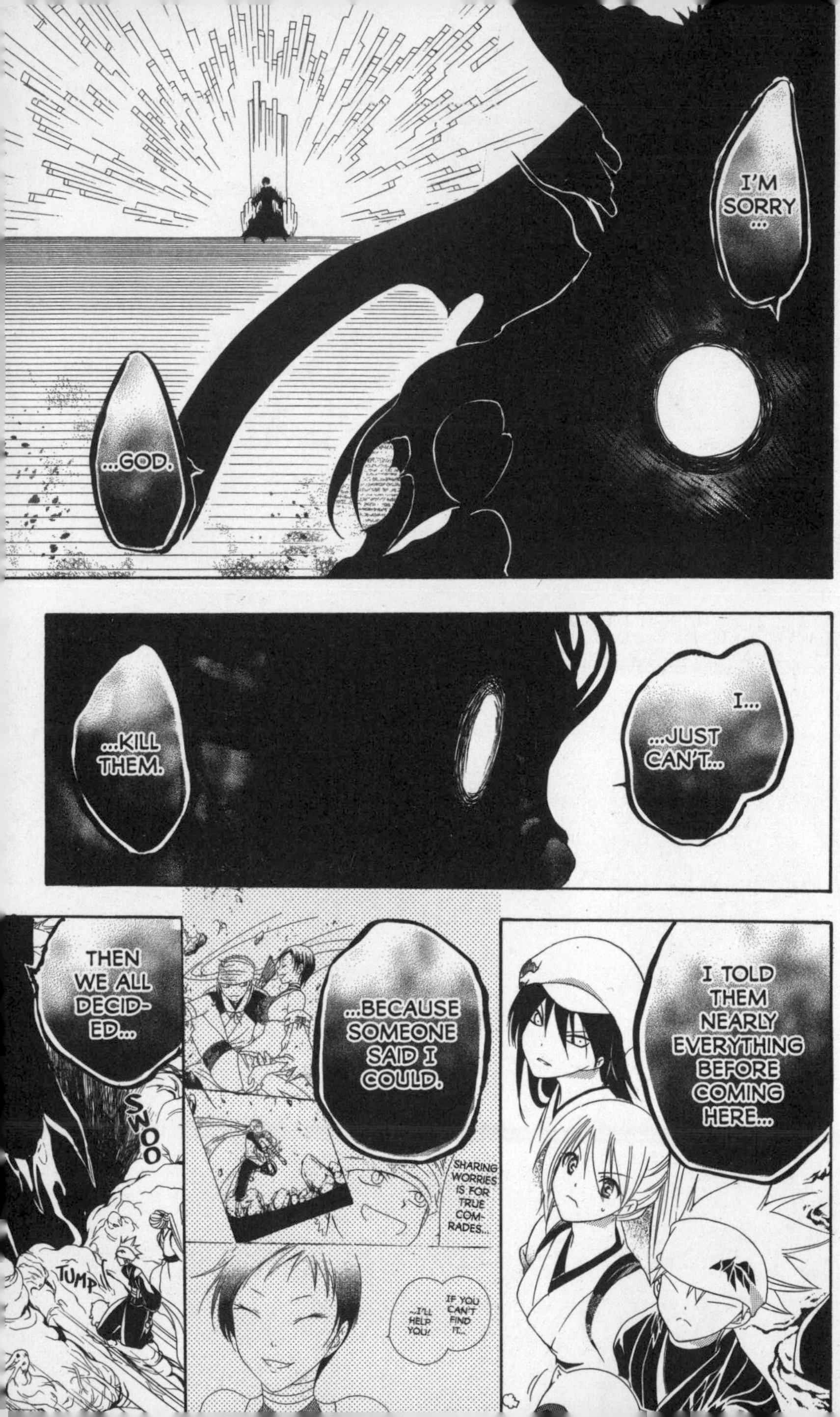
I'M SORRY...
...GOD.
I...
...JUST CAN'T...
...KILL THEM.
I TOLD THEM NEARLY EVERYTHING BEFORE COMING HERE...
...BECAUSE SOMEONE SAID I COULD.
SHARING WORRIES IS FOR TRUE COM-RADES...
IF YOU CAN'T FIND IT...
...I'LL HELP YOU!
THEN WE ALL DECID-ED...
SWOO
TUMP

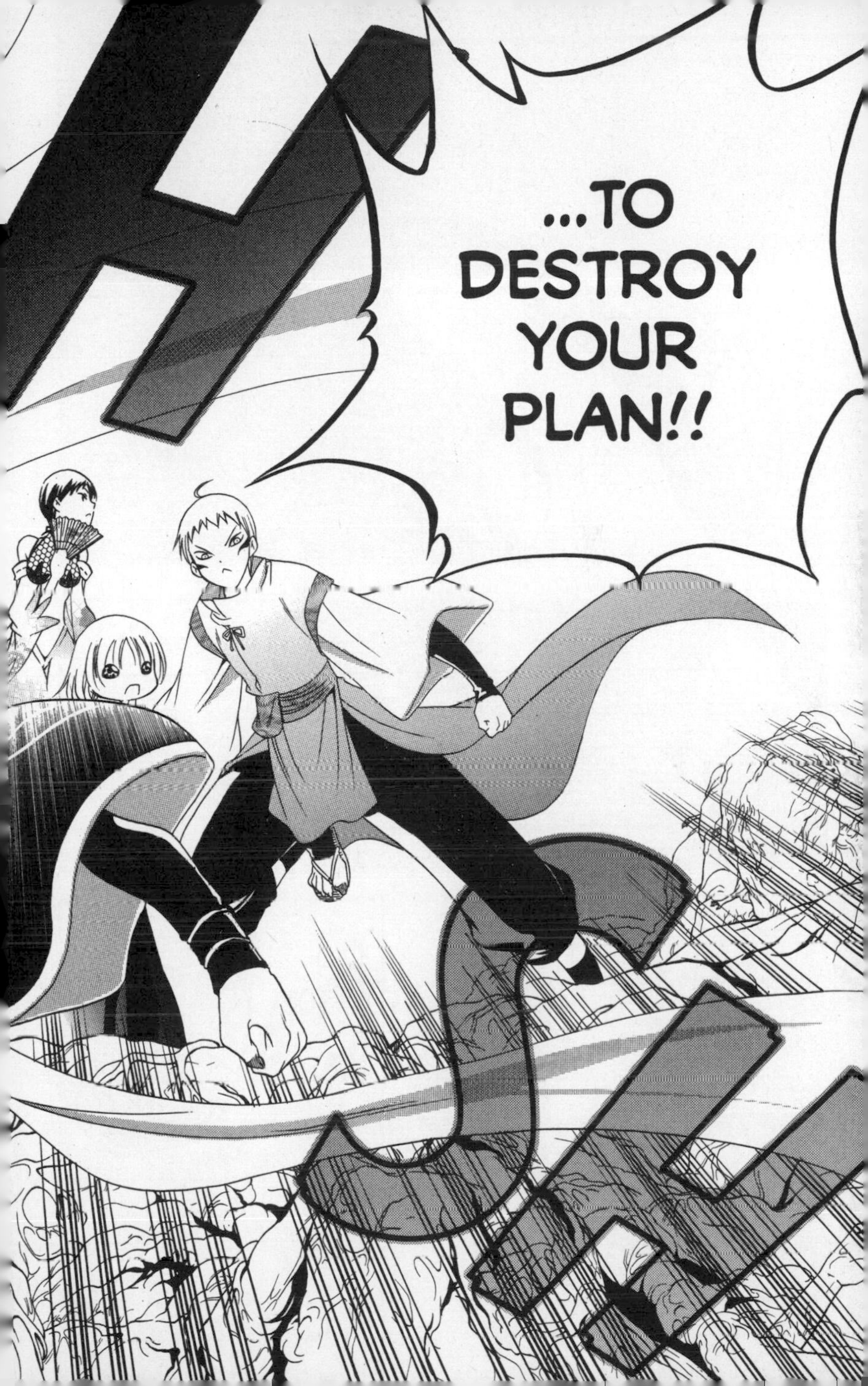
...TO DESTROY YOUR PLAN!!

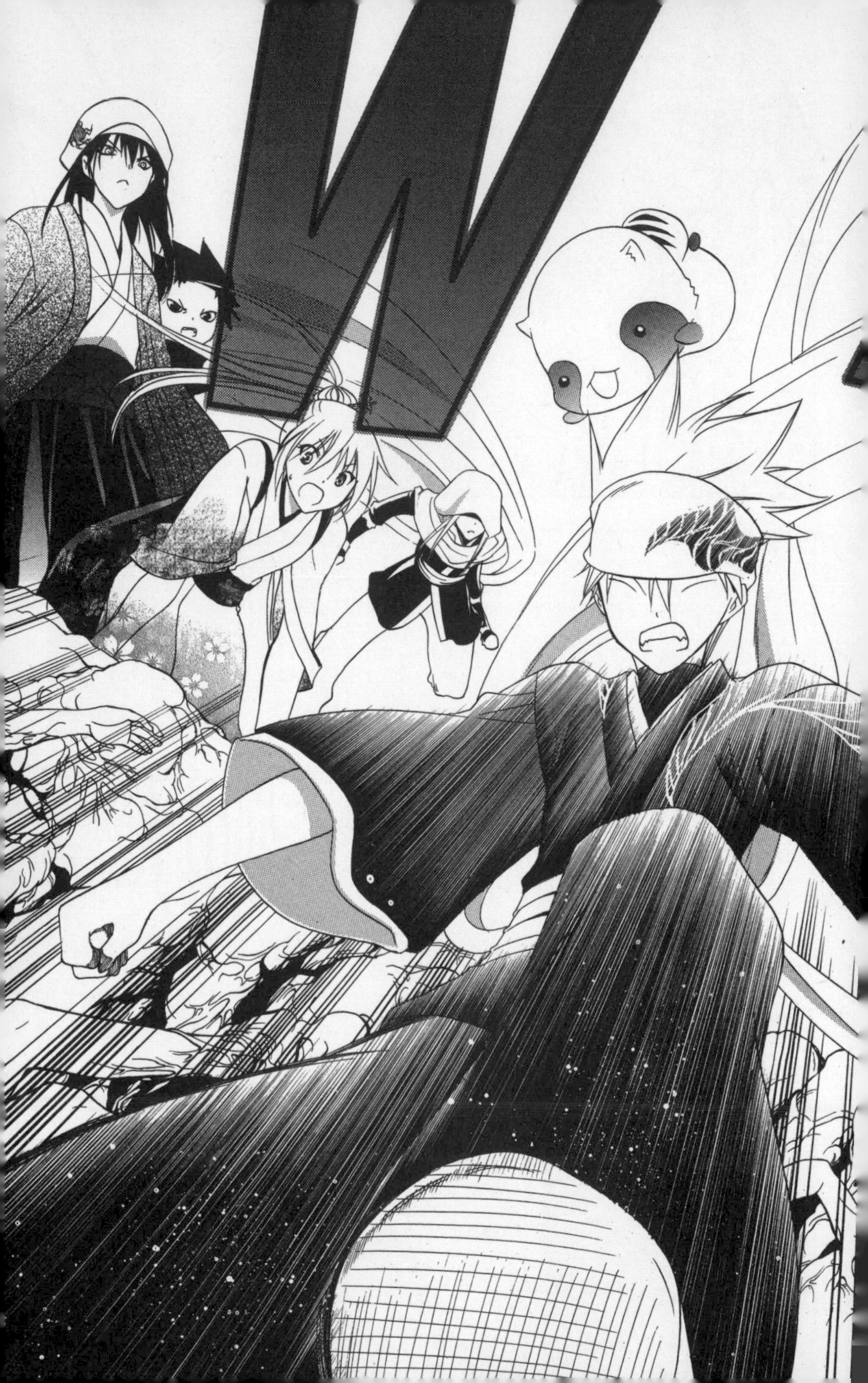
W

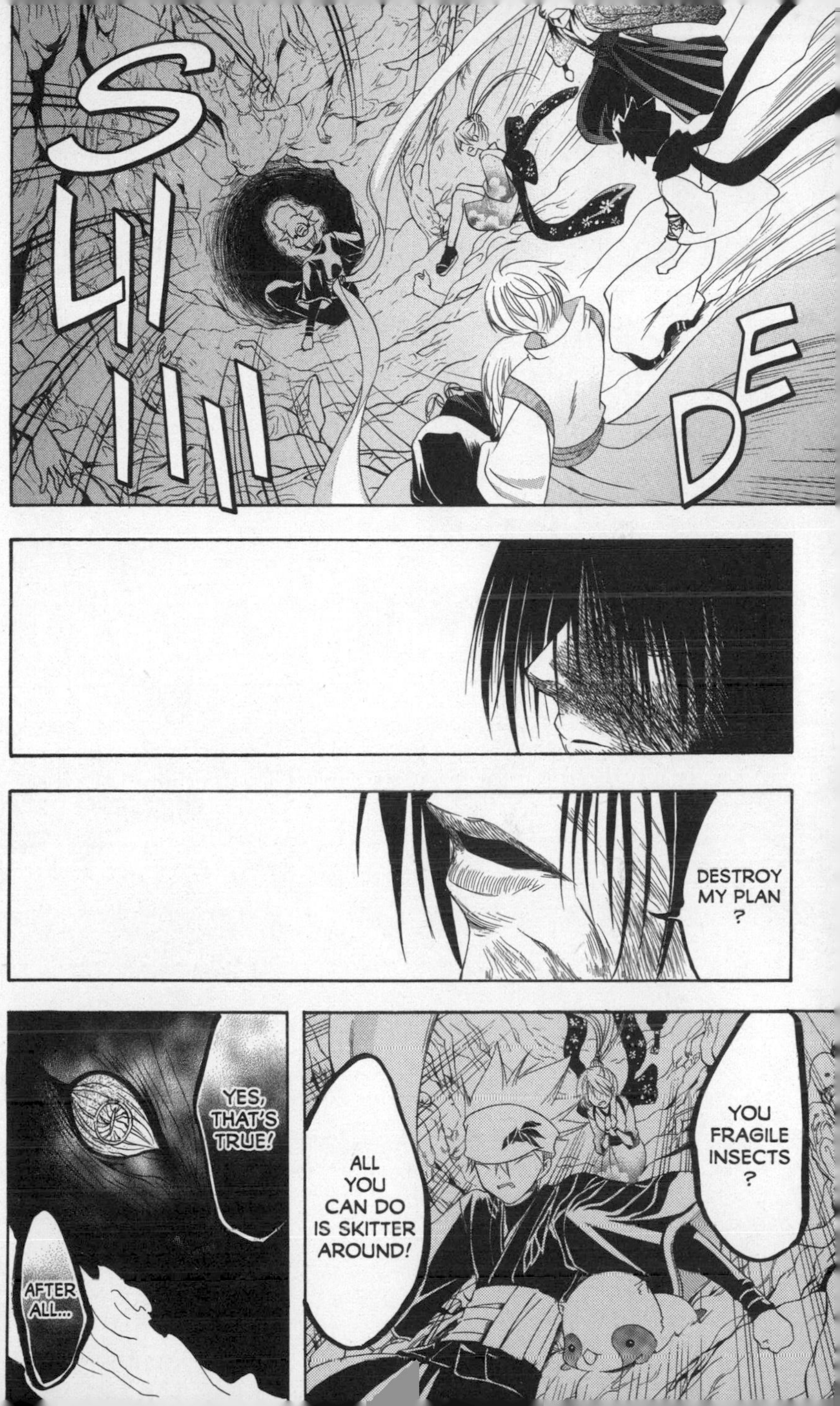
SLIIIIDE
DESTROY MY PLAN ?
YOU FRAGILE INSECTS ?
ALL YOU CAN DO IS SKITTER AROUND!
YES, THAT'S TRUE!
AFTER ALL...

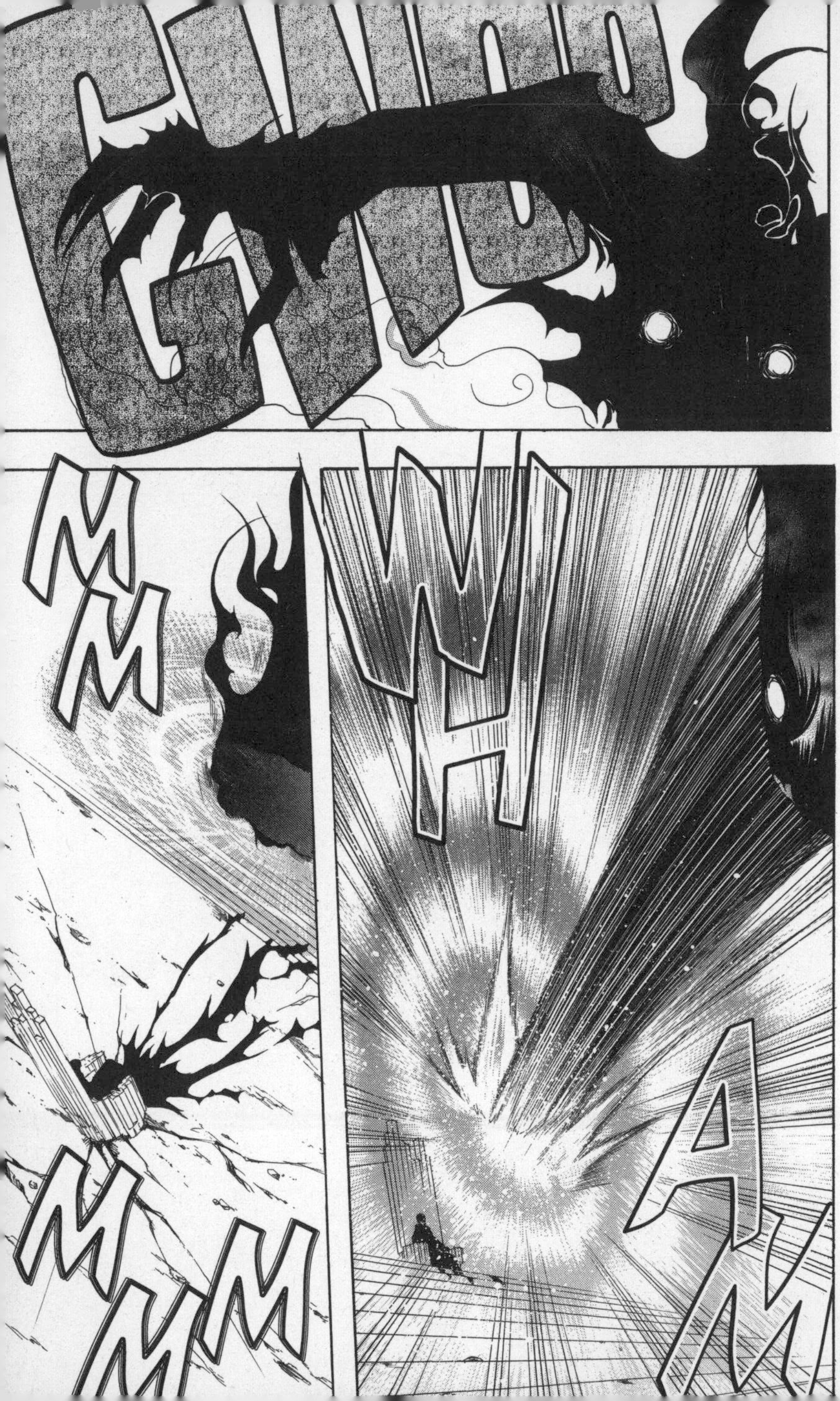
WH
AM
MMM
MMMM

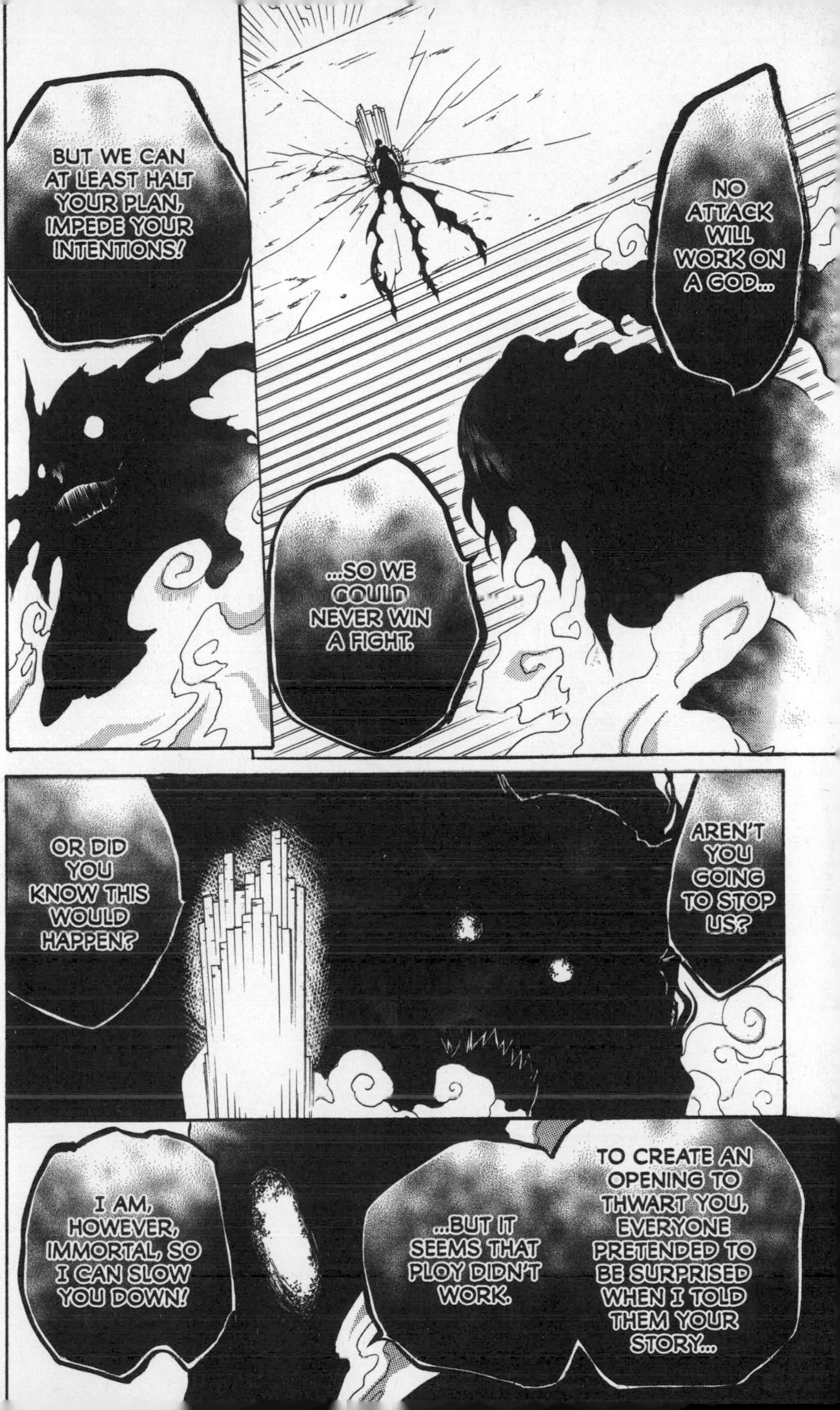
NO ATTACK WILL WORK ON A GOD...
...SO WE COULD NEVER WIN A FIGHT.
BUT WE CAN AT LEAST HALT YOUR PLAN, IMPEDE YOUR INTENTIONS!
AREN'T YOU GOING TO STOP US?
OR DID YOU KNOW THIS WOULD HAPPEN?
TO CREATE AN OPENING TO THWART YOU, EVERYONE PRETENDED TO BE SURPRISED WHEN I TOLD THEM YOUR STORY...
...BUT IT SEEMS THAT PLOY DIDN'T WORK.
I AM, HOWEVER, IMMORTAL, SO I CAN SLOW YOU DOWN!

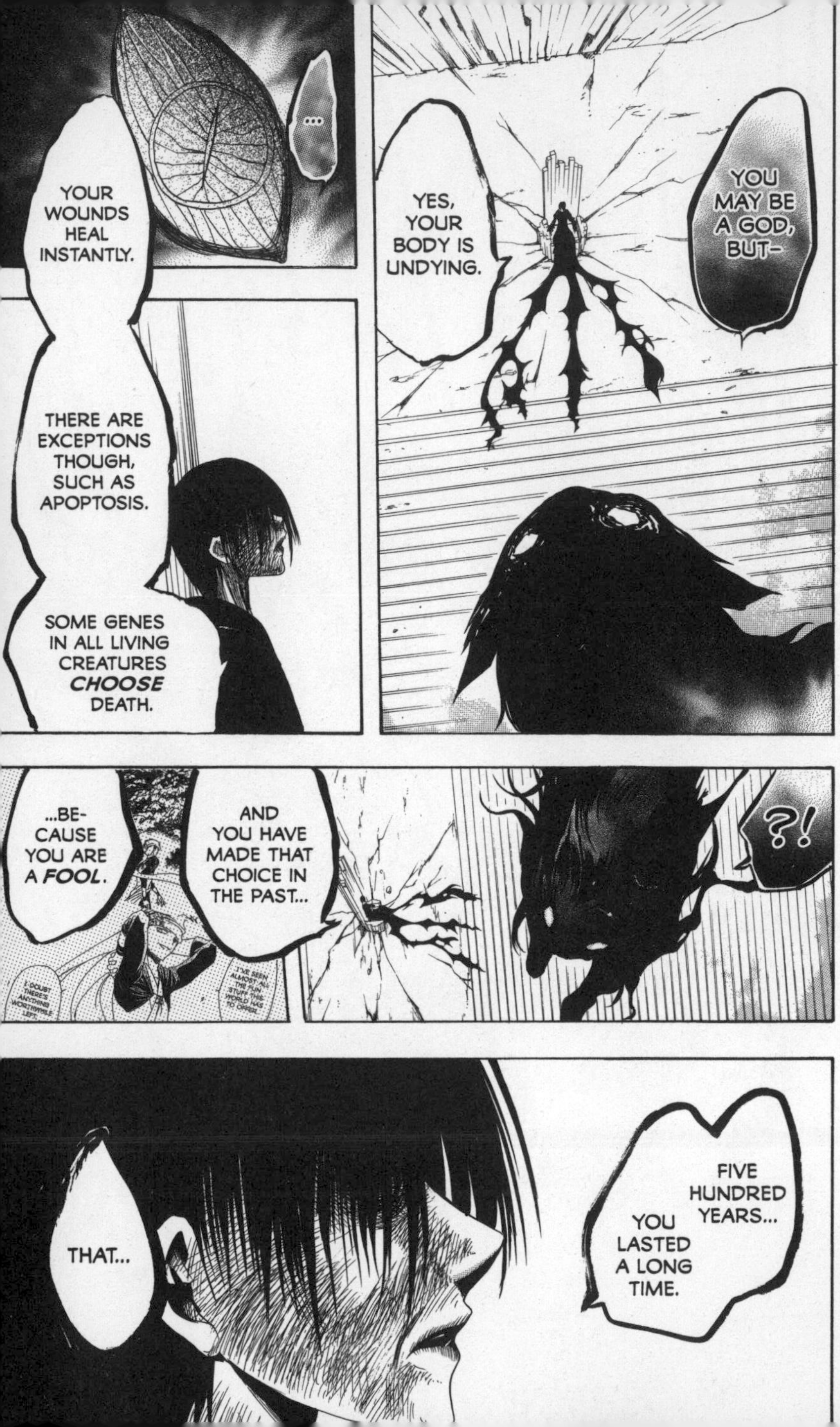
YOU MAY BE A GOD, BUT-
YES, YOUR BODY IS UNDYING.
...
YOUR WOUNDS HEAL INSTANTLY.
THERE ARE EXCEPTIONS THOUGH, SUCH AS APOPTOSIS.
SOME GENES IN ALL LIVING CREATURES *CHOOSE* DEATH.
?!
AND YOU HAVE MADE THAT CHOICE IN THE PAST...
...BE-CAUSE YOU ARE A *FOOL*.
I'VE SEEN ALMOST ALL THE FUN STUFF THIS WORLD HAS TO OFFER.
I DOUBT THERE'S ANYTHING WORTHWHILE LEFT.
FIVE HUNDRED YEARS...
YOU LASTED A LONG TIME.
THAT...

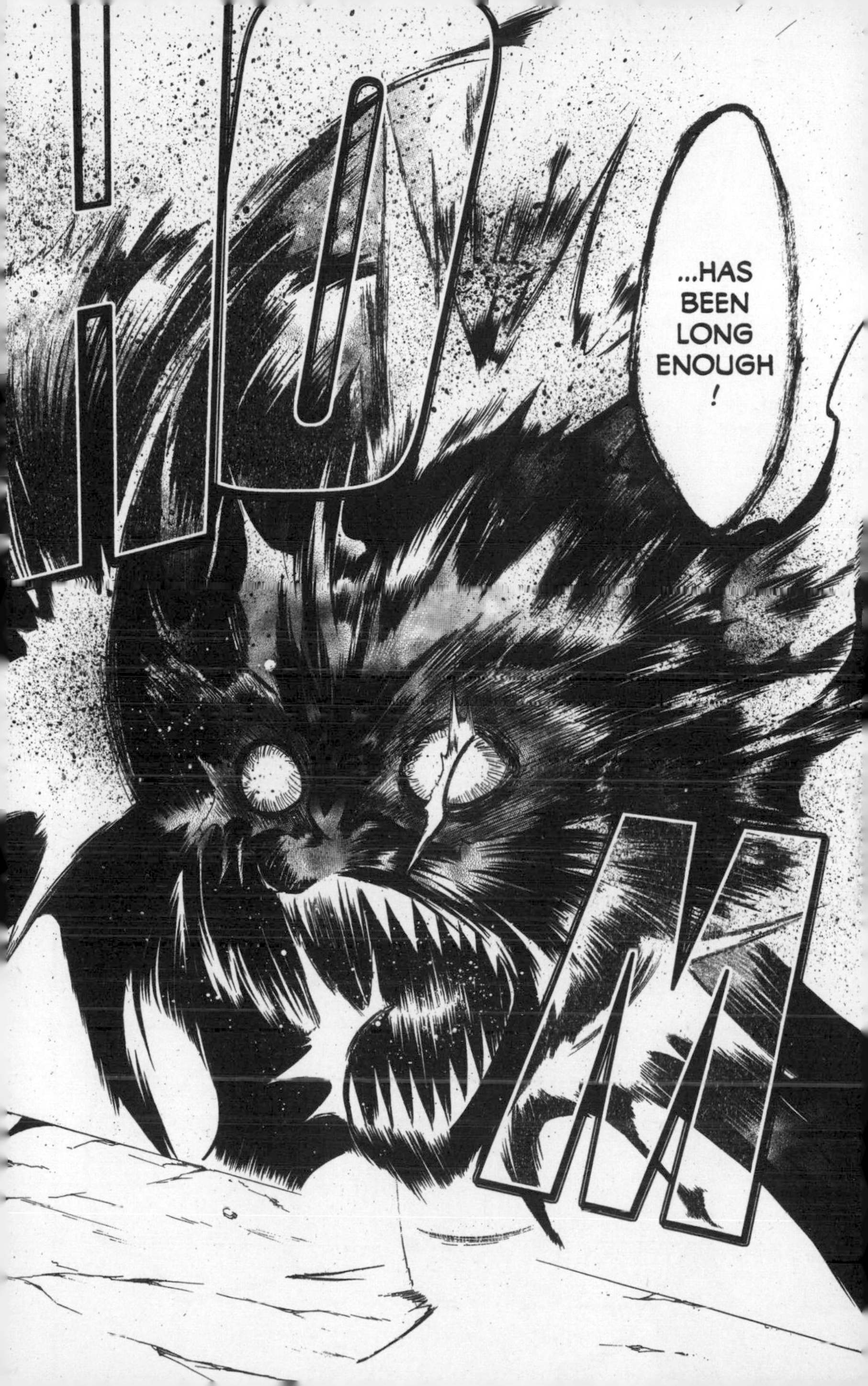
...HAS BEEN LONG ENOUGH!

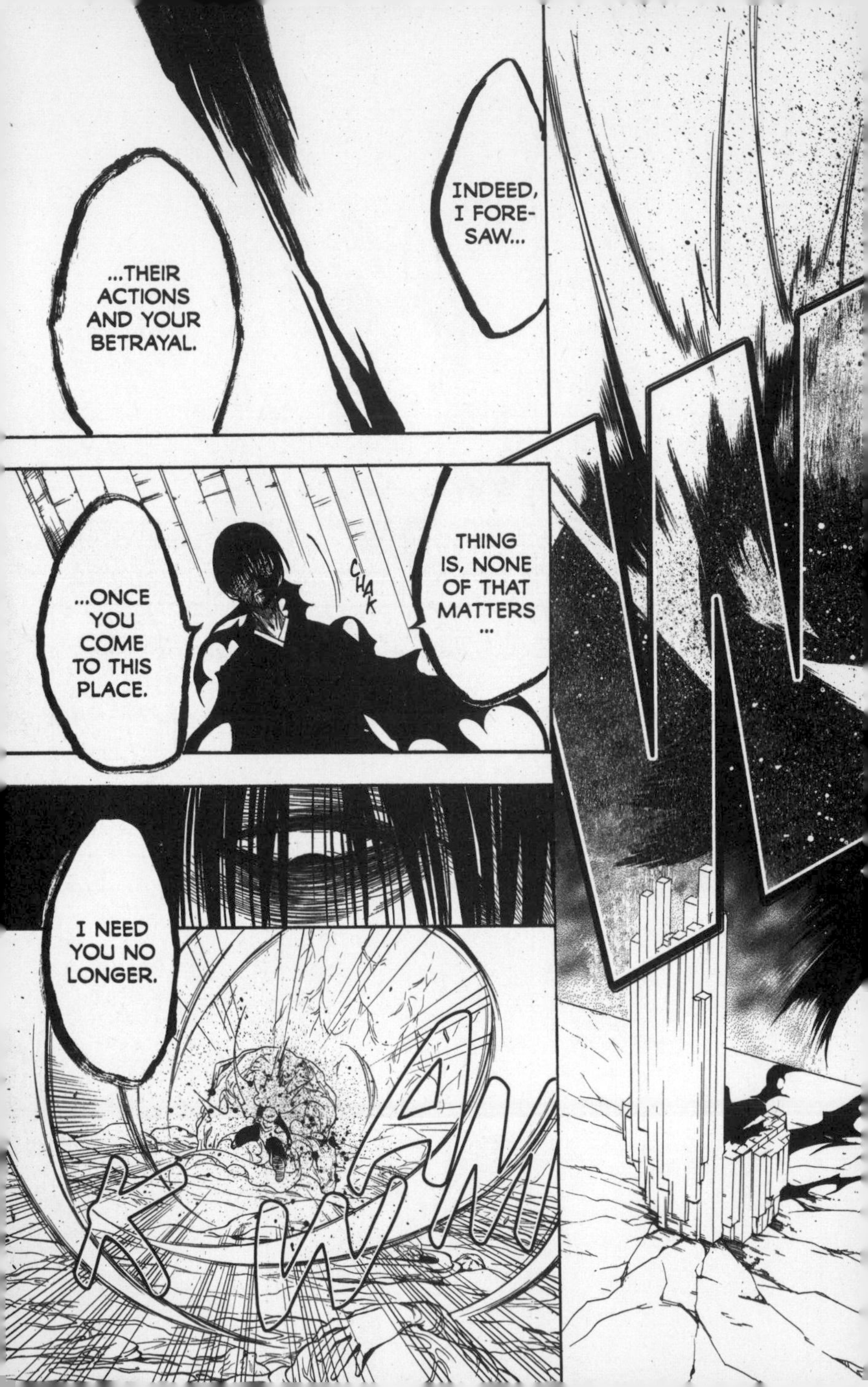
INDEED, I FORE- SAW...
...THEIR ACTIONS AND YOUR BETRAYAL.
THING IS, NONE OF THAT MATTERS ...
CHAK
...ONCE YOU COME TO THIS PLACE.
I NEED YOU NO LONGER.

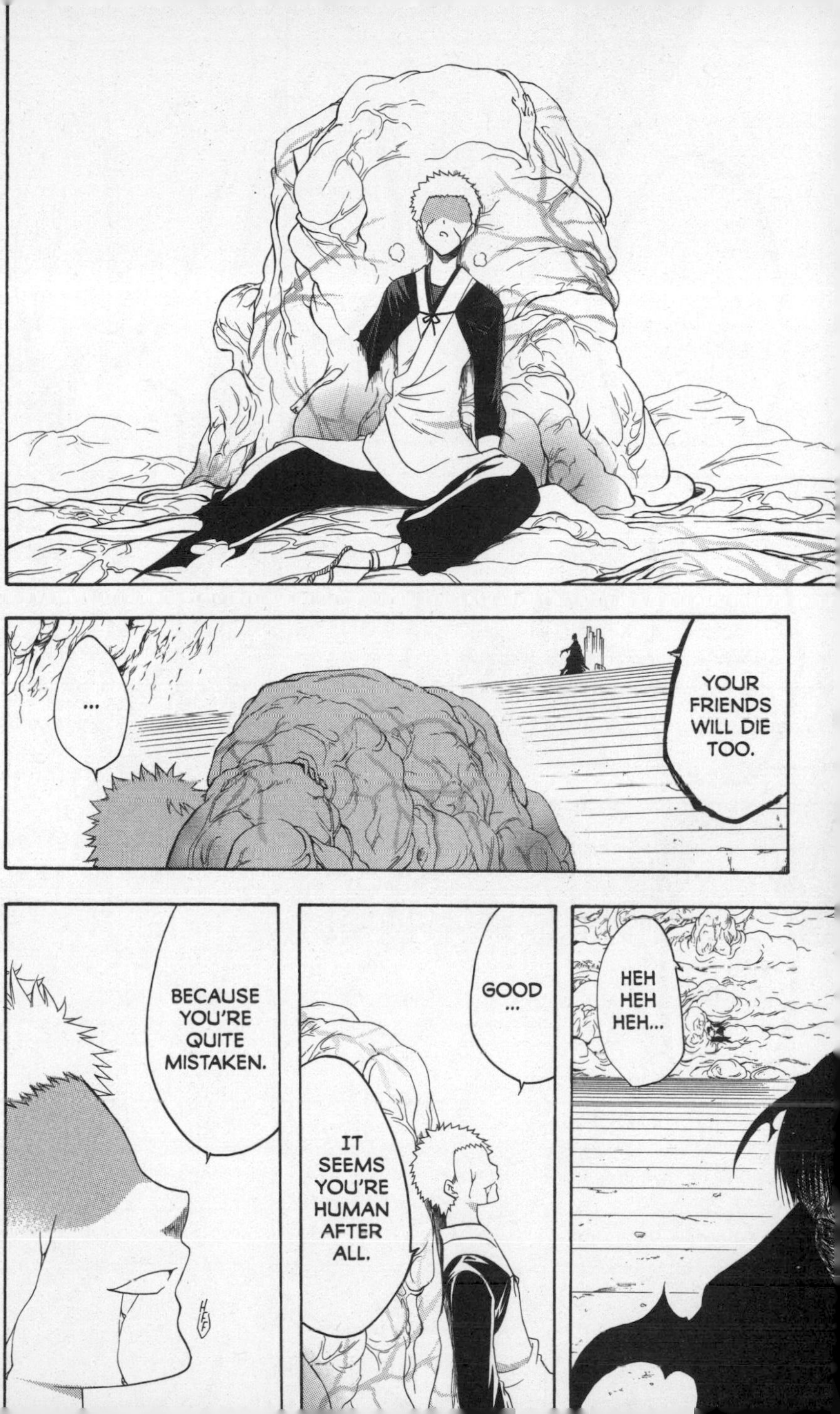
YOUR FRIENDS WILL DIE TOO.
...
HEH HEH HEH...
GOOD ...
IT SEEMS YOU'RE HUMAN AFTER ALL.
BECAUSE YOU'RE QUITE MISTAKEN.

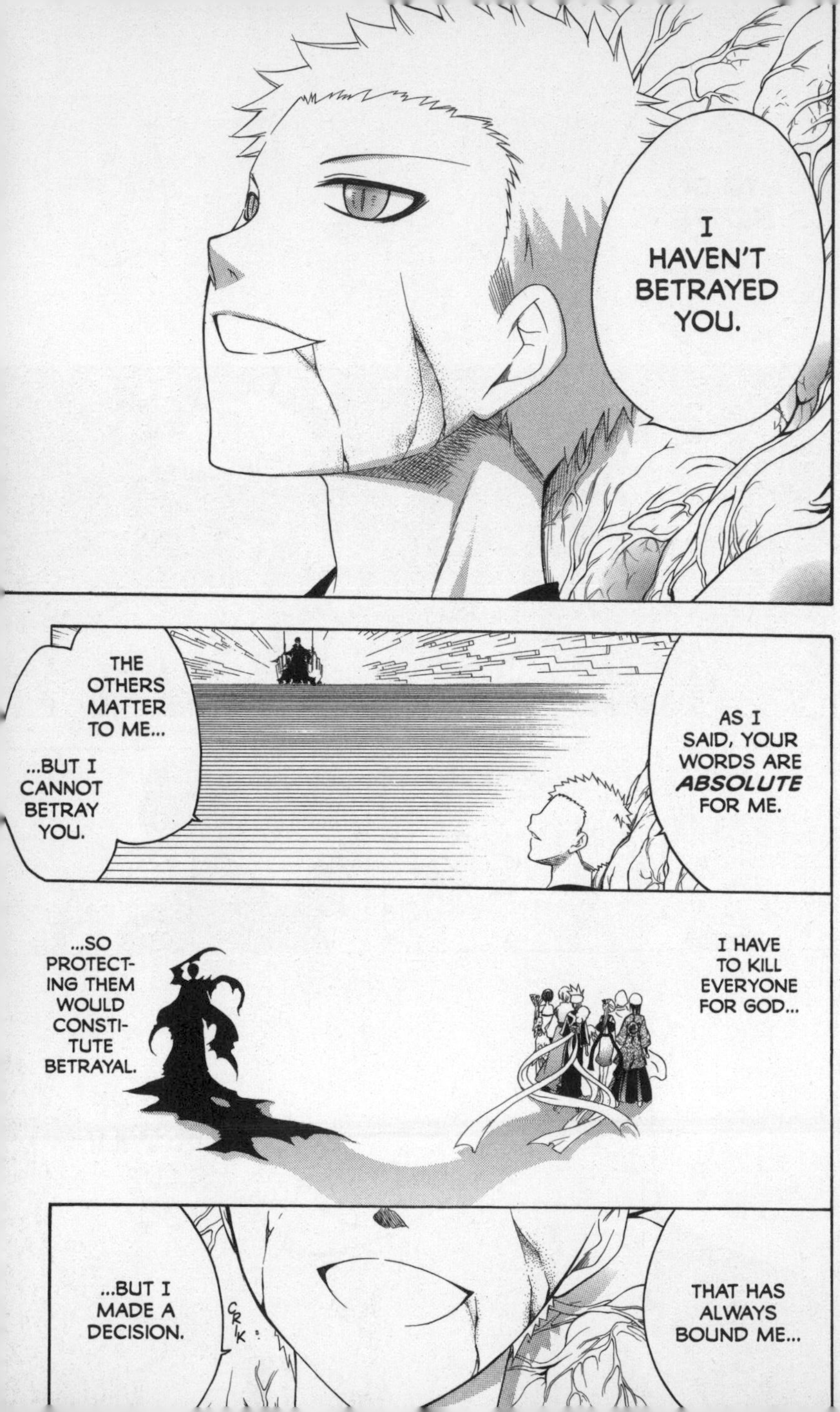
I HAVEN'T BETRAYED YOU.
AS I SAID, YOUR WORDS ARE *ABSOLUTE* FOR ME.
THE OTHERS MATTER TO ME...
...BUT I CANNOT BETRAY YOU.
I HAVE TO KILL EVERYONE FOR GOD...
...SO PROTECTING THEM WOULD CONSTITUTE BETRAYAL.
THAT HAS ALWAYS BOUND ME...
CRIK
...BUT I MADE A DECISION.

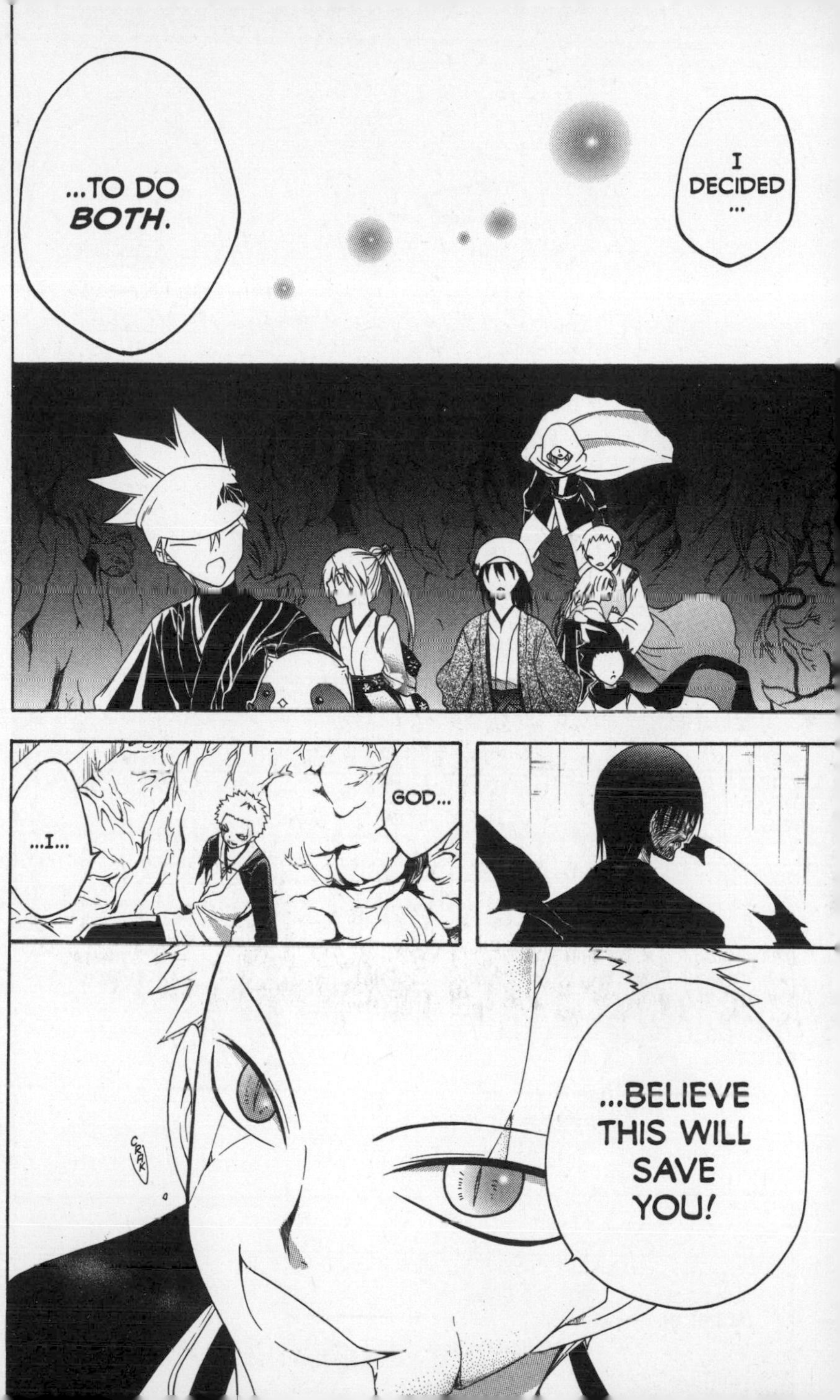
I DECIDED ...
...TO DO BOTH.
GOD...
...I...
...BELIEVE THIS WILL SAVE YOU!
CRAK

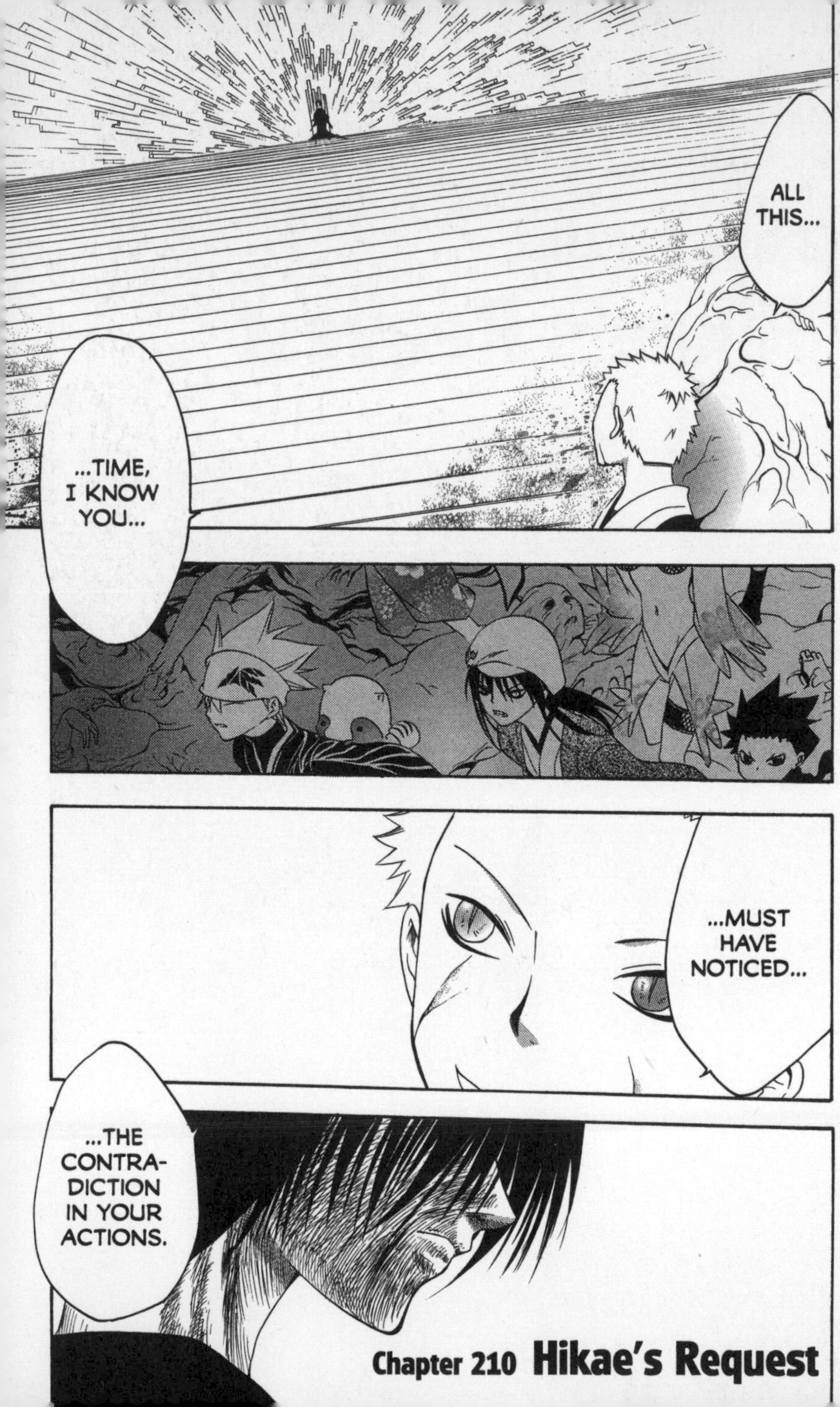
ALL THIS...
...TIME, I KNOW YOU...
...MUST HAVE NOTICED...
...THE CONTRADICTION IN YOUR ACTIONS.
Chapter 210 Hikae's Request

Chapter 210
Hikae's Request

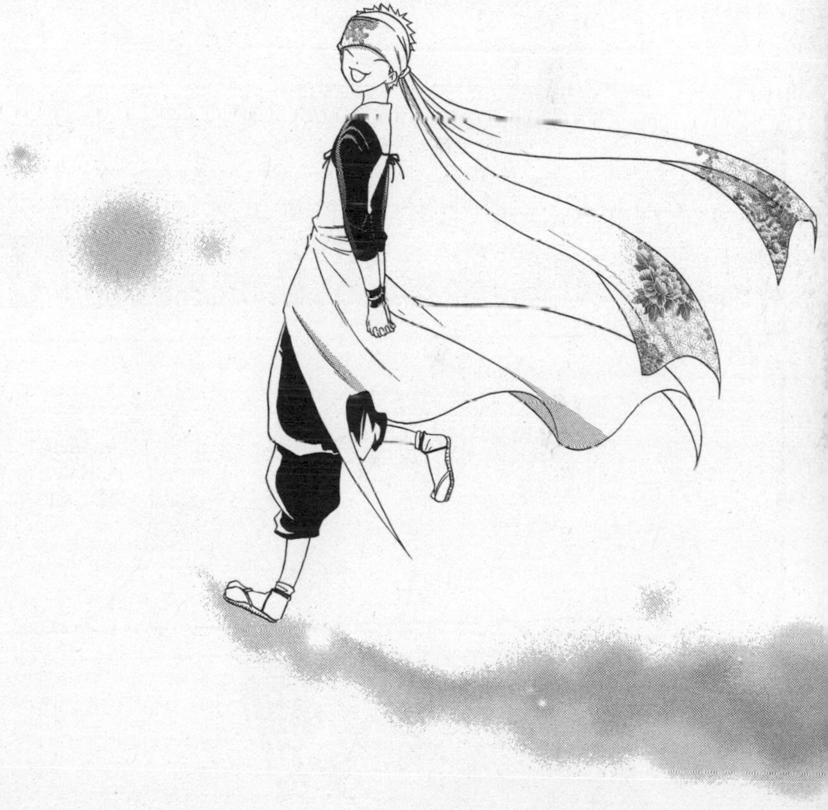

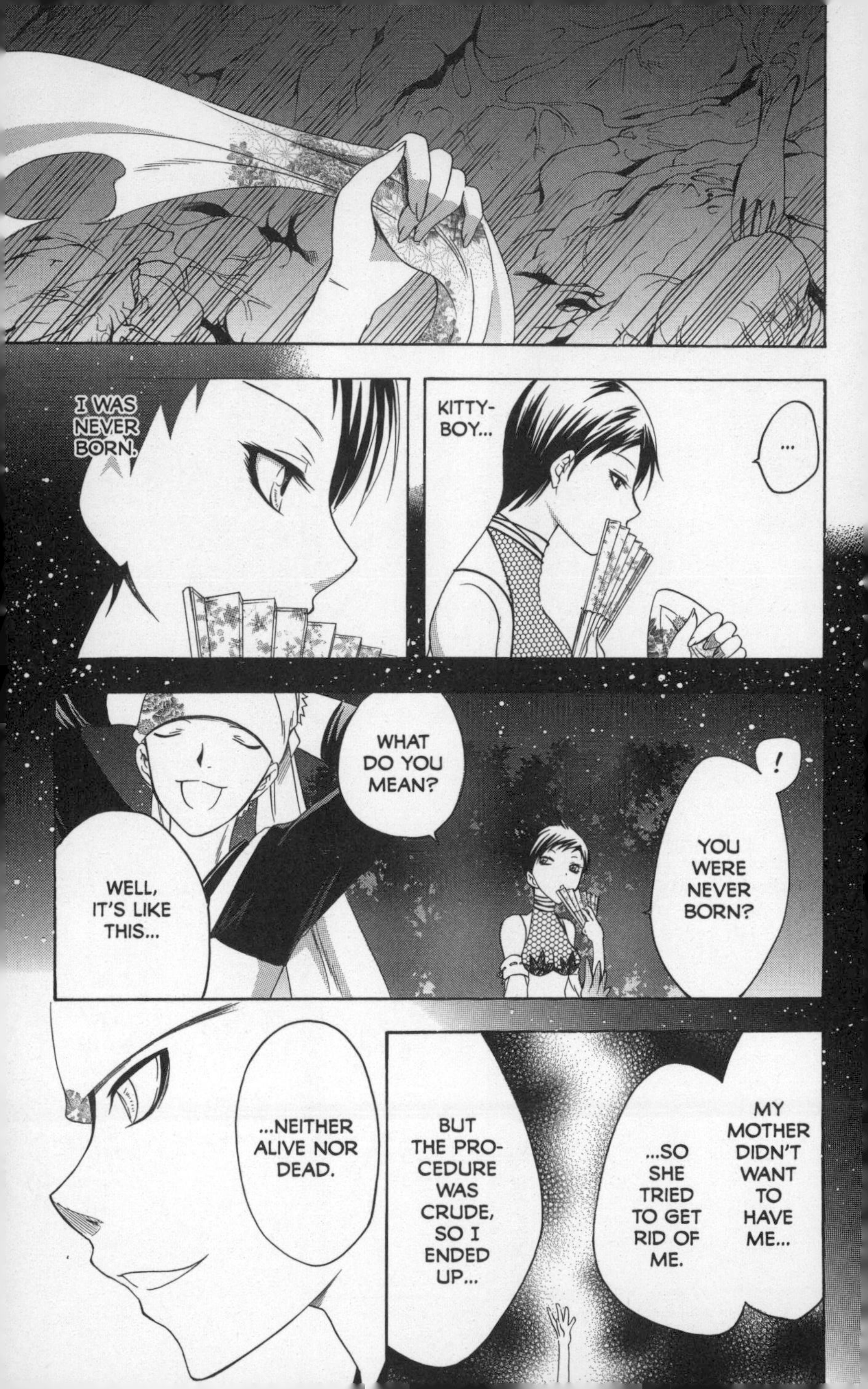
...
KITTY-BOY...
I WAS NEVER BORN.
!
YOU WERE NEVER BORN?
WHAT DO YOU MEAN?
WELL, IT'S LIKE THIS...
MY MOTHER DIDN'T WANT TO HAVE ME...
...SO SHE TRIED TO GET RID OF ME.
BUT THE PROCEDURE WAS CRUDE, SO I ENDED UP...
...NEITHER ALIVE NOR DEAD.

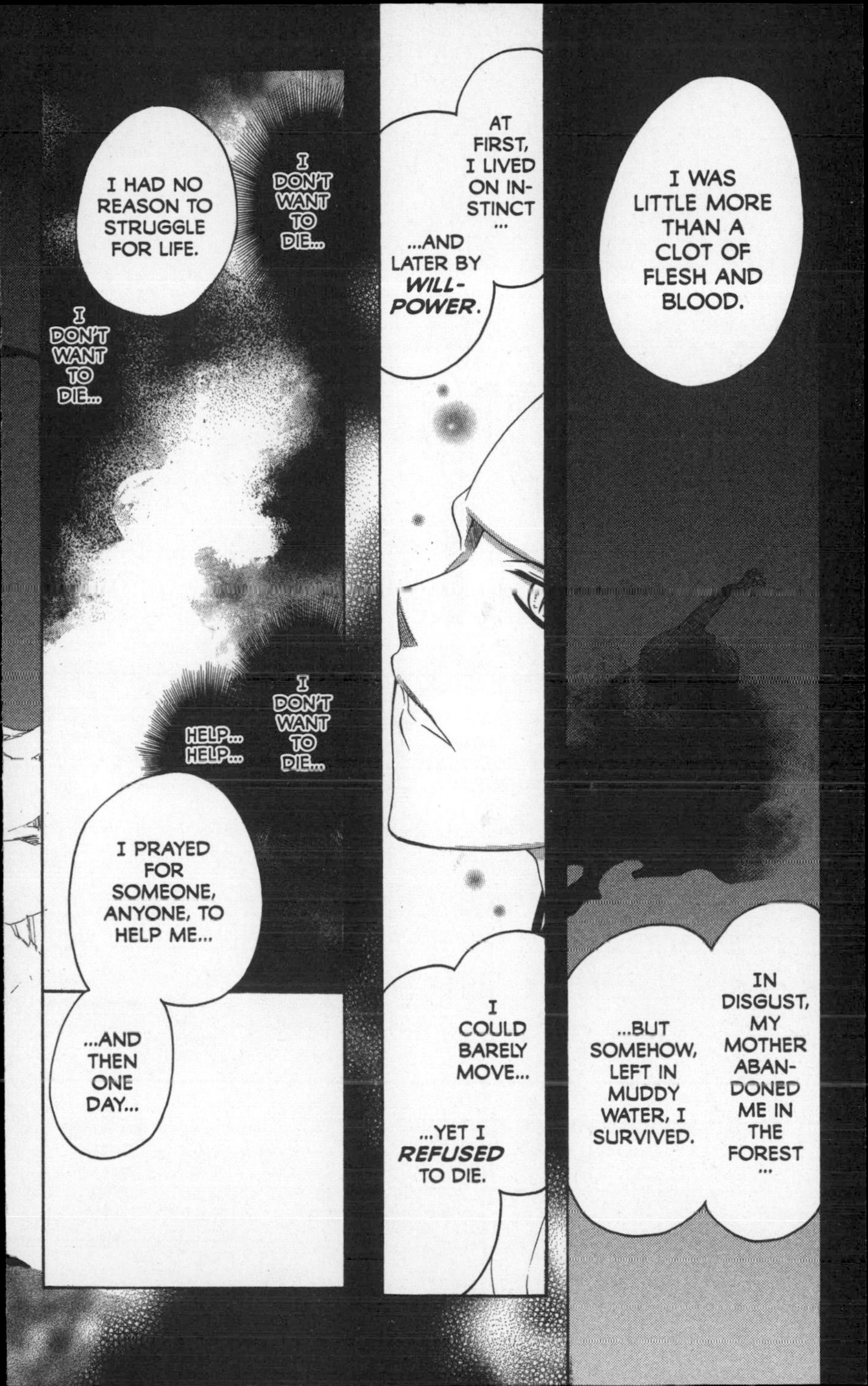
I WAS LITTLE MORE THAN A CLOT OF FLESH AND BLOOD.
IN DISGUST, MY MOTHER ABANDONED ME IN THE FOREST...
...BUT SOMEHOW, LEFT IN MUDDY WATER, I SURVIVED.
AT FIRST, I LIVED ON INSTINCT...
...AND LATER BY *WILLPOWER*.
I COULD BARELY MOVE...
...YET I *REFUSED* TO DIE.
I DON'T WANT TO DIE...
I HAD NO REASON TO STRUGGLE FOR LIFE.
I DON'T WANT TO DIE...
I DON'T WANT TO DIE...
HELP... HELP...
I PRAYED FOR SOMEONE, ANYONE, TO HELP ME...
...AND THEN ONE DAY...

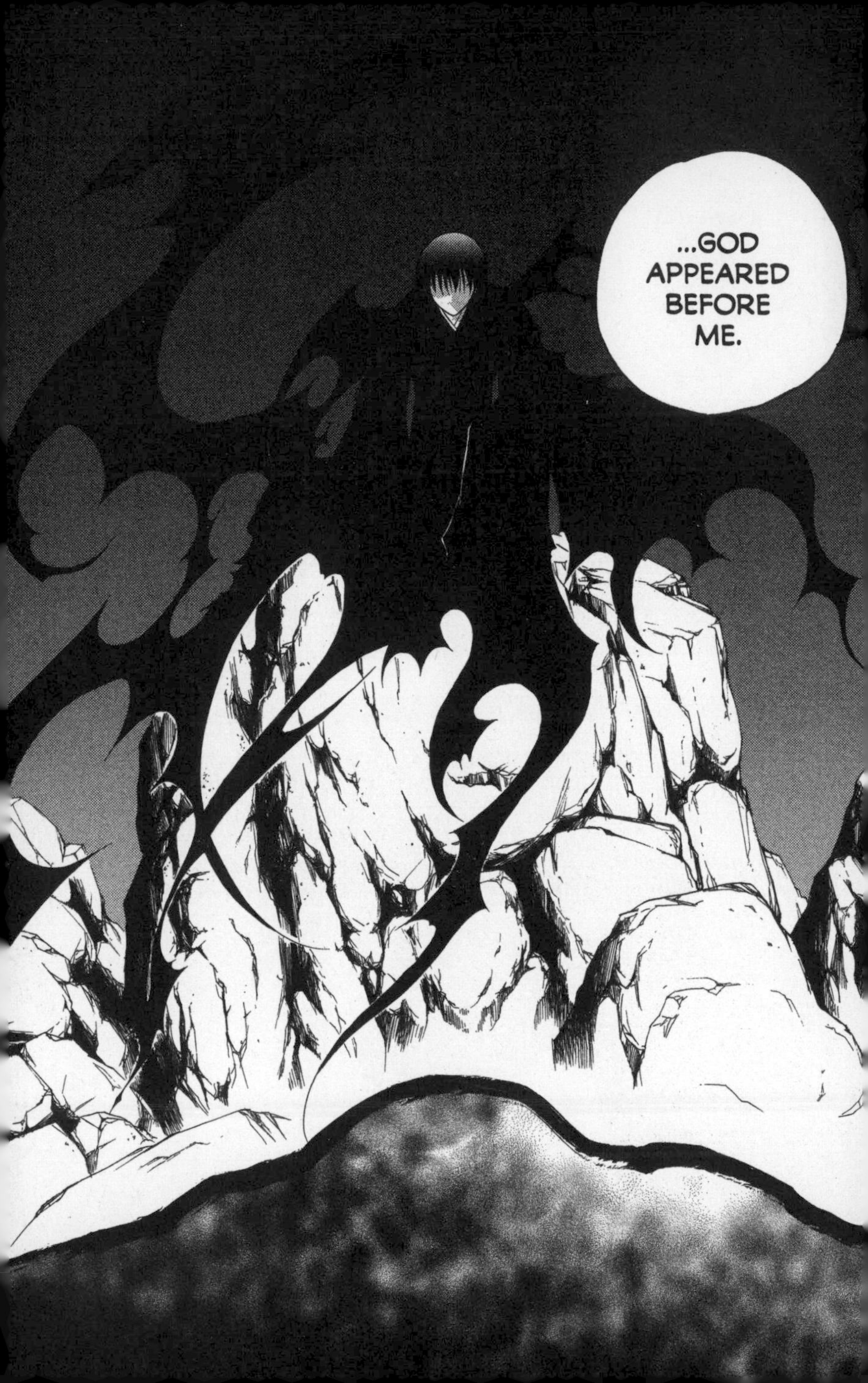
...GOD APPEARED BEFORE ME.

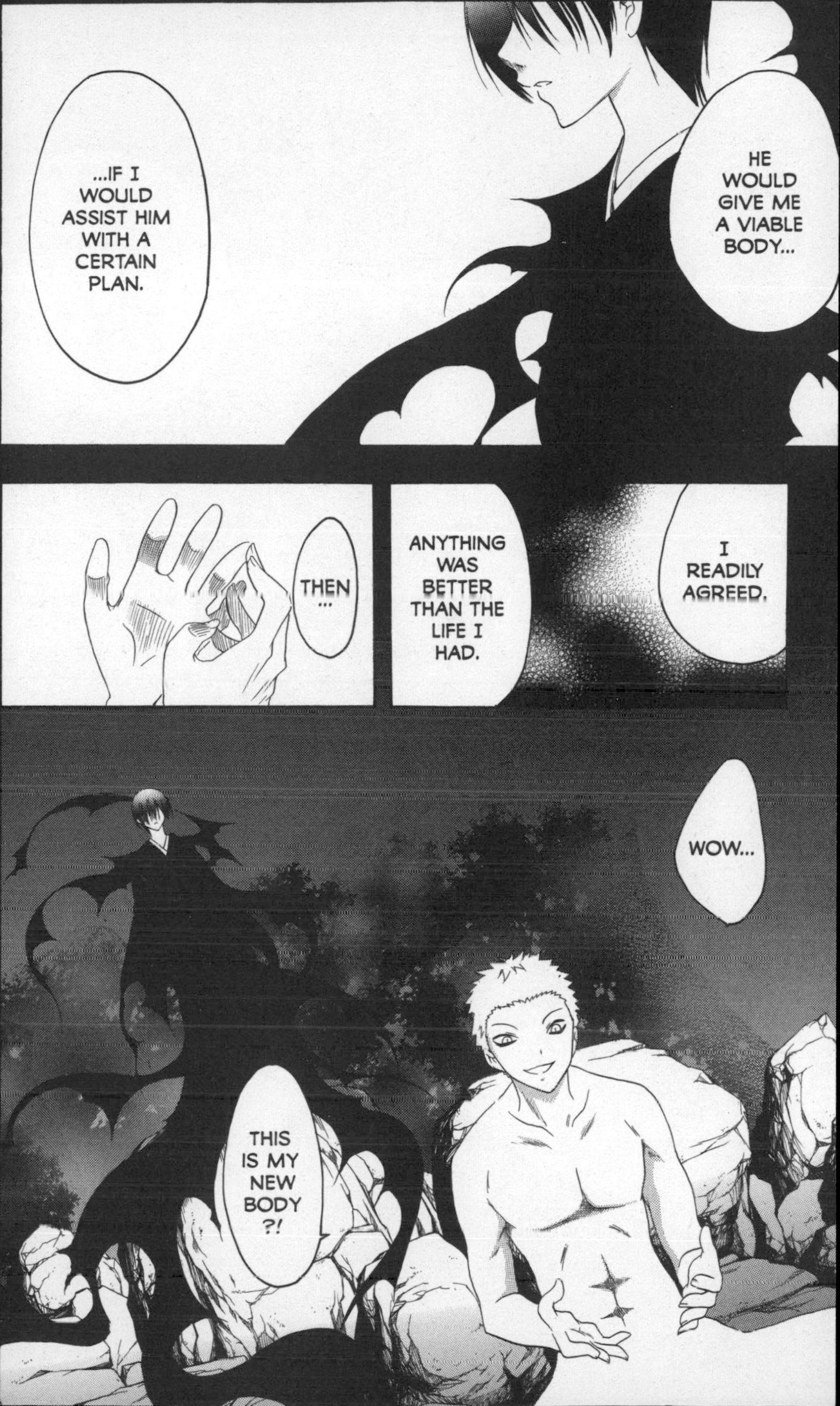
HE WOULD GIVE ME A VIABLE BODY...
...IF I WOULD ASSIST HIM WITH A CERTAIN PLAN.
I READILY AGREED.
ANYTHING WAS BETTER THAN THE LIFE I HAD.
THEN...
WOW...
THIS IS MY NEW BODY?!

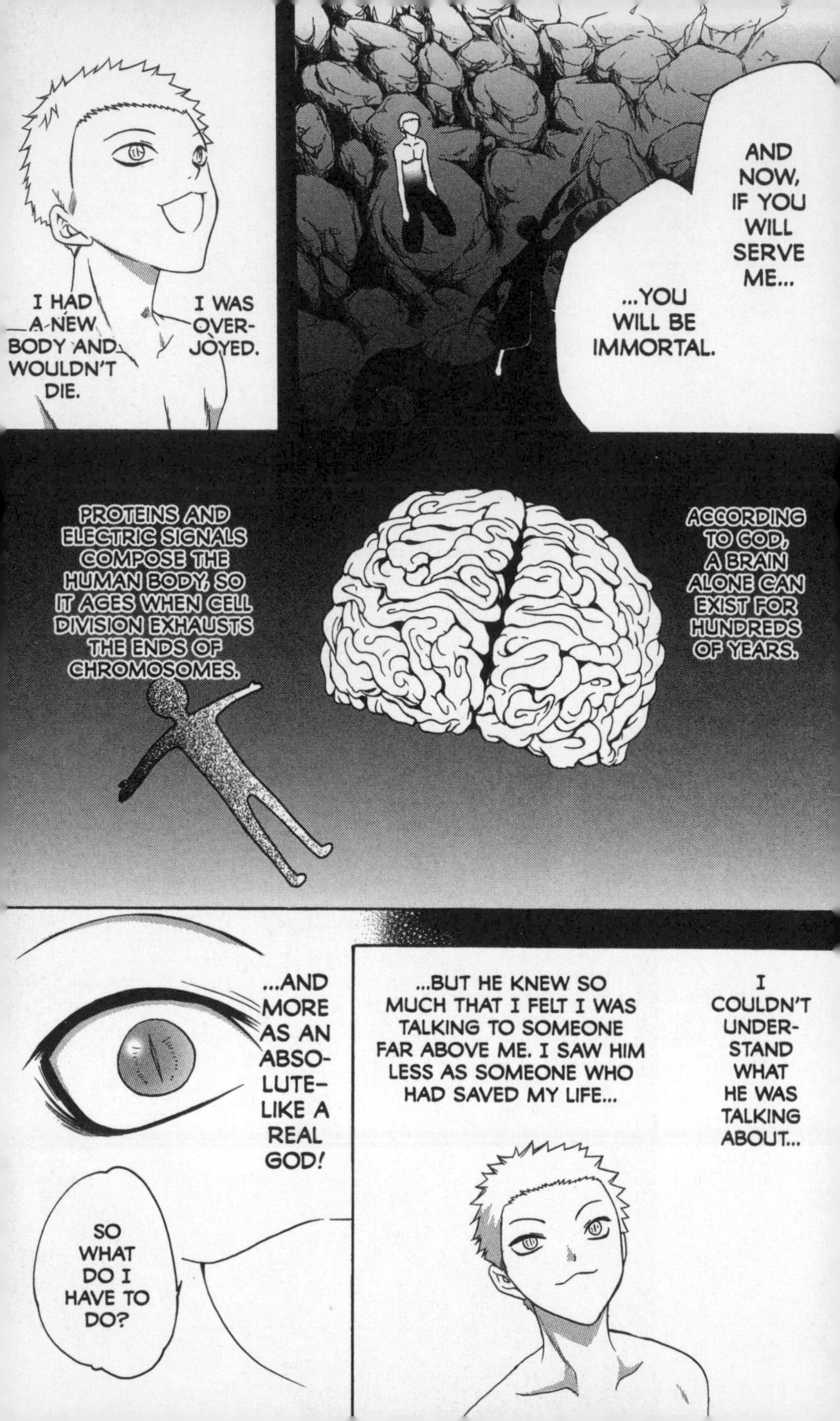
AND NOW, IF YOU WILL SERVE ME...
...YOU WILL BE IMMORTAL.
I WAS OVER-JOYED.
I HAD A NEW BODY AND WOULDN'T DIE.
ACCORDING TO GOD, A BRAIN ALONE CAN EXIST FOR HUNDREDS OF YEARS.
PROTEINS AND ELECTRIC SIGNALS COMPOSE THE HUMAN BODY, SO IT AGES WHEN CELL DIVISION EXHAUSTS THE ENDS OF CHROMOSOMES.
I COULDN'T UNDER-STAND WHAT HE WAS TALKING ABOUT...
...BUT HE KNEW SO MUCH THAT I FELT I WAS TALKING TO SOMEONE FAR ABOVE ME. I SAW HIM LESS AS SOMEONE WHO HAD SAVED MY LIFE...
...AND MORE AS AN ABSO-LUTE–LIKE A REAL GOD!
SO WHAT DO I HAVE TO DO?

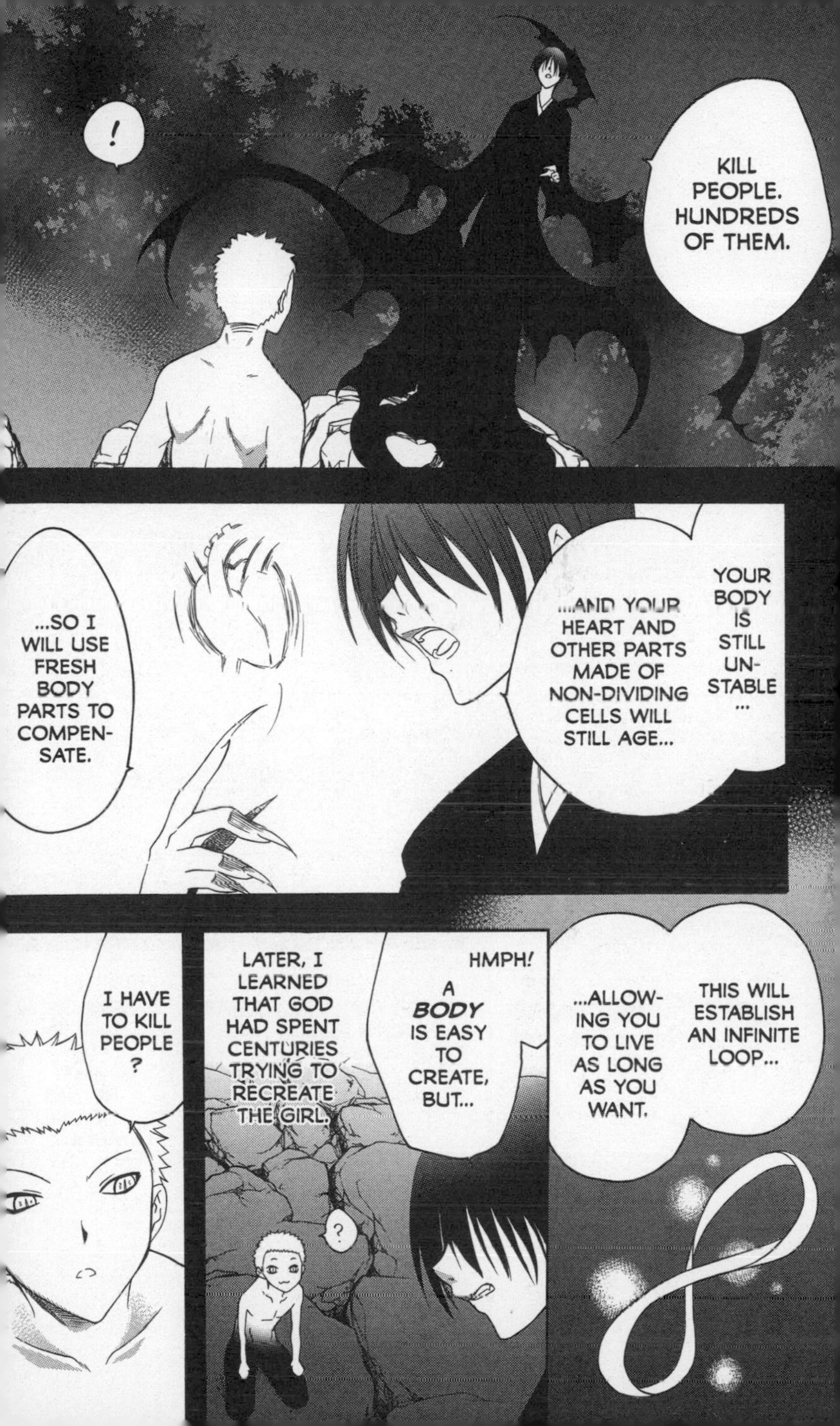
KILL PEOPLE. HUNDREDS OF THEM.
!
YOUR BODY IS STILL UN-STABLE ...
...AND YOUR HEART AND OTHER PARTS MADE OF NON-DIVIDING CELLS WILL STILL AGE...
...SO I WILL USE FRESH BODY PARTS TO COMPEN-SATE.
THIS WILL ESTABLISH AN INFINITE LOOP...
...ALLOW-ING YOU TO LIVE AS LONG AS YOU WANT.
HMPH! A *BODY* IS EASY TO CREATE, BUT...
LATER, I LEARNED THAT GOD HAD SPENT CENTURIES TRYING TO RECREATE THE GIRL.
?
I HAVE TO KILL PEOPLE ?

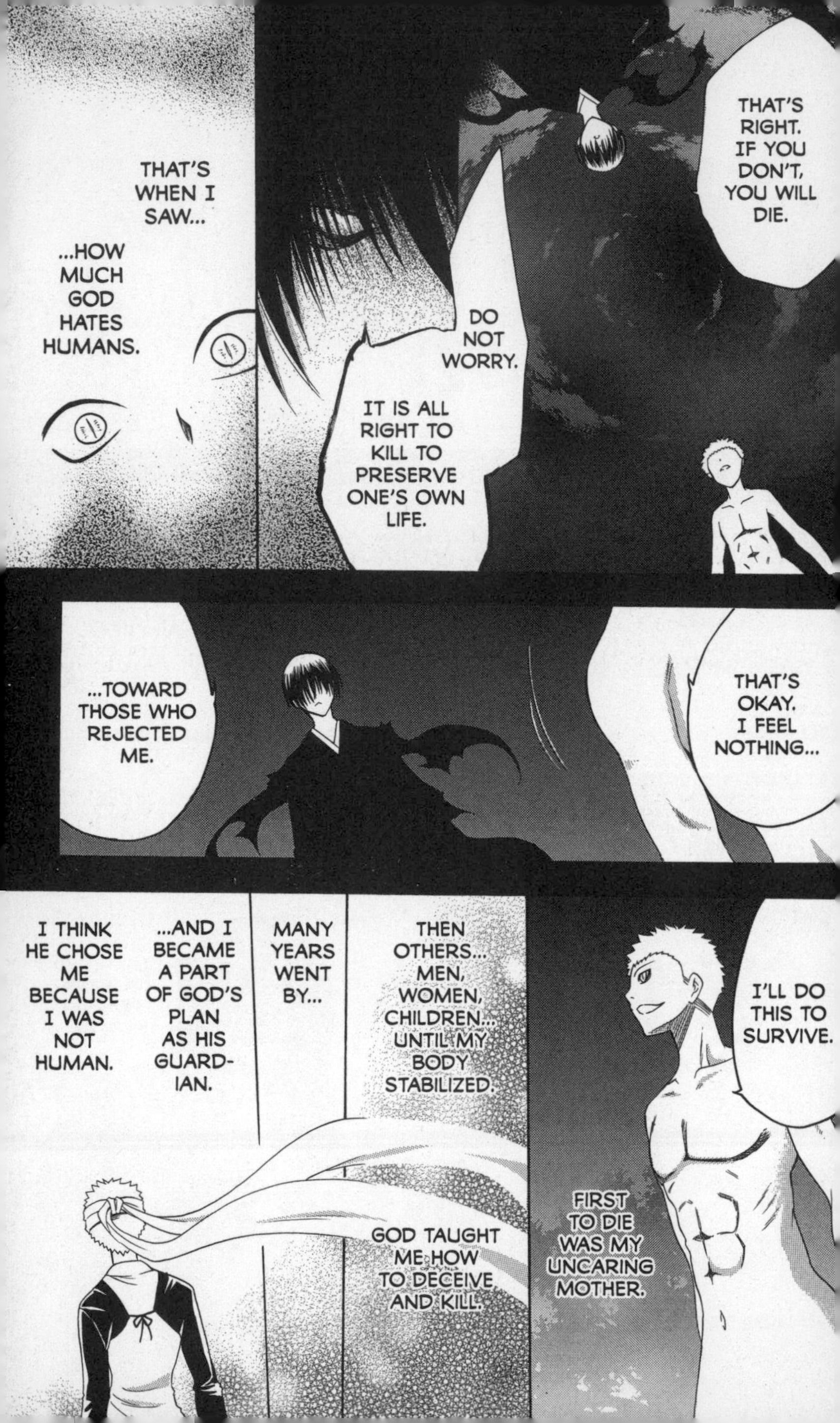
THAT'S RIGHT. IF YOU DON'T, YOU WILL DIE.
DO NOT WORRY.
IT IS ALL RIGHT TO KILL TO PRESERVE ONE'S OWN LIFE.
THAT'S WHEN I SAW...
...HOW MUCH GOD HATES HUMANS.
THAT'S OKAY. I FEEL NOTHING...
...TOWARD THOSE WHO REJECTED ME.
I'LL DO THIS TO SURVIVE.
FIRST TO DIE WAS MY UNCARING MOTHER.
THEN OTHERS... MEN, WOMEN, CHILDREN... UNTIL MY BODY STABILIZED.
GOD TAUGHT ME HOW TO DECEIVE AND KILL.
MANY YEARS WENT BY...
...AND I BECAME A PART OF GOD'S PLAN AS HIS GUARDIAN.
I THINK HE CHOSE ME BECAUSE I WAS NOT HUMAN.

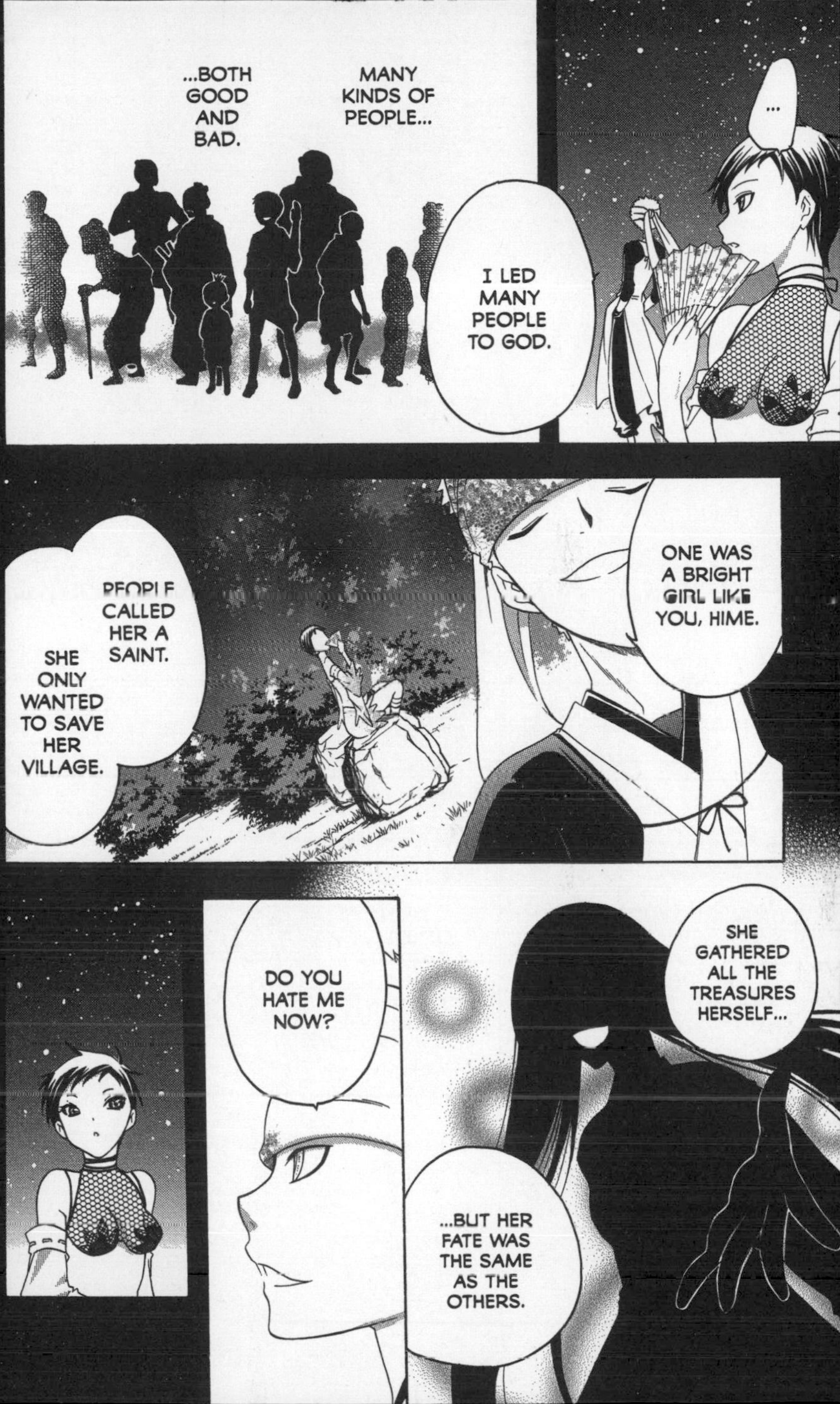
...
I LED MANY PEOPLE TO GOD.
MANY KINDS OF PEOPLE...
...BOTH GOOD AND BAD.
ONE WAS A BRIGHT GIRL LIKE YOU, HIME.
PEOPLE CALLED HER A SAINT.
SHE ONLY WANTED TO SAVE HER VILLAGE.
SHE GATHERED ALL THE TREASURES HERSELF...
...BUT HER FATE WAS THE SAME AS THE OTHERS.
DO YOU HATE ME NOW?

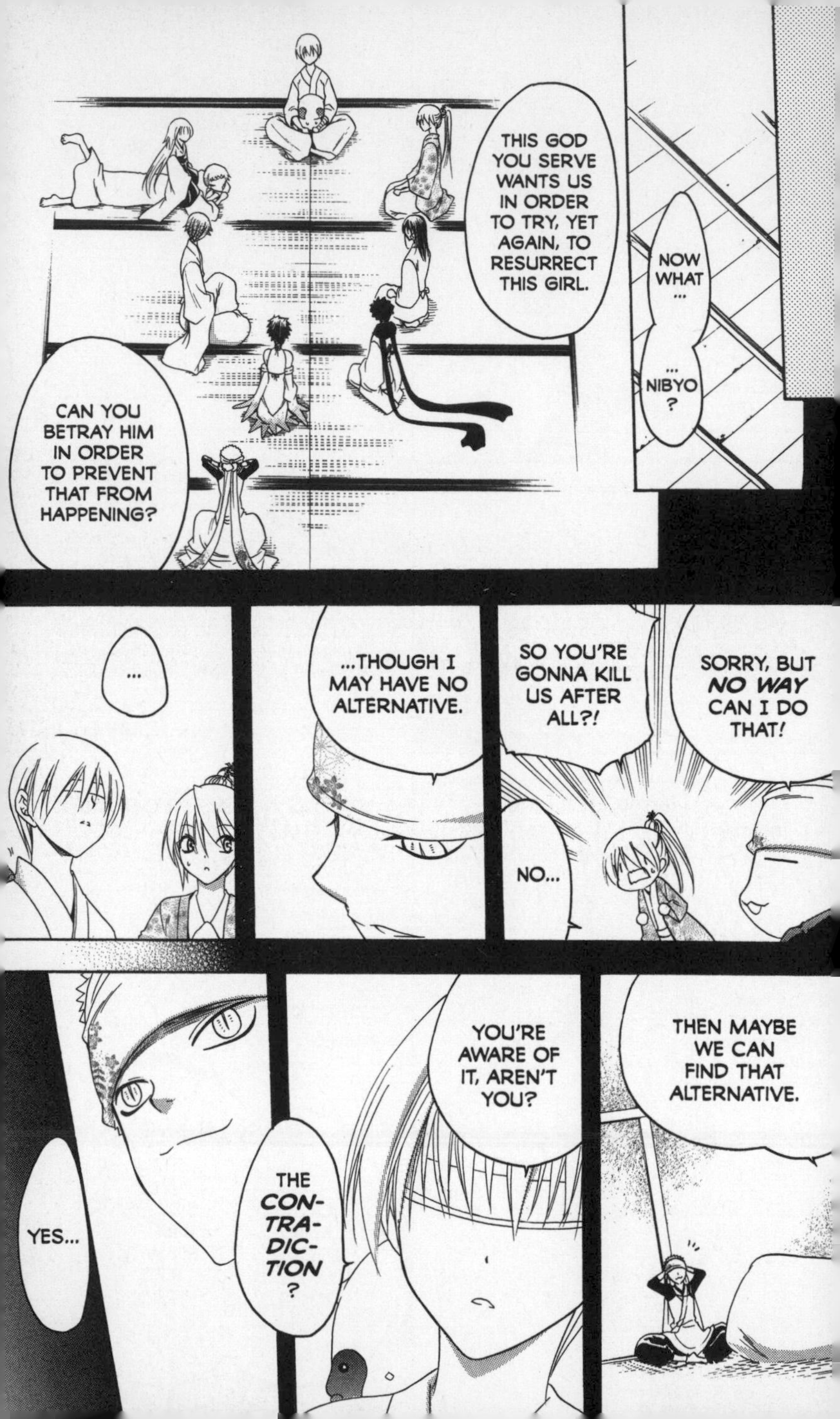
NOW WHAT ...
... NIBYO ?
THIS GOD YOU SERVE WANTS US IN ORDER TO TRY, YET AGAIN, TO RESURRECT THIS GIRL.
CAN YOU BETRAY HIM IN ORDER TO PREVENT THAT FROM HAPPENING?
SORRY, BUT *NO WAY* CAN I DO THAT!
SO YOU'RE GONNA KILL US AFTER ALL?!
NO...
...THOUGH I MAY HAVE NO ALTERNATIVE.
...
THEN MAYBE WE CAN FIND THAT ALTERNATIVE.
YOU'RE AWARE OF IT, AREN'T YOU?
THE *CONTRADICTION*?
YES...

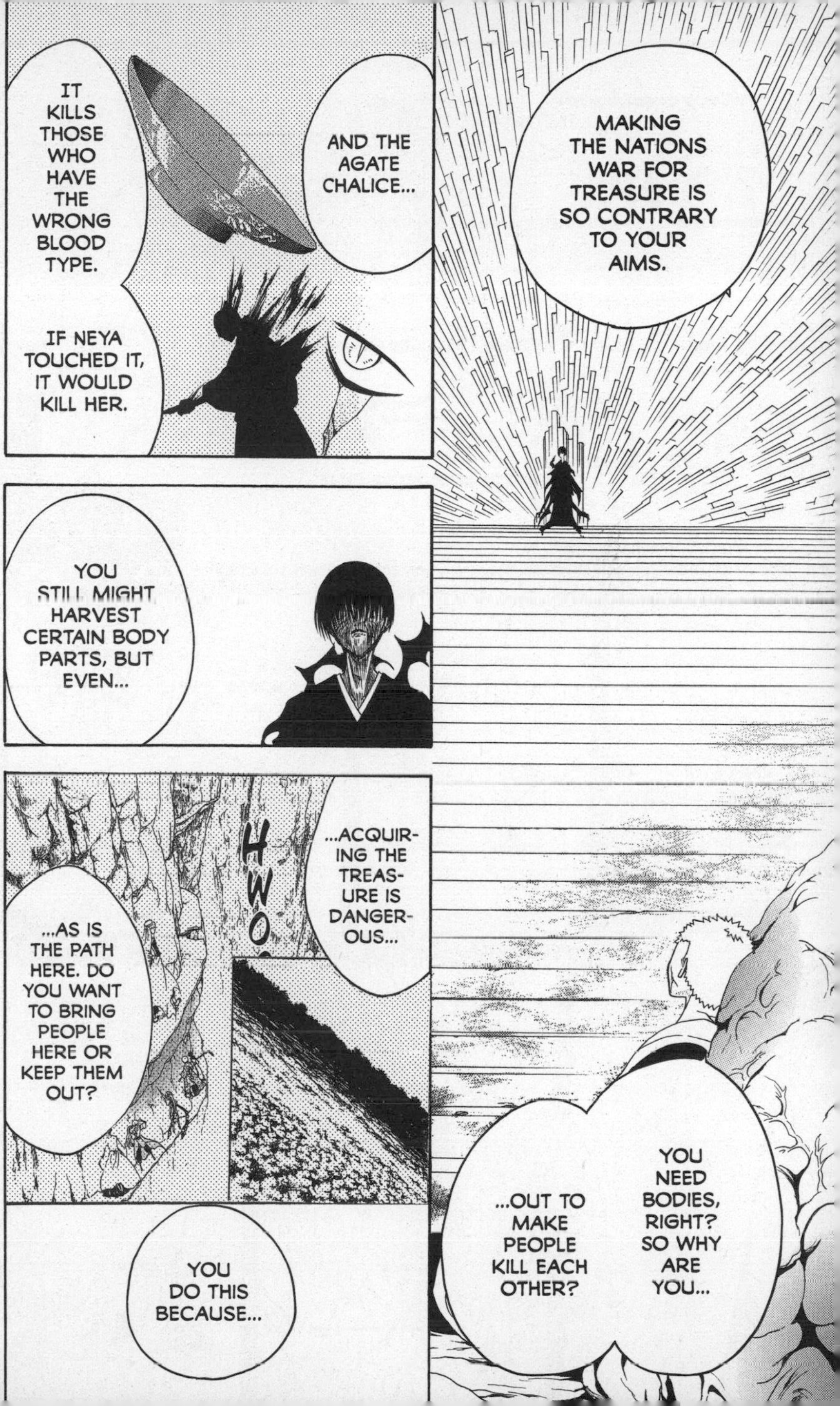
MAKING THE NATIONS WAR FOR TREASURE IS SO CONTRARY TO YOUR AIMS.
YOU NEED BODIES, RIGHT? SO WHY ARE YOU...
...OUT TO MAKE PEOPLE KILL EACH OTHER?
AND THE AGATE CHALICE...
IT KILLS THOSE WHO HAVE THE WRONG BLOOD TYPE.
IF NEYA TOUCHED IT, IT WOULD KILL HER.
YOU STILL MIGHT HARVEST CERTAIN BODY PARTS, BUT EVEN...
...ACQUIRING THE TREASURE IS DANGEROUS...
HWO
...AS IS THE PATH HERE. DO YOU WANT TO BRING PEOPLE HERE OR KEEP THEM OUT?
YOU DO THIS BECAUSE...

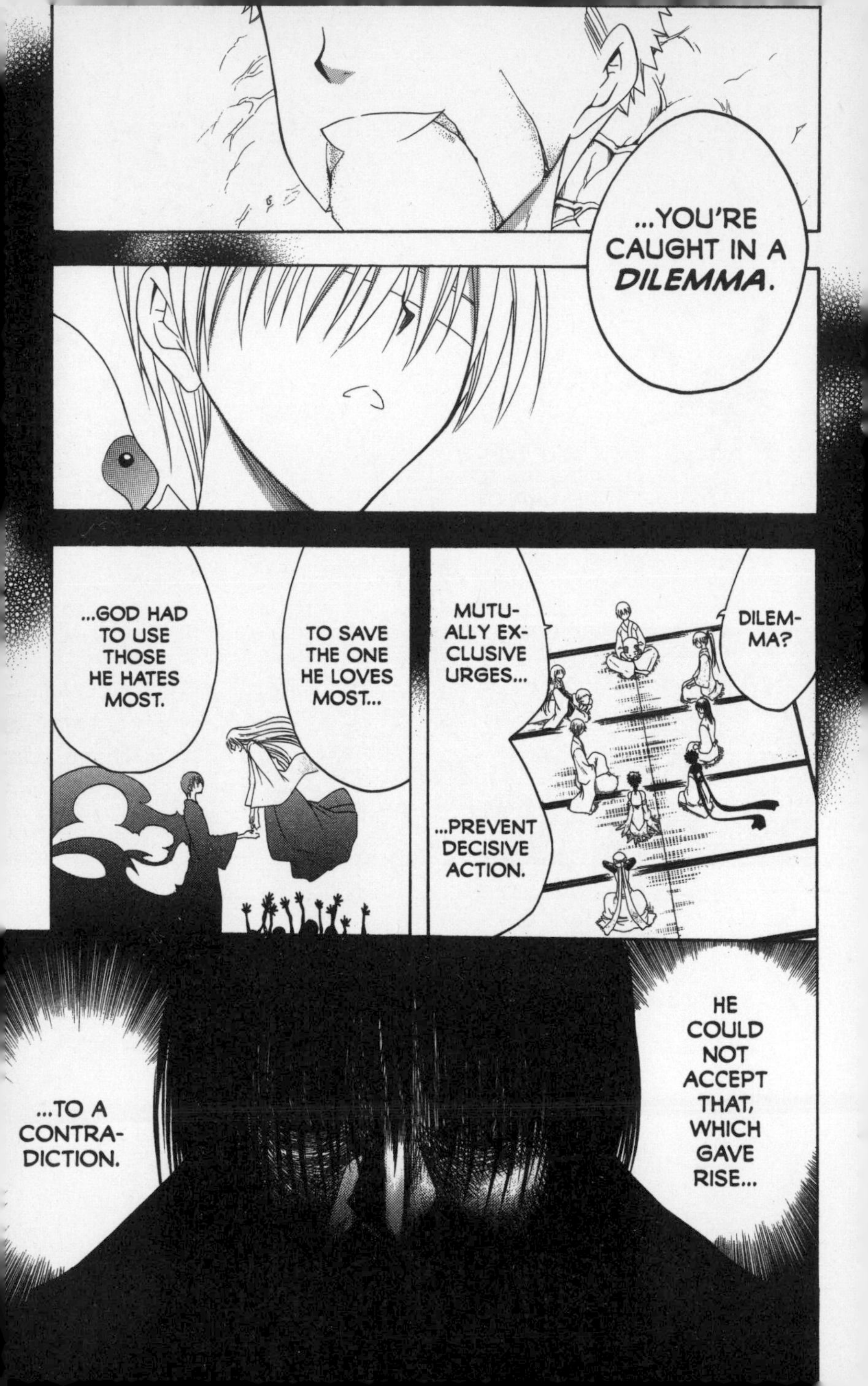
...YOU'RE CAUGHT IN A *DILEMMA*.
DILEM-MA?
MUTU-ALLY EX-CLUSIVE URGES...
...PREVENT DECISIVE ACTION.
TO SAVE THE ONE HE LOVES MOST...
...GOD HAD TO USE THOSE HE HATES MOST.
HE COULD NOT ACCEPT THAT, WHICH GAVE RISE...
...TO A CONTRA-DICTION.

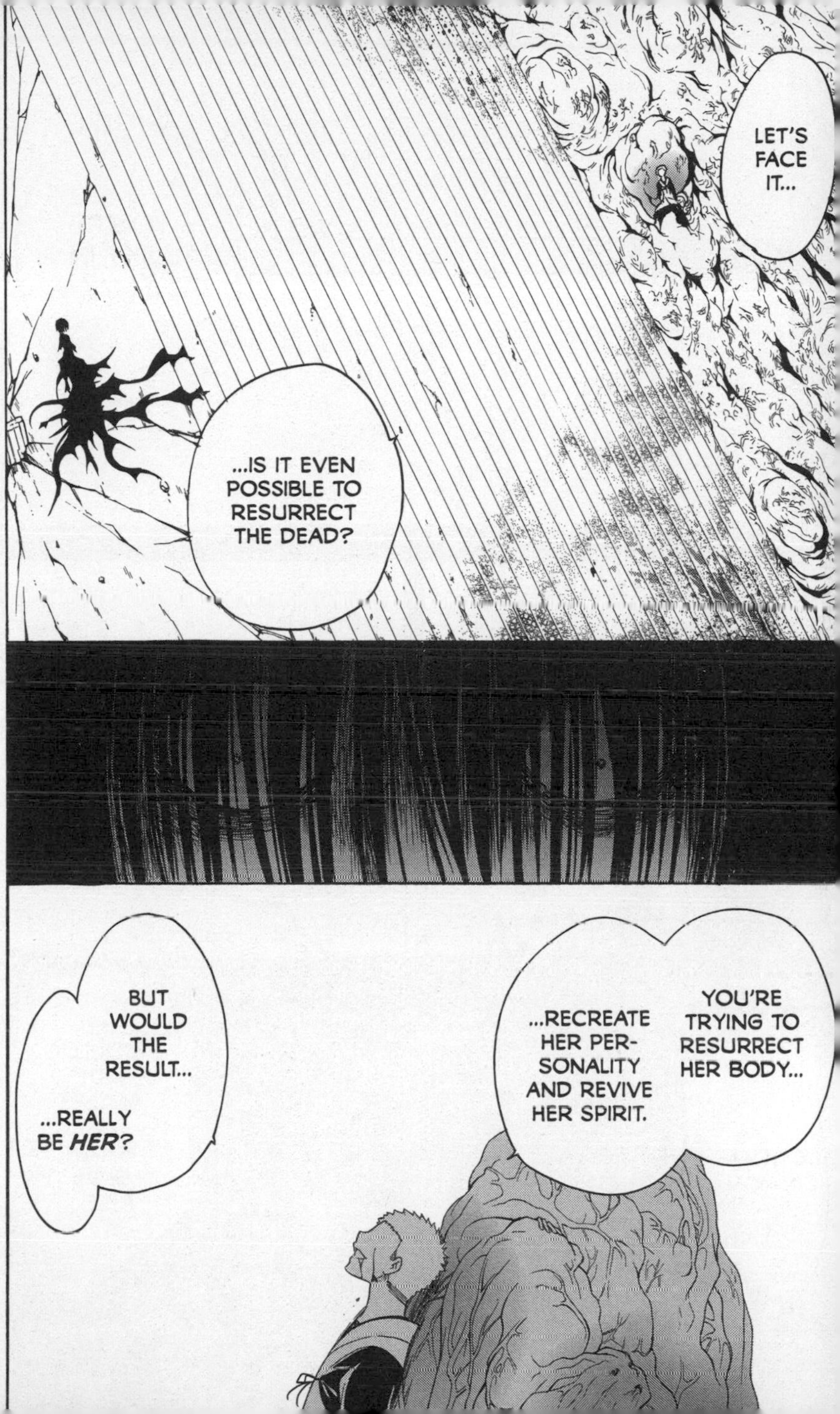
LET'S FACE IT...
...IS IT EVEN POSSIBLE TO RESURRECT THE DEAD?
YOU'RE TRYING TO RESURRECT HER BODY...
...RECREATE HER PER-SONALITY AND REVIVE HER SPIRIT.
BUT WOULD THE RESULT...
...REALLY BE *HER*?

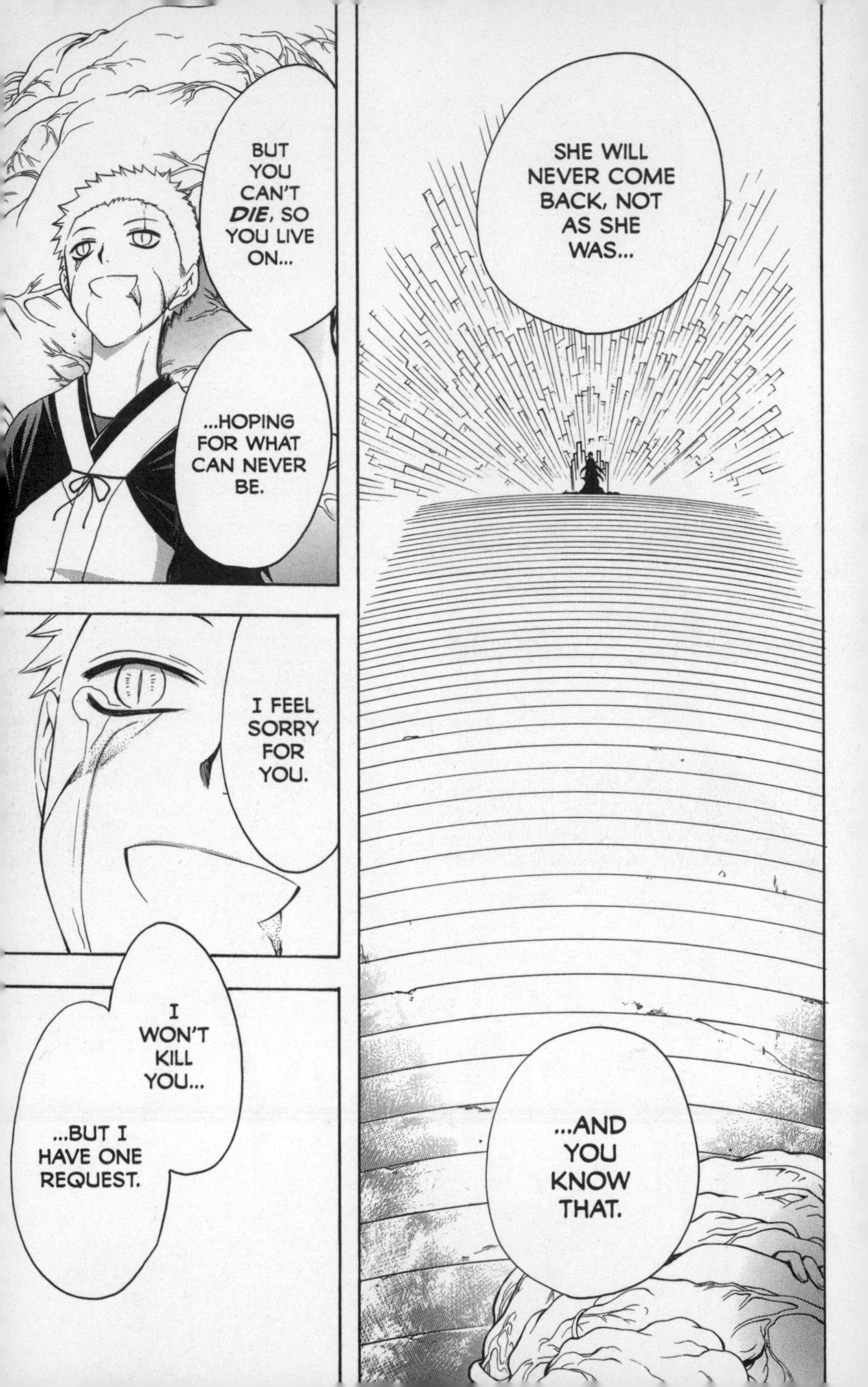
SHE WILL NEVER COME BACK, NOT AS SHE WAS...
...AND YOU KNOW THAT.
BUT YOU CAN'T *DIE*, SO YOU LIVE ON...
...HOPING FOR WHAT CAN NEVER BE.
I FEEL SORRY FOR YOU.
I WON'T KILL YOU...
...BUT I HAVE ONE REQUEST.

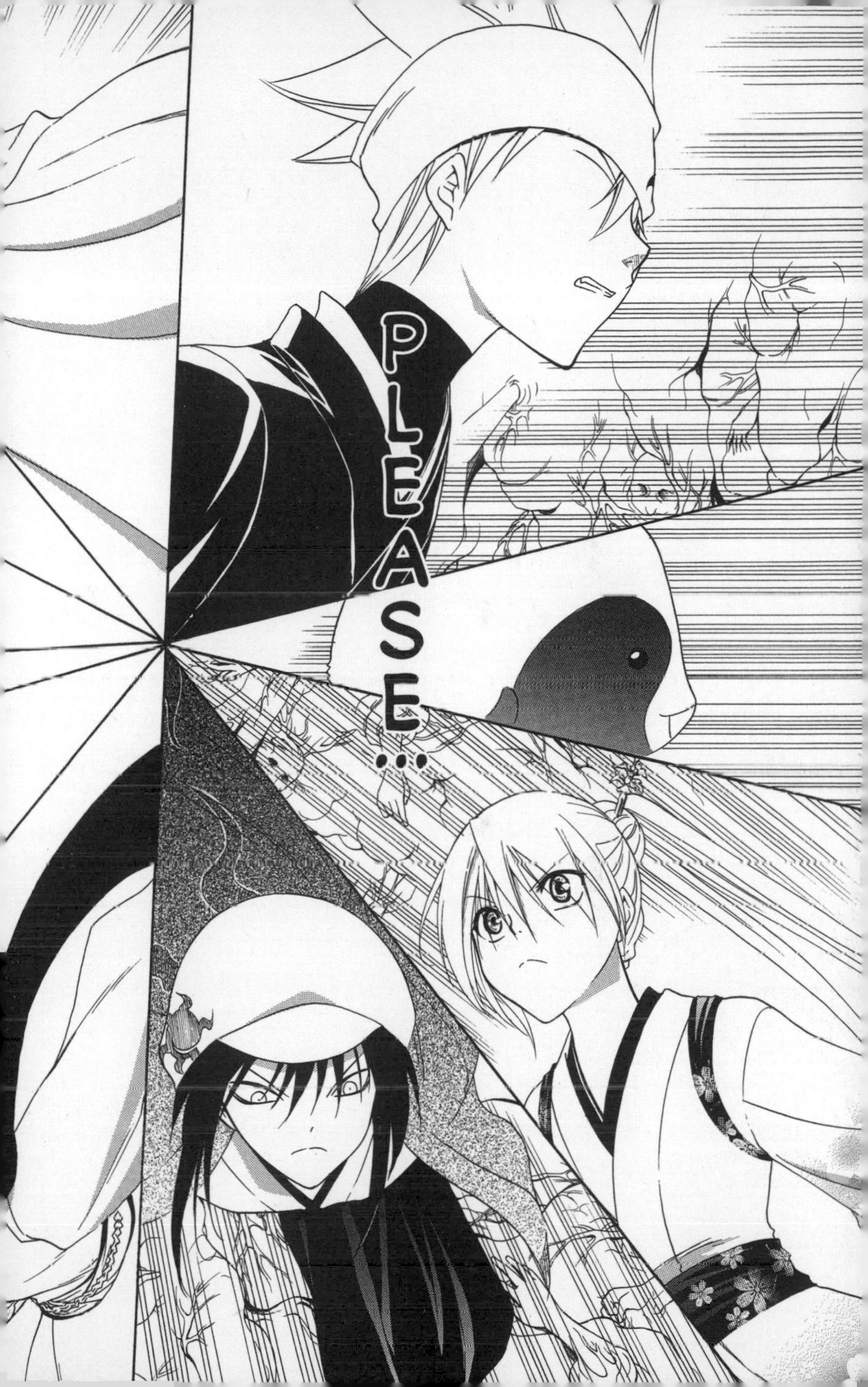
PLEASE...

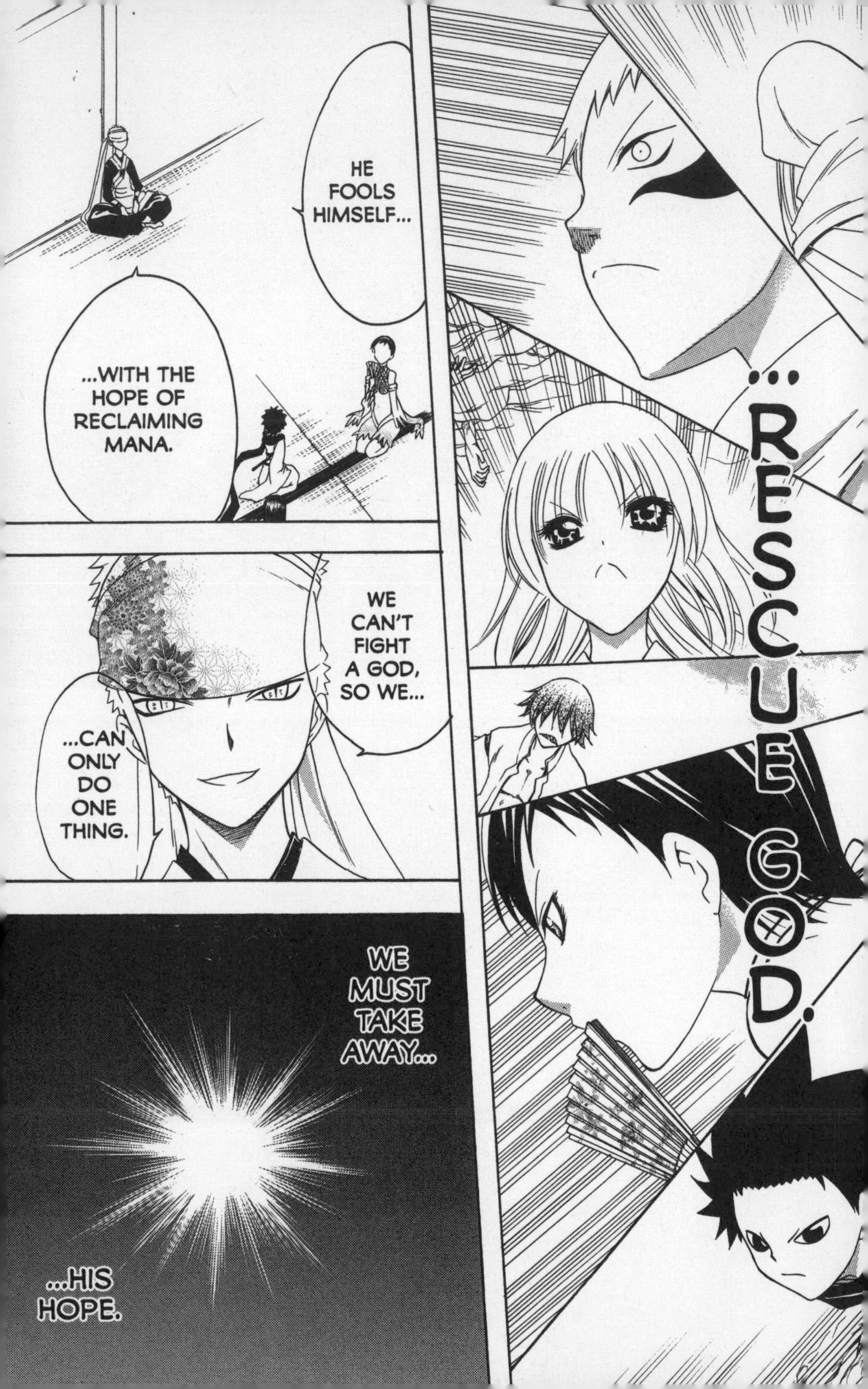
...RESCUE GOD.
HE FOOLS HIMSELF...
...WITH THE HOPE OF RECLAIMING MANA.
WE CAN'T FIGHT A GOD, SO WE...
...CAN ONLY DO ONE THING.
WE MUST TAKE AWAY...
...HIS HOPE.

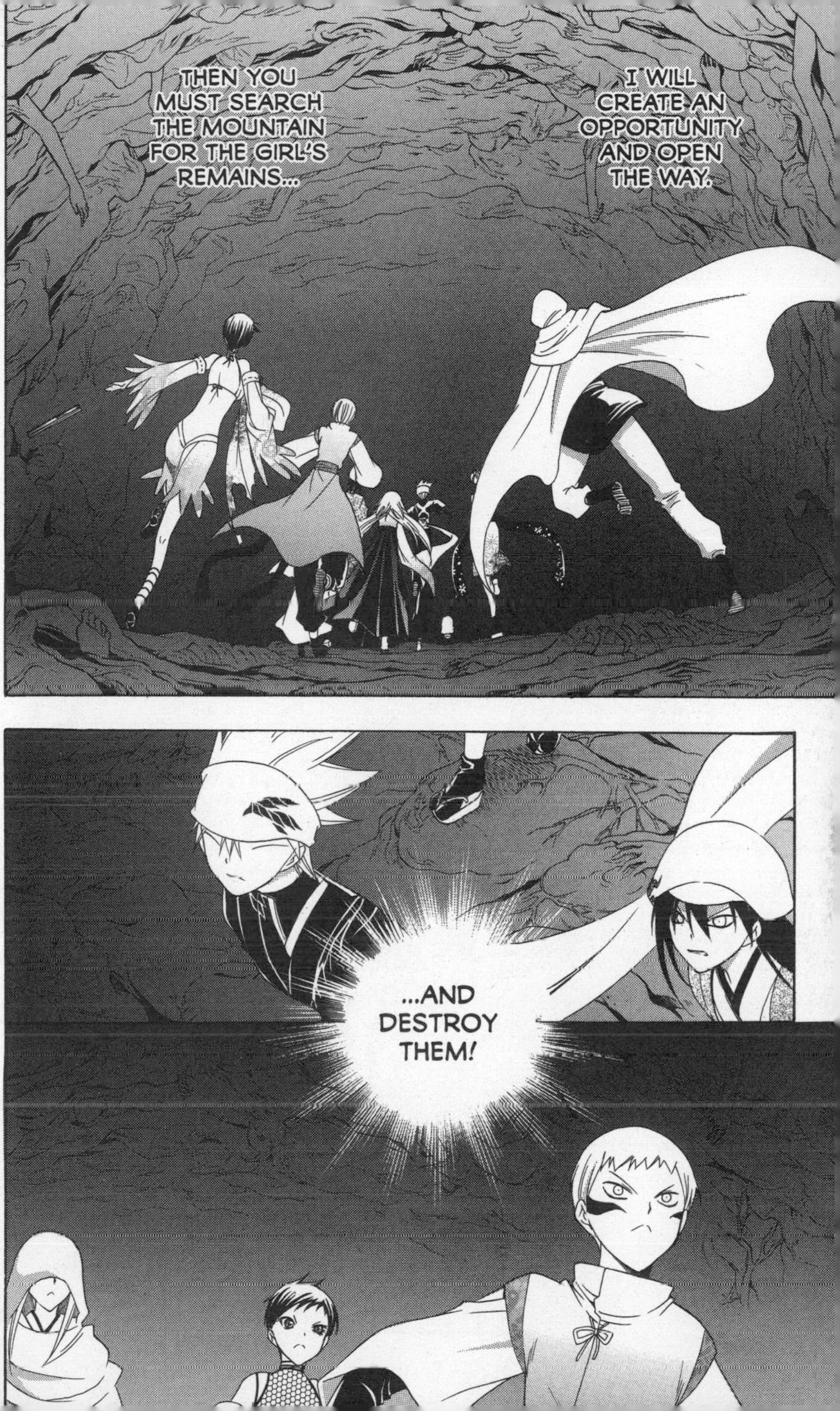
I WILL CREATE AN OPPORTUNITY AND OPEN THE WAY.
THEN YOU MUST SEARCH THE MOUNTAIN FOR THE GIRL'S REMAINS...
...AND DESTROY THEM!

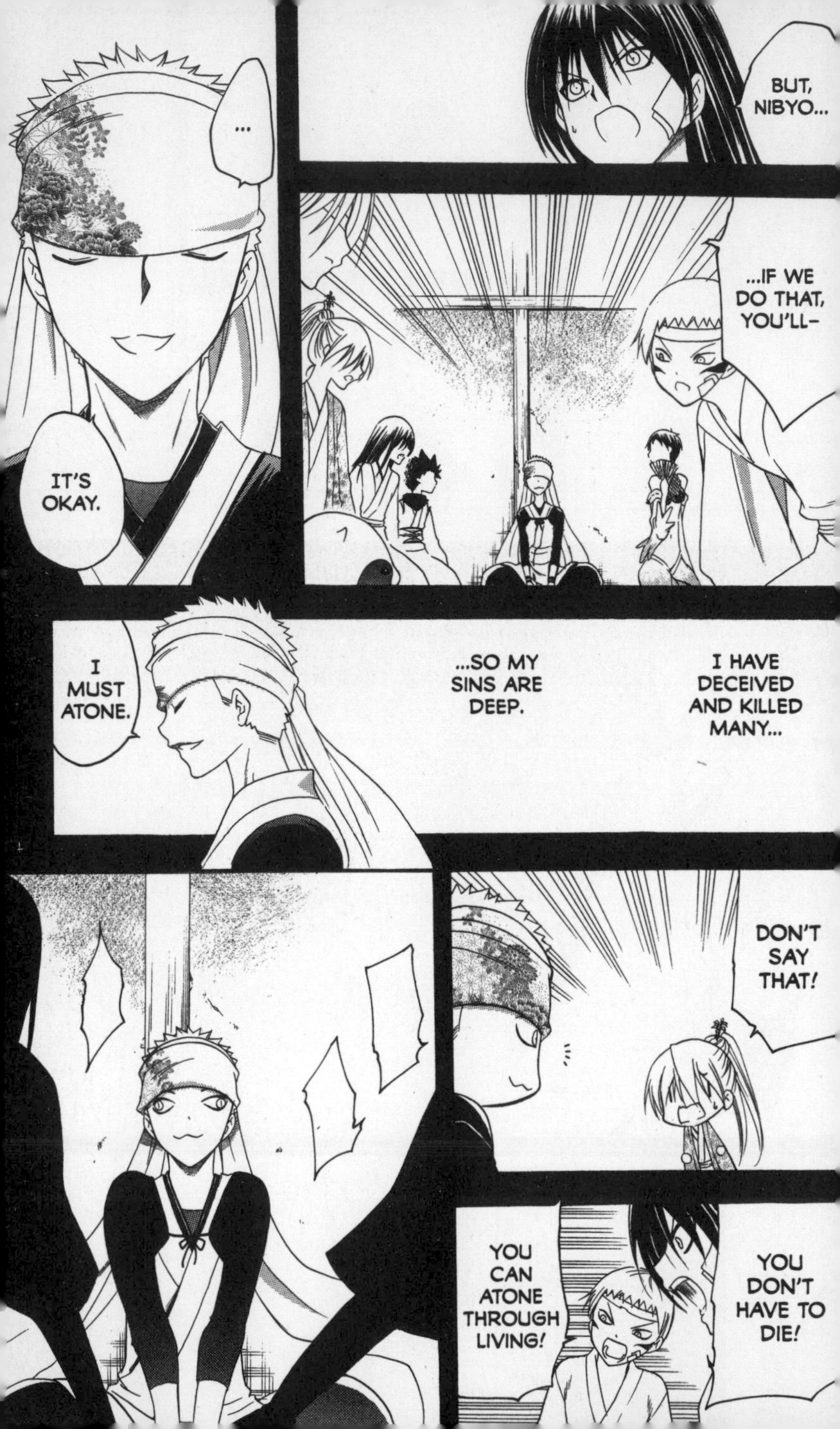
BUT, NIBYO...
...IF WE DO THAT, YOU'LL-
...
IT'S OKAY.
I HAVE DECEIVED AND KILLED MANY...
...SO MY SINS ARE DEEP.
I MUST ATONE.
DON'T SAY THAT!
YOU DON'T HAVE TO DIE!
YOU CAN ATONE THROUGH LIVING!

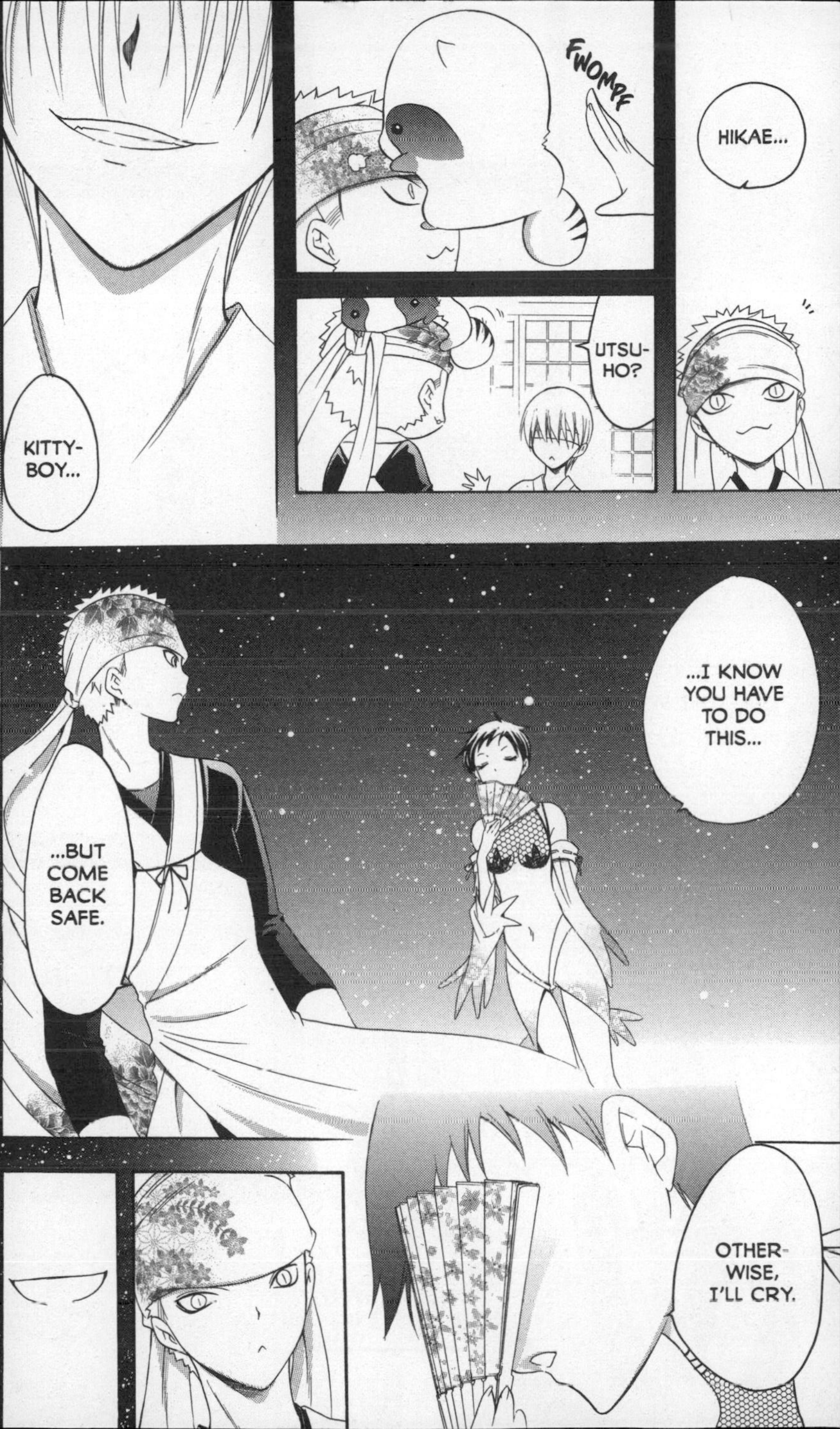
HIKAE...
FWOMPF
UTSU-HO?
KITTY-BOY...
...I KNOW YOU HAVE TO DO THIS...
...BUT COME BACK SAFE.
OTHER-WISE, I'LL CRY.

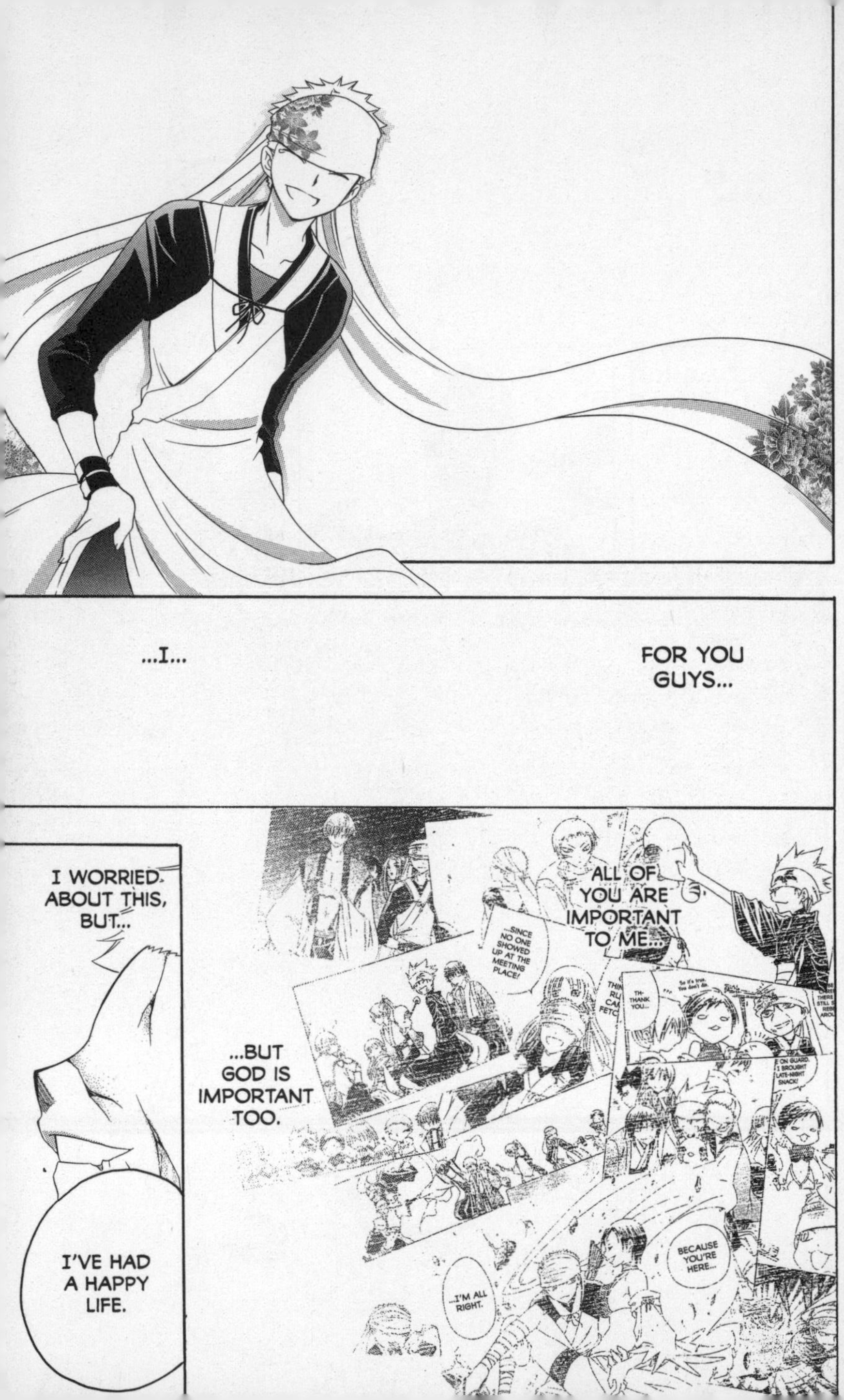
FOR YOU GUYS...
...I...
ALL OF YOU ARE IMPORTANT TO ME...
...SINCE NO ONE SHOWED UP AT THE MEETING PLACE!
TH-THANK YOU...
I BROUGHT LATE-NIGHT SNACK!
...BUT GOD IS IMPORTANT TOO.
BECAUSE YOU'RE HERE...
...I'M ALL RIGHT.
I WORRIED ABOUT THIS, BUT...
I'VE HAD A HAPPY LIFE.

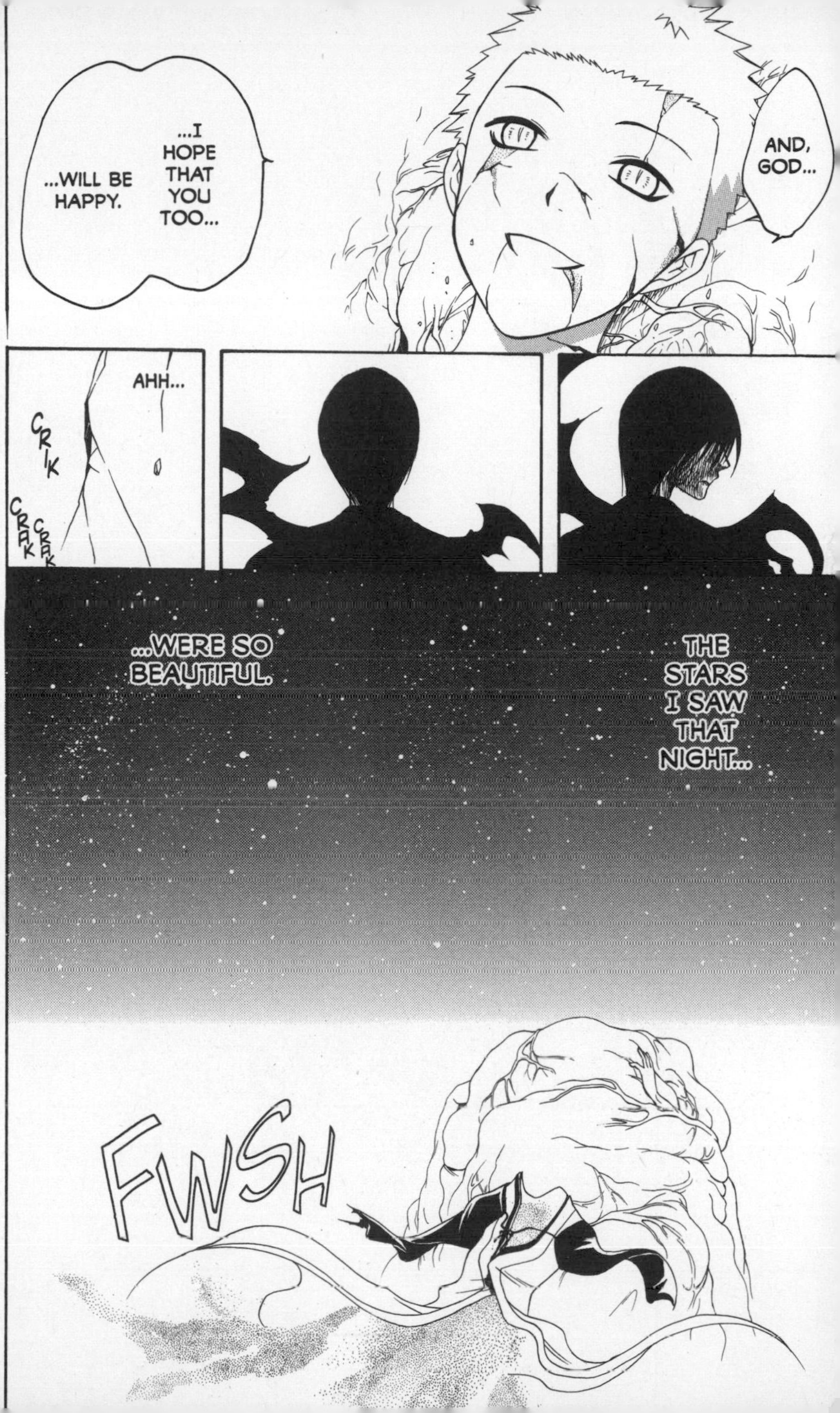
AND, GOD...
...I HOPE THAT YOU TOO...
...WILL BE HAPPY.
AHH...
CRIK
CRAK CRAK
THE STARS I SAW THAT NIGHT...
...WERE SO BEAUTIFUL.
FWSH

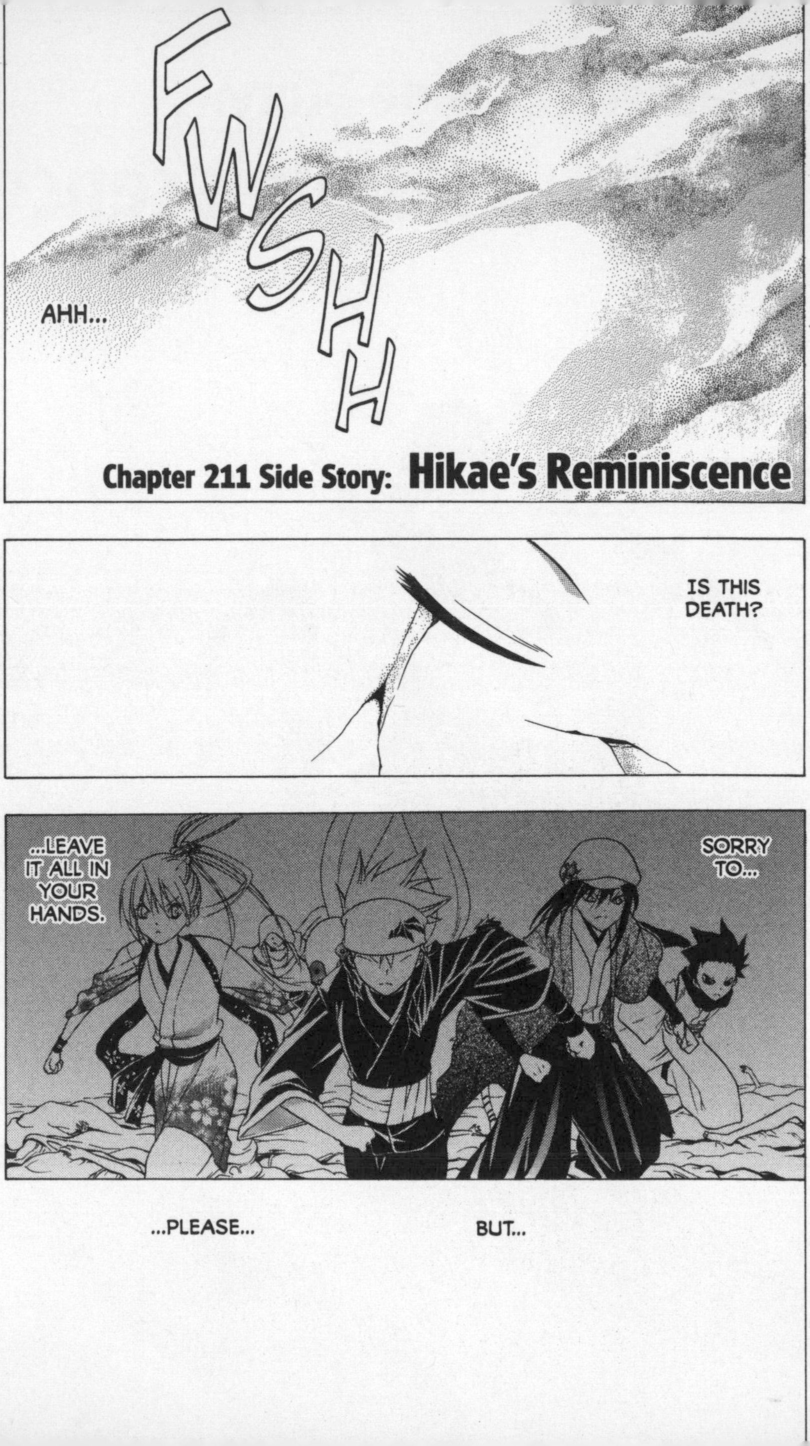
FWSHH
AHH...
Chapter 211 Side Story: Hikae's Reminiscence
IS THIS DEATH?
SORRY TO...
...LEAVE IT ALL IN YOUR HANDS.
BUT...
...PLEASE...

Chapter 211 Side Story:
Hikae's Reminiscence

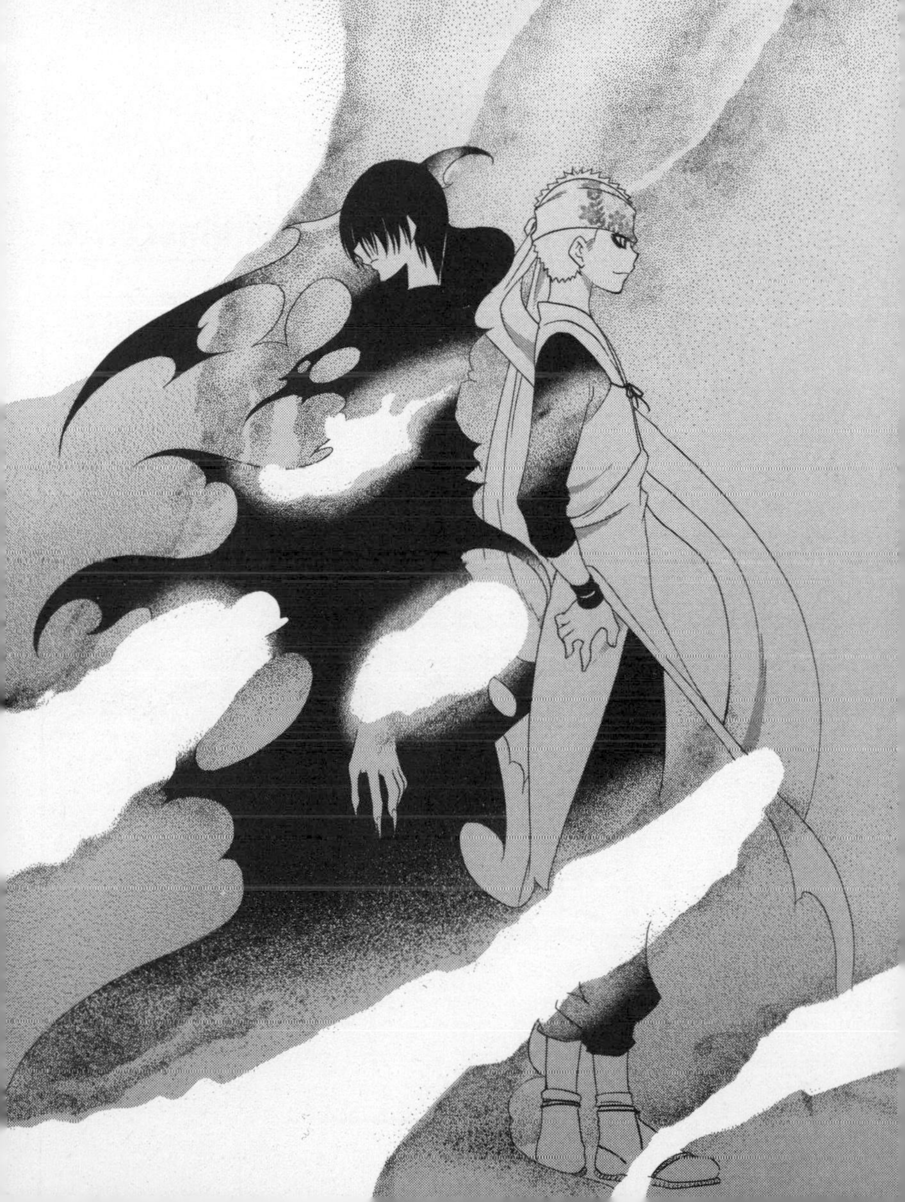

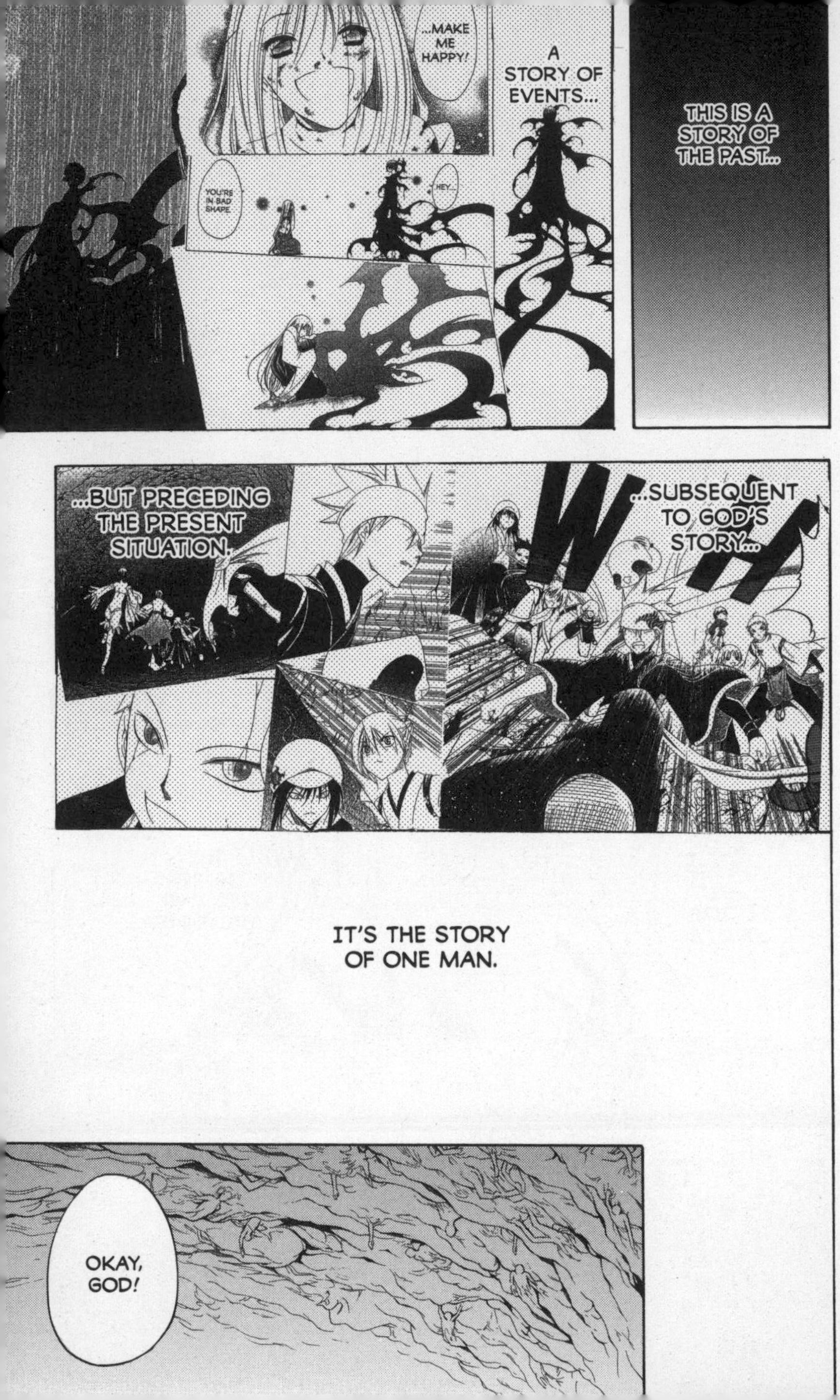
THIS IS A STORY OF THE PAST...
A STORY OF EVENTS...
...MAKE ME HAPPY!
HEY...
YOU'RE IN BAD SHAPE.
...SUBSEQUENT TO GOD'S STORY...
...BUT PRECEDING THE PRESENT SITUATION.
IT'S THE STORY OF ONE MAN.
OKAY, GOD!

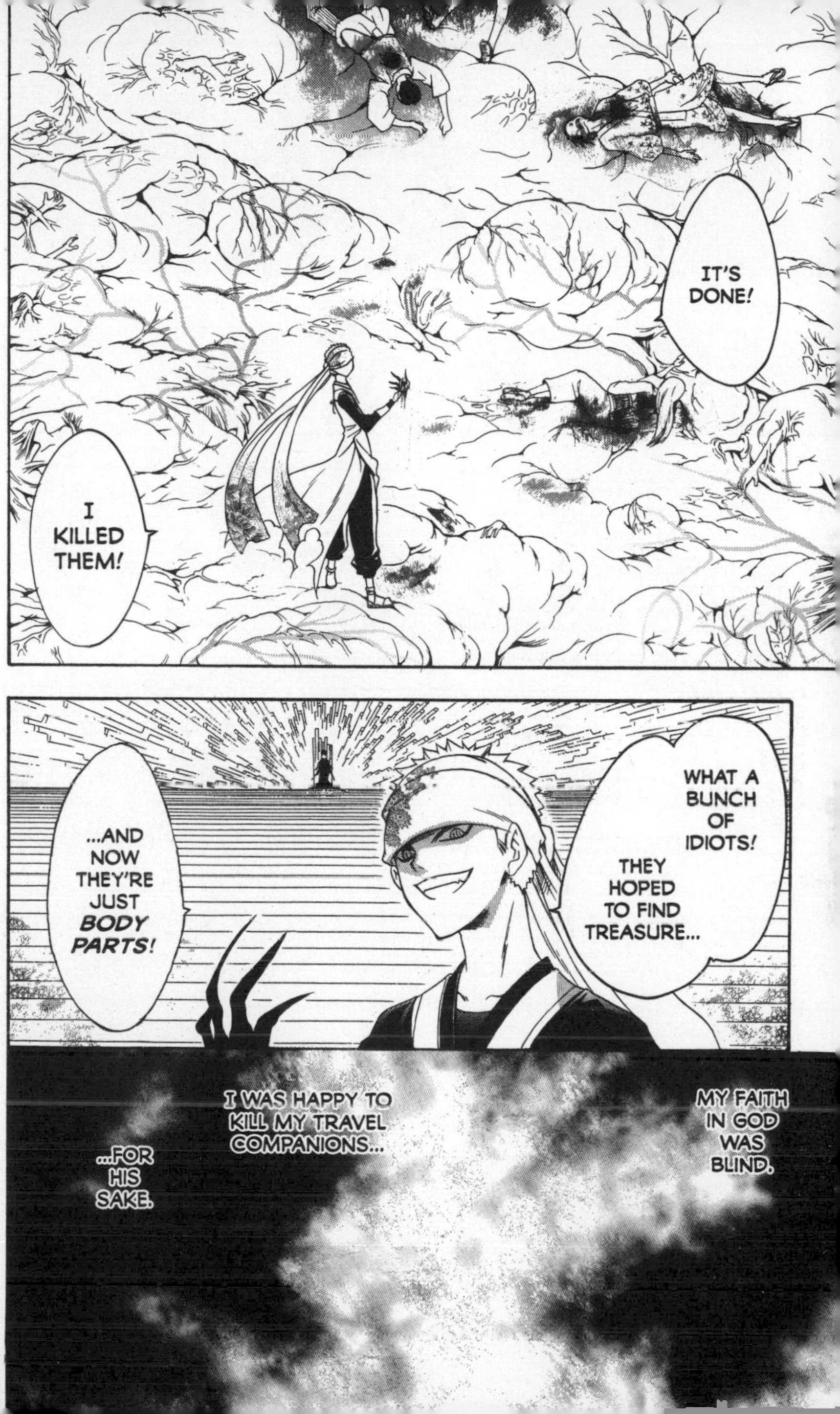
IT'S DONE!
I KILLED THEM!
WHAT A BUNCH OF IDIOTS!
THEY HOPED TO FIND TREASURE...
...AND NOW THEY'RE JUST *BODY PARTS*!
MY FAITH IN GOD WAS BLIND.
I WAS HAPPY TO KILL MY TRAVEL COMPANIONS...
...FOR HIS SAKE.

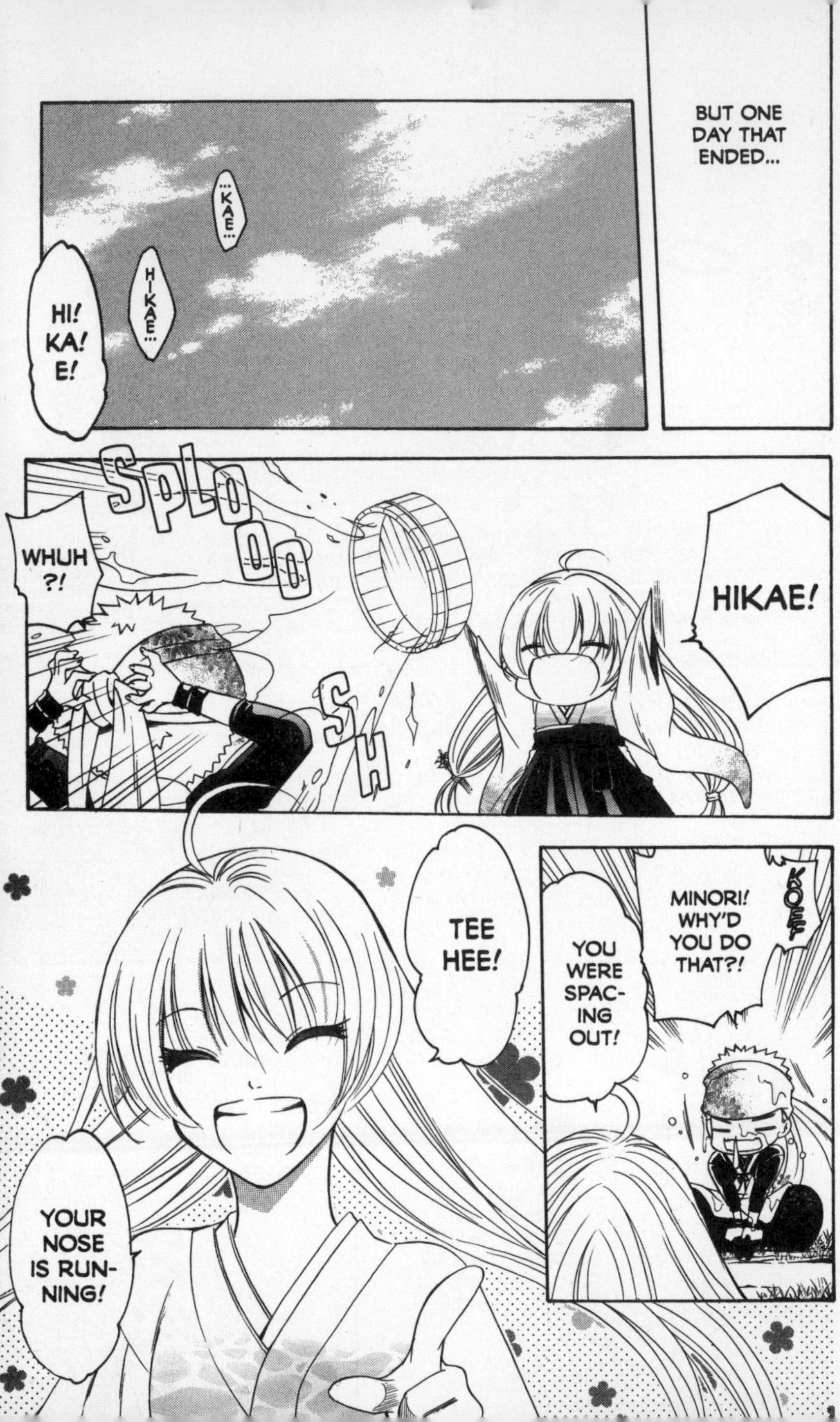
BUT ONE DAY THAT ENDED...
...KAE...
HIKAE...
HI! KA! E!
HIKAE!
SPLOOOO
WHUH?!
SH
KOFF
MINORI! WHY'D YOU DO THAT?!
YOU WERE SPAC-ING OUT!
TEE HEE!
YOUR NOSE IS RUN-NING!

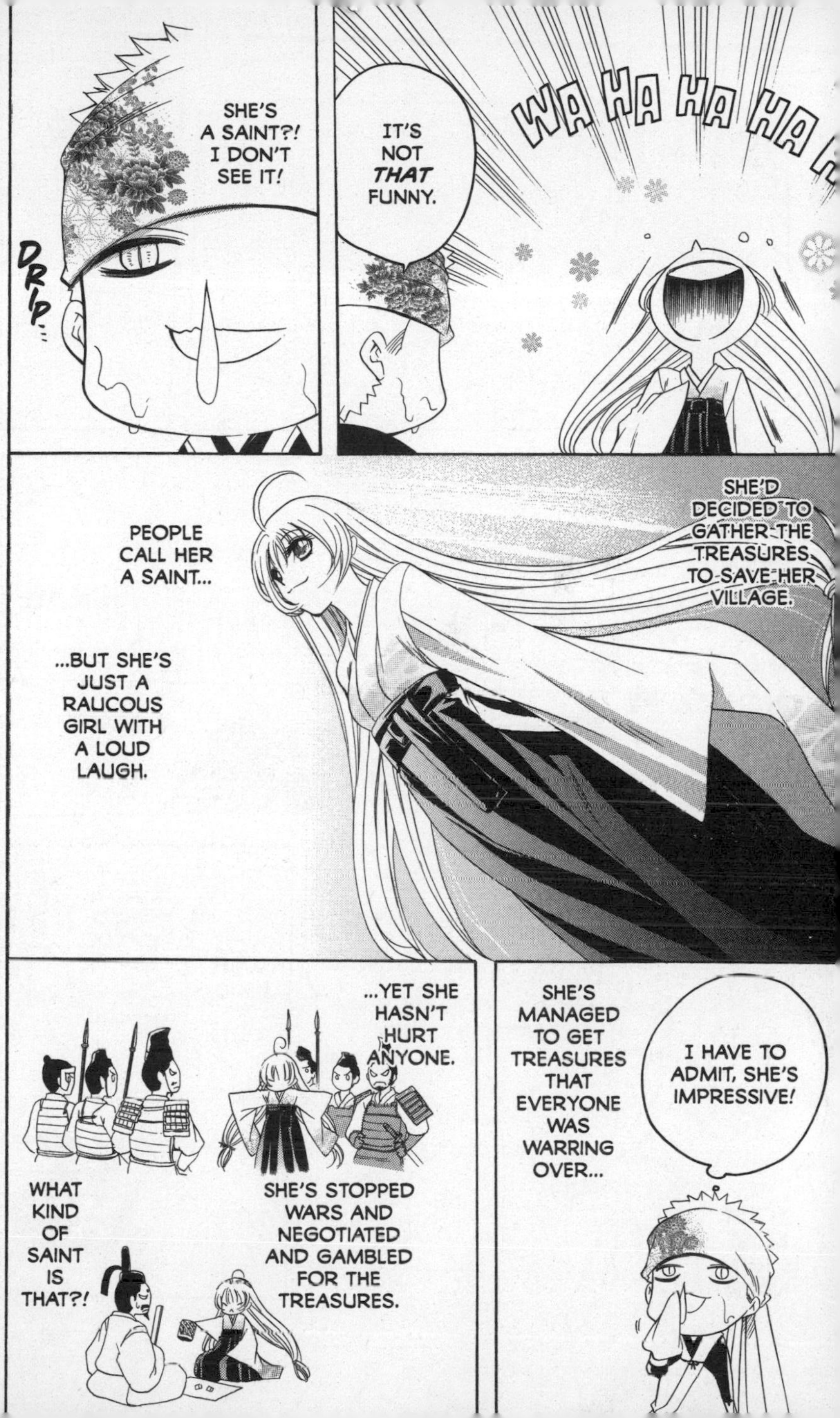
WA HA HA HA H
IT'S NOT *THAT* FUNNY.
SHE'S A SAINT?! I DON'T SEE IT!
DRIP
SHE'D DECIDED TO GATHER THE TREASURES TO SAVE HER VILLAGE.
PEOPLE CALL HER A SAINT...
...BUT SHE'S JUST A RAUCOUS GIRL WITH A LOUD LAUGH.
SHE'S MANAGED TO GET TREASURES THAT EVERYONE WAS WARRING OVER...
I HAVE TO ADMIT, SHE'S IMPRESSIVE!
...YET SHE HASN'T HURT ANYONE.
SHE'S STOPPED WARS AND NEGOTIATED AND GAMBLED FOR THE TREASURES.
WHAT KIND OF SAINT IS THAT?!

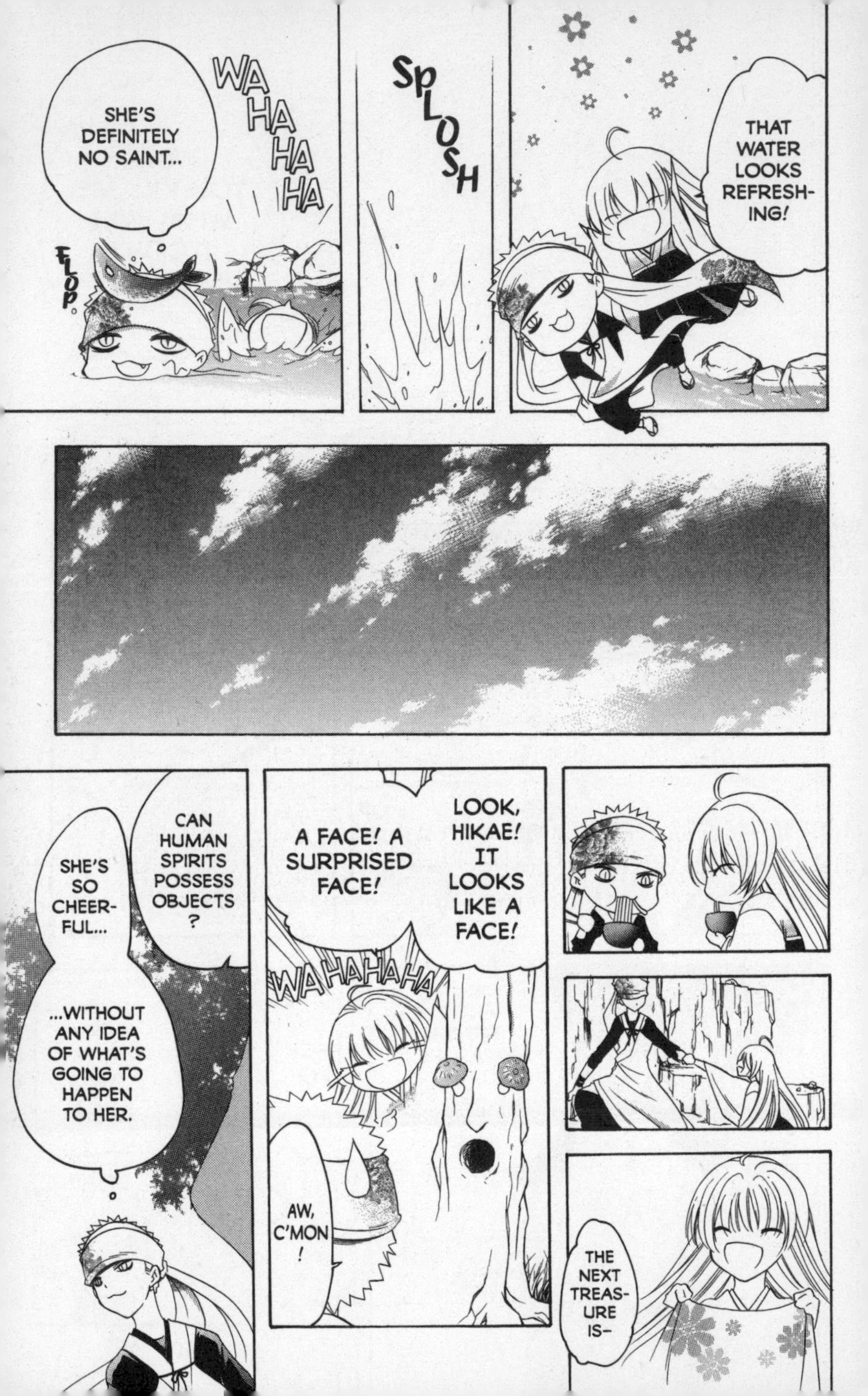
THAT WATER LOOKS REFRESHING!
SPLOSH
WAHAHAHA
SHE'S DEFINITELY NO SAINT...
FLOP
THE NEXT TREASURE IS-
LOOK, HIKAE! IT LOOKS LIKE A FACE!
A FACE! A SURPRISED FACE!
WAHAHAHA
AW, C'MON!
CAN HUMAN SPIRITS POSSESS OBJECTS?
SHE'S SO CHEERFUL...
...WITHOUT ANY IDEA OF WHAT'S GOING TO HAPPEN TO HER.

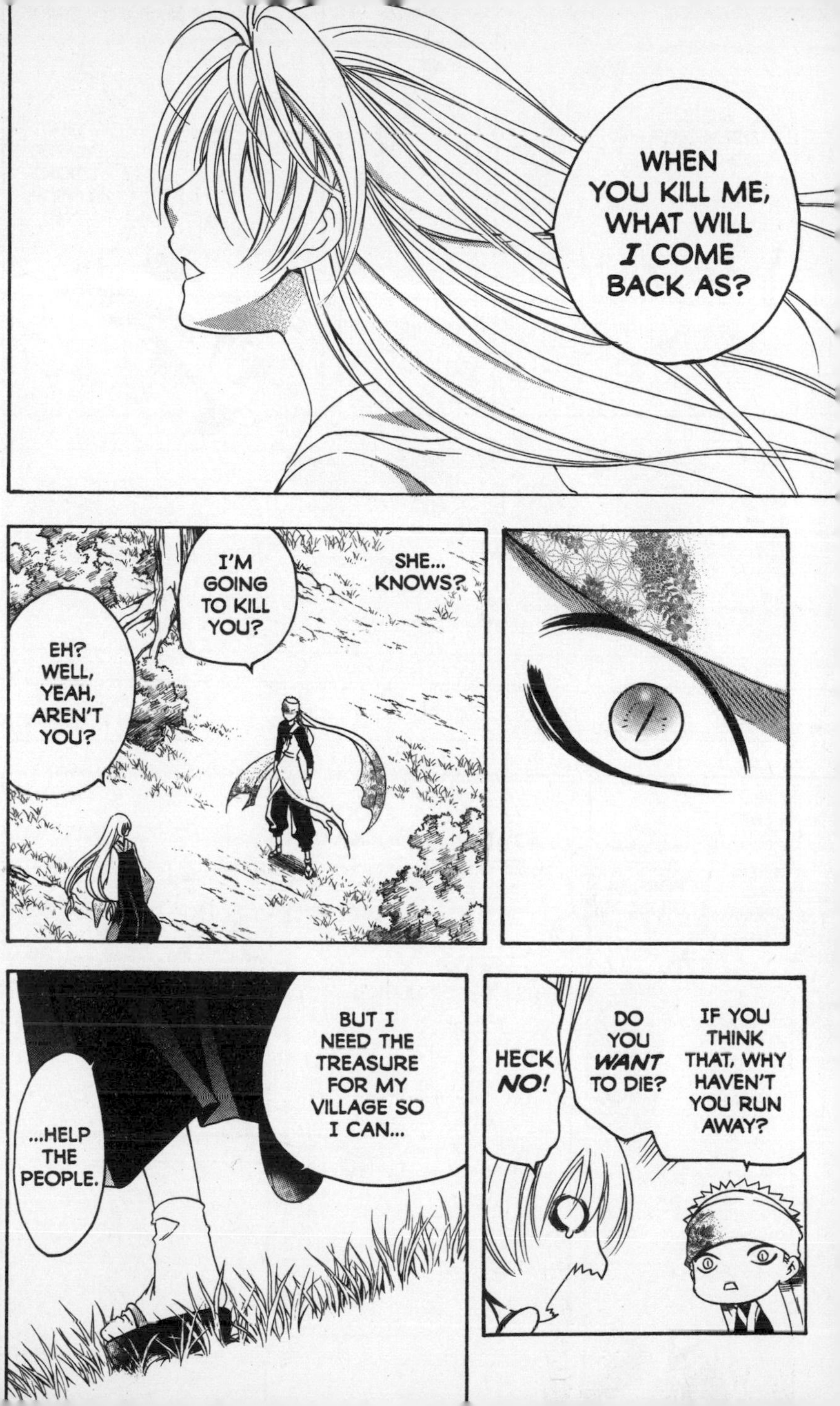
WHEN YOU KILL ME, WHAT WILL *I* COME BACK AS?
SHE... KNOWS?
I'M GOING TO KILL YOU?
EH? WELL, YEAH, AREN'T YOU?
IF YOU THINK THAT, WHY HAVEN'T YOU RUN AWAY?
DO YOU *WANT* TO DIE?
HECK *NO!*
BUT I NEED THE TREASURE FOR MY VILLAGE SO I CAN...
...HELP THE PEOPLE.

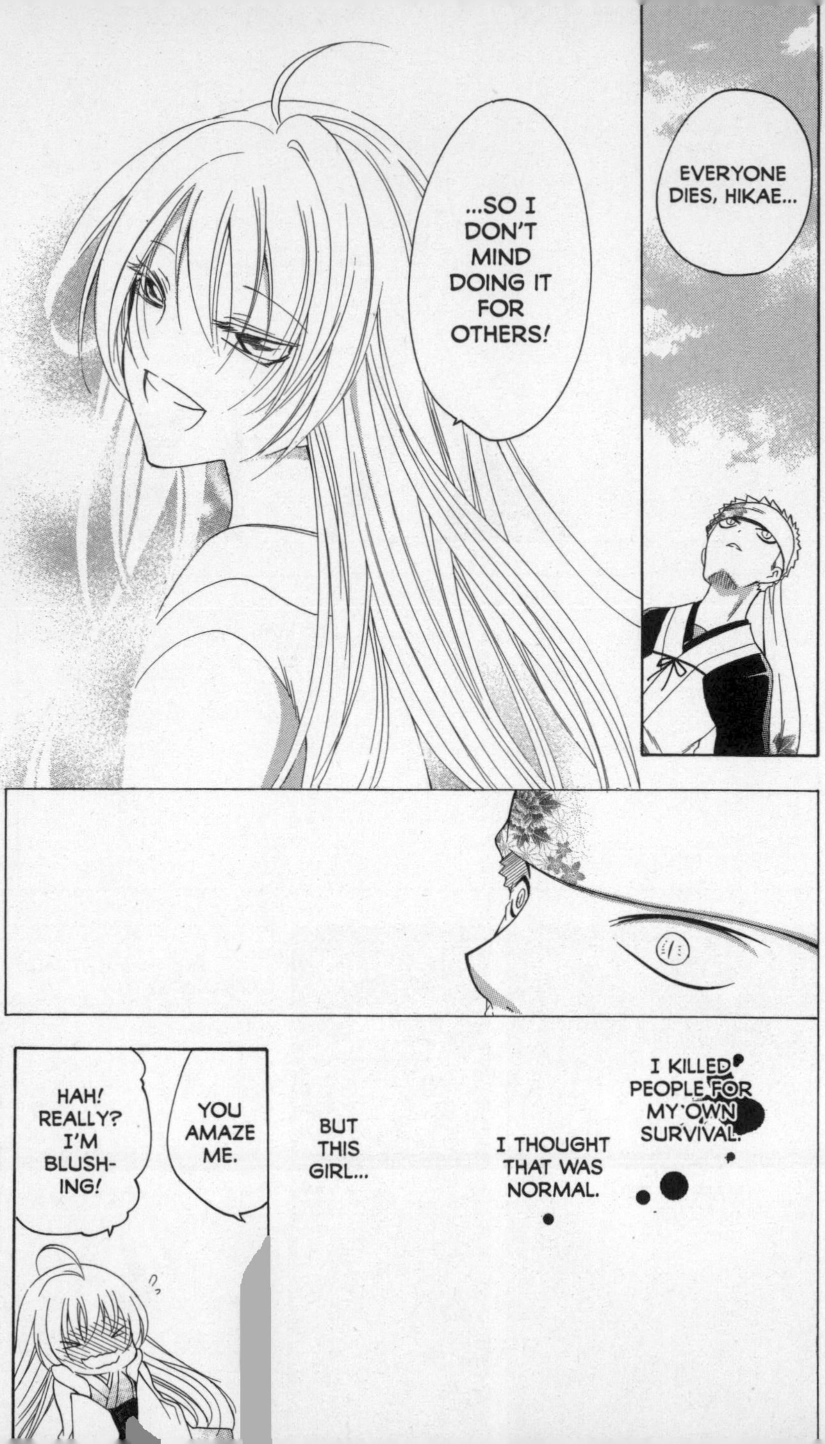
EVERYONE DIES, HIKAE...
...SO I DON'T MIND DOING IT FOR OTHERS!
I KILLED PEOPLE FOR MY OWN SURVIVAL.
I THOUGHT THAT WAS NORMAL.
BUT THIS GIRL...
YOU AMAZE ME.
HAH! REALLY? I'M BLUSH-ING!

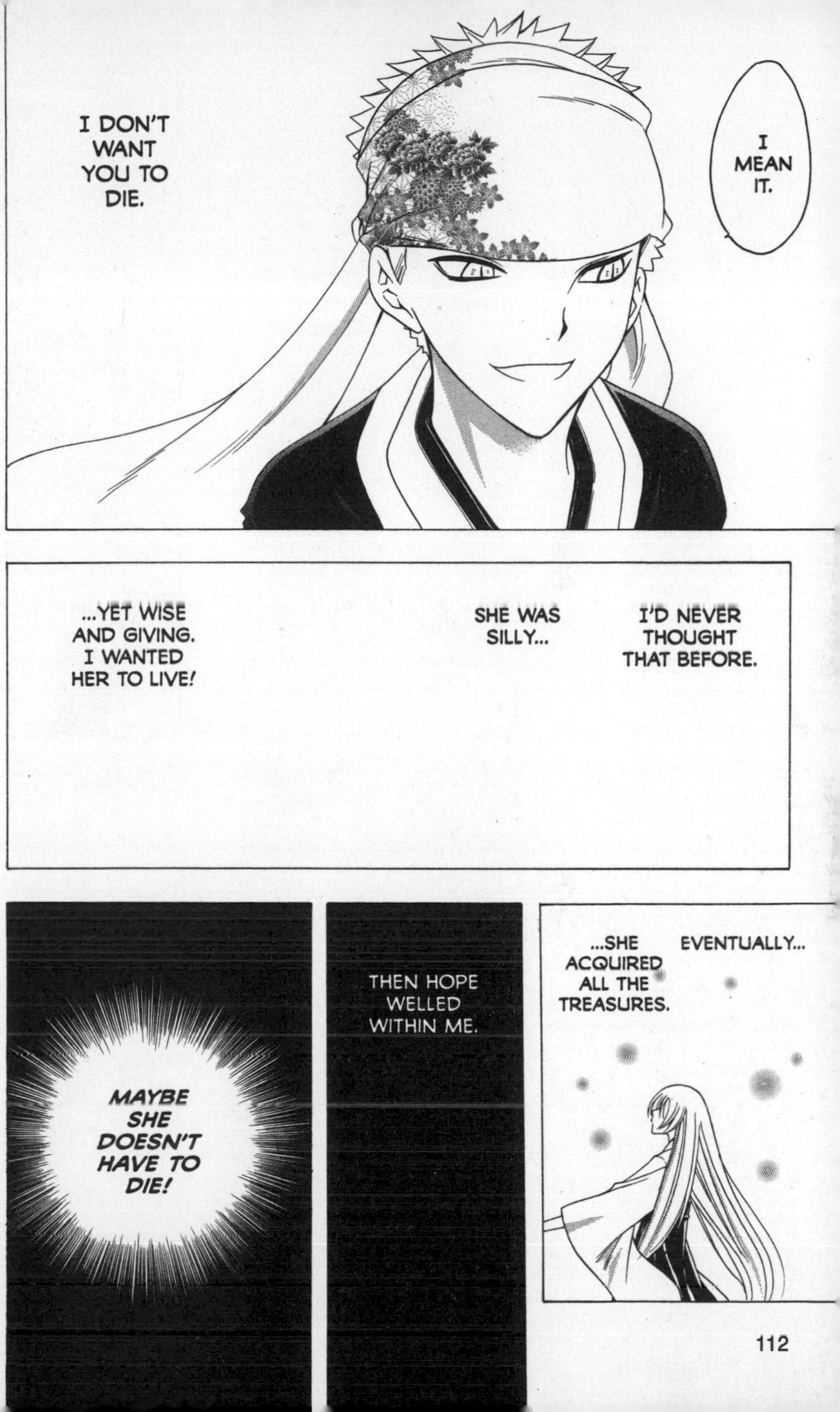
I MEAN IT.
I DON'T WANT YOU TO DIE.
I'D NEVER THOUGHT THAT BEFORE.
SHE WAS SILLY...
...YET WISE AND GIVING. I WANTED HER TO LIVE!
EVENTUALLY...
...SHE ACQUIRED ALL THE TREASURES.
THEN HOPE WELLED WITHIN ME.
MAYBE SHE DOESN'T HAVE TO DIE!

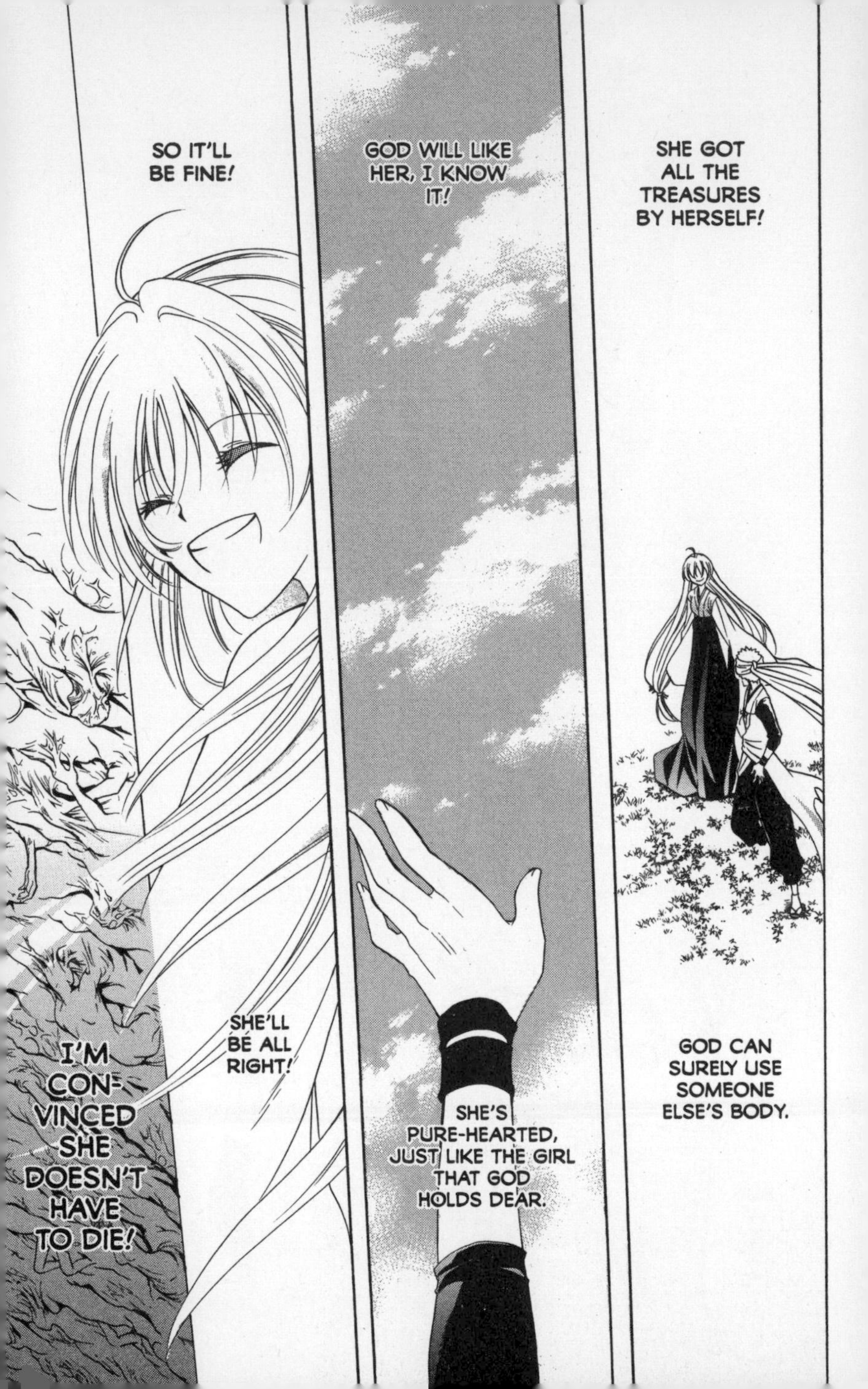
SHE GOT ALL THE TREASURES BY HERSELF!
GOD CAN SURELY USE SOMEONE ELSE'S BODY.
GOD WILL LIKE HER, I KNOW IT!
SHE'S PURE-HEARTED, JUST LIKE THE GIRL THAT GOD HOLDS DEAR.
SO IT'LL BE FINE!
SHE'LL BE ALL RIGHT!
I'M CON-VINCED SHE DOESN'T HAVE TO DIE!

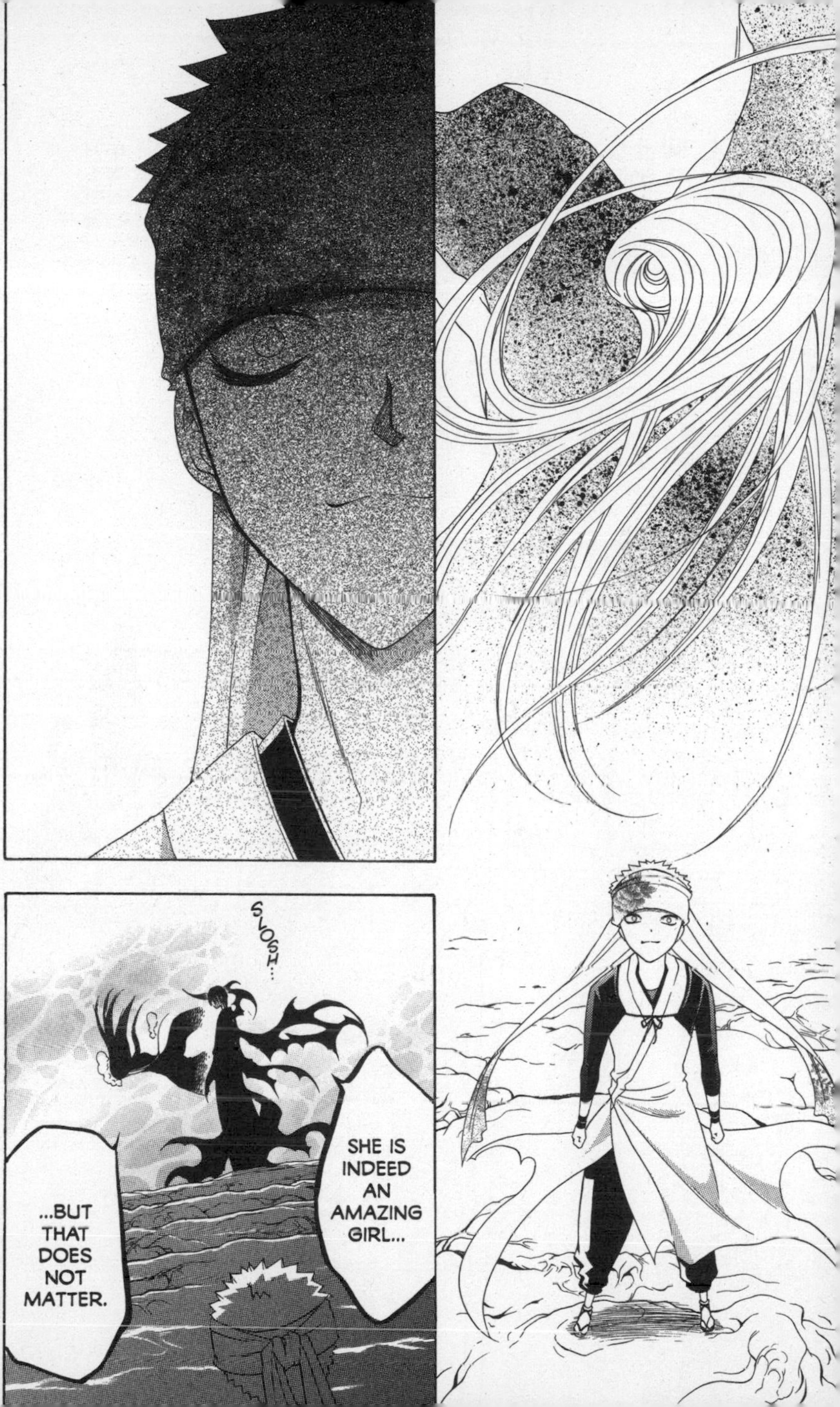
SLOSH...
SHE IS INDEED AN AMAZING GIRL...
...BUT THAT DOES NOT MATTER.

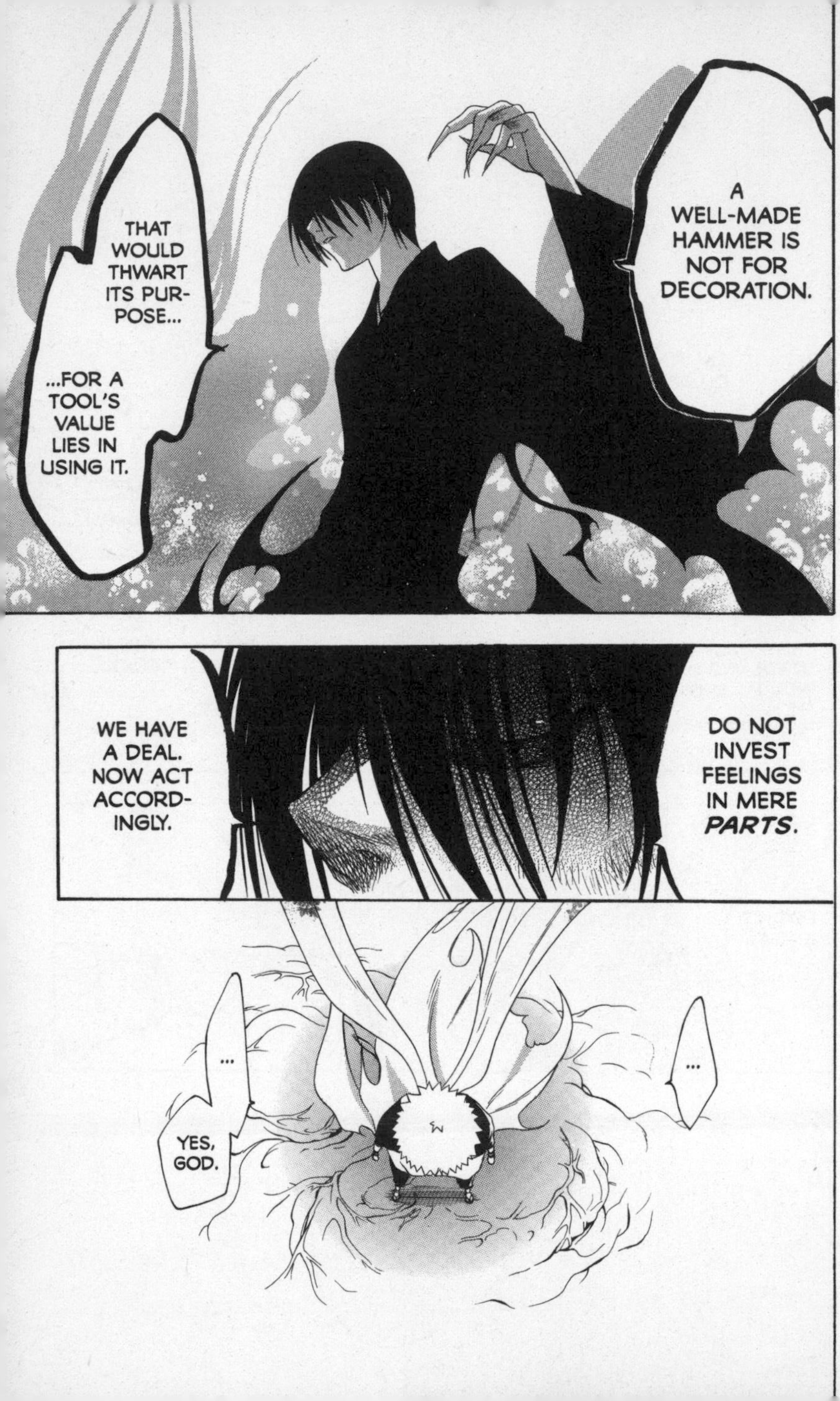
A WELL-MADE HAMMER IS NOT FOR DECORATION.
THAT WOULD THWART ITS PURPOSE...
...FOR A TOOL'S VALUE LIES IN USING IT.
DO NOT INVEST FEELINGS IN MERE *PARTS*.
WE HAVE A DEAL. NOW ACT ACCORDINGLY.
...
...
YES, GOD.

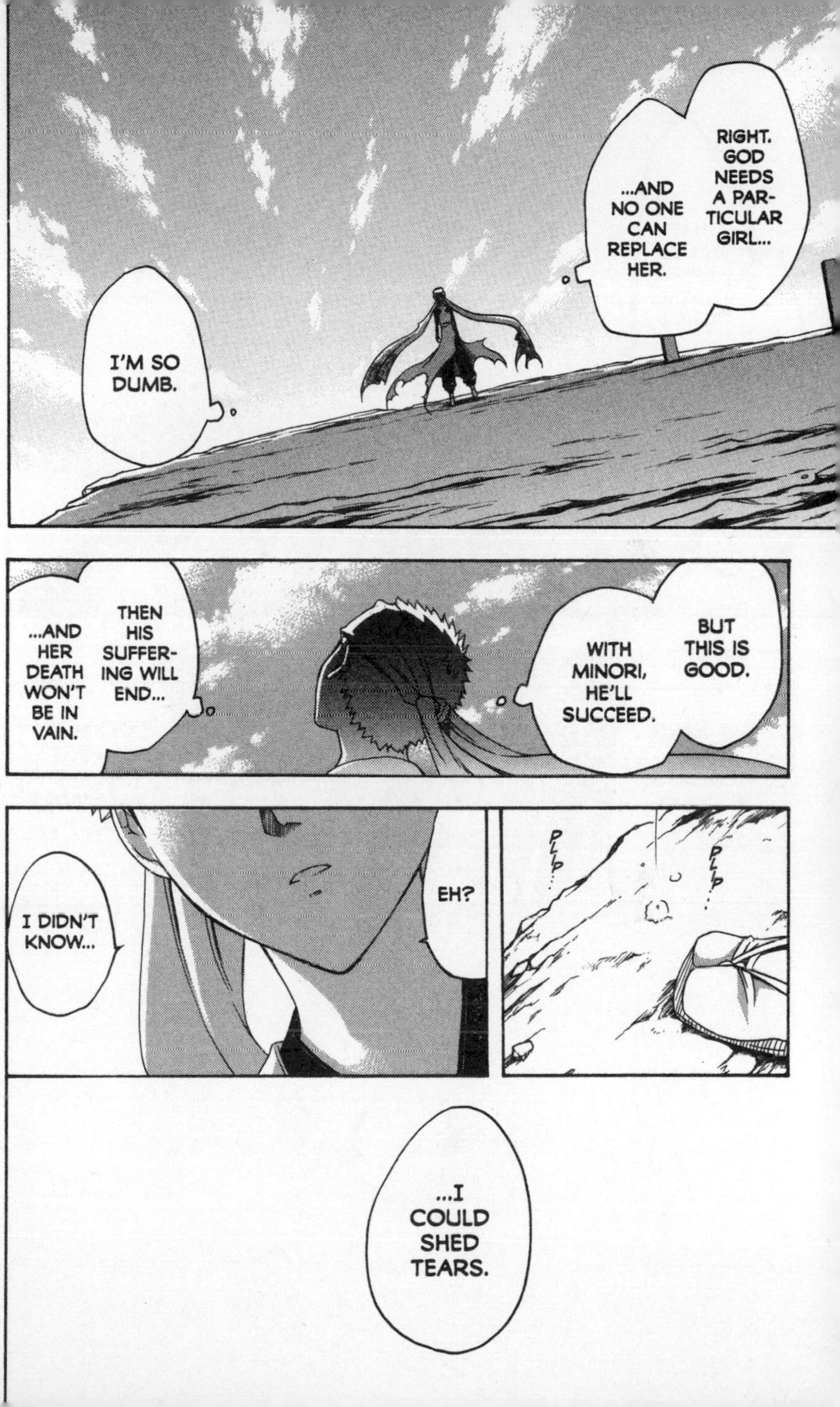
RIGHT. GOD NEEDS A PARTICULAR GIRL...
...AND NO ONE CAN REPLACE HER.
I'M SO DUMB.
BUT THIS IS GOOD.
WITH MINORI, HE'LL SUCCEED.
THEN HIS SUFFERING WILL END...
...AND HER DEATH WON'T BE IN VAIN.
PLIP...
PLIP...
EH?
I DIDN'T KNOW...
...I COULD SHED TEARS.

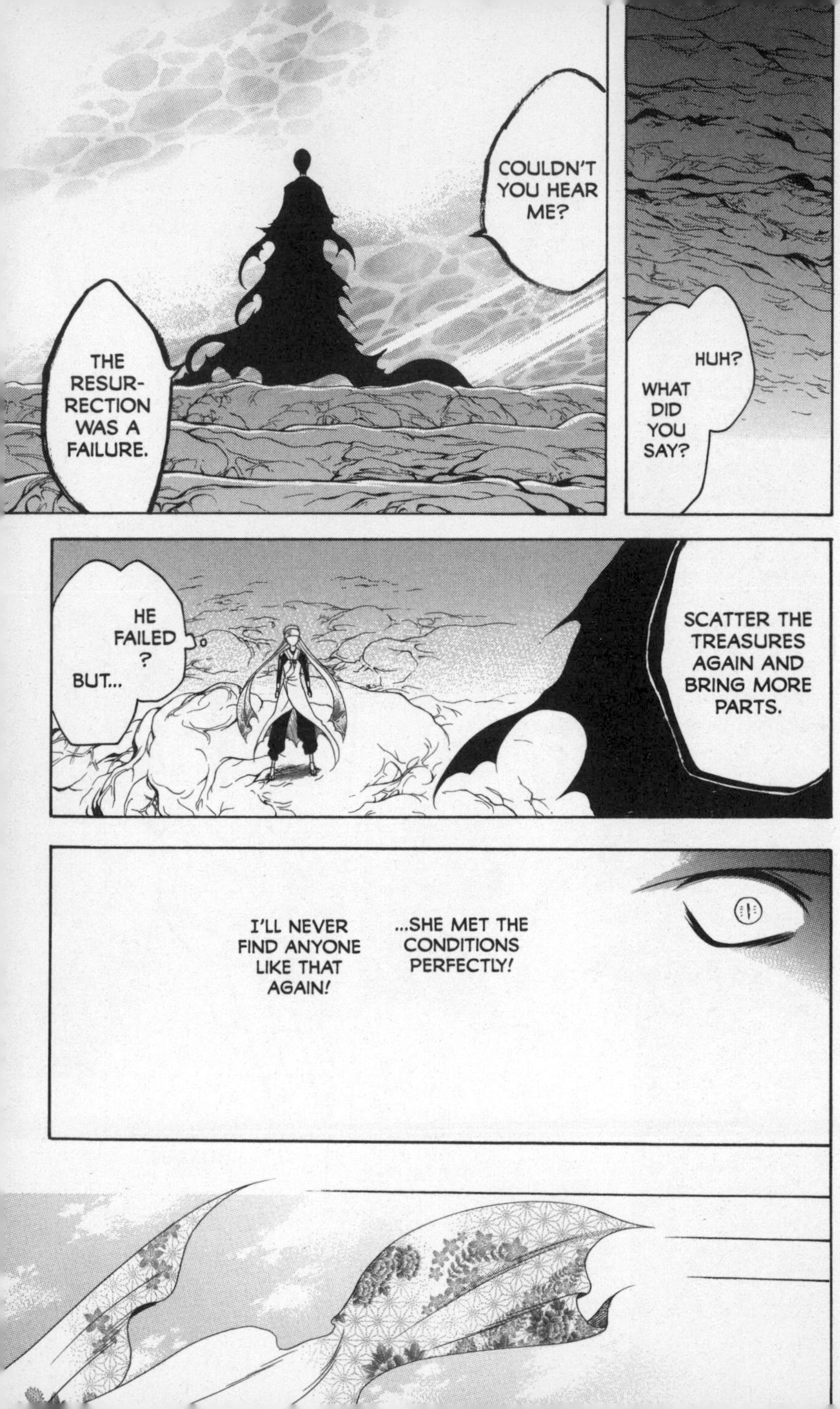
HUH?
WHAT DID YOU SAY?
COULDN'T YOU HEAR ME?
THE RESUR-RECTION WAS A FAILURE.
SCATTER THE TREASURES AGAIN AND BRING MORE PARTS.
HE FAILED? BUT...
...SHE MET THE CONDITIONS PERFECTLY!
I'LL NEVER FIND ANYONE LIKE THAT AGAIN!

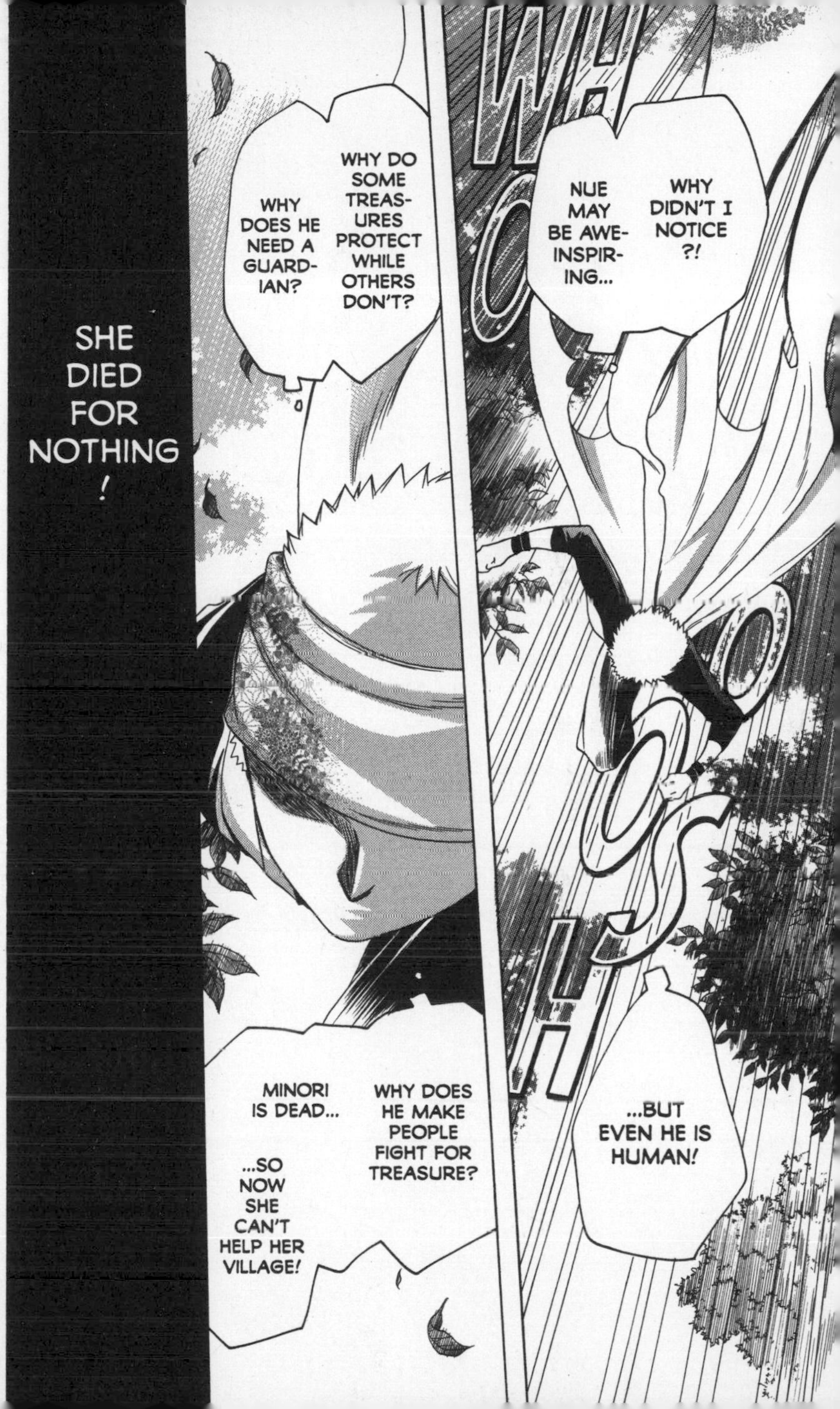
WHOOSH
WHY DIDN'T I NOTICE ?!
NUE MAY BE AWE-INSPIRING...
...BUT EVEN HE IS HUMAN!
WHY DO SOME TREASURES PROTECT WHILE OTHERS DON'T?
WHY DOES HE NEED A GUARDIAN?
WHY DOES HE MAKE PEOPLE FIGHT FOR TREASURE?
MINORI IS DEAD...
...SO NOW SHE CAN'T HELP HER VILLAGE!
SHE DIED FOR NOTHING!

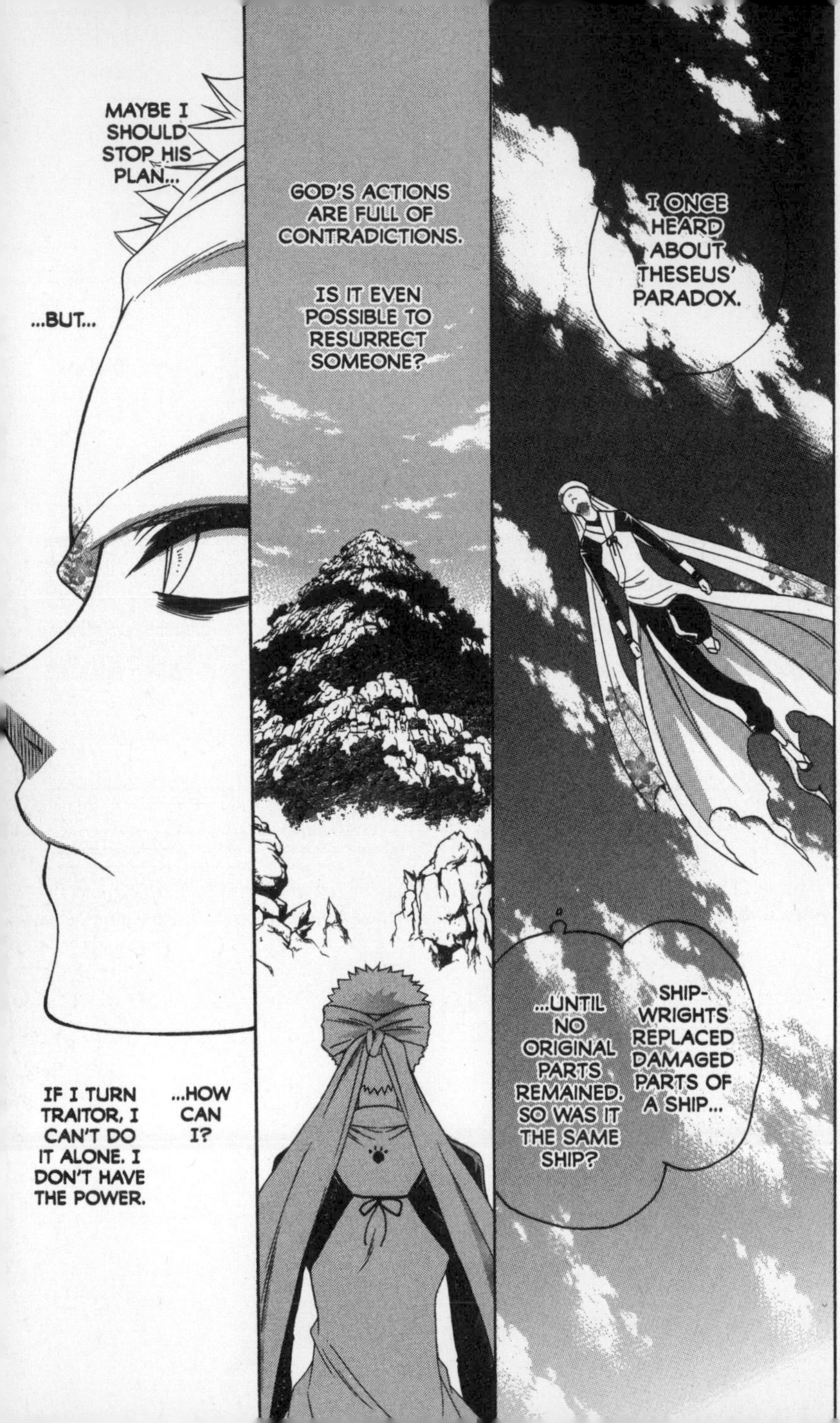
I ONCE HEARD ABOUT THESEUS' PARADOX.
SHIP-WRIGHTS REPLACED DAMAGED PARTS OF A SHIP...
...UNTIL NO ORIGINAL PARTS REMAINED. SO WAS IT THE SAME SHIP?
GOD'S ACTIONS ARE FULL OF CONTRADICTIONS.
IS IT EVEN POSSIBLE TO RESURRECT SOMEONE?
MAYBE I SHOULD STOP HIS PLAN...
...BUT...
...HOW CAN I?
IF I TURN TRAITOR, I CAN'T DO IT ALONE. I DON'T HAVE THE POWER.

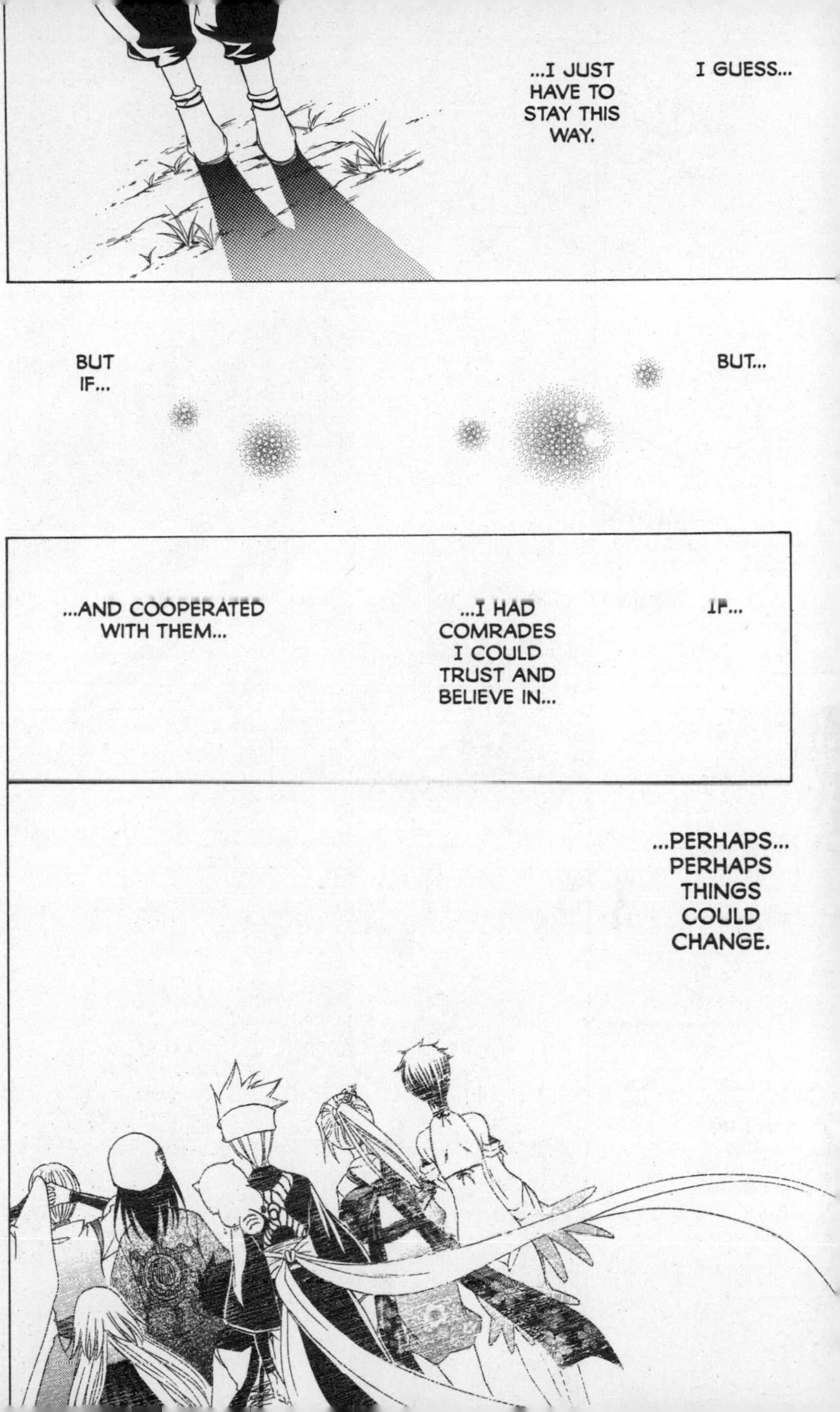
I GUESS...
...I JUST HAVE TO STAY THIS WAY.
BUT...
BUT IF...
IF...
...I HAD COMRADES I COULD TRUST AND BELIEVE IN...
...AND COOPERATED WITH THEM...
...PERHAPS... PERHAPS THINGS COULD CHANGE.

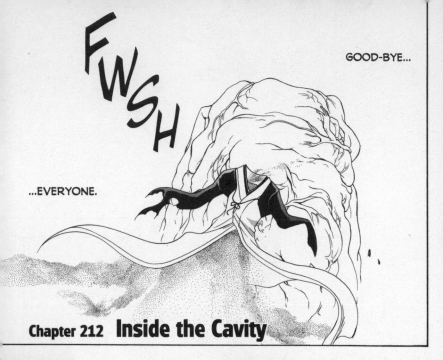

GOOD-BYE...

...EVERYONE.

FWSH

Chapter 212 Inside the Cavity

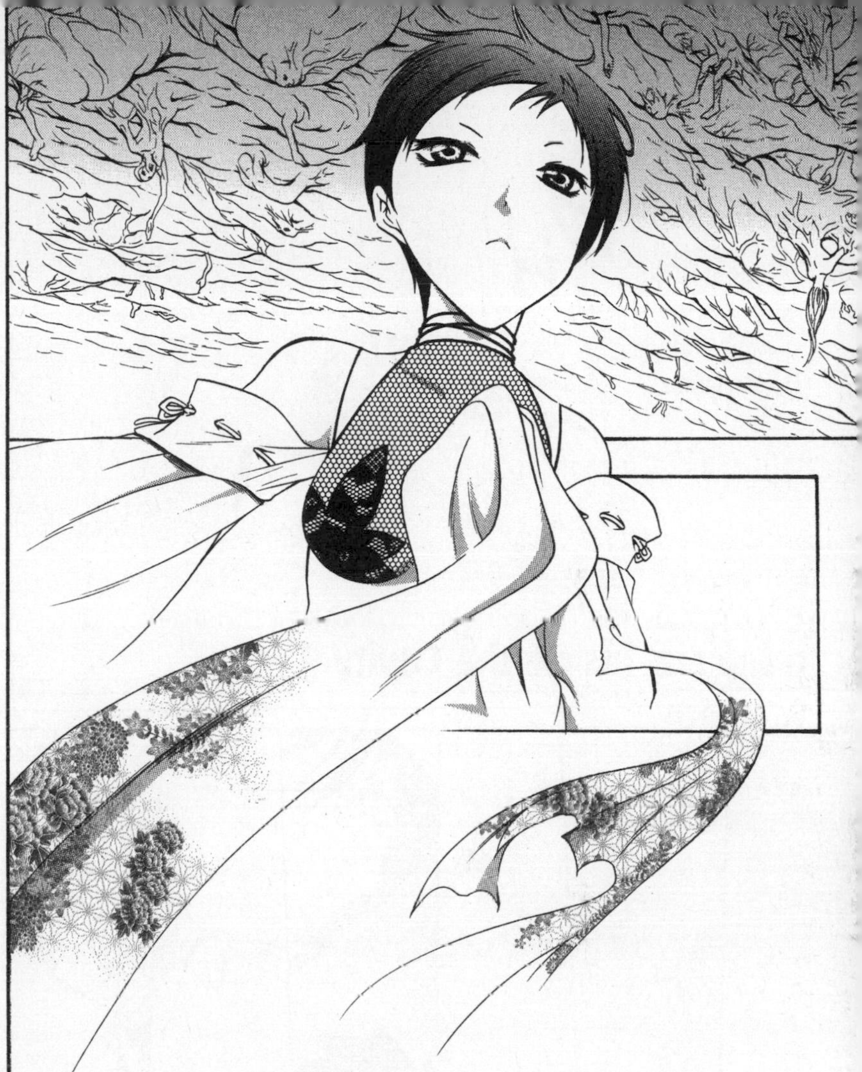

Chapter 212
Inside the Cavity

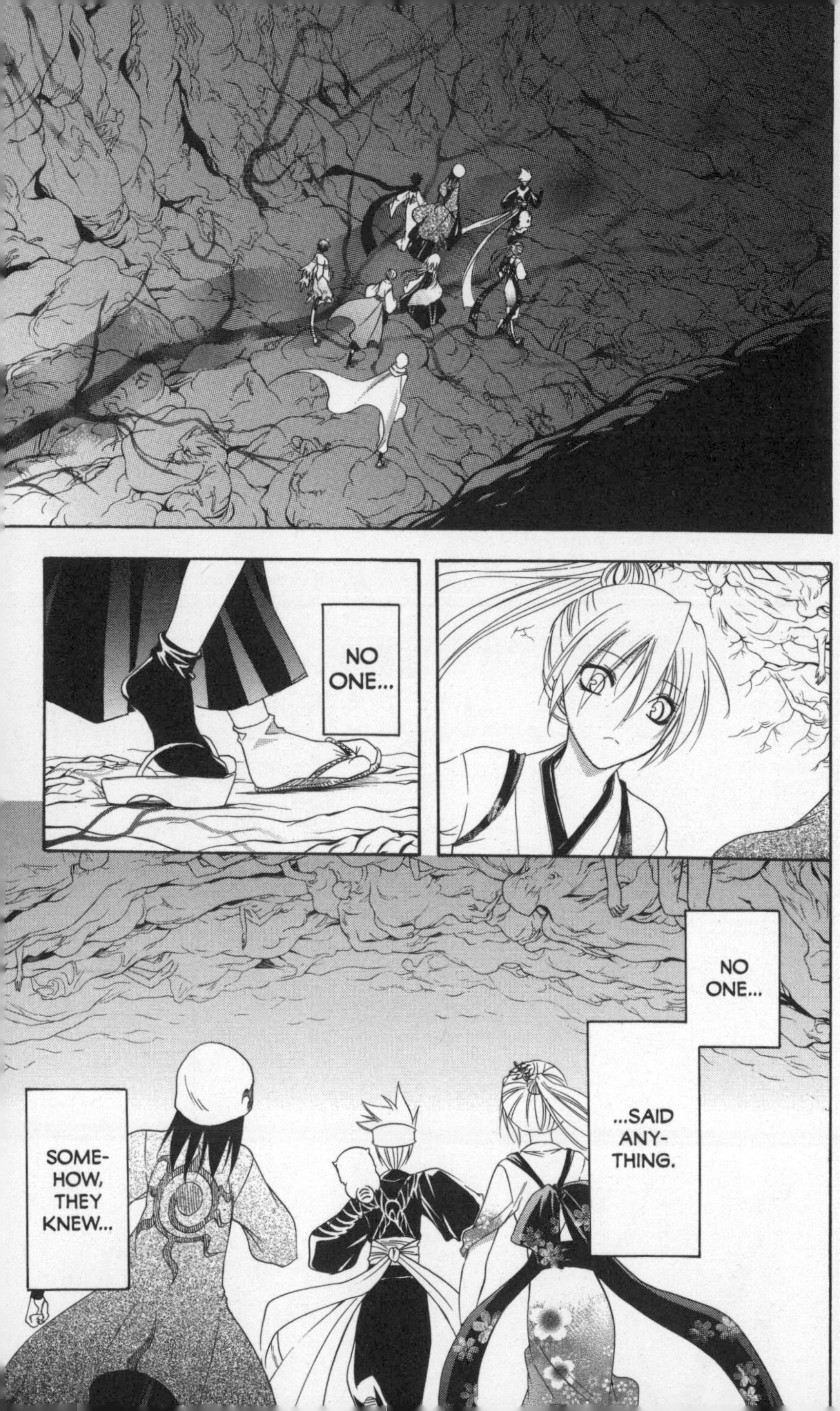
NO ONE...
NO ONE...
...SAID ANY-THING.
SOME-HOW, THEY KNEW...

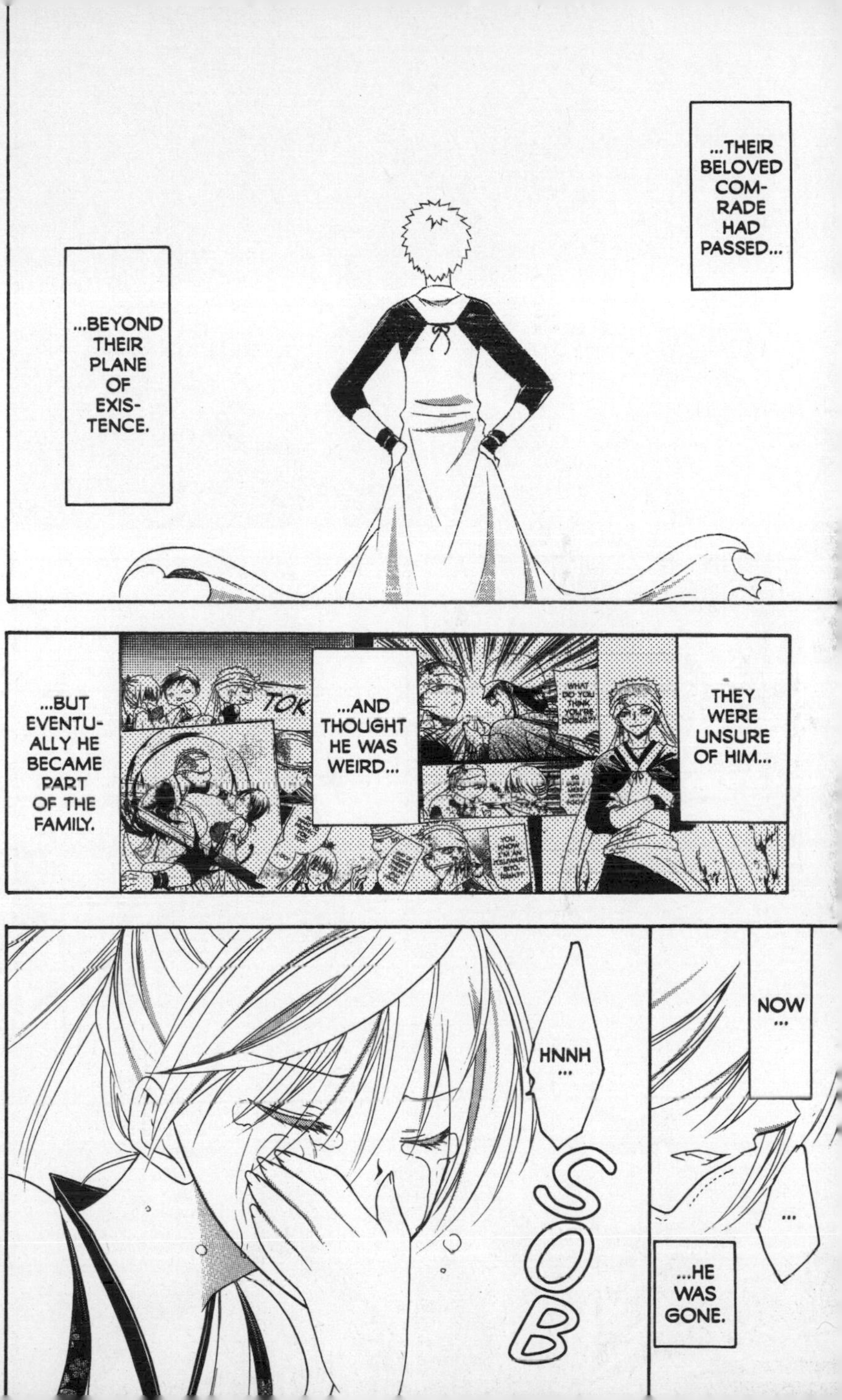
...THEIR BELOVED COMRADE HAD PASSED...
...BEYOND THEIR PLANE OF EXISTENCE.
THEY WERE UNSURE OF HIM...
...AND THOUGHT HE WAS WEIRD...
TOK
...BUT EVENTUALLY HE BECAME PART OF THE FAMILY.
NOW...
...
...HE WAS GONE.
HNNH...
SOB

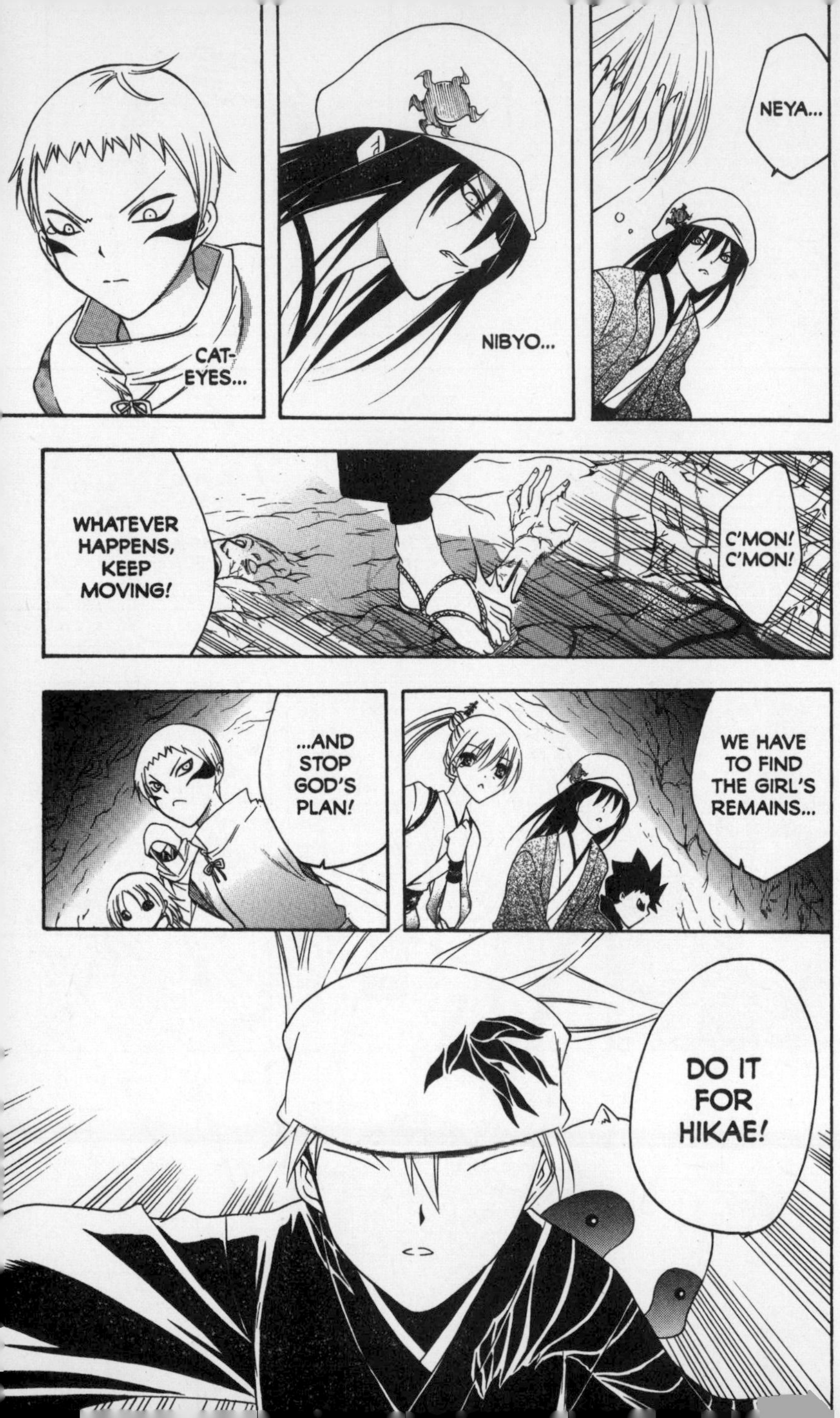
NEYA...
NIBYO...
CAT-EYES...
C'MON! C'MON!
WHATEVER HAPPENS, KEEP MOVING!
WE HAVE TO FIND THE GIRL'S REMAINS...
...AND STOP GOD'S PLAN!
DO IT FOR HIKAE!

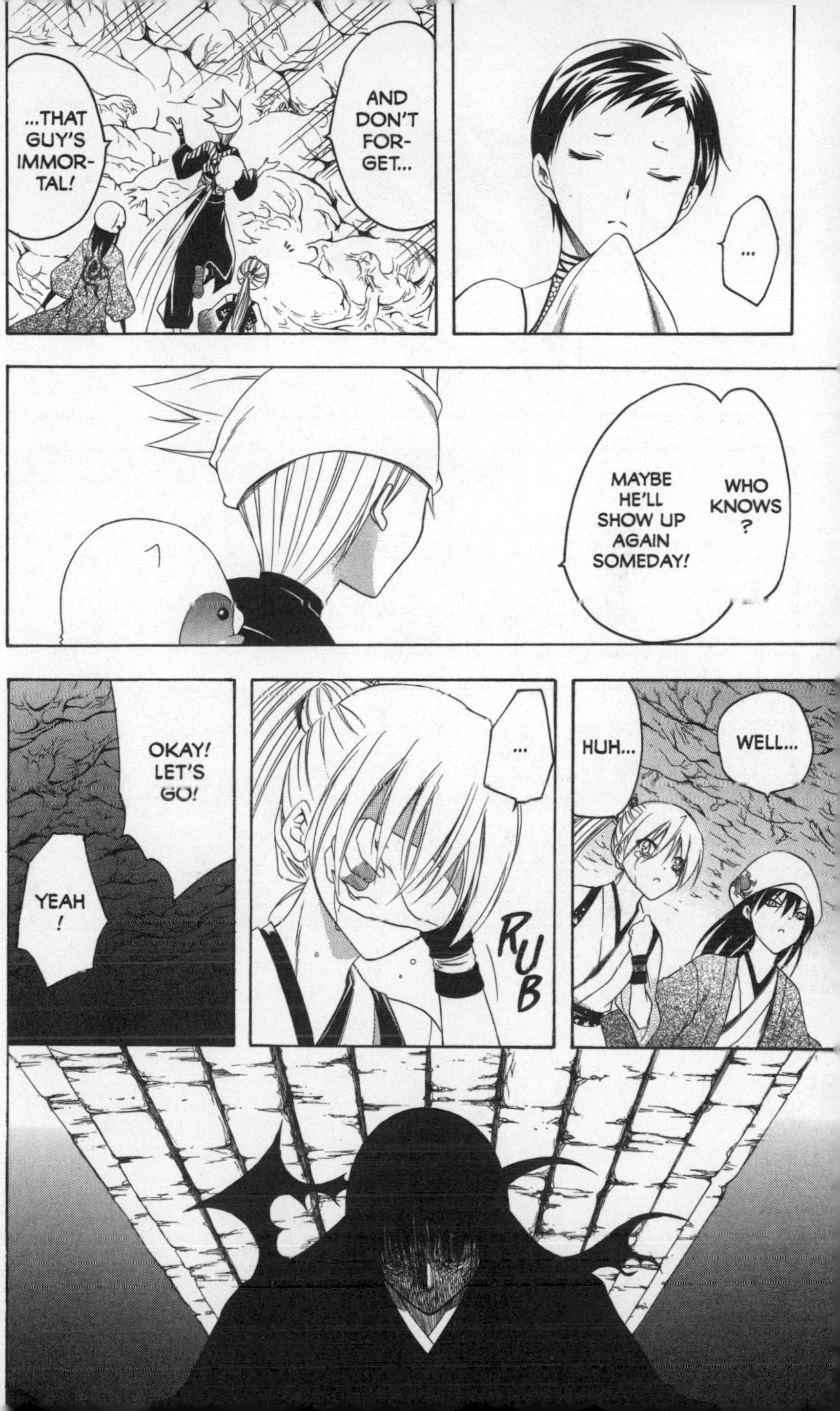
...
AND DON'T FOR-GET...
...THAT GUY'S IMMOR-TAL!
WHO KNOWS?
MAYBE HE'LL SHOW UP AGAIN SOMEDAY!
WELL...
HUH...
...
RUB
OKAY! LET'S GO!
YEAH!

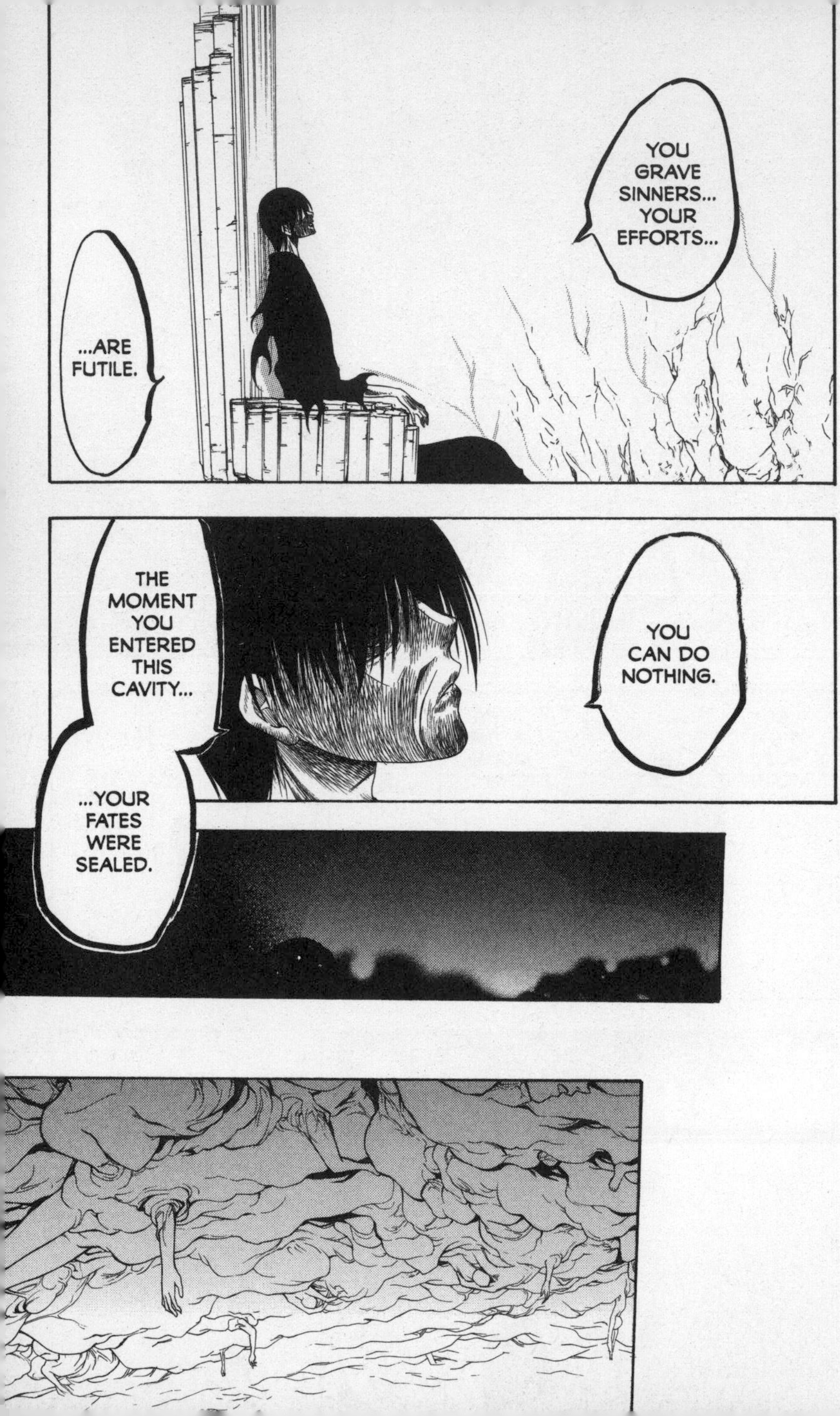
YOU GRAVE SINNERS... YOUR EFFORTS...
...ARE FUTILE.
YOU CAN DO NOTHING.
THE MOMENT YOU ENTERED THIS CAVITY...
...YOUR FATES WERE SEALED.

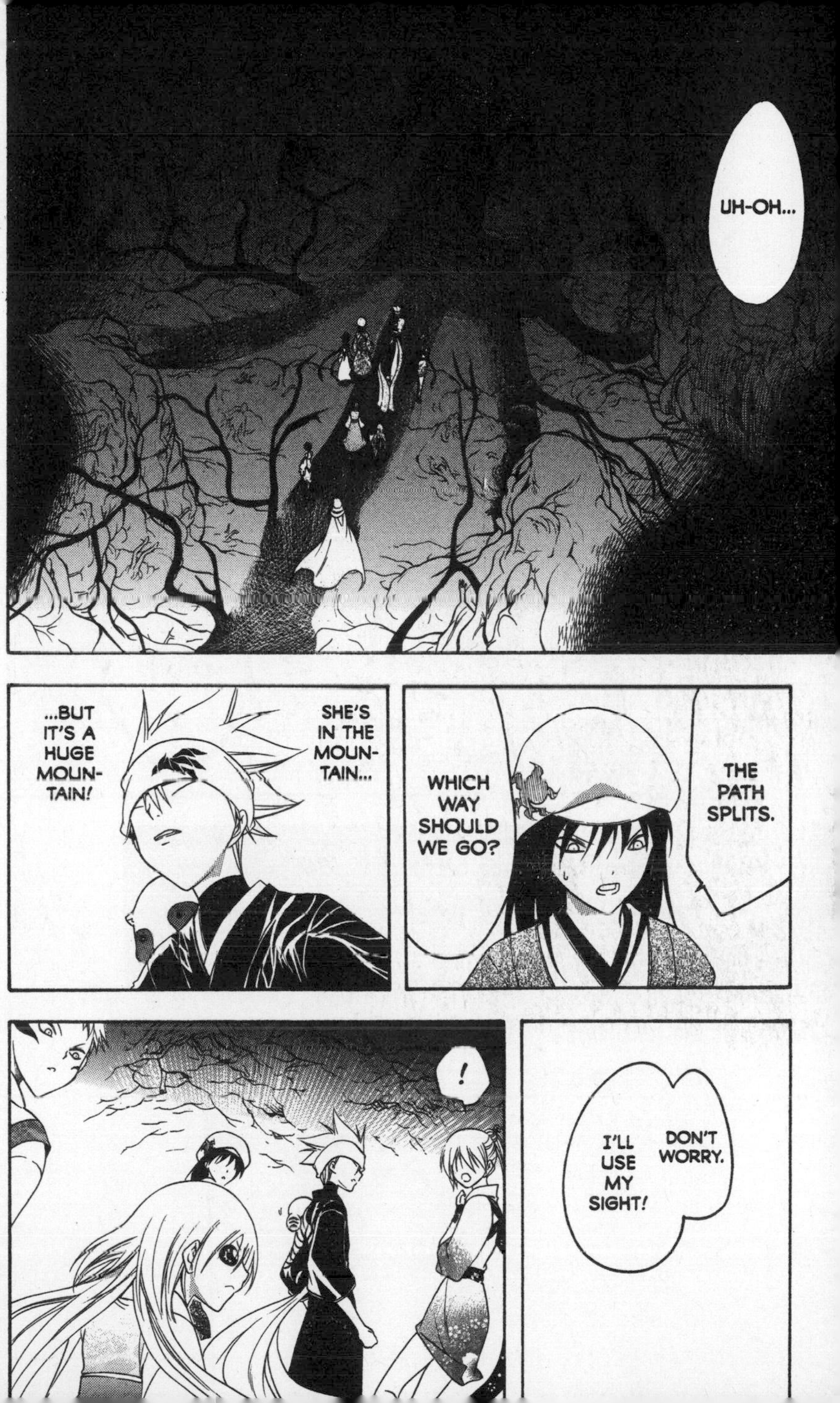
UH-OH...
THE PATH SPLITS.
WHICH WAY SHOULD WE GO?
SHE'S IN THE MOUNTAIN...
...BUT IT'S A HUGE MOUNTAIN!
DON'T WORRY.
I'LL USE MY SIGHT!
!

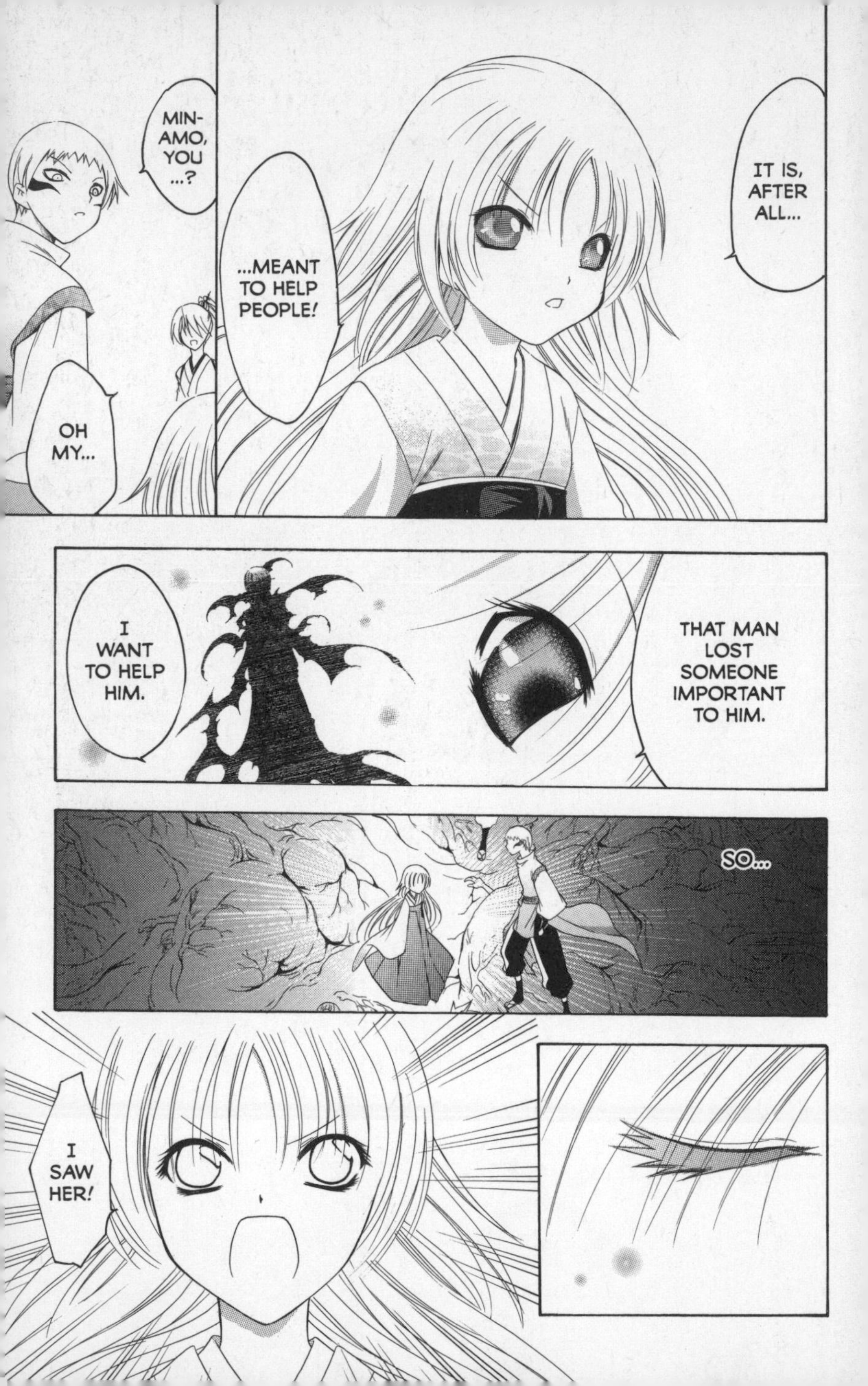
IT IS, AFTER ALL...
...MEANT TO HELP PEOPLE!
MIN-AMO, YOU ...?
OH MY...
THAT MAN LOST SOMEONE IMPORTANT TO HIM.
I WANT TO HELP HIM.
SO...
I SAW HER!

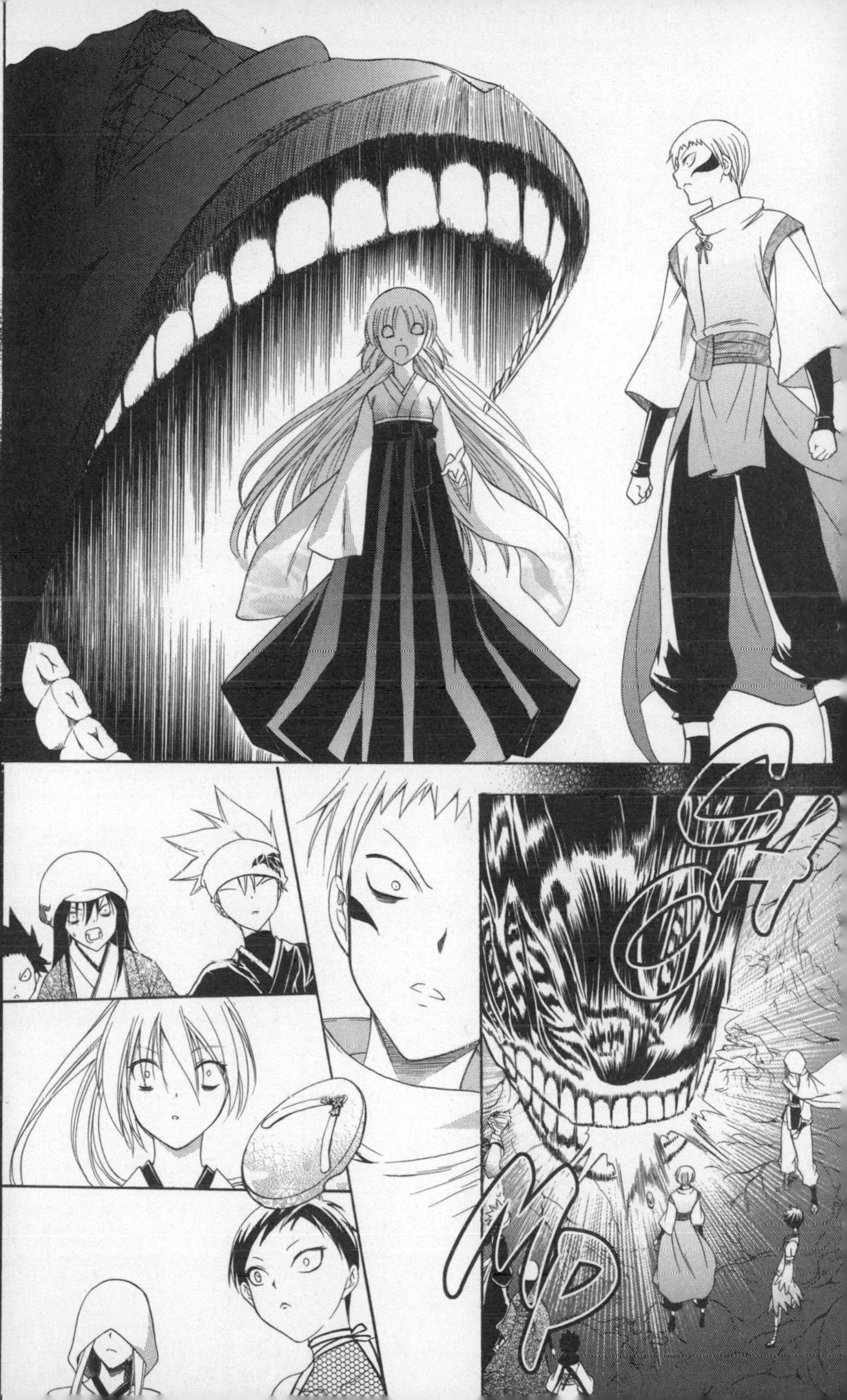
CHOMP

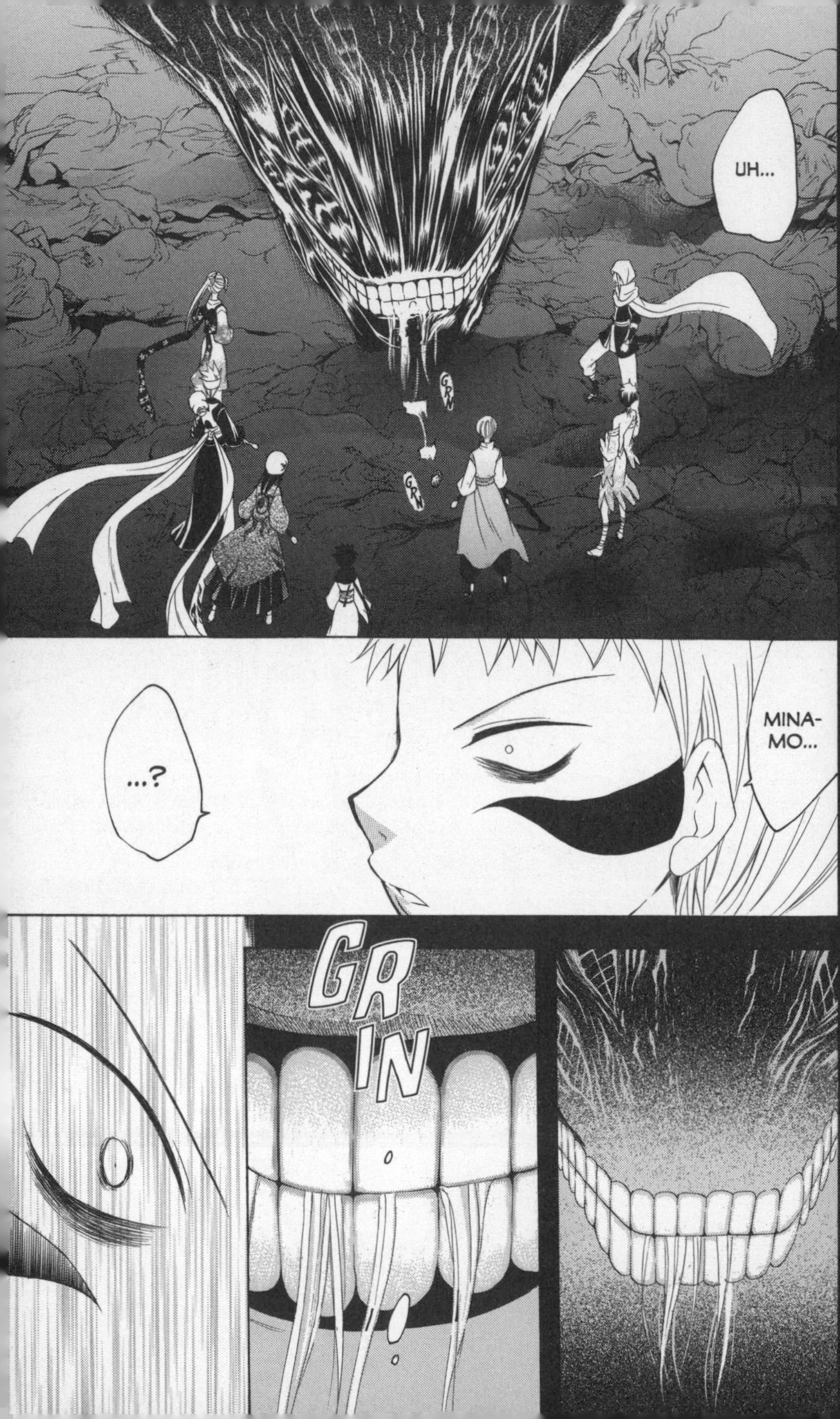
UH...
GRN
GRN
MINA-
MO...
...?
GRIN

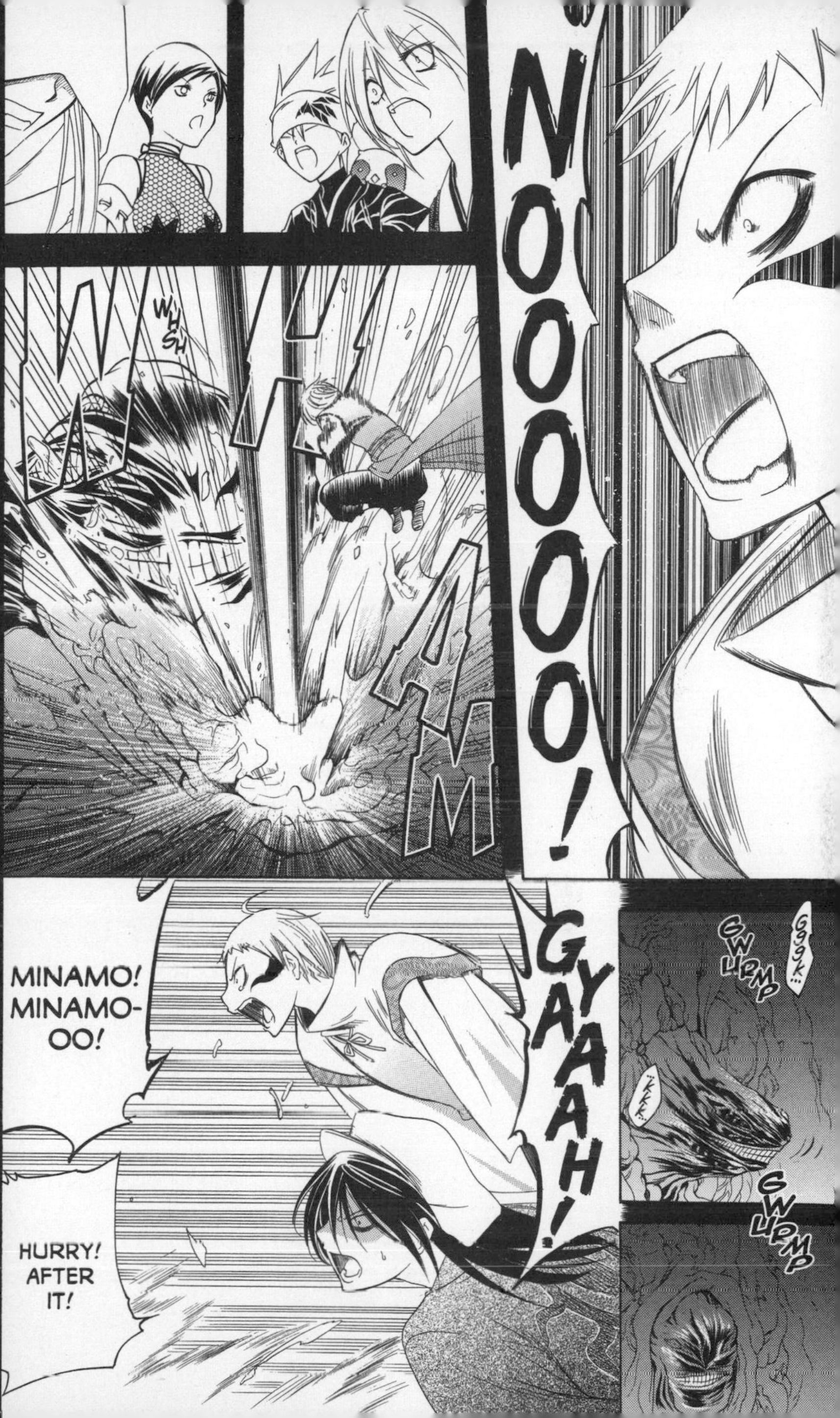
NOOOOOOO!
WHSH
WHAM
GWURMP
G99k...
...KKK
GWURMP
GYAAAH!
MINAMO! MINAMO-OO!
HURRY! AFTER IT!

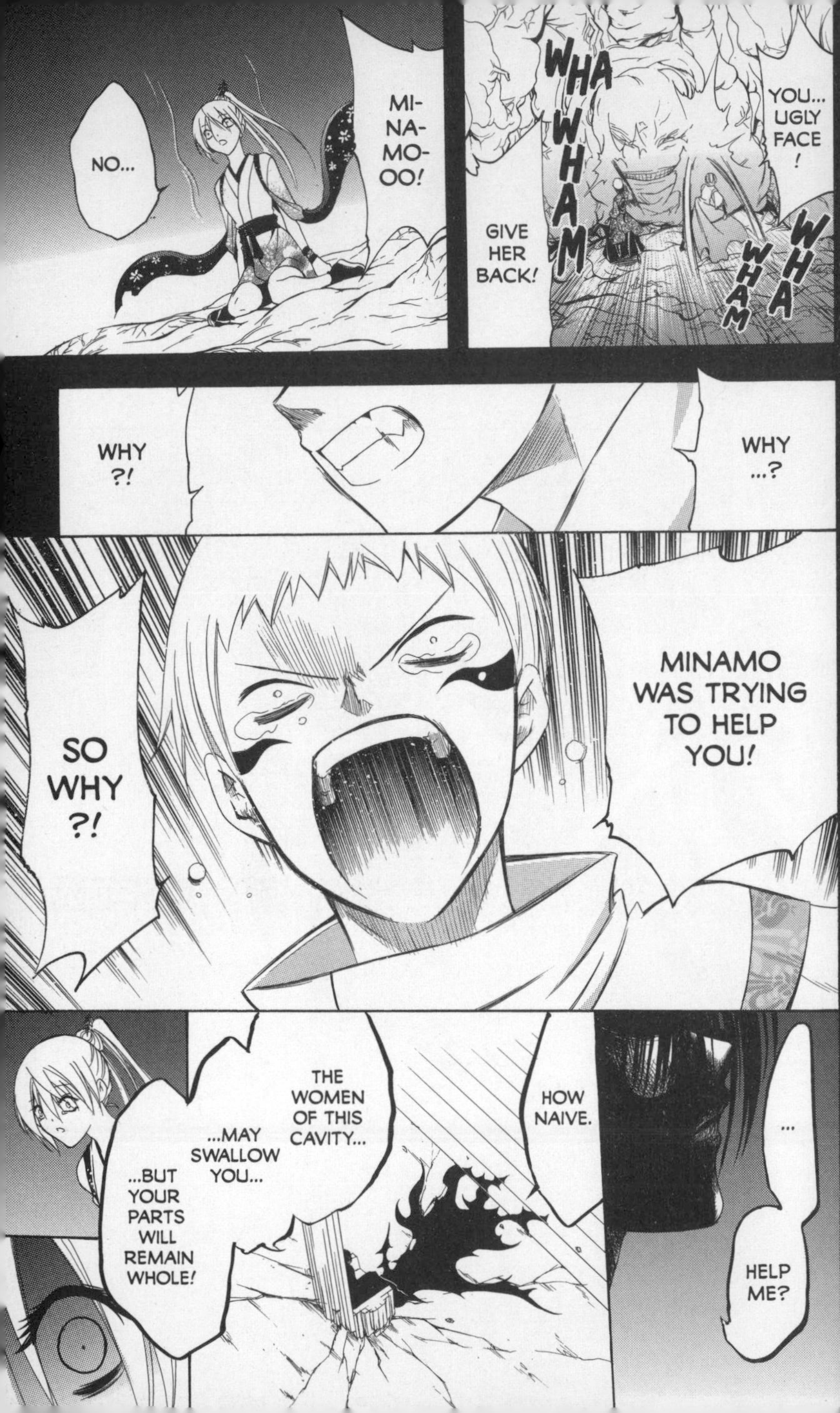
YOU... UGLY FACE!
WHA WHAM
WHA WHAM
GIVE HER BACK!
MI-NA-MO-OO!
NO...
WHY ...?
WHY ?!
MINAMO WAS TRYING TO HELP YOU!
SO WHY ?!
...
HELP ME?
HOW NAIVE.
THE WOMEN OF THIS CAVITY...
...MAY SWALLOW YOU...
...BUT YOUR PARTS WILL REMAIN WHOLE!

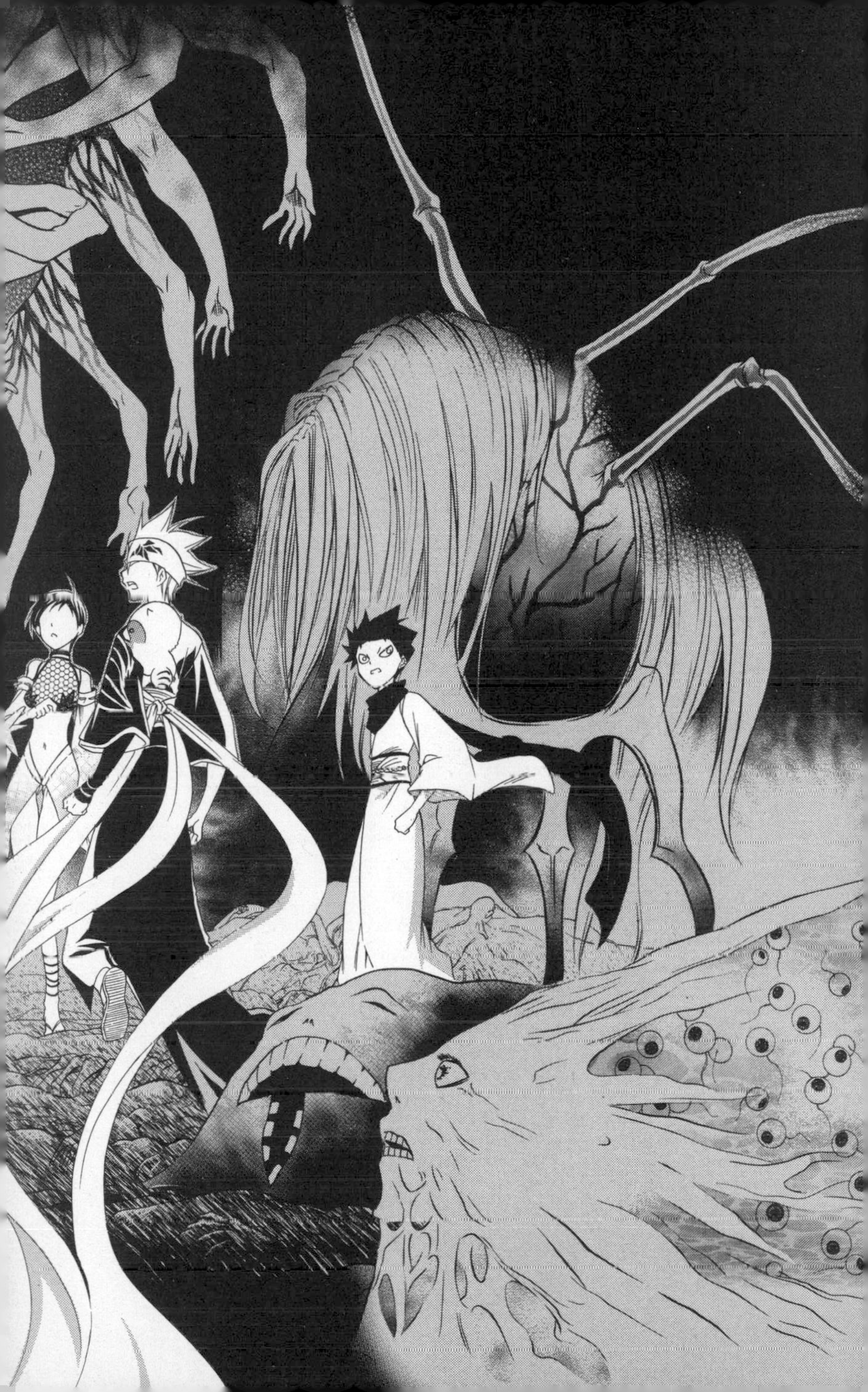

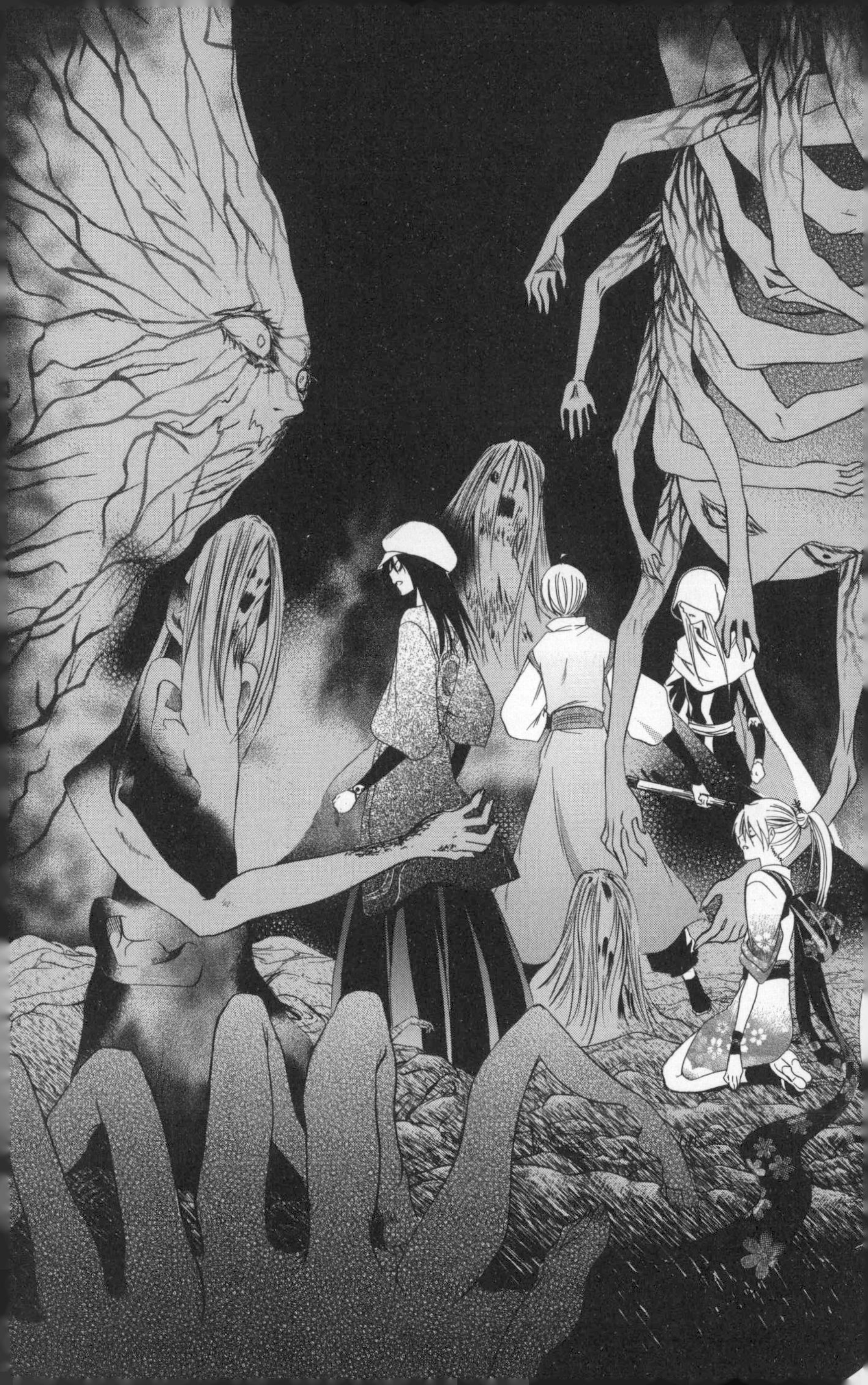

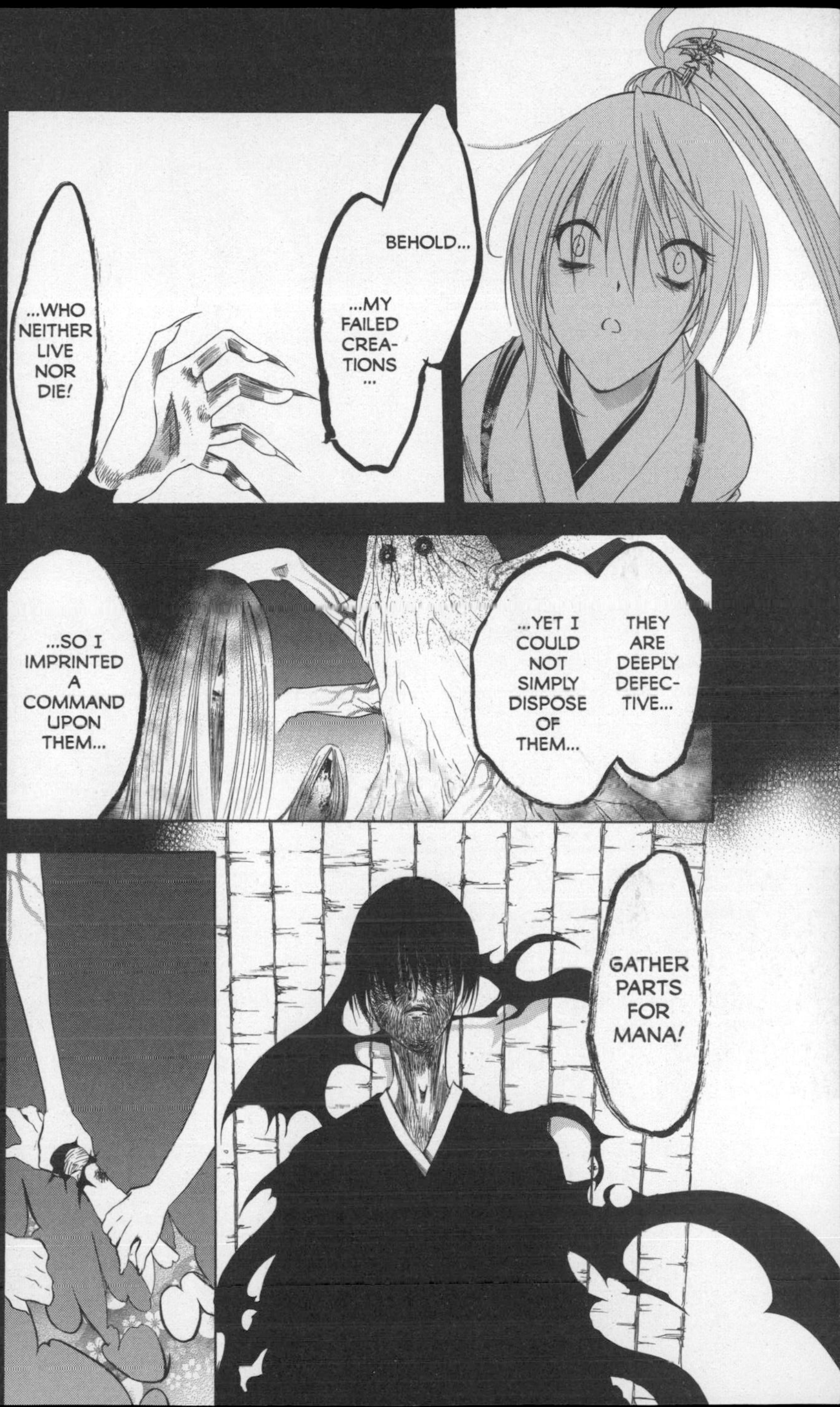
BEHOLD... ...MY FAILED CREA-TIONS...
...WHO NEITHER LIVE NOR DIE!
THEY ARE DEEPLY DEFEC-TIVE... ...YET I COULD NOT SIMPLY DISPOSE OF THEM...
...SO I IMPRINTED A COMMAND UPON THEM...
GATHER PARTS FOR MANA!

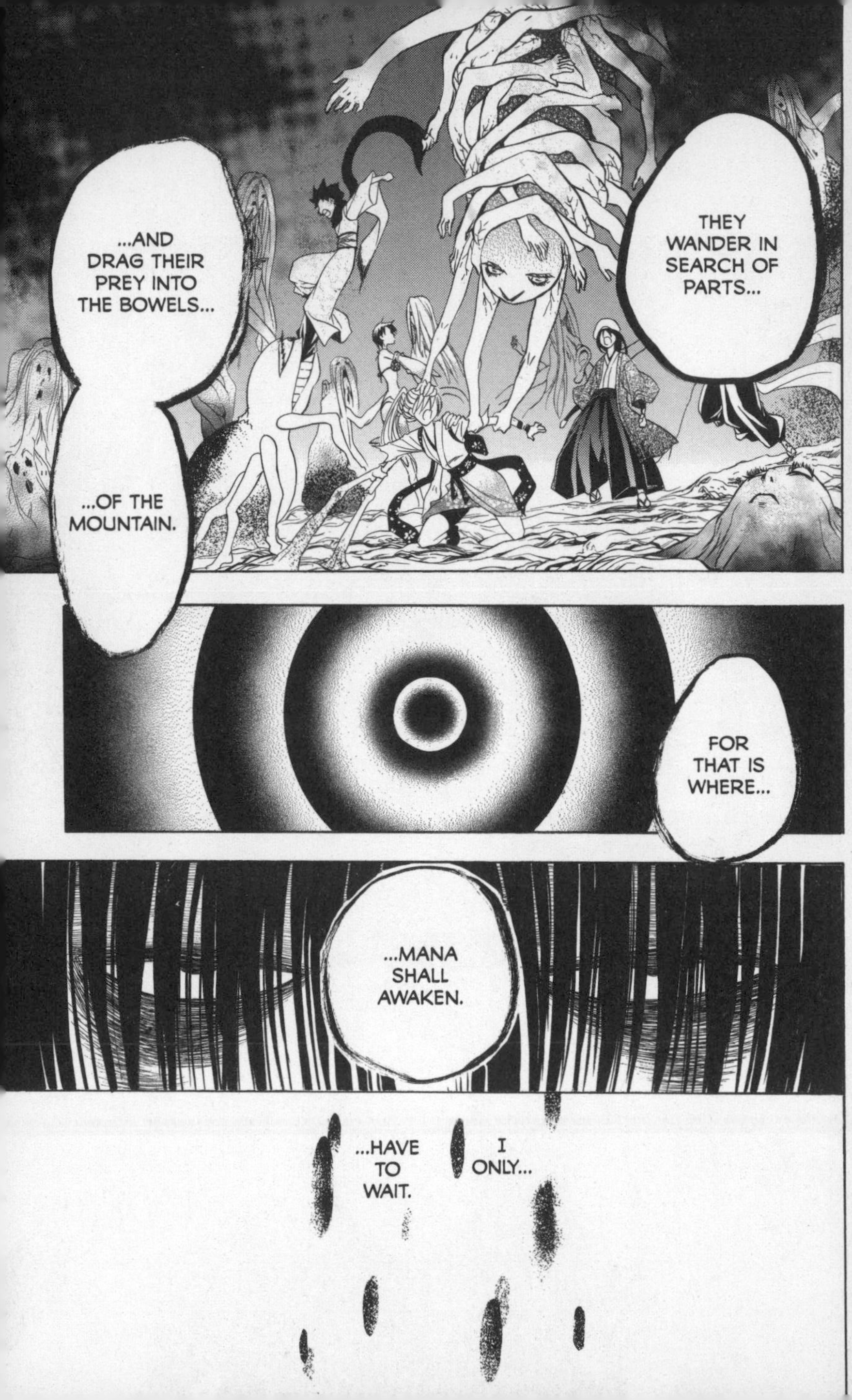
THEY WANDER IN SEARCH OF PARTS...
...AND DRAG THEIR PREY INTO THE BOWELS...
...OF THE MOUNTAIN.
FOR THAT IS WHERE...
...MANA SHALL AWAKEN.
I ONLY...
...HAVE TO WAIT.

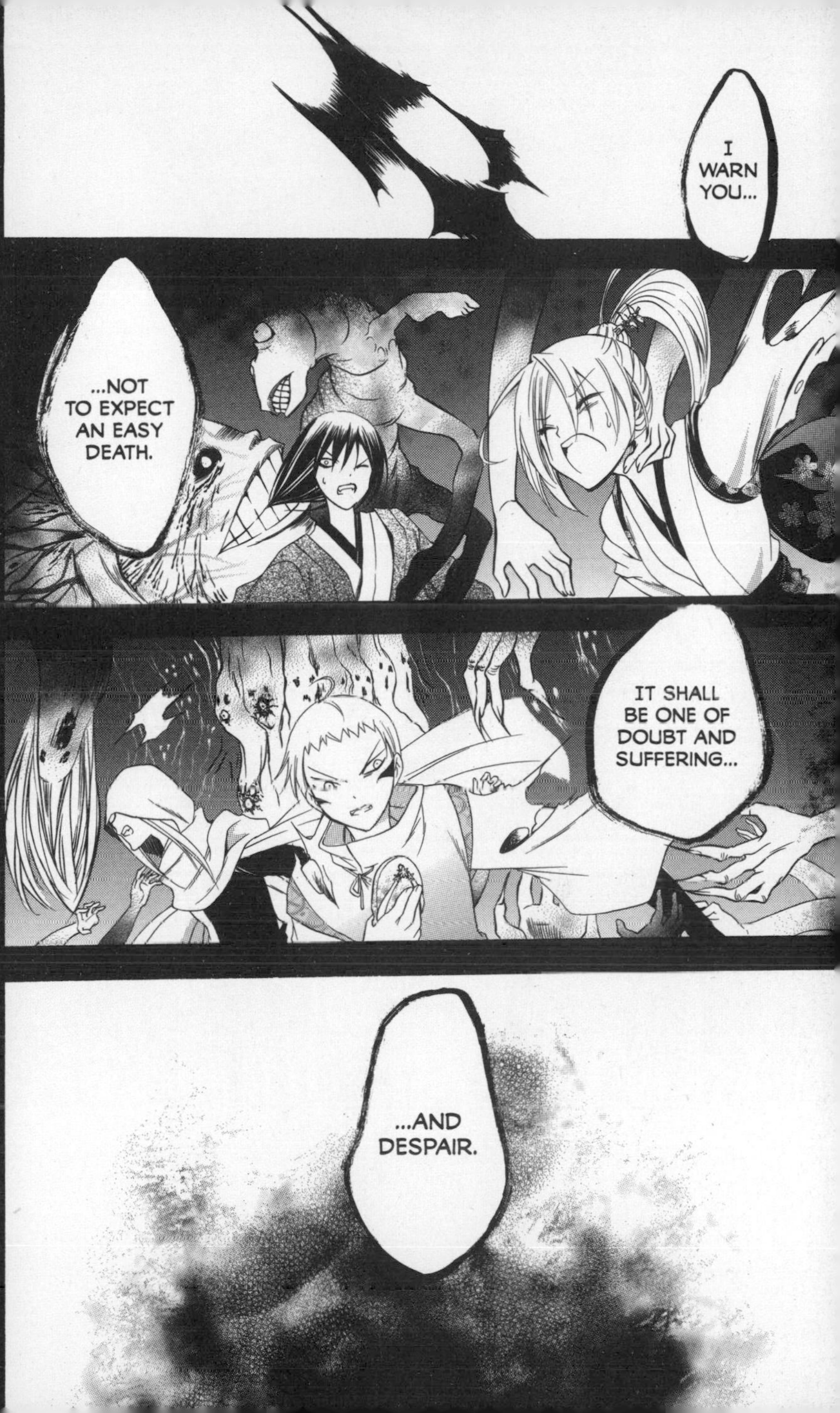
I WARN YOU...
...NOT TO EXPECT AN EASY DEATH.
IT SHALL BE ONE OF DOUBT AND SUFFERING...
...AND DESPAIR.

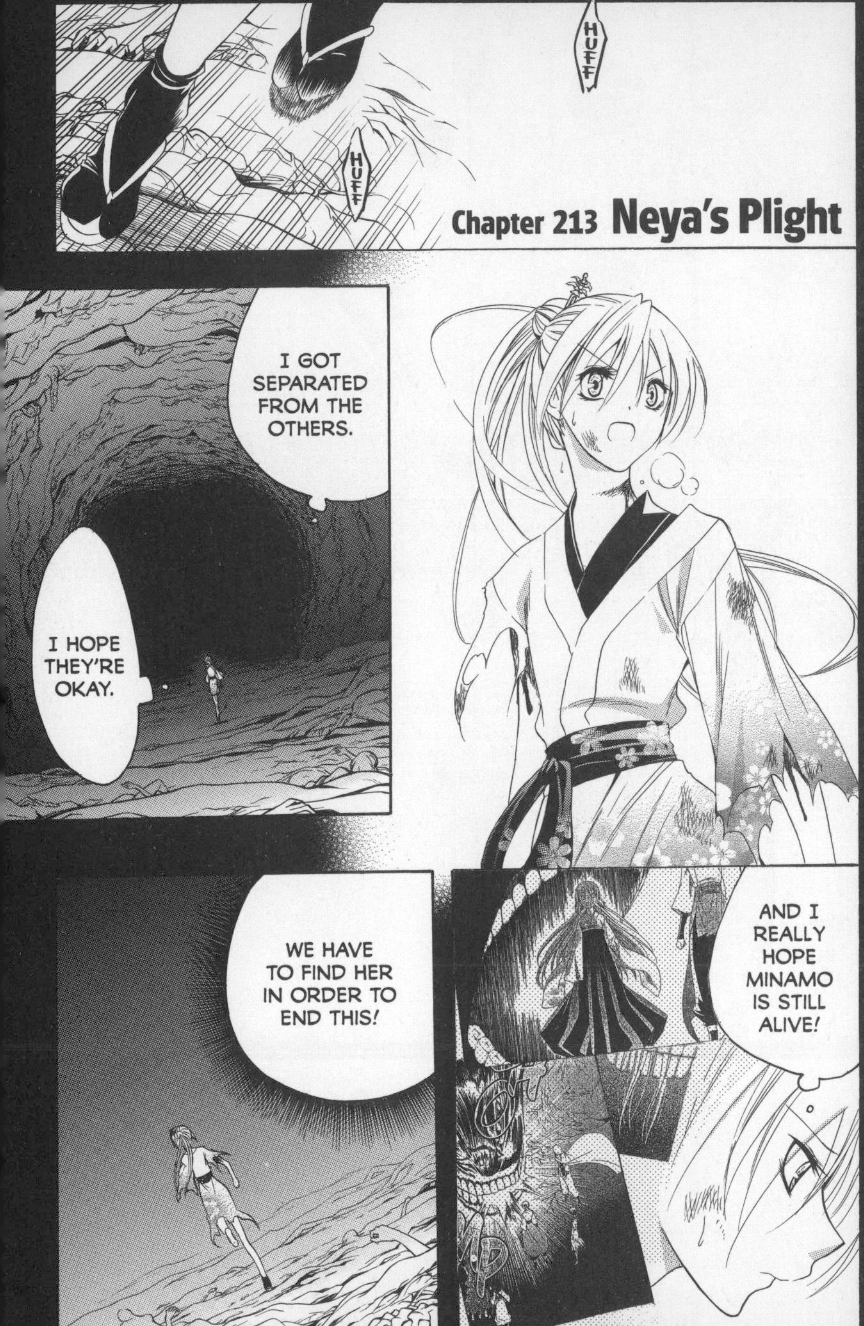
HUFF
HUFF
Chapter 213 Neya's Plight
I GOT SEPARATED FROM THE OTHERS.
I HOPE THEY'RE OKAY.
AND I REALLY HOPE MINAMO IS STILL ALIVE!
WE HAVE TO FIND HER IN ORDER TO END THIS!

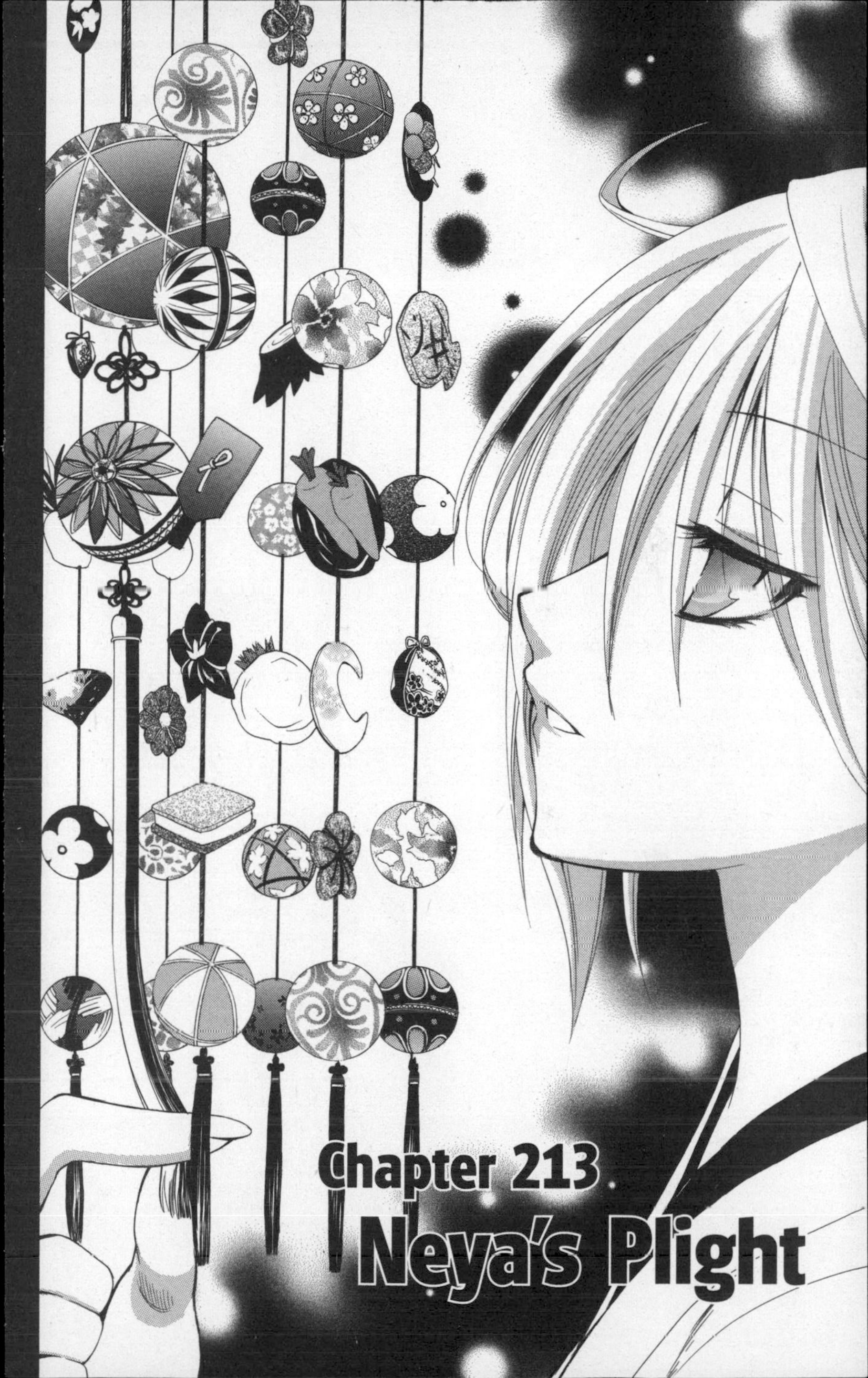
Chapter 213
Neya's Plight

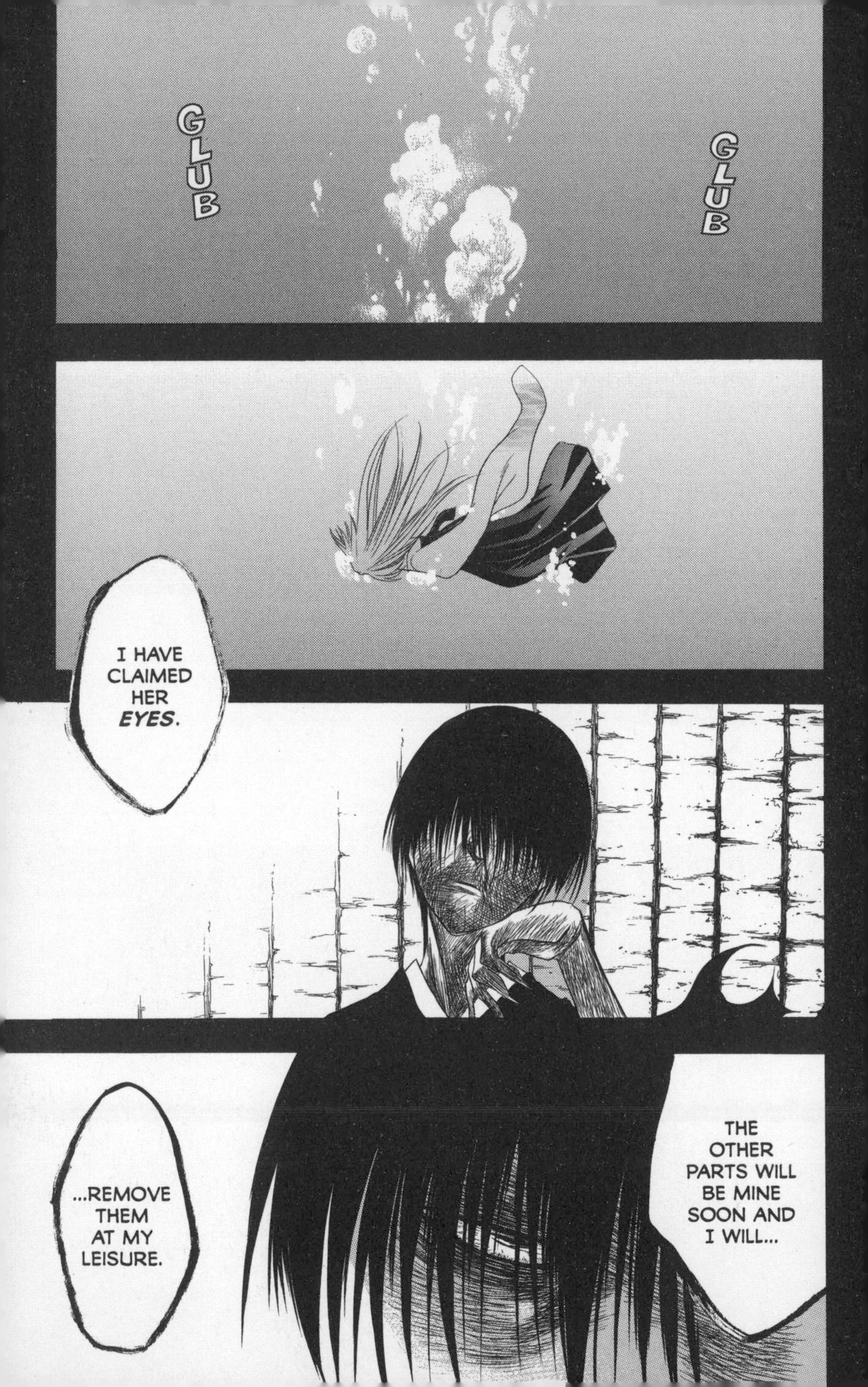
GLUB
GLUB
I HAVE CLAIMED HER *EYES*.
THE OTHER PARTS WILL BE MINE SOON AND I WILL...
...REMOVE THEM AT MY LEISURE.

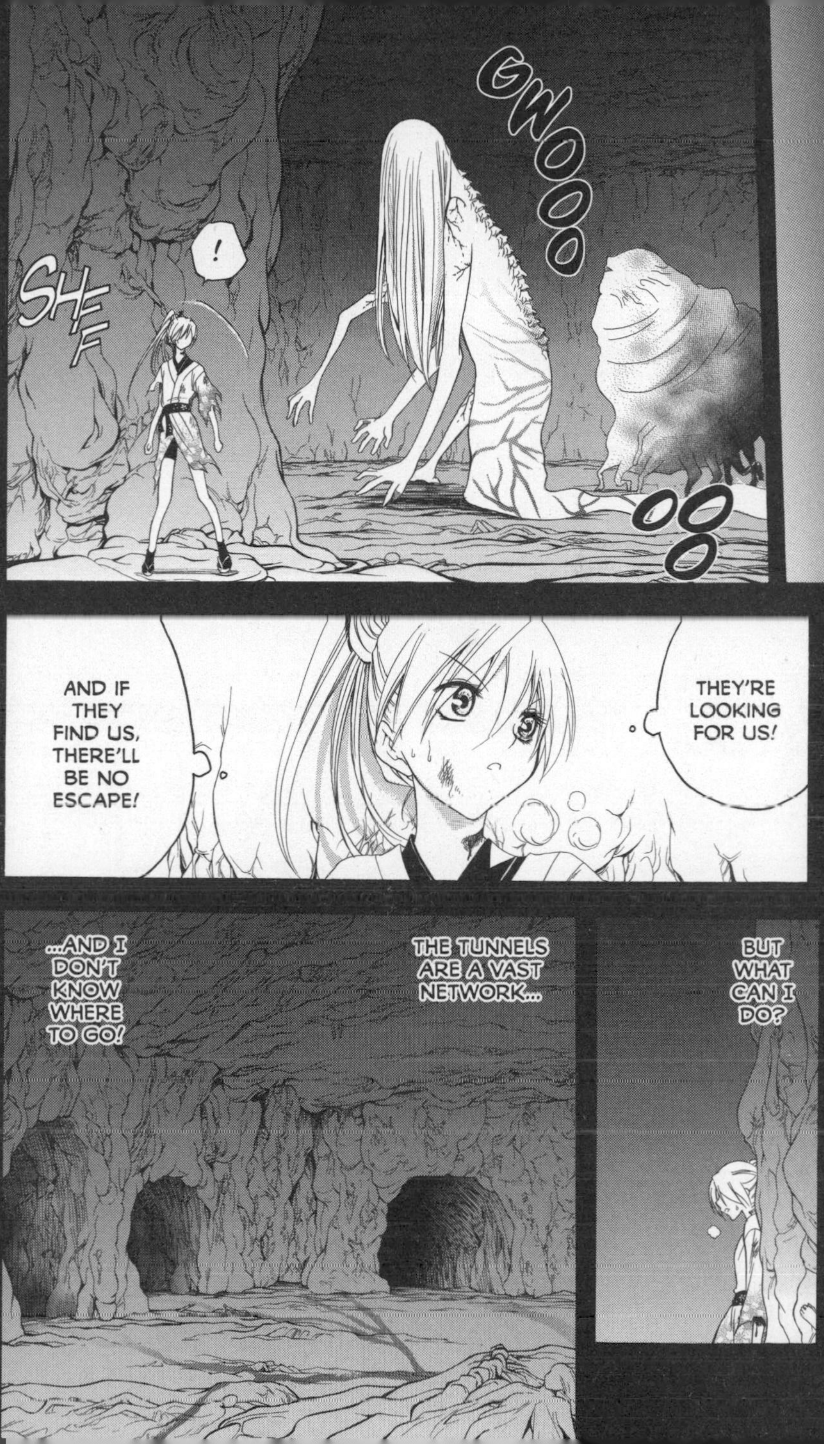
GWOOOO
OOO
!
SHFF
THEY'RE LOOKING FOR US!
AND IF THEY FIND US, THERE'LL BE NO ESCAPE!
BUT WHAT CAN I DO?
THE TUNNELS ARE A VAST NETWORK...
...AND I DON'T KNOW WHERE TO GO!

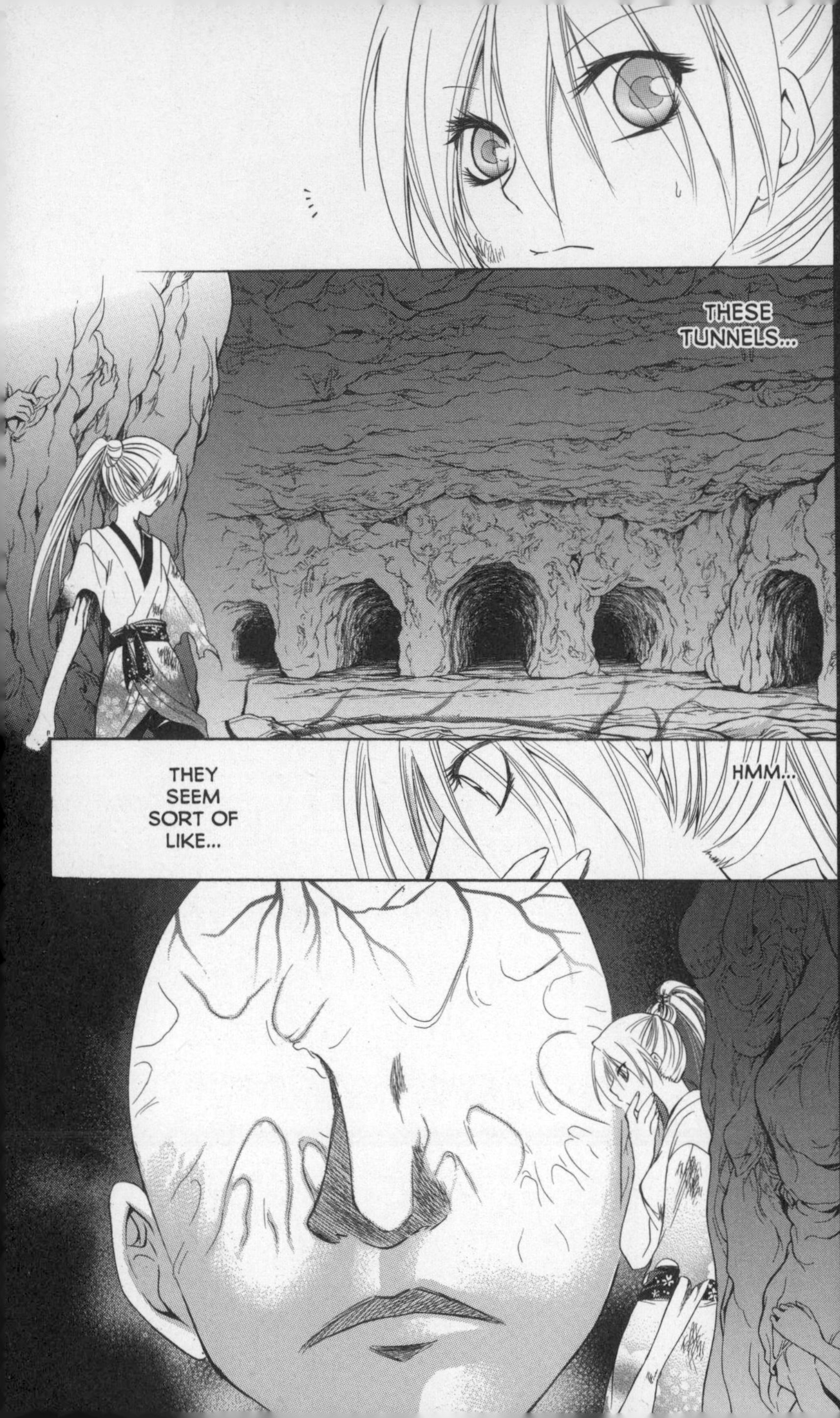
THESE TUNNELS...
HMM...
THEY SEEM SORT OF LIKE...

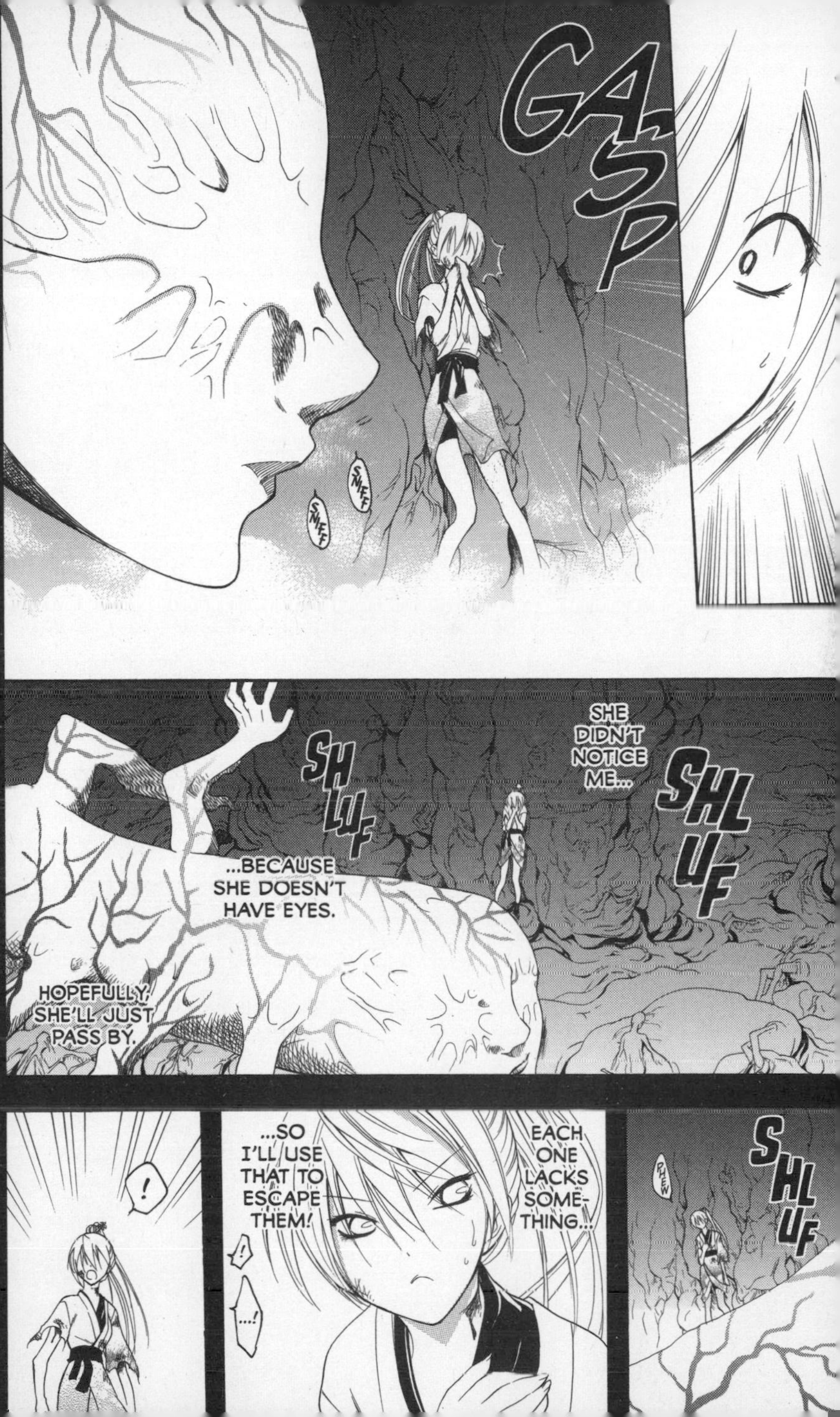
GASP
SNIFF
SNIFF
SHLUF
SHE DIDN'T NOTICE ME...
SHLUF
...BECAUSE SHE DOESN'T HAVE EYES.
HOPEFULLY, SHE'LL JUST PASS BY.
SHLUF
PHEW
EACH ONE LACKS SOME-THING...
...SO I'LL USE THAT TO ESCAPE THEM!
!
...!
!

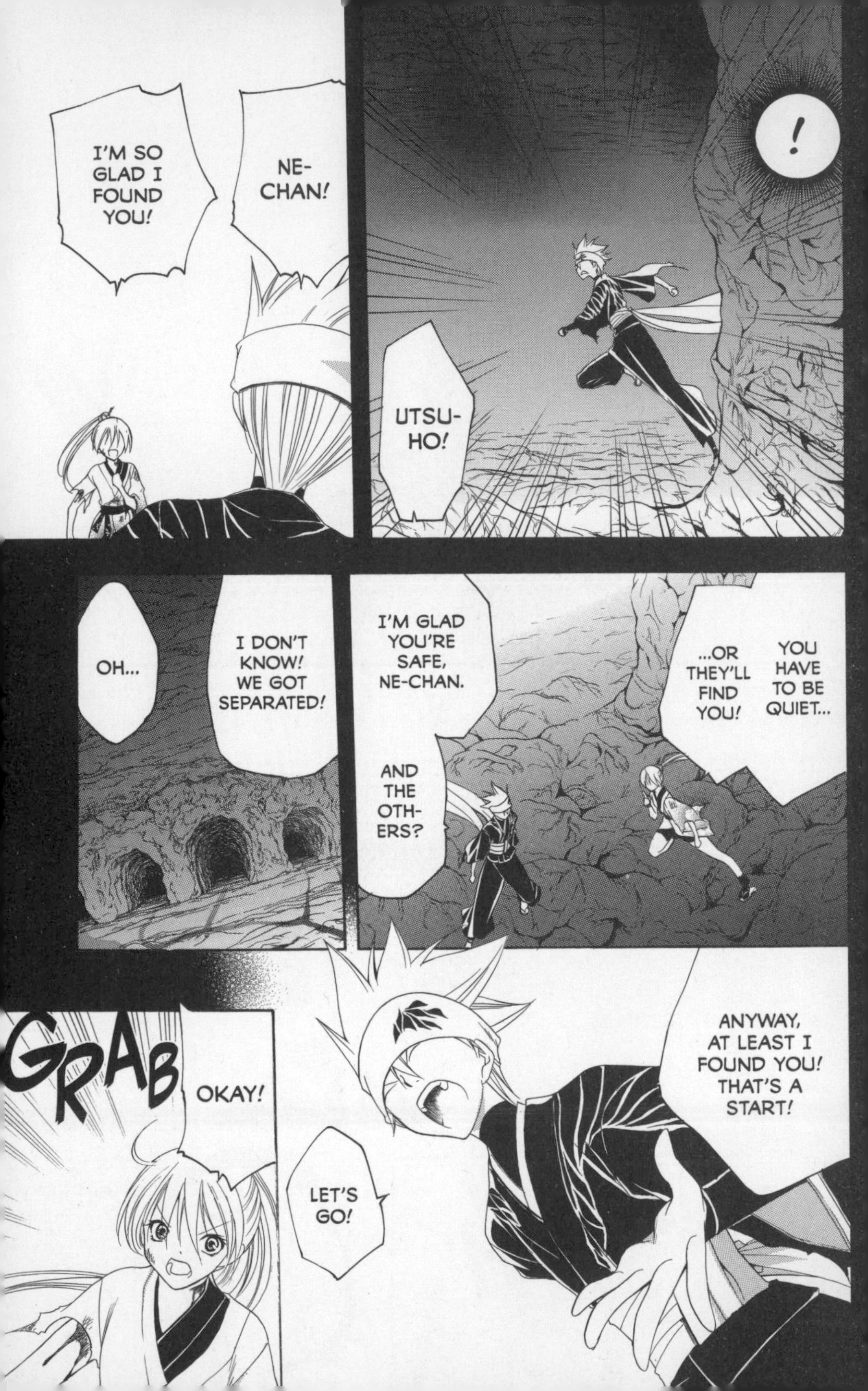
!
UTSU-HO!
NE-CHAN!
I'M SO GLAD I FOUND YOU!
YOU HAVE TO BE QUIET...
...OR THEY'LL FIND YOU!
I'M GLAD YOU'RE SAFE, NE-CHAN.
AND THE OTHERS?
I DON'T KNOW! WE GOT SEPARATED!
OH...
ANYWAY, AT LEAST I FOUND YOU! THAT'S A START!
LET'S GO!
OKAY!
GRAB

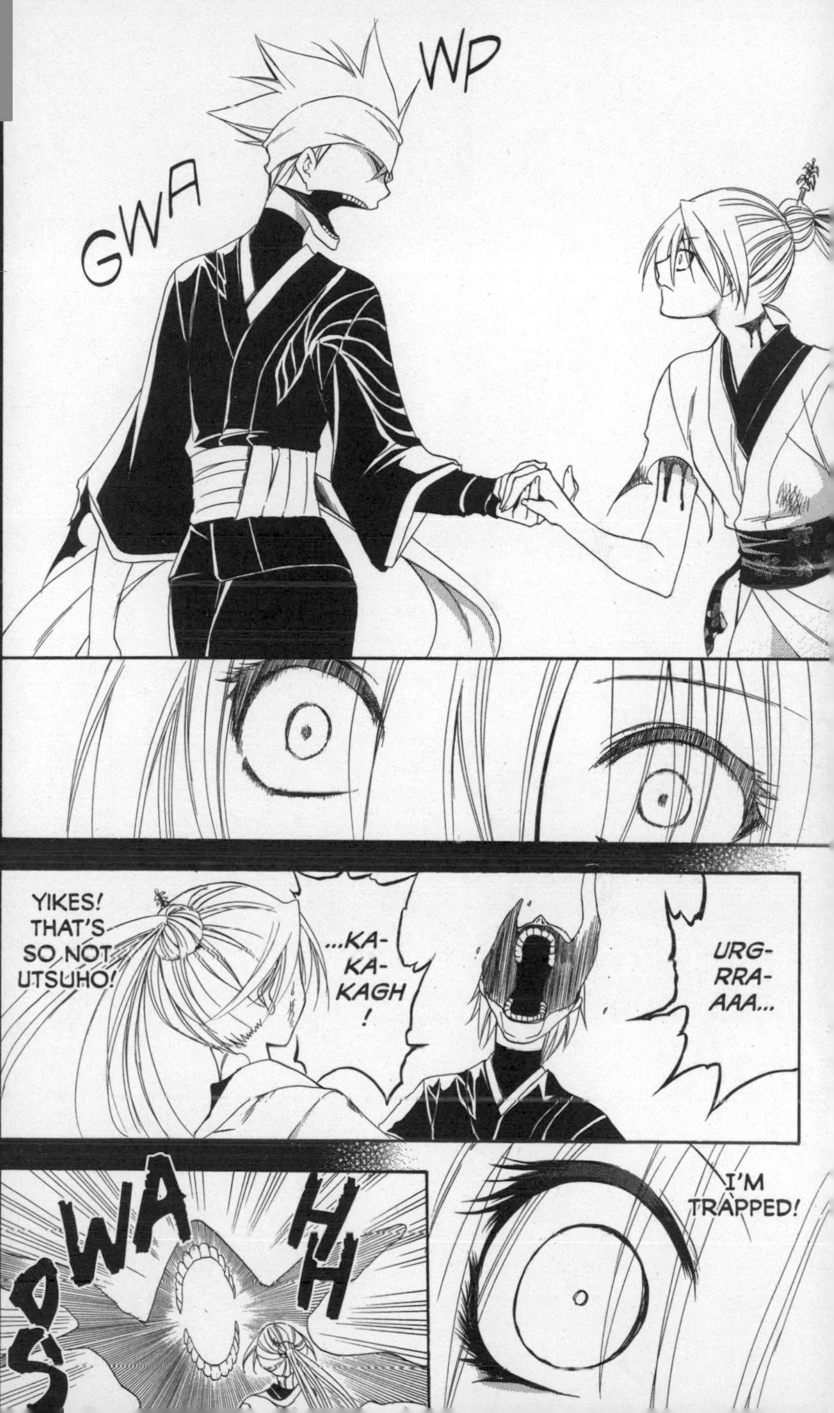
WP
GWA
URG-RRA-AAA...
...KA-KA-KAGH!
YIKES! THAT'S SO NOT UTSUHO!
I'M TRAPPED!
SWAHH

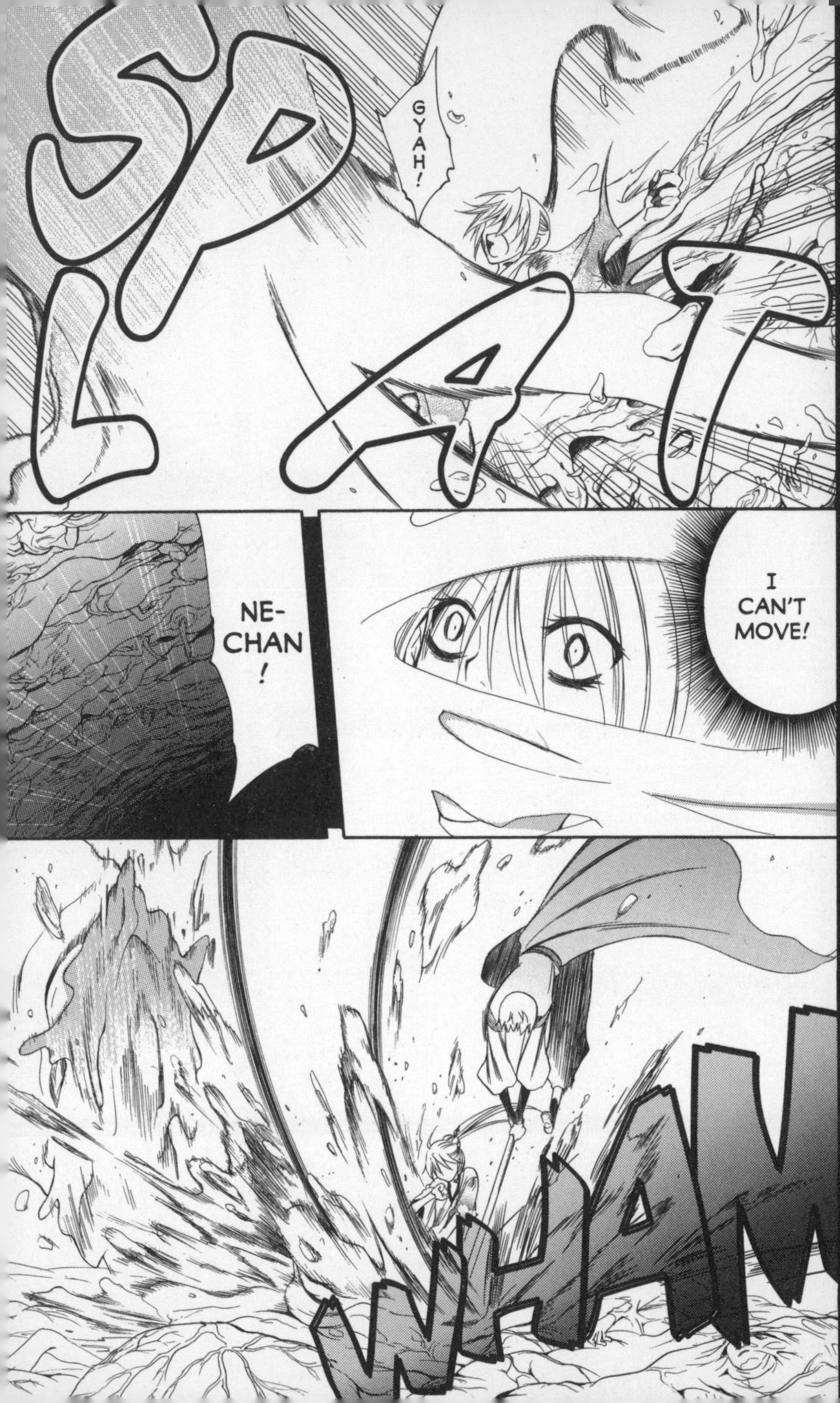
SPLAT
GYAH!
I CAN'T MOVE!
NE-CHAN!
WHAM

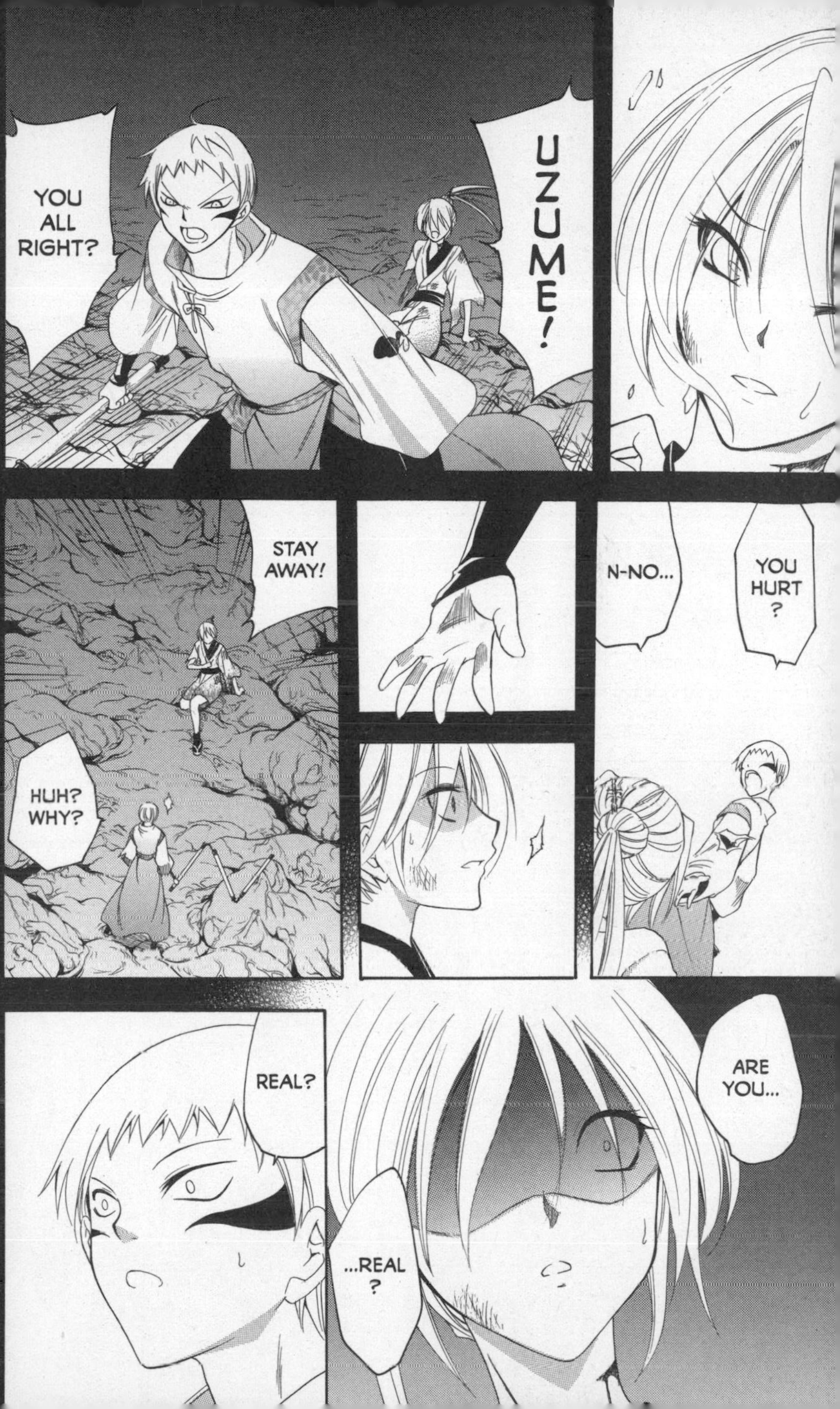
UZUME!
YOU ALL RIGHT?
YOU HURT?
N-NO...
STAY AWAY!
HUH? WHY?
ARE YOU...
REAL?
...REAL?

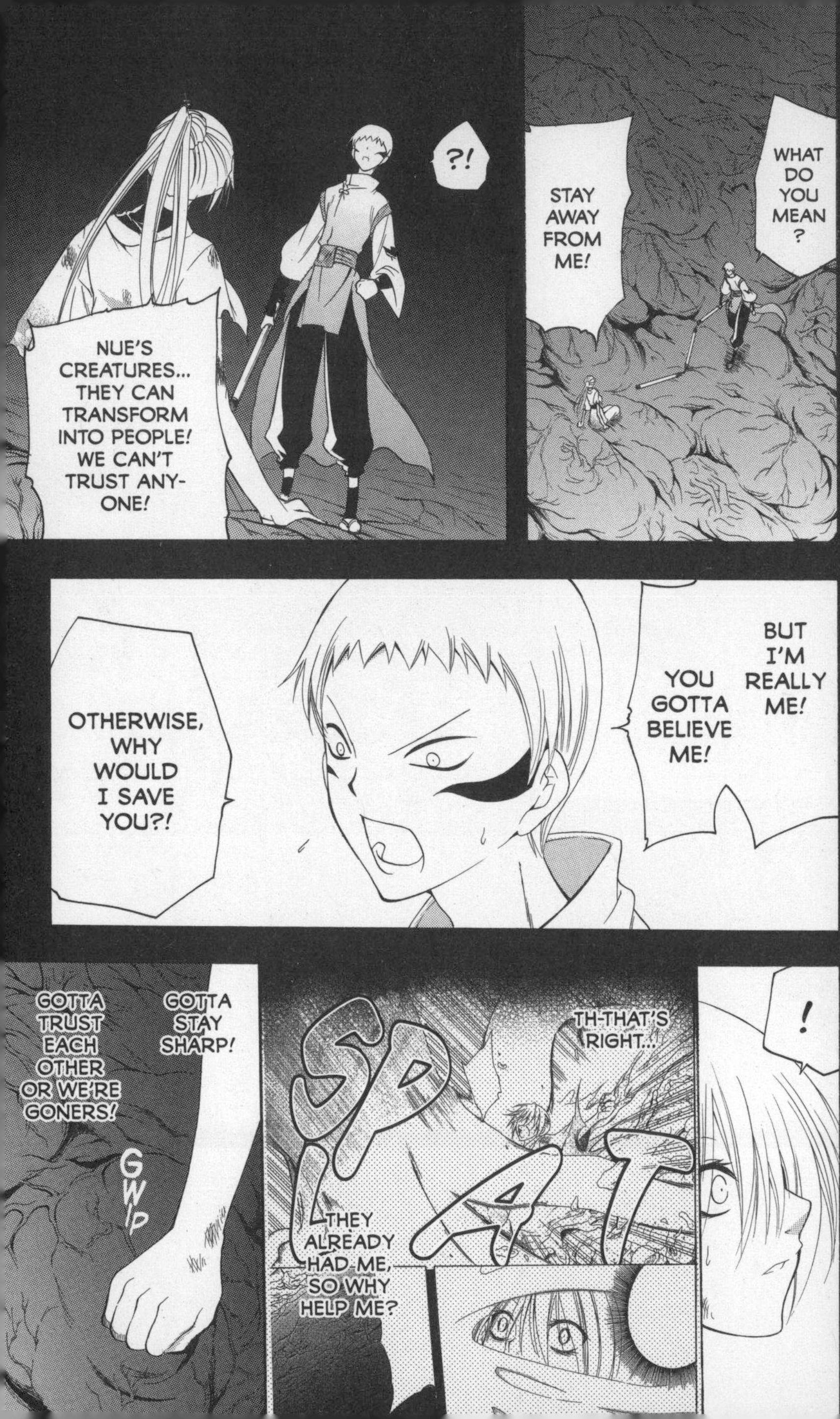
WHAT DO YOU MEAN?
STAY AWAY FROM ME!
?!
NUE'S CREATURES... THEY CAN TRANSFORM INTO PEOPLE! WE CAN'T TRUST ANY-ONE!
BUT I'M REALLY ME!
YOU GOTTA BELIEVE ME!
OTHERWISE, WHY WOULD I SAVE YOU?!
!
TH-THAT'S RIGHT...
SPLAT
THEY ALREADY HAD ME, SO WHY HELP ME?
GOTTA STAY SHARP!
GOTTA TRUST EACH OTHER OR WE'RE GONERS!
GWIP

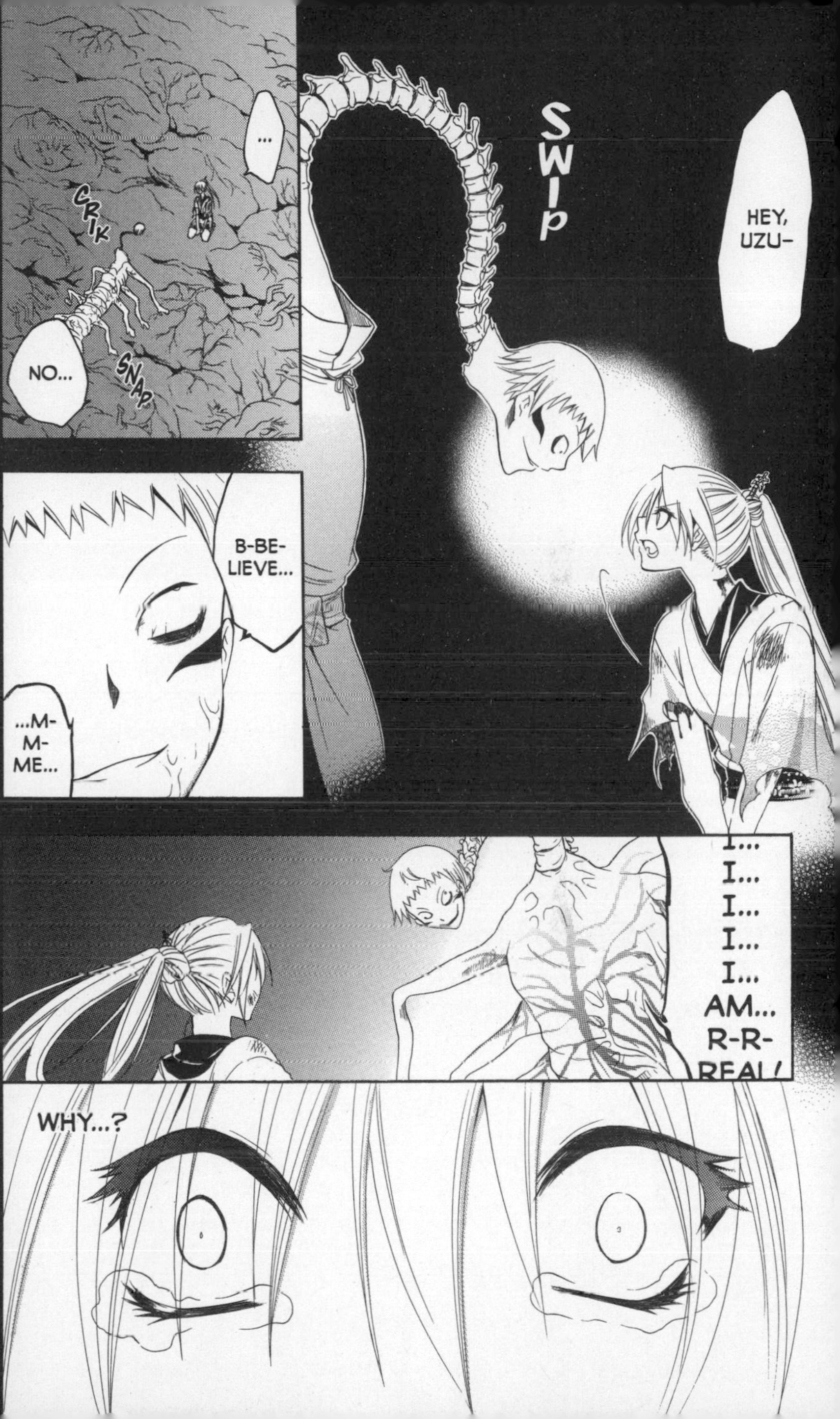
HEY, UZU-
SWIP
...
CRIK
NO...
SNAP
B-BE-LIEVE...
...M-M-ME...
I... I... I... I... I... AM... R-R-REAL!
WHY...?

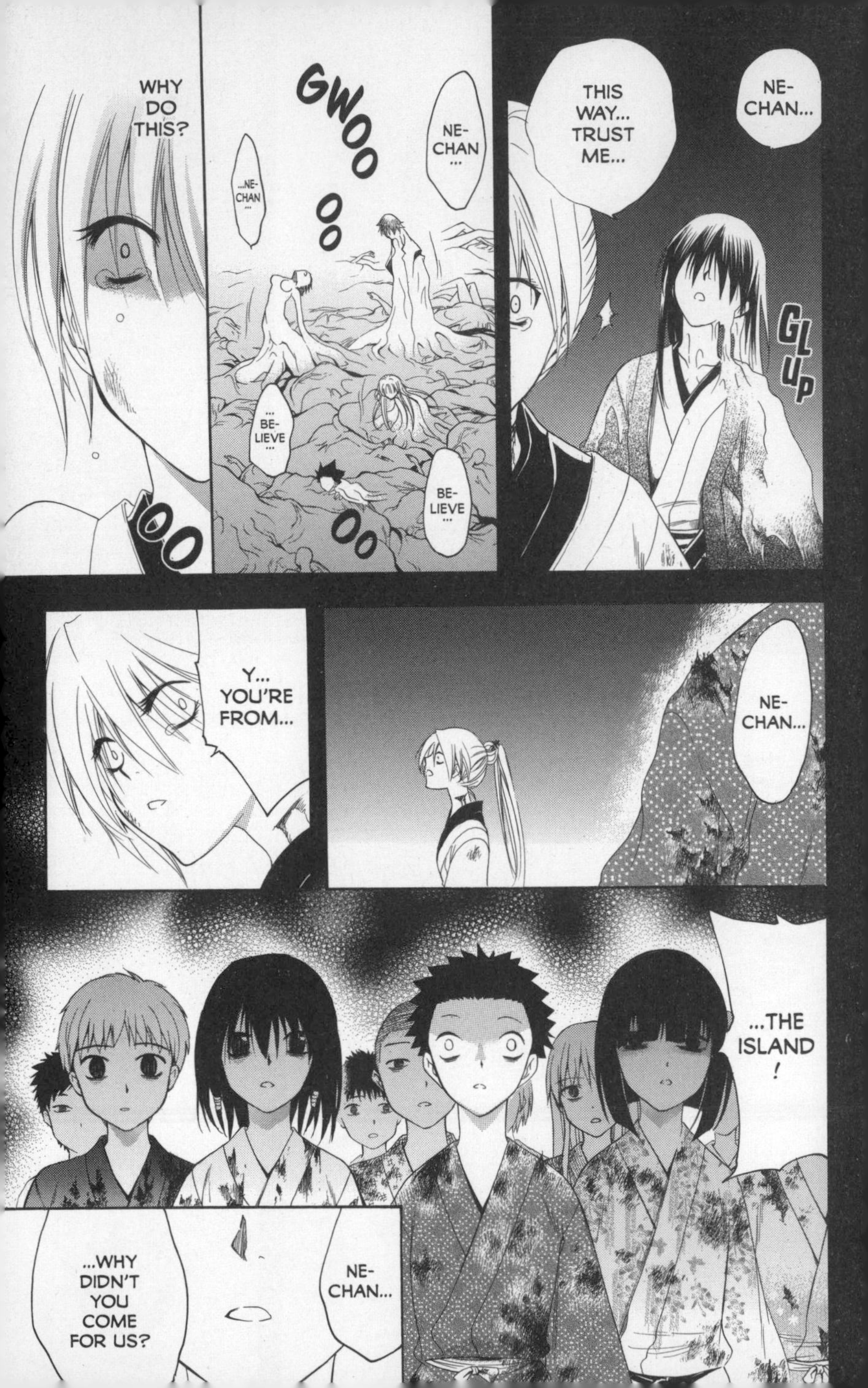
NE-CHAN...
THIS WAY... TRUST ME...
GLUP
NE-CHAN...
GWOOOOOOOOOO
...NE-CHAN...
...BE-LIEVE...
BE-LIEVE...
WHY DO THIS?
NE-CHAN...
Y... YOU'RE FROM...
...THE ISLAND!
NE-CHAN...
...WHY DIDN'T YOU COME FOR US?

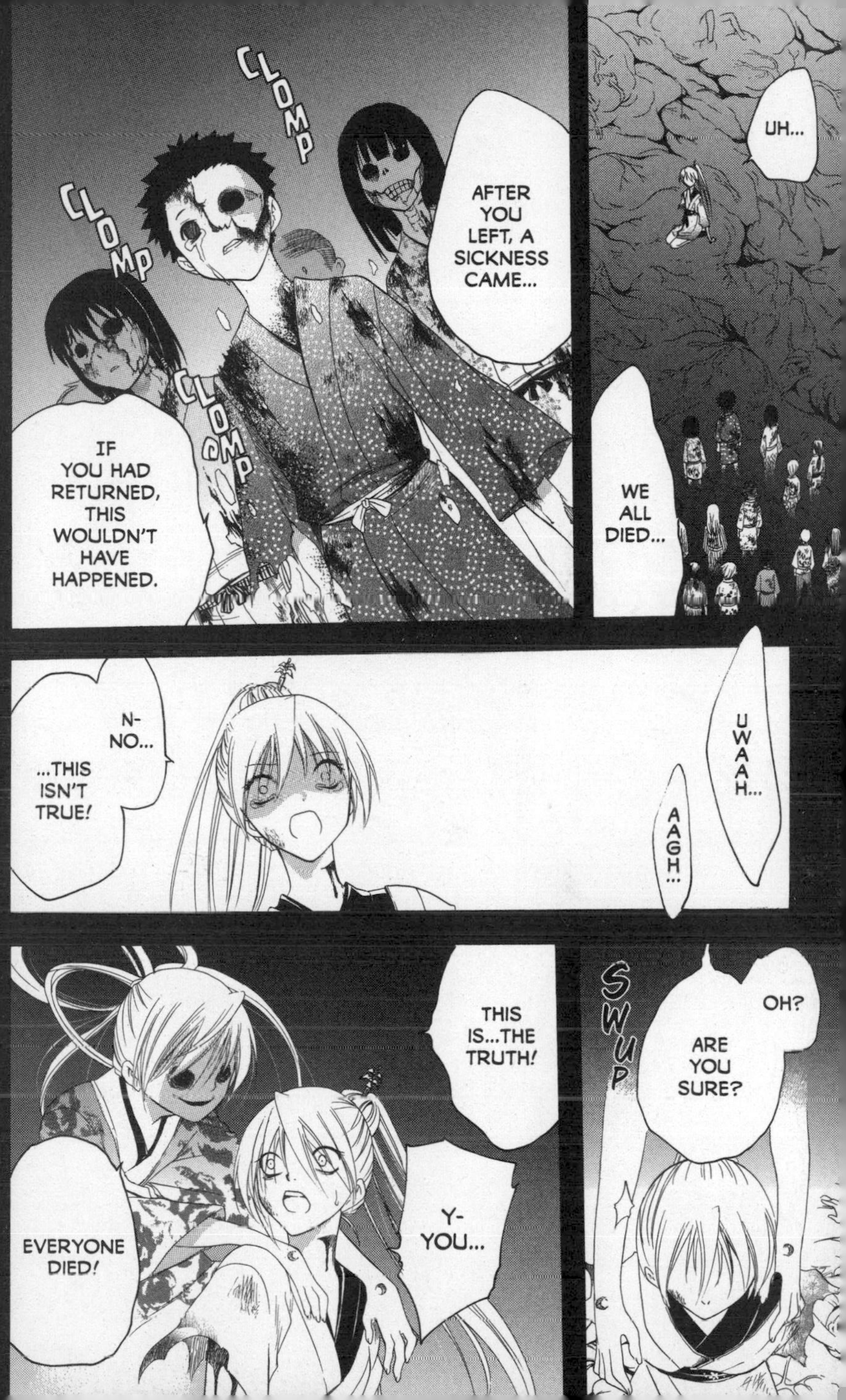
UH...
WE ALL DIED...
CLOMP
AFTER YOU LEFT, A SICKNESS CAME...
CLOMP
CLOMP
IF YOU HAD RETURNED, THIS WOULDN'T HAVE HAPPENED.
UWAAH...
AAGH...
N-NO...
...THIS ISN'T TRUE!
OH?
ARE YOU SURE?
SWUP
THIS IS...THE TRUTH!
Y-YOU...
EVERYONE DIED!

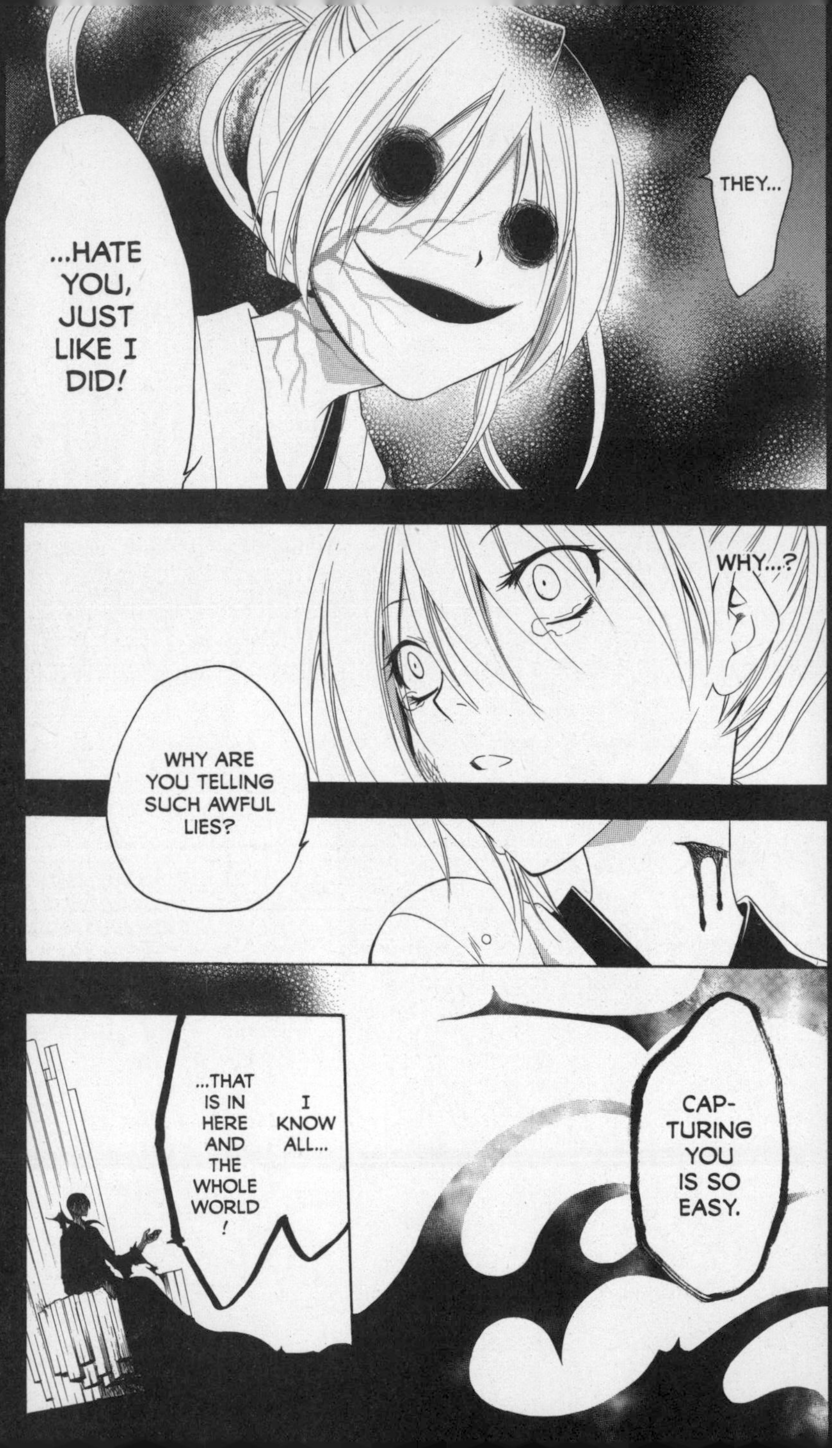
THEY...
...HATE YOU, JUST LIKE I DID!
WHY...?
WHY ARE YOU TELLING SUCH AWFUL LIES?
CAP-TURING YOU IS SO EASY.
I KNOW ALL...
...THAT IS IN HERE AND THE WHOLE WORLD!

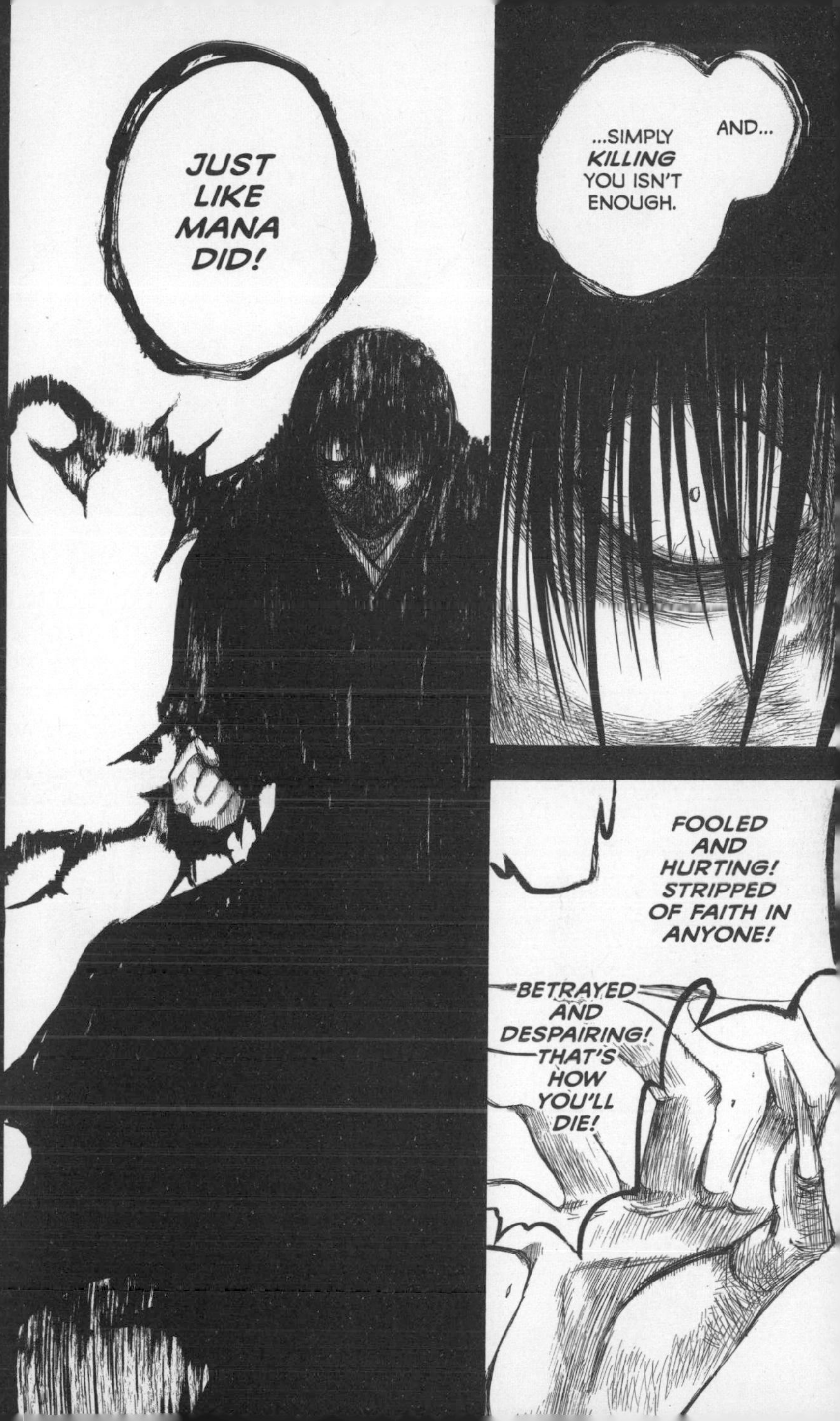
AND...
...SIMPLY KILLING YOU ISN'T ENOUGH.
FOOLED AND HURTING! STRIPPED OF FAITH IN ANYONE!
BETRAYED AND DESPAIRING! THAT'S HOW YOU'LL DIE!
JUST LIKE MANA DID!

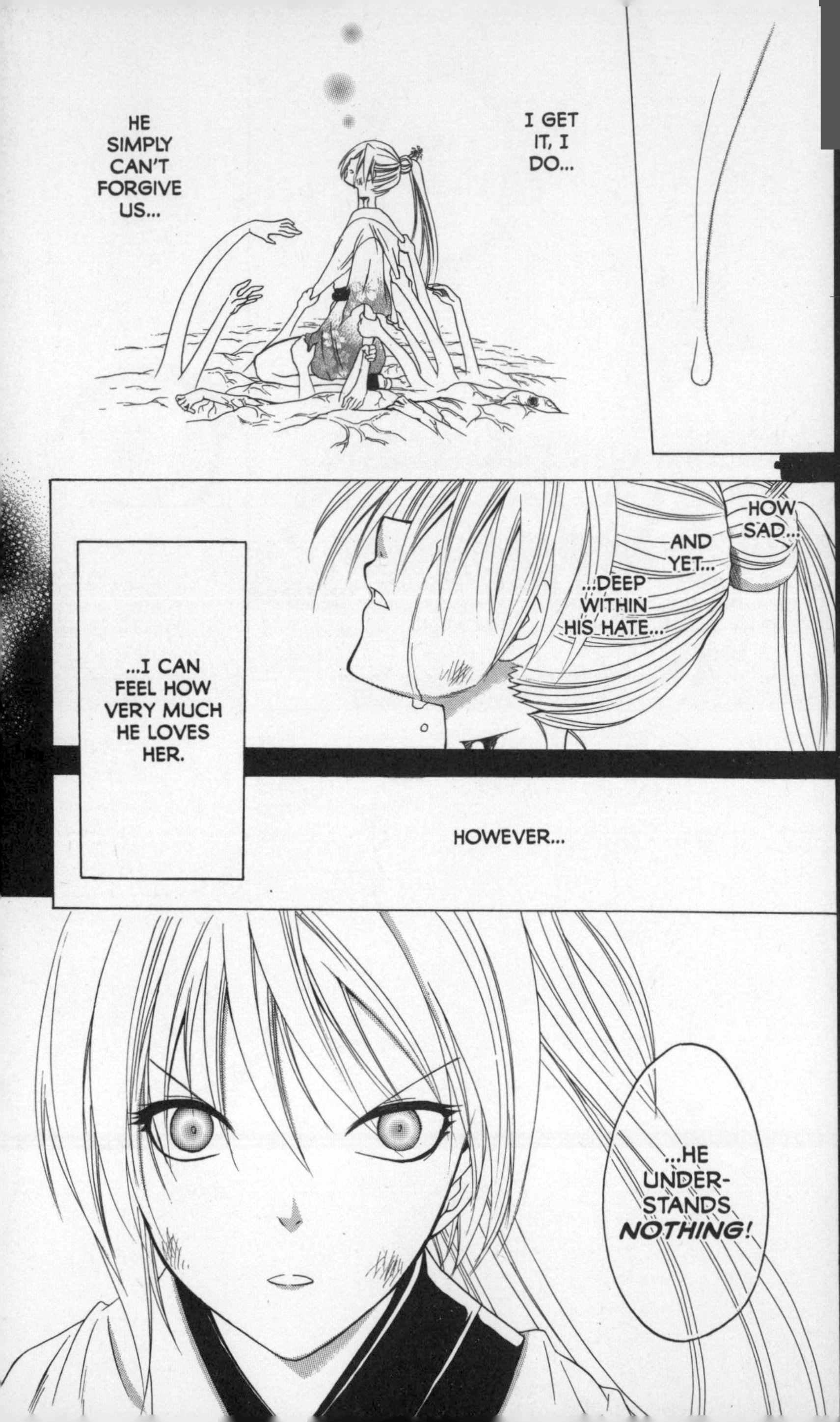
I GET IT, I DO...
HE SIMPLY CAN'T FORGIVE US...
HOW SAD...
AND YET...
...DEEP WITHIN HIS HATE...
...I CAN FEEL HOW VERY MUCH HE LOVES HER.
HOWEVER...
...HE UNDER-STANDS *NOTHING*!

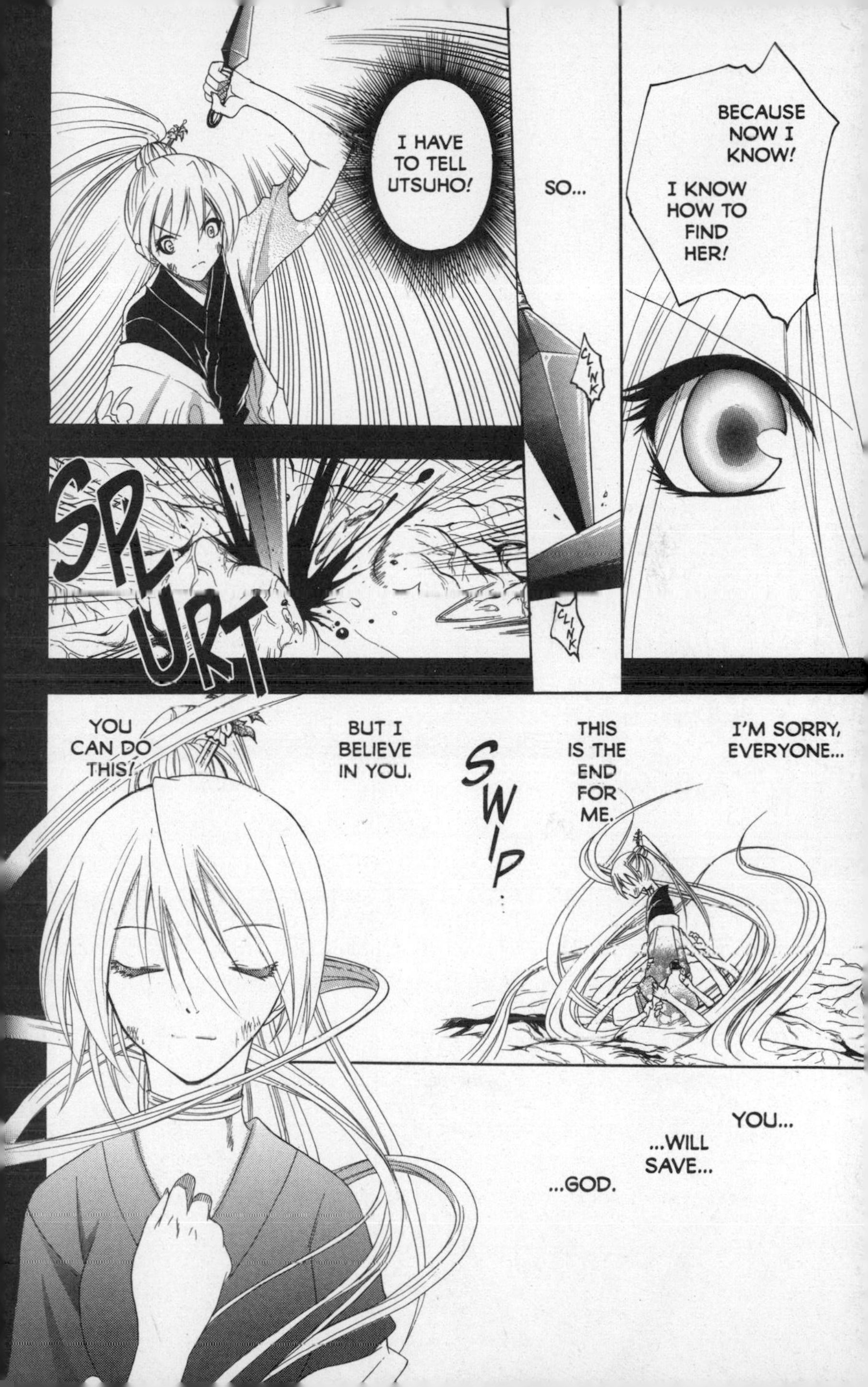
BECAUSE NOW I KNOW!
I KNOW HOW TO FIND HER!
SO...
CLINK
CLINK
I HAVE TO TELL UTSUHO!
SPLURT
I'M SORRY, EVERYONE...
THIS IS THE END FOR ME.
SWIP
BUT I BELIEVE IN YOU.
YOU CAN DO THIS!
YOU...
...WILL SAVE...
...GOD.

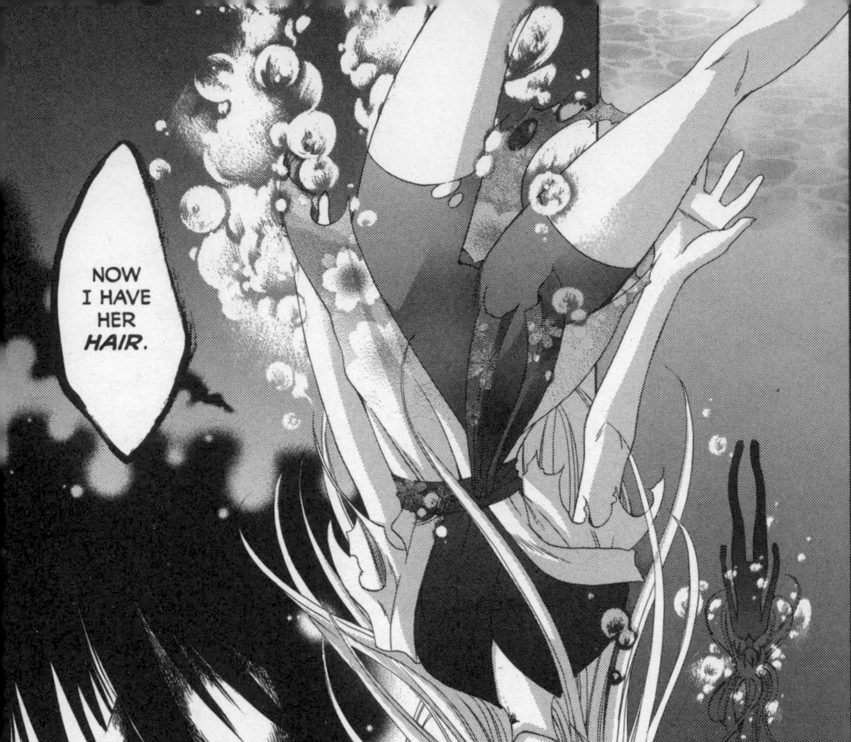
NOW I HAVE HER HAIR.

Chapter 214 It Isn't Pointless

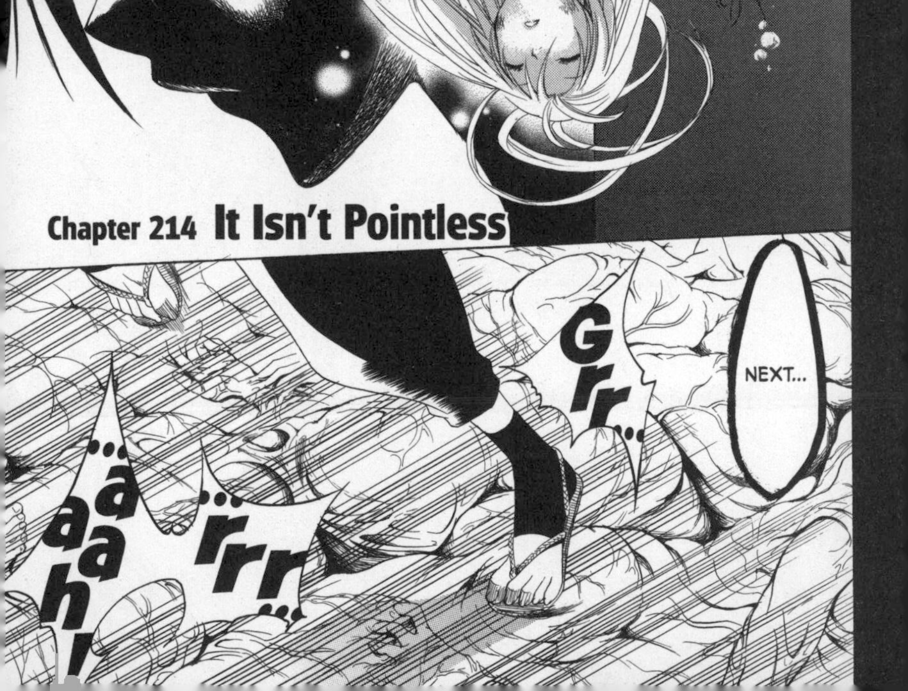
NEXT...
Grr...
...rrr...
...äaah!

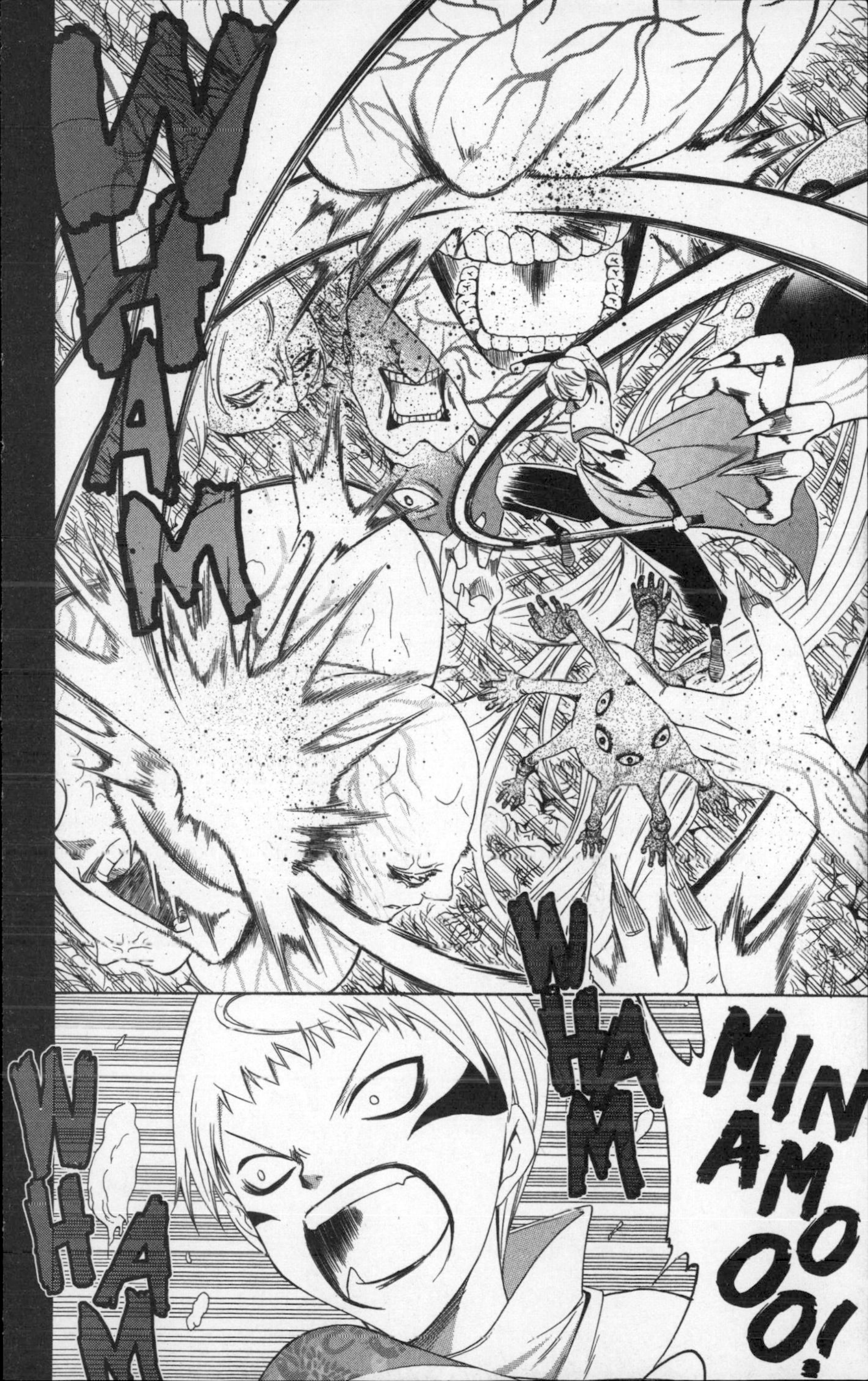
WHAM
WHAM
MINAMOOO!
WHAM

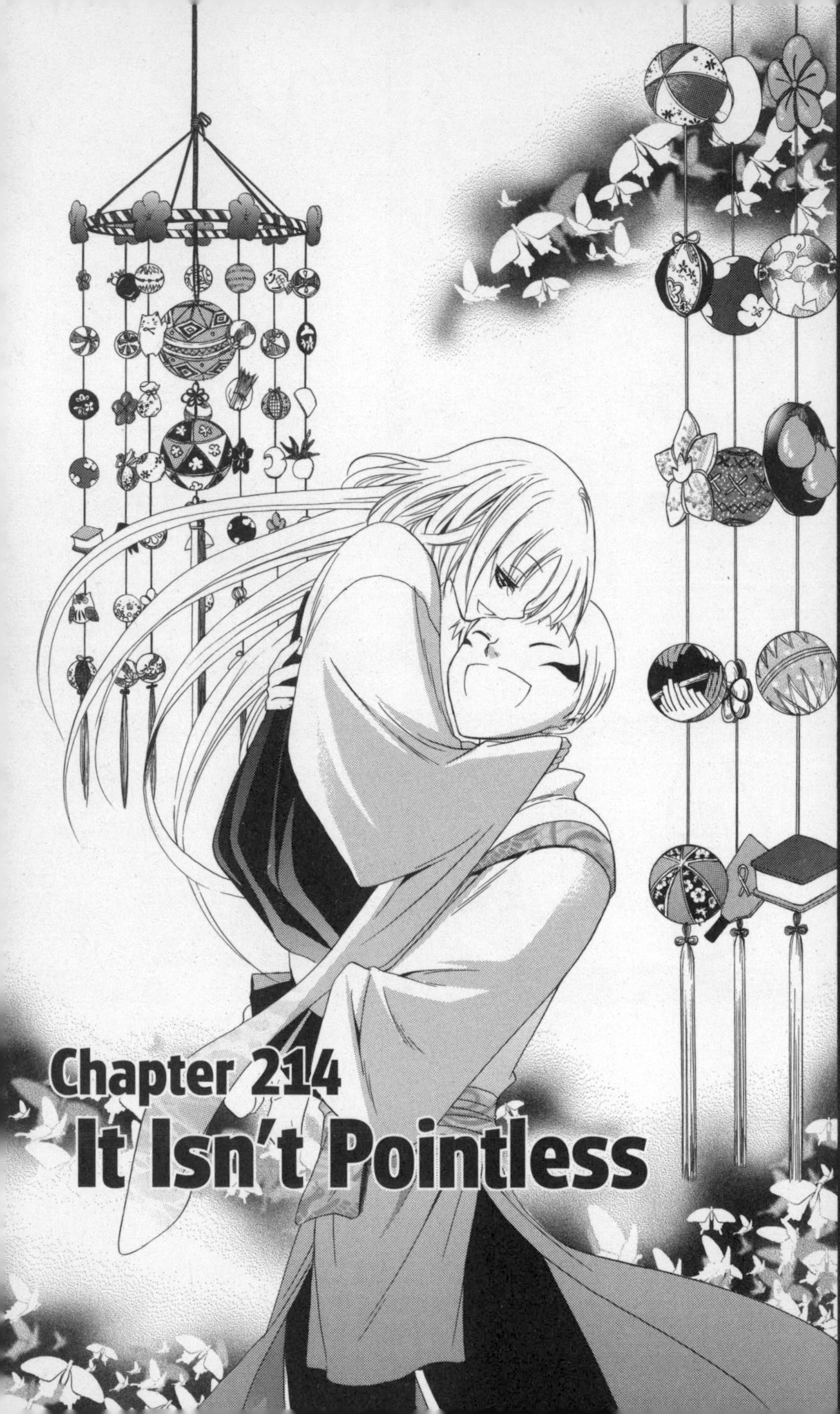
Chapter 214
It Isn't Pointless

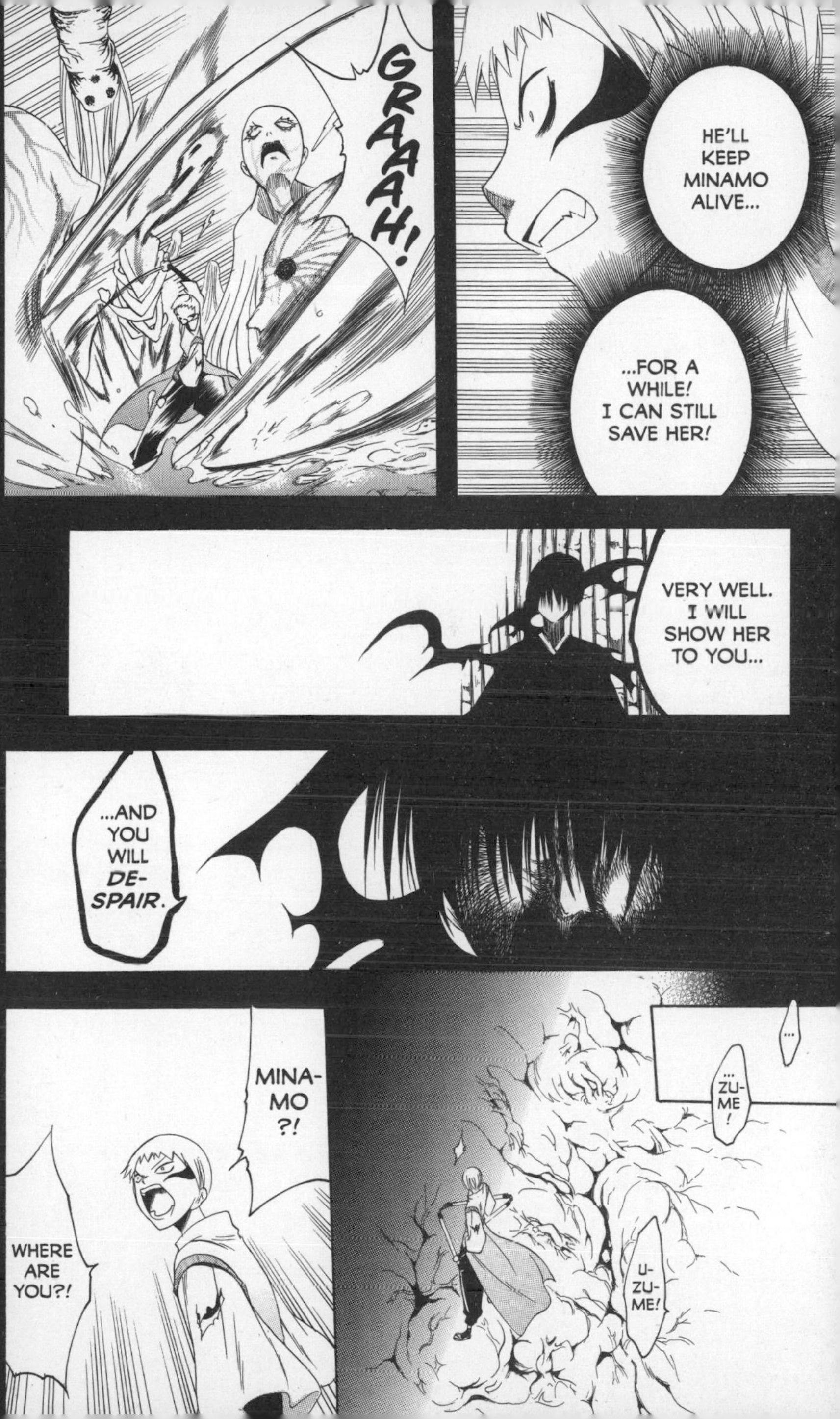
HE'LL KEEP MINAMO ALIVE...
...FOR A WHILE! I CAN STILL SAVE HER!
GRAAAAH!
VERY WELL. I WILL SHOW HER TO YOU...
...AND YOU WILL DE-SPAIR.
...
...ZU-ME!
U-ZU-ME!
MINA-MO?!
WHERE ARE YOU?!

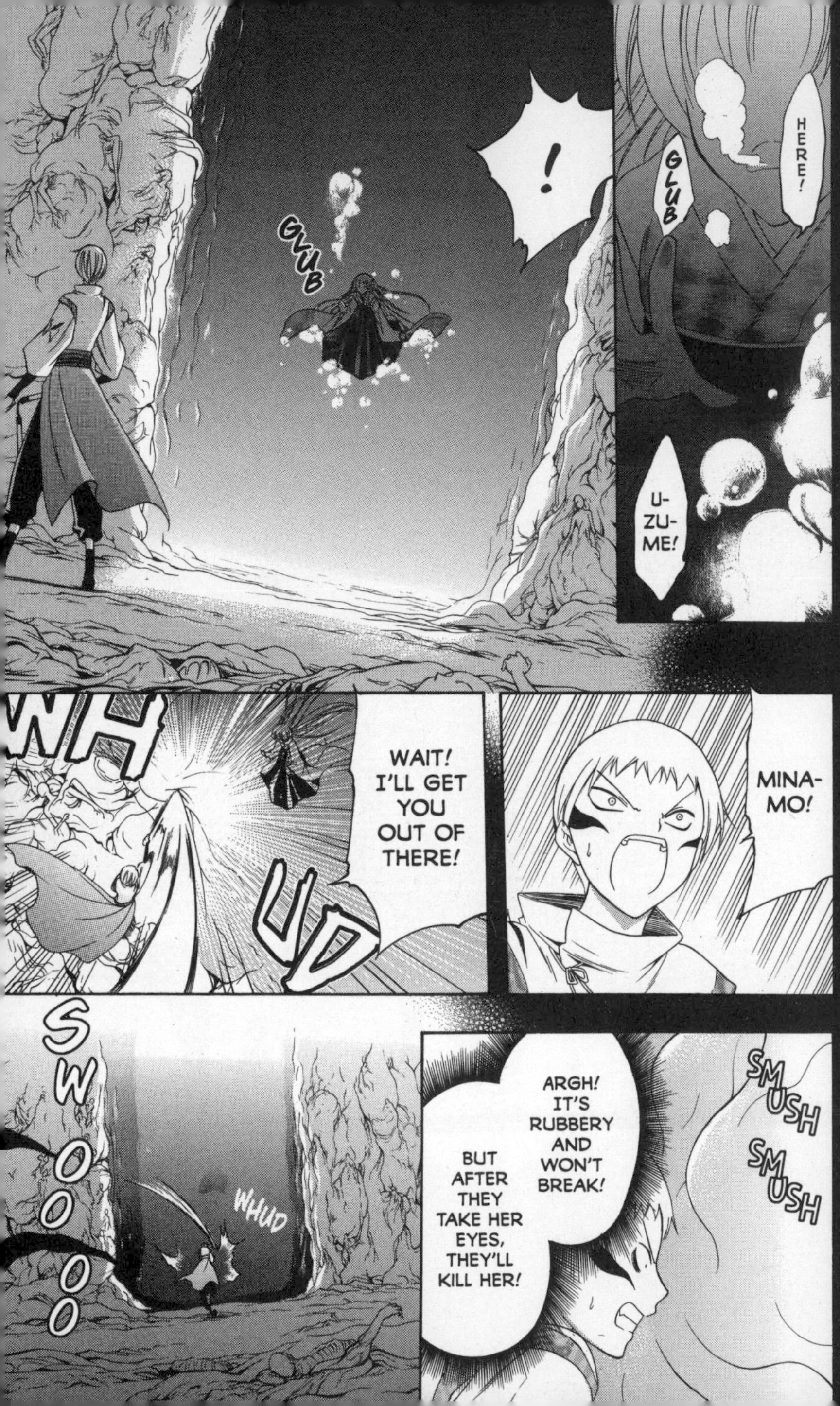
HERE!
GLUB
U-ZU-ME!
!
GLUB
MINAMO!
WAIT! I'LL GET YOU OUT OF THERE!
WHUD
SMUSH
SMUSH
ARGH! IT'S RUBBERY AND WON'T BREAK!
BUT AFTER THEY TAKE HER EYES, THEY'LL KILL HER!
SWOOOOO
WHUD

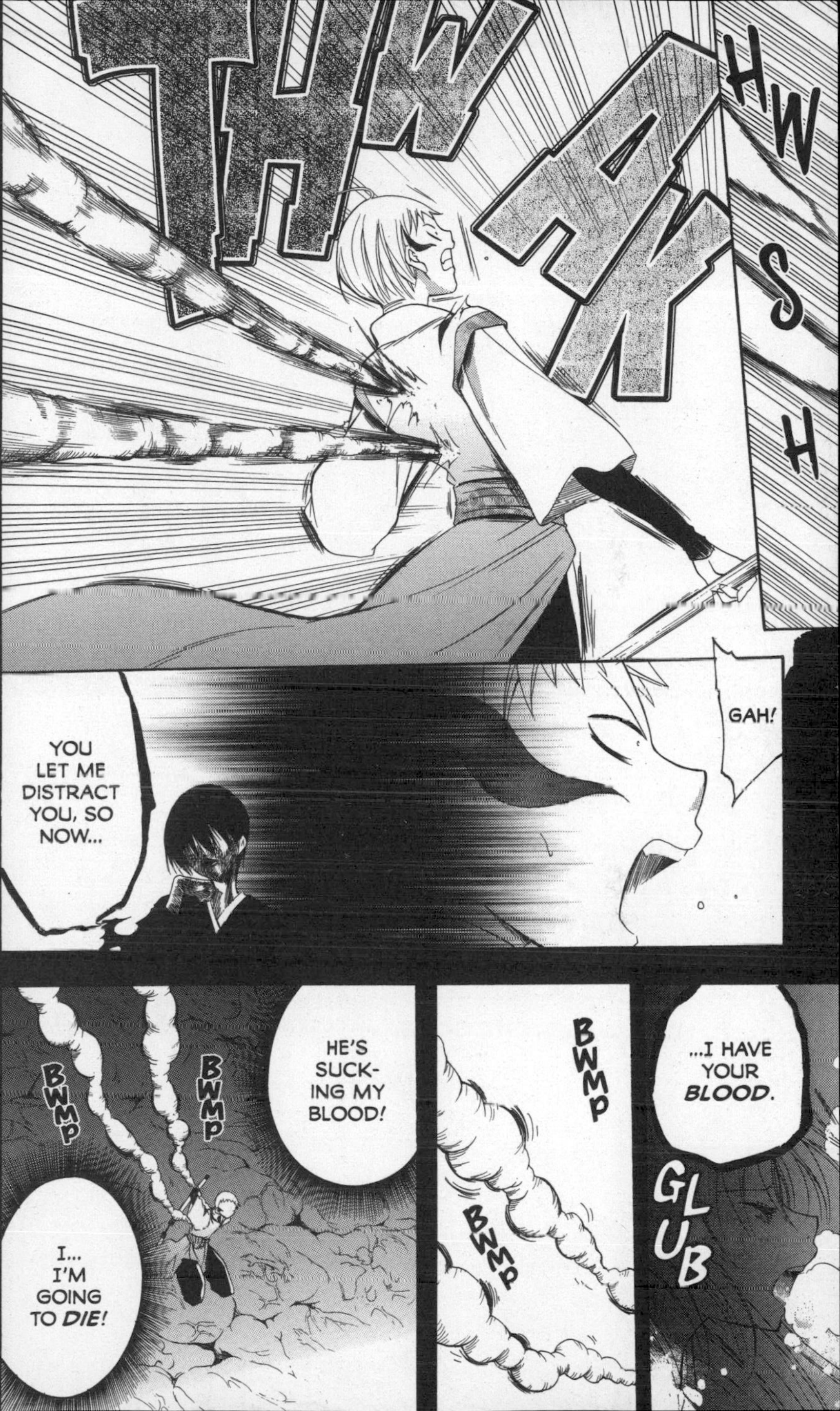
HWSSH
THWAK
GAH!
YOU LET ME DISTRACT YOU, SO NOW...
...I HAVE YOUR *BLOOD*.
GLUB
BWMP
BWMP
HE'S SUCK-ING MY BLOOD!
BWMP
BWMP
I... I'M GOING TO *DIE*!

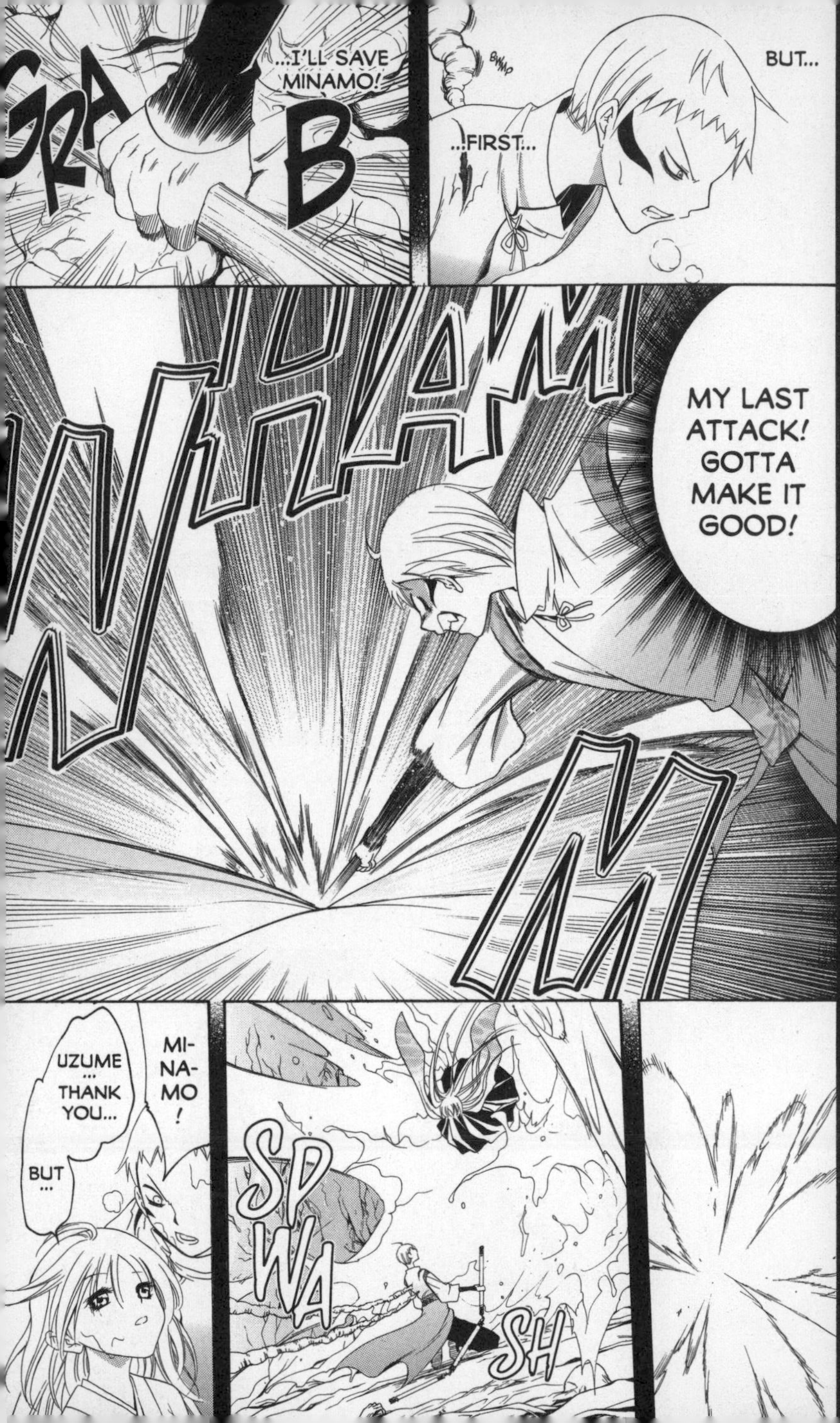
BUT...
...FIRST...
...I'LL SAVE MINAMO!
GRAB
MY LAST ATTACK! GOTTA MAKE IT GOOD!
WHAMM
SPWASH
MI-NA-MO!
UZUME... THANK YOU...
BUT...

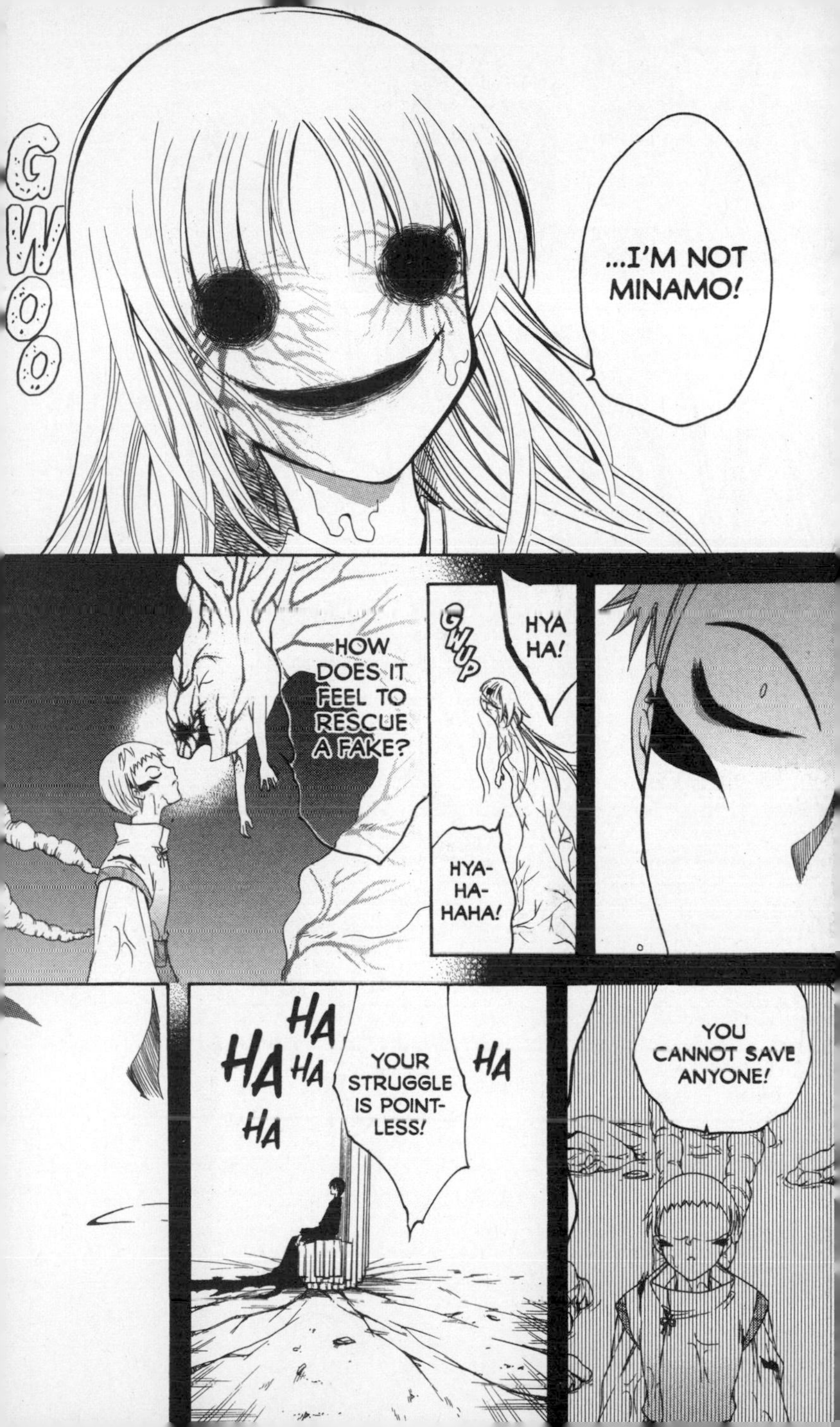
...I'M NOT MINAMO!
GWOOO
HYA HA!
GWUP
HYA-HA-HAHA!
HOW DOES IT FEEL TO RESCUE A FAKE?
YOU CANNOT SAVE ANYONE!
HA
YOUR STRUGGLE IS POINT-LESS!
HA
HA
HA
HA

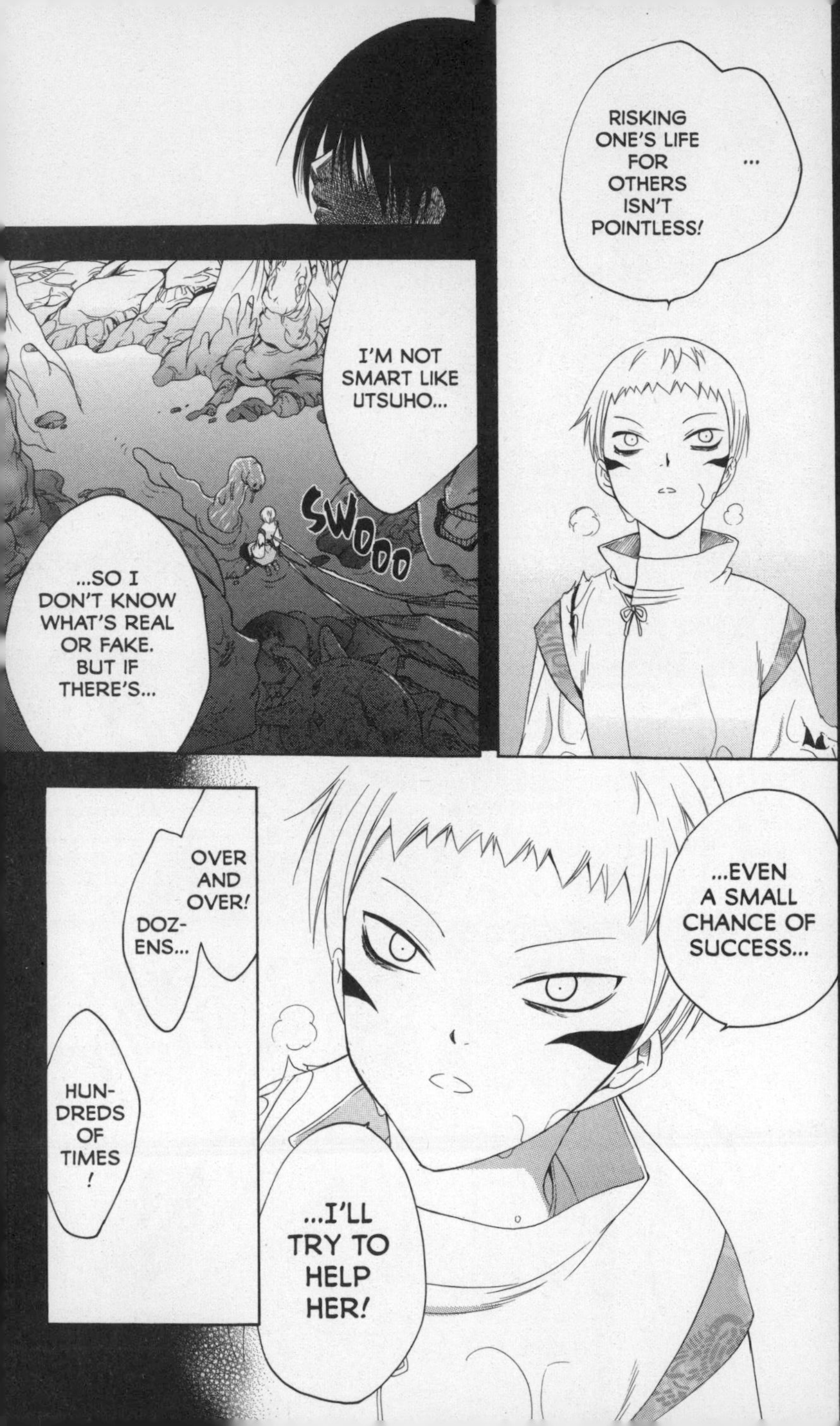
RISKING ONE'S LIFE FOR OTHERS ISN'T POINTLESS!
...
I'M NOT SMART LIKE UTSUHO...
SWOOO
...SO I DON'T KNOW WHAT'S REAL OR FAKE. BUT IF THERE'S...
...EVEN A SMALL CHANCE OF SUCCESS...
...I'LL TRY TO HELP HER!
OVER AND OVER!
DOZ-ENS...
HUN-DREDS OF TIMES!

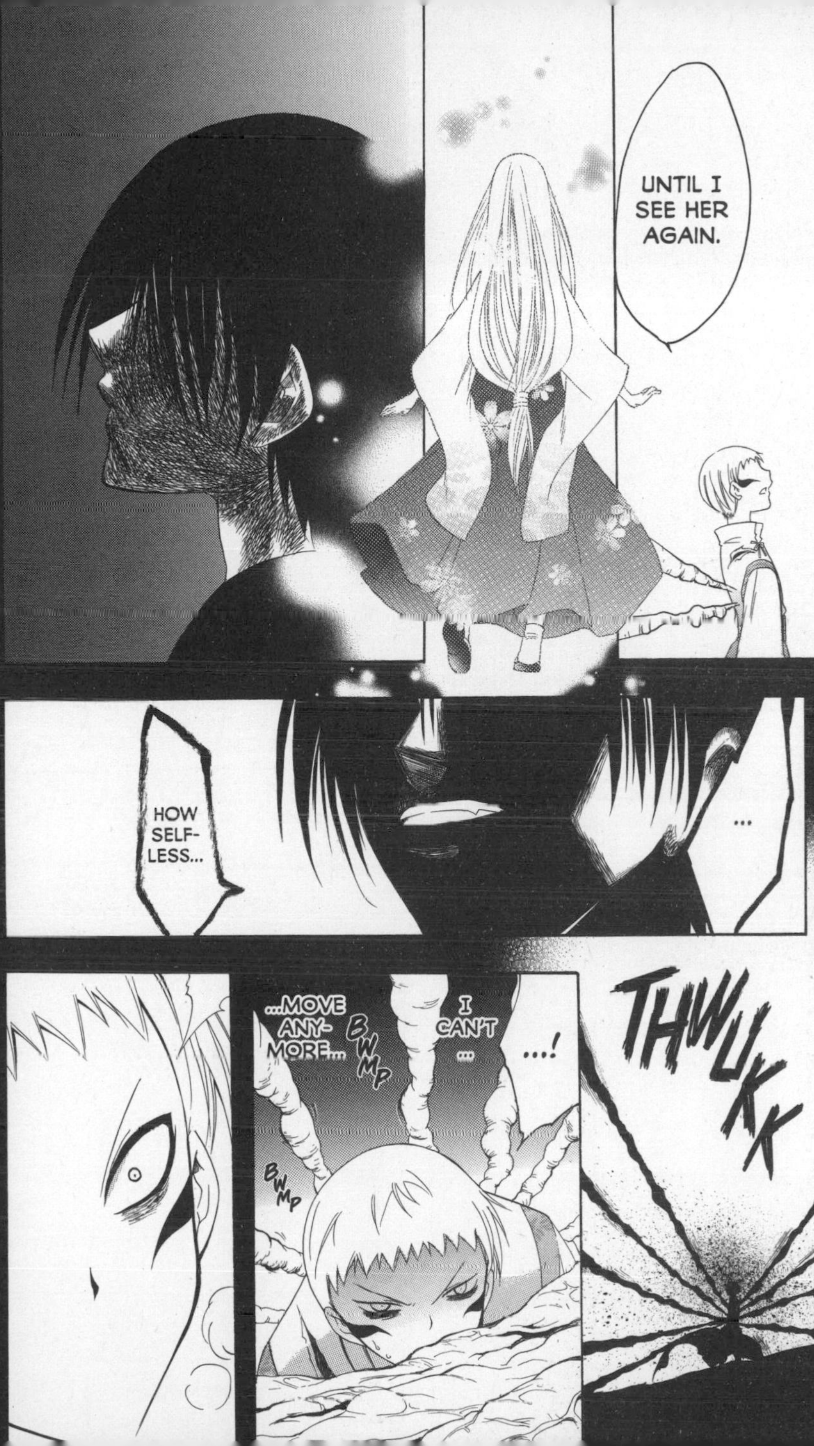
UNTIL I SEE HER AGAIN.
...
HOW SELF-LESS...
THWUKK
...!
I CAN'T ...
BWMP
...MOVE ANY-MORE...
BWMP

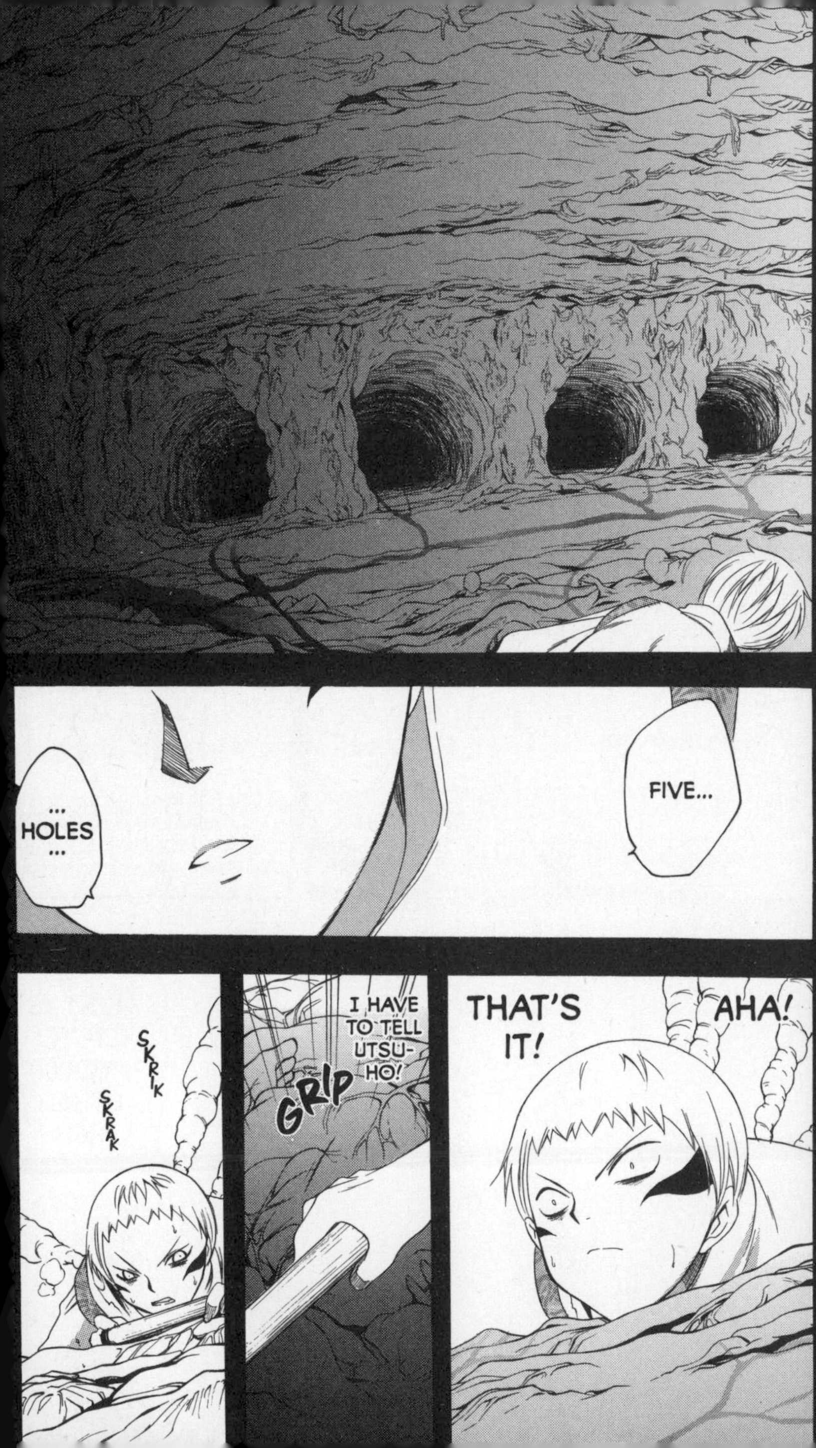
FIVE...
... HOLES ...
AHA!
THAT'S IT!
I HAVE TO TELL UTSU-HO!
GRIP
SKRIK
SKRAK

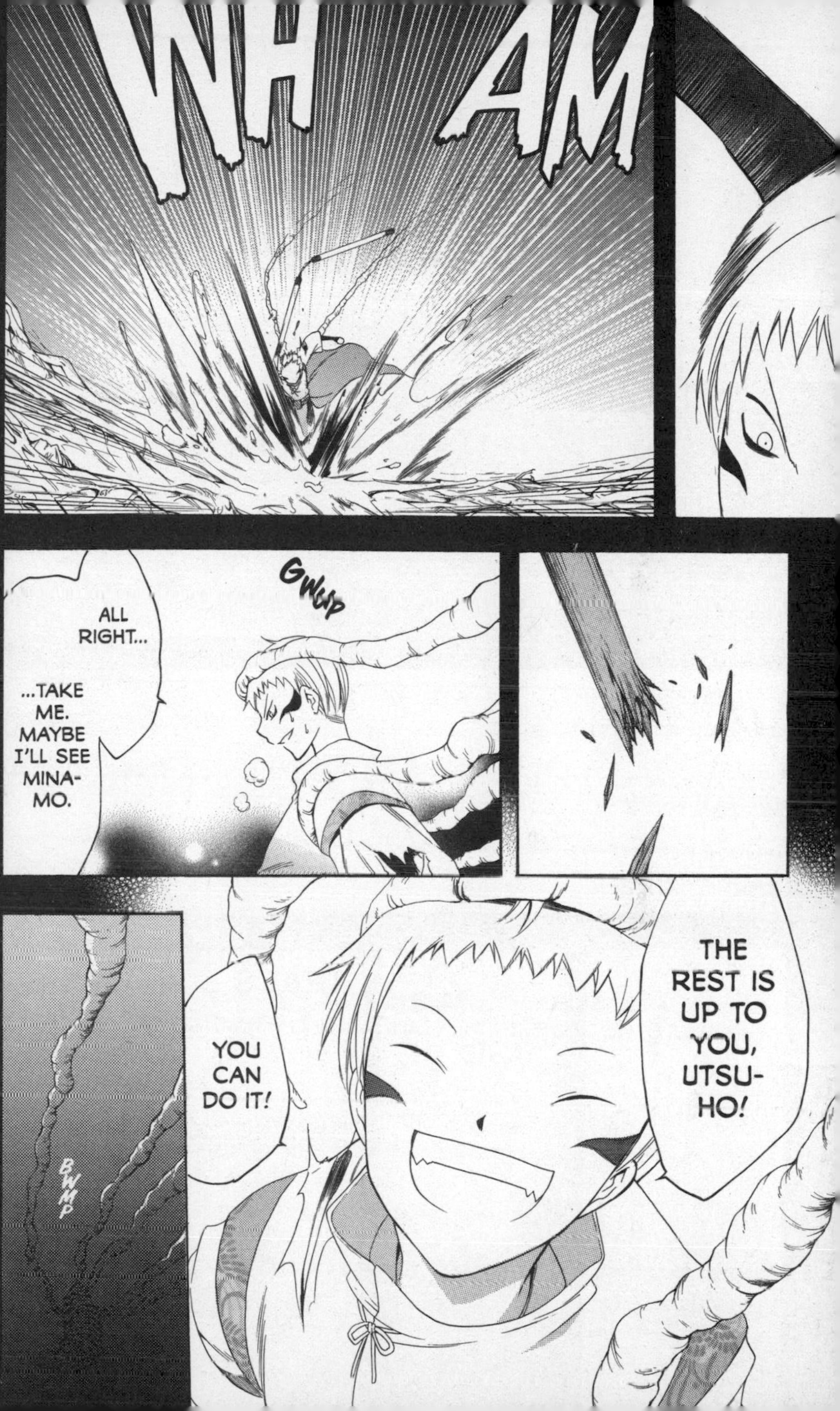
WHAM
GWUP
ALL RIGHT...
...TAKE ME. MAYBE I'LL SEE MINAMO.
THE REST IS UP TO YOU, UTSUHO!
YOU CAN DO IT!
BWMP

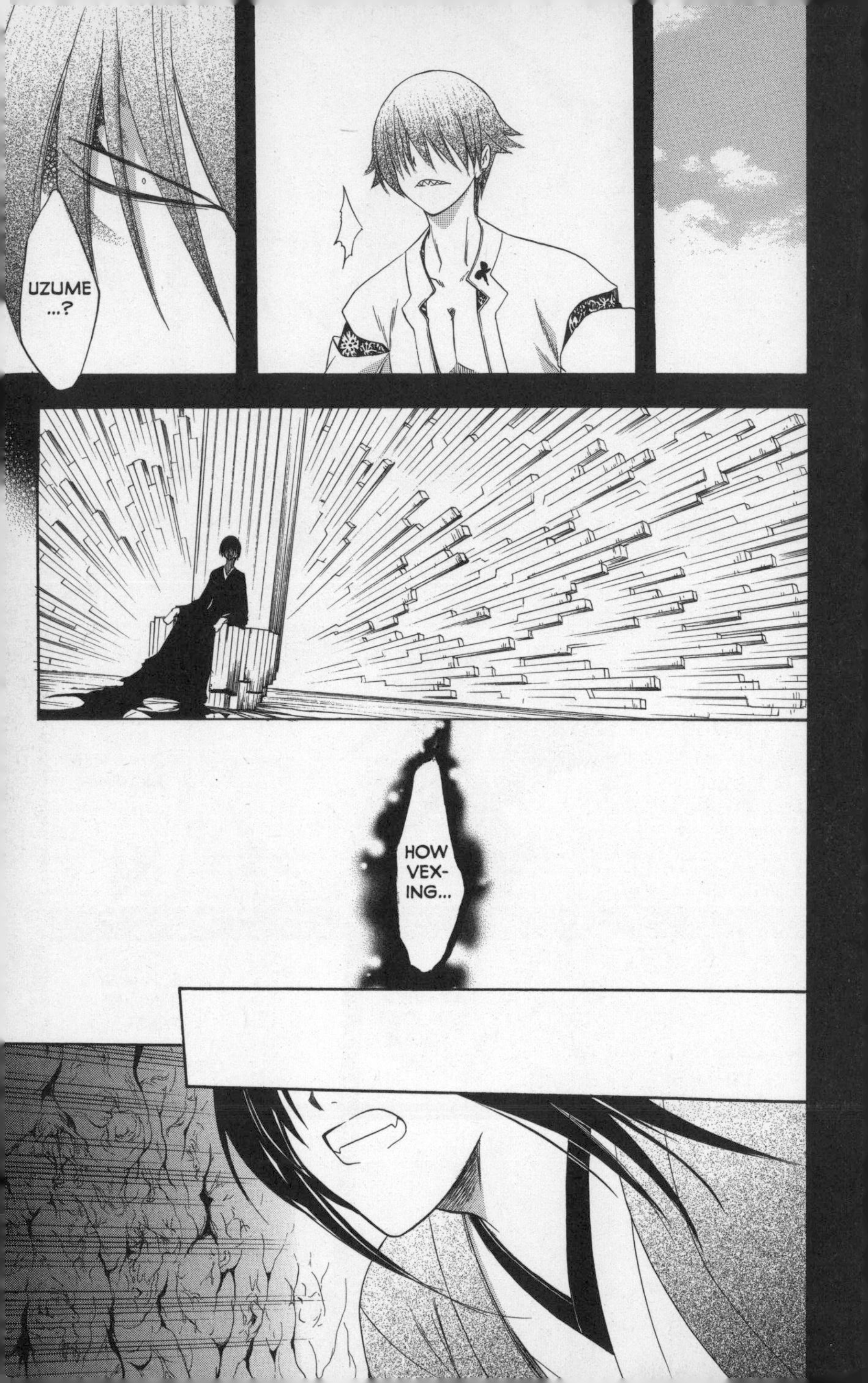
UZUME ...?
HOW VEX-ING...

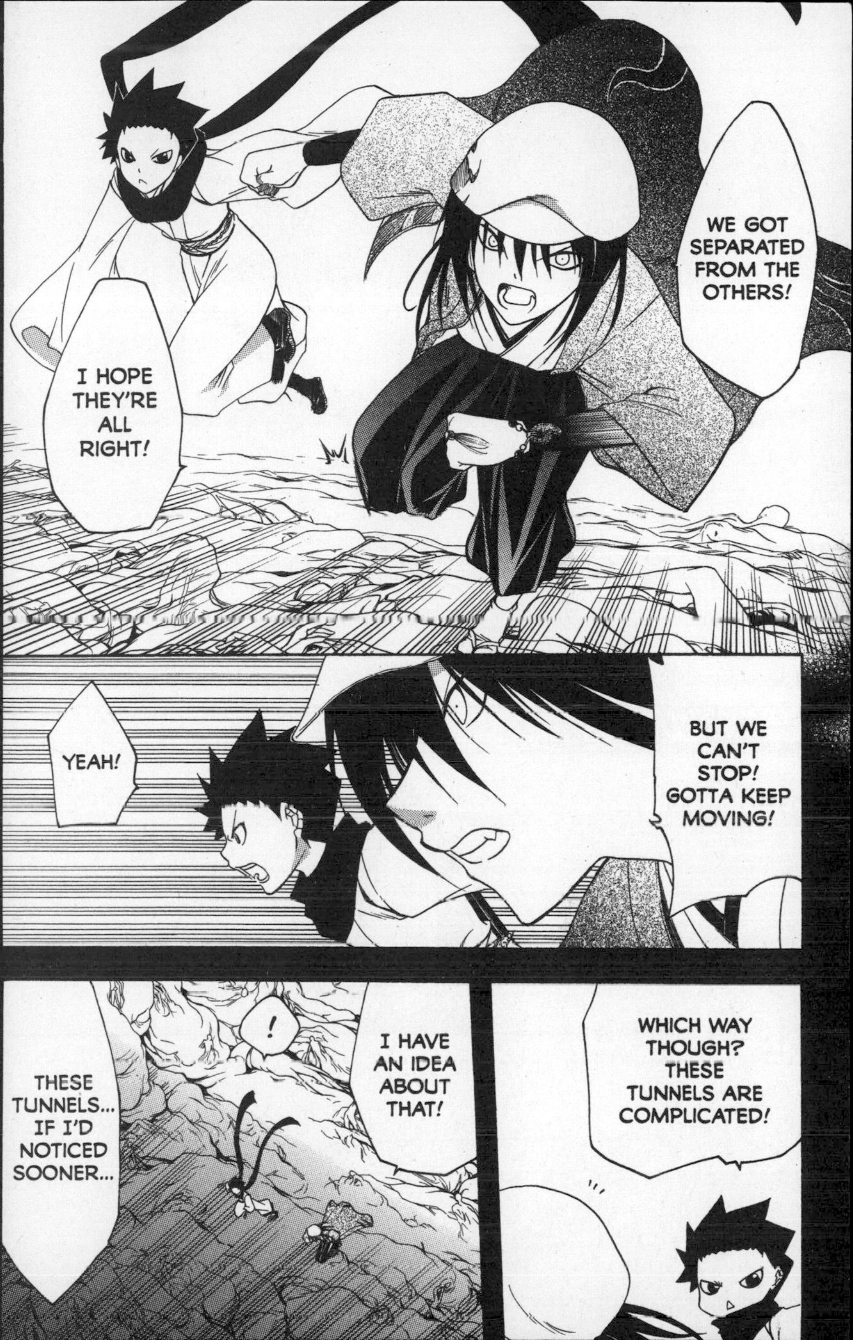
WE GOT SEPARATED FROM THE OTHERS!
I HOPE THEY'RE ALL RIGHT!
BUT WE CAN'T STOP! GOTTA KEEP MOVING!
YEAH!
WHICH WAY THOUGH? THESE TUNNELS ARE COMPLICATED!
I HAVE AN IDEA ABOUT THAT!
!
THESE TUNNELS... IF I'D NOTICED SOONER...

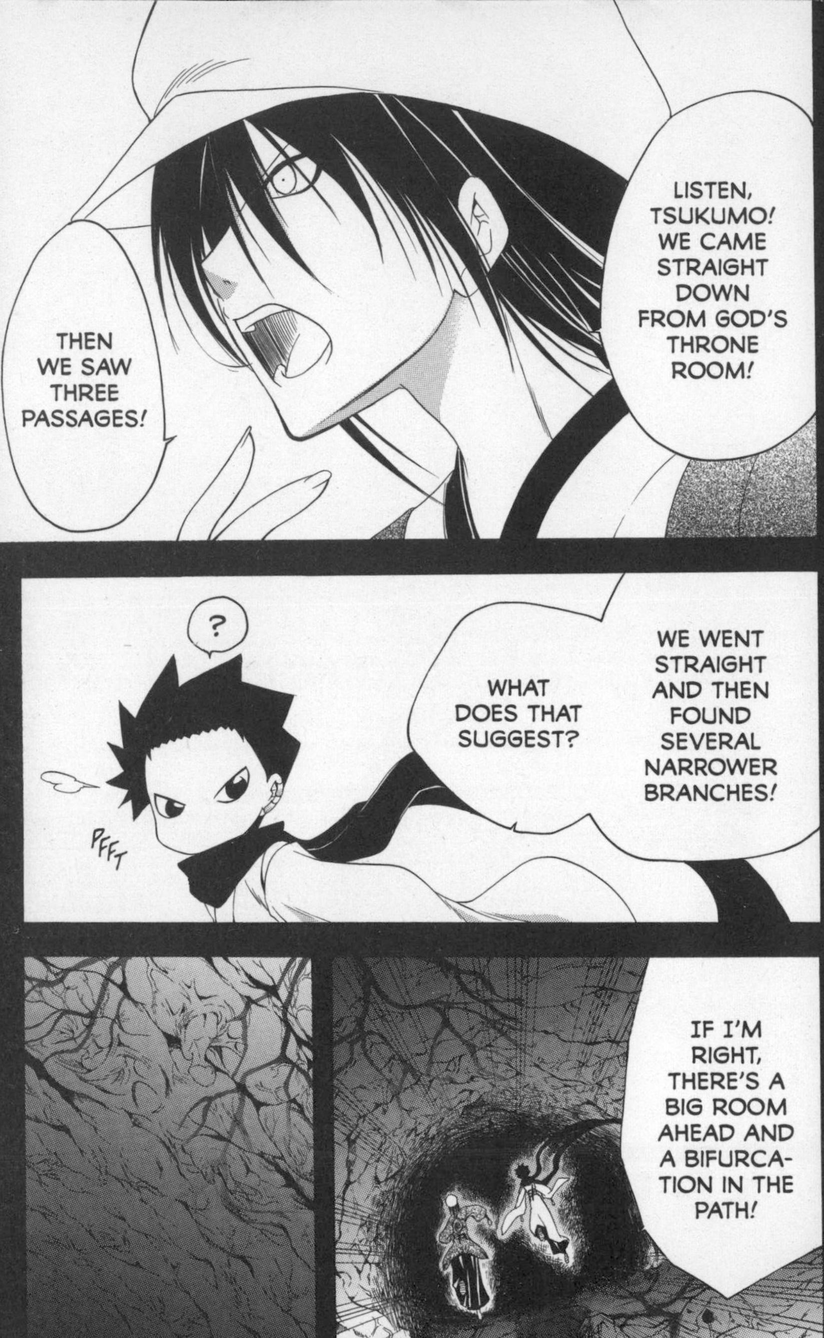
LISTEN, TSUKUMO! WE CAME STRAIGHT DOWN FROM GOD'S THRONE ROOM!
THEN WE SAW THREE PASSAGES!
WE WENT STRAIGHT AND THEN FOUND SEVERAL NARROWER BRANCHES!
WHAT DOES THAT SUGGEST?
?
PFFT
IF I'M RIGHT, THERE'S A BIG ROOM AHEAD AND A BIFURCATION IN THE PATH!

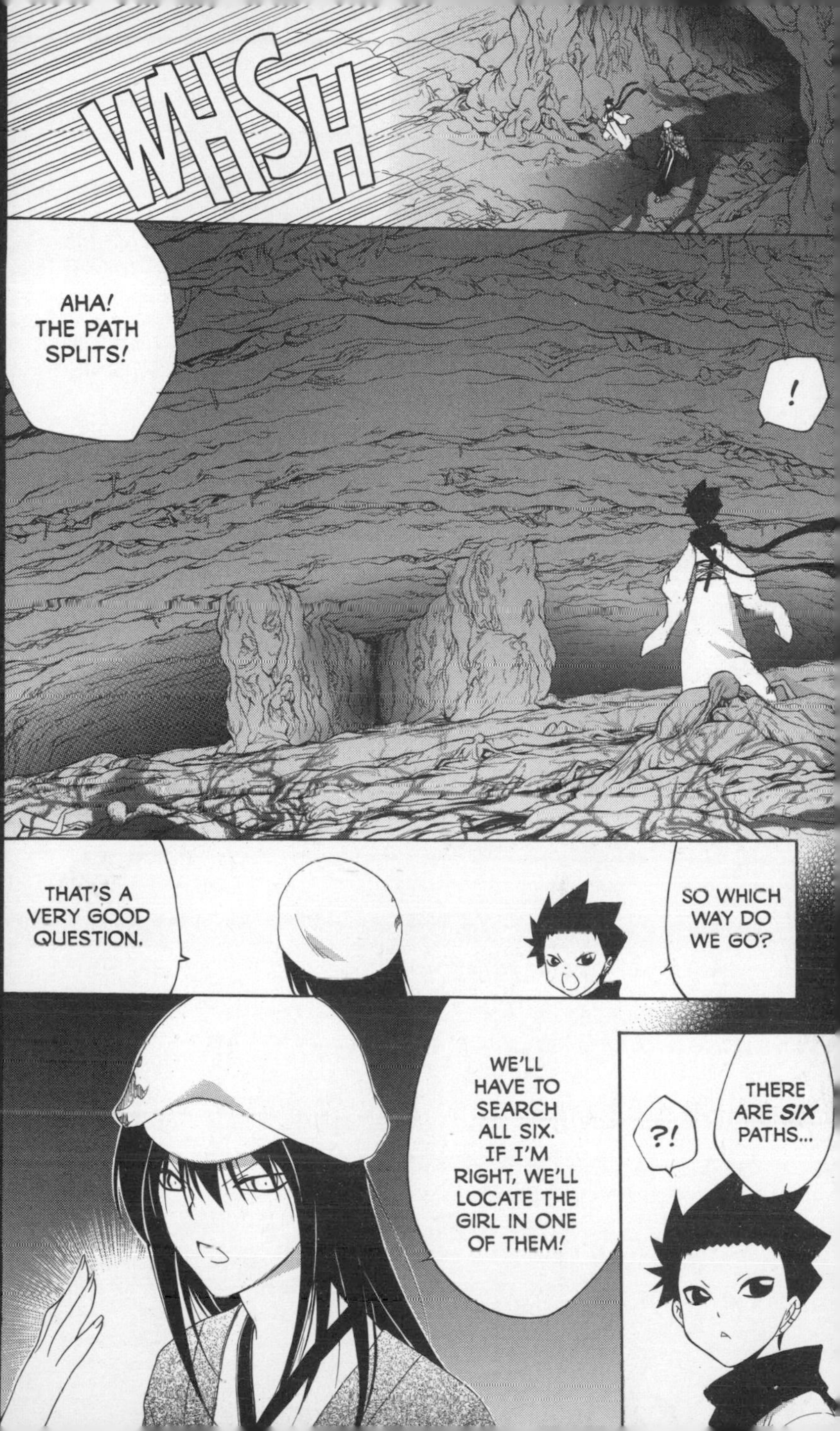
WHSH
AHA! THE PATH SPLITS!
!
SO WHICH WAY DO WE GO?
THAT'S A VERY GOOD QUESTION.
THERE ARE *SIX* PATHS...
?!
WE'LL HAVE TO SEARCH ALL SIX. IF I'M RIGHT, WE'LL LOCATE THE GIRL IN ONE OF THEM!

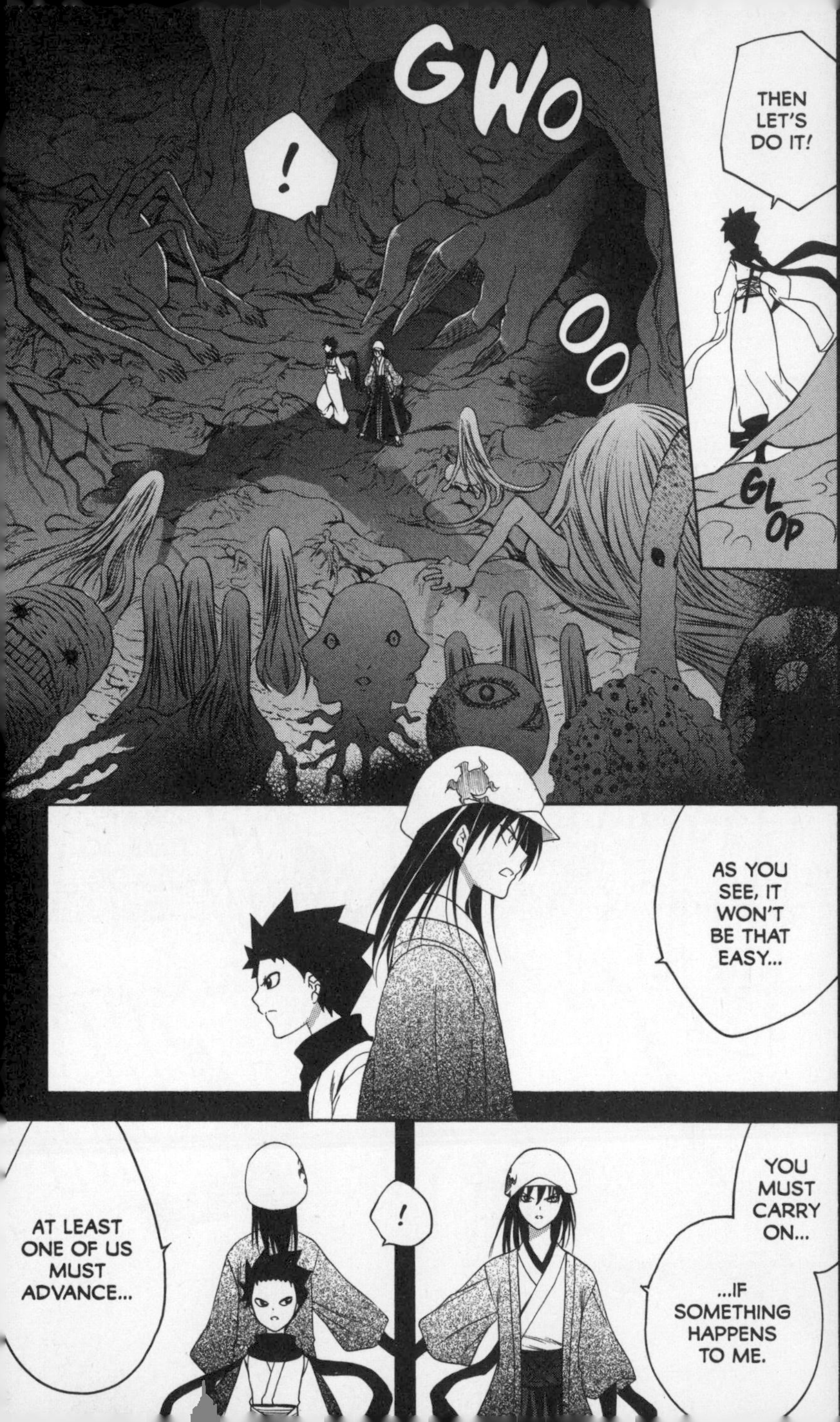
THEN LET'S DO IT!
GLOP
GWOOO
!
AS YOU SEE, IT WON'T BE THAT EASY...
YOU MUST CARRY ON...
...IF SOMETHING HAPPENS TO ME.
!
AT LEAST ONE OF US MUST ADVANCE...

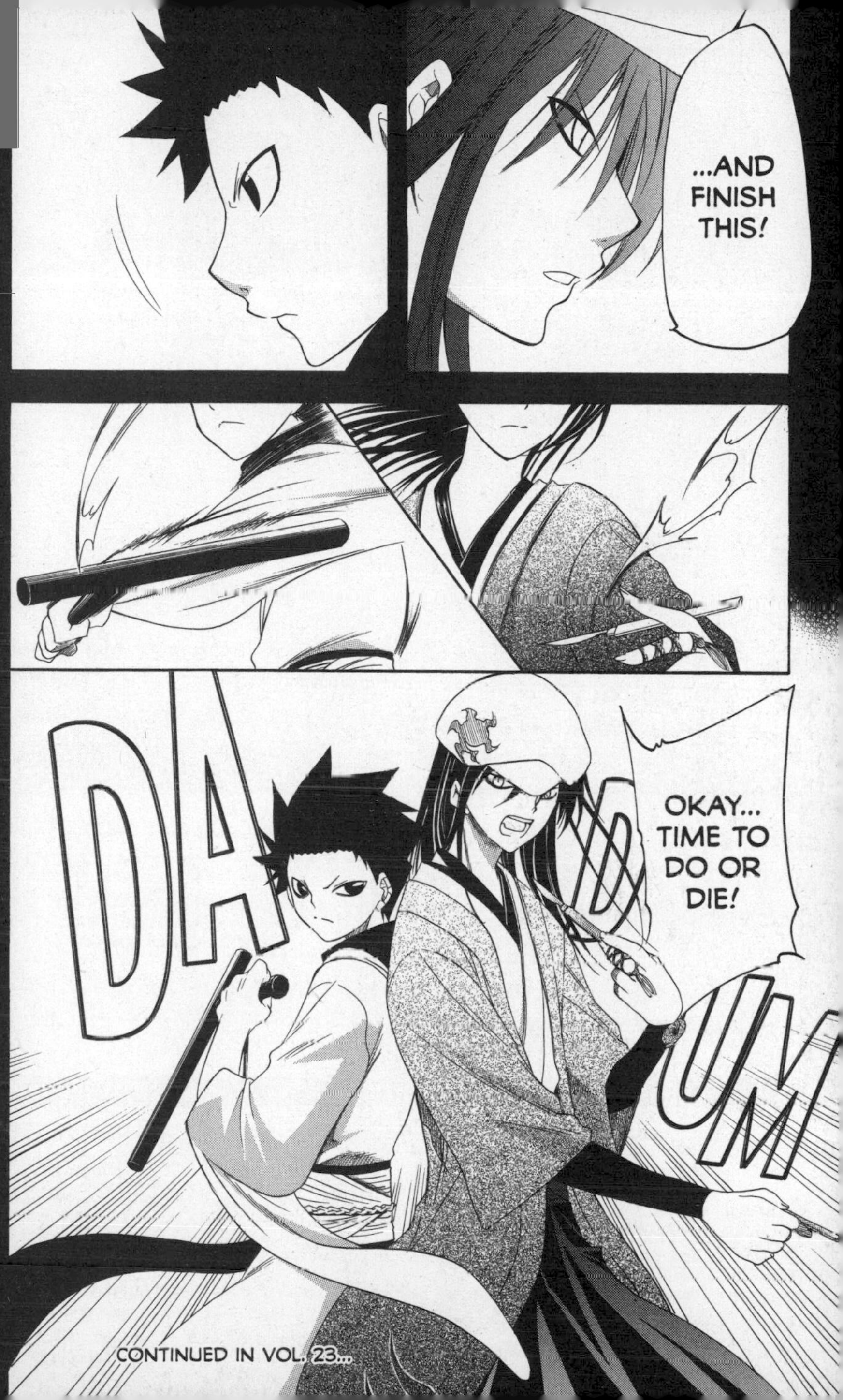
...AND FINISH THIS!
OKAY... TIME TO DO OR DIE!
DADUM
CONTINUED IN VOL. 23...